DATE DUE

~~MR 1 7 02~~ AP 24 '02		
~~JE 1 '04~~		
~~AP 6 0~~		

Language
and
Liberation

SUNY Series in
Contemporary Continental Philosophy

Dennis J. Schmidt, editor

Language
and
Liberation

Feminism, Philosophy, and Language

Edited by
Christina Hendricks
and
Kelly Oliver

State University of New York Press

The artwork on the front cover is "Breaking the Vicious Circle"
by Remedios Varo. Reprinted courtesy of Walter Gruen.

Production by Ruth Fisher
Marketing by Fran Keneston

Published by
State University of New York Press, Albany

© 1999 State University of New York

For information, address State University of New York Press,
State University Plaza, Albany, NY 12246

Library of Congress Cataloging-in-Publication Data

Language and liberation : Feminism, Philosophy, and Language / edited
    by Christina Hendricks and Kelly Oliver
        p. cm.
    ISBN 0-7914-4051-6 (hc : alk. paper). — ISBN 0-7914-4052-4 (pb :
alk. paper)
    1. Language and languages—Sex differences. 2. Feminism.
P120.S48L344   1999
408'.2—dc21   98-27369
                                                         CIP

10 9 8 7 6 5 4 3 2 1

Contents

Acknowledgments

This collection of essays began in 1990 when Kelly Oliver and Dale Bauer put together a special issue of *Hypatia* on Philosophy and Language which was published as *Hypatia* volume 7, number 2, Spring 1992. The editors of *Language and Liberation* would like to thank Dale Bauer for all of the work that she did on the original *Hypatia* issue that made our present collection possible. Thanks also to *Hypatia* and especially Linda Lopez McAlister for printing the original collection of essays. In addition, we would like to thank Sara Mills, Andrea Nye, Jane Hedley, Ewa Ziarek, Susan Bernstein, and Elissa Marder for agreeing to let us reprint their *Hypatia* articles free of charge. A special thanks to SUNY Press for agreeing to make a donation to *Hypatia* in the name of each of these authors.

Although six of the thirteen essays published in *Language and Liberation* were originally published in *Hypatia*, most of them have been revised and updated for this collection. The majority of essays in this collection have never before been published. We would like to thank the authors of these new essays for their continued patience and faith in us while we were converting the *Hypatia* volume into a book.

Christina Hendricks and Kelly Oliver

Introduction

How to Do (Feminist) Things with Words[1]

E lissa Marder writes in regard to feminism that "its necessity, its reason for being as discursive praxis, is as political response."[2] If feminism is irreducibly political, and if, as Marder claims, "[t]o intervene politically is to speak punctually, performatively, and strategically," then the words of feminists may need to be more than mere lifeless vehicles for the communication of ideas. Language is sometimes characterized as reflective, as a neutral mirror for an objective reality. But feminist language, if it is to effect social and political change, must be active—we must use feminist words to *do* things. This collection of essays is devoted to exploring the possibilities of using language as an important means for reaching feminist goals of liberation. These diverse essays criticize theories of language that suppose it to express rigid, closed truths about reality. Instead, the authors here emphasize the *creative* capacity of language, its ability to help shape our conceptions of self and of the world. They urge that attention to language must be an important part of any feminist political agenda, and they share a confidence in the power of language to help liberate women from oppressive circumstances and identities. The authors in this anthology each show, in different ways, how words can also be deeds.

This collection is divided into four parts. The first, entitled "The Power of Words: Changing Meanings, Changing Social Spaces," addresses the possibility that changing the way we use language may have profound effects in a larger social context. The essays by Lynne Tirrell, Sara Mills, Jane Hedley, and Georganna Ulary each consider different ways of using words in pursuit of liberation. The

1

essays in the second section, entitled "The Power to Speak: Who Is Speaking, from Where?" consider how changes in language use may affect not only the social and political status of women, but also their very identity. Of major concern in this context are questions involving both the "we" of feminist group identity as well as the "I" of individual identity. For example, how might feminists use terms such as "women" and "feminists" in ways that preserve their strategic power while avoiding their oppressive exclusionary potential? In addition, should feminists try to avoid presenting a singular, uniform notion of individual identity, since this may form an oppressive notion of self? The essays by Elissa Marder, Susan David Bernstein, and Sangeeta Ray address such concerns by considering uses of language that facilitate an openness to difference and change rather than emphasizing a closed, exclusionary view of identity. The authors in the third section, "The Power of Masculinist Metaphors: Words that Keep Women in Place," emphasize the power of metaphor to shape our conceptions of, and accepted truths about, the world. Natalie Alexander, Andrea Nye, and Roberta Weston each analyze the metaphors used by prominent philosophers and consider the consequences of these metaphors in a feminist context. The fourth section, "The Power of Feminist Metaphors: Words That Open Spaces for Women," focuses on the ways that metaphors can be deployed to meet feminist ends. Ewa Płonowska Ziarek, Lisa Walsh, and Cynthia Baker each address the power and pitfalls of using feminist metaphors of fluidity and maternity.

The essays in this collection span not only a range of topics in the vast area of feminism and language, but also a range of philosophical approaches. In order to help bring together such diversity as part of a larger, feminist concern with language, this Introduction provides some historical background for the issues addressed in each of the four parts. In the Introduction we present a short overview of the literature forming the background for the current work presented in this collection. We consider the crucial questions and issues at stake in each of the four parts, situating these essays in the history of the field and showing how they take older inquiries into important new directions. The Introduction is therefore divided into four sections paralleling the divisions of the book, and a short description of the essays in each part is included.

Part I
The Power of Words:
Changing Meanings, Changing Social Spaces

The essays in the first part of this volume address how changes in language use might affect women's circumstances and identities. An important question in such discussions is whether or not there is a difference in language use between men and women. In other words, is it possible to distinguish a kind of "female" language from a "male" one? Among those feminists who have answered this question in the affirmative, there are differences of opinion as to what should be done about it.[3] Some, such as Robin Lakoff, argue that women's speech exhibits a powerlessness that is detrimental to feminist goals, and that women should therefore try to adopt the more powerful speech patterns used by men.[4] Others, such as Dale Spender and Luce Irigaray, claim that women's language needs to be reclaimed and valorized because its use may help us to avoid some of the oppressive tendencies of the language developed by males. The issues presented in the following brief, historical account of this debate underlie the work being done now on the power of words to change women's social circumstances, as presented in the first part of this collection. These essays extend, refuse, and/or go beyond many of the questions considered by feminist language theorists in the past.

Robin Lakoff, Casey Miller, Kate Swift, and Cheris Kramarae published empirical studies in the 1970s and '80s suggesting the existence of a specifically feminine way of using language. Following roughly the methods of the American structuralists studying Native American languages in the 1950s, they gathered samples from women and catalogued them in order to determine patterns in sounds, words, and grammatical structures, as well as conventions for the distribution of these fundamental elements. But unlike the American structuralists, Lakoff, Miller/Swift, and Kramarae did not work from a random sampling of the group of speakers under investigation. Rather, as part of the sociolinguistic movement of the 1960s, they proceeded under the claim that random sampling smoothes over the differences in language use corresponding to social categories such as race, class, and gender. These feminists argued that there is an important relationship between language use and social status, and they brought such social differences to the fore in their works. They focused on specific, nonrandom groups of women and determined how their speech differed from what was considered the (male) norm.

These theorists reported that women did indeed use language in a significantly different way than men. In *Language and Woman's Place*, Lakoff argues that " 'Women's language' shows up in all levels of the grammar of English" (Lakoff 1975, 8). She finds that in general women are more likely than men to use "tag" questions, "hedges," and "super polite" forms as devices for deferring to men and avoiding responsibility. The use of "tag" questions is a linguistic tactic that combines an assertion with a yes-or-no question, such as: "The movie does start at seven-thirty, doesn't it?" Such questions suggest that the speaker is sure enough about the answer to avoid asking for information, yet unsure enough to require confirmation from a respondent. Lakoff suggests that this move, though it can signal a desire to avoid conflict within discourse, can also give the impression of powerlessness. In addition, "hedging," or being overly "polite" may reinforce a view of women as lacking in confidence, as being afraid to express their own views (or perhaps even as incapable of *having* views of their own). Lakoff argues that such differences in language use between men and women provides "black and white" evidence of sexism (Lakoff 1975, 4).

This discrepancy in language use between the sexes is, however, a complex problem for which Lakoff does not provide a clear solution in her work. On the one hand, she proposes that women give up their "lady-like" language, but on the other she seems also to argue that this "feminine" language is symptomatic of a more pervasive sexism that cannot be eliminated by a simple change in word use. Still, even if women's language alone doesn't cause sexism, Lakoff suggests that it does perpetuate it. Discrepancies in language use between men and women may be rooted in deep biological, sociopolitical, and economic relations, but "[t]he ultimate effect of these discrepancies is that women are systematically denied access to power, on the grounds that they are not capable of holding it as demonstrated by their linguistic behavior . . ." (Lakoff 1975, 7). To help break the cycle, Lakoff urges women to adopt the language used by people in power (men). Though this step may not be enough to gain women immediate access to power, Lakoff seems to be saying that it will at least remove one of the hindrances to it. Thus, for Lakoff, it seems a change in language use has the potential to change women's social status in a limited way.

In *Words and Women*, Casey Miller and Kate Swift also suggest that a change in language use will lead to a change in the social position of women (Miller and Swift 1977). They argue that our language is riddled with sexist elements that work to suppress the role of women in society. Miller/Swift catalogue the sexism in our language (such as idioms, derogatory terms associated with women, and the generic use of "he" and "man") and conclude that the rejection of such elements will lead to more accuracy in language use. For example, both men and women participate in human activities, but the use of the generic "he/man" does not reflect this. Further, the use of such pronouns can perpetuate sexist circumstances by supporting the view that he/man constitutes "humanity," from which she/woman is excluded. Miller/Swift argue that any change in language use that will "contribute to clarity and accuracy" rather than "fudge them" should be made.

Cheris Kramarae follows the sociolinguistic tradition in finding differences between women's and men's speech, arguing that differences in the use of language reflect differences in social status (Kramarae 1981).[5] Kramarae endorses what she calls the "strategy model" of language: she maintains that variations in language use develop as strategies for dealing with social situations. For women, this means that differences between their speech and that of men is the result of adaptive behavior through which women learn to operate within oppressive social circumstances. Experiencing a deficiency of social power in relation to that of men, women learn to use different language strategies in order to exercise what power they do have. For Kramarae, language itself is not responsible for women's oppression, it is merely a reflection of that oppression. Moreover, language is a useful strategic tool for operating within an oppressive culture. This picture of feminine speech seems more positive than that presented by Lakoff, for it accords women's language some strategic value. Still, Kramarae finds feminine language to be powerless in comparison to that of men.[6]

English feminist Dale Spender uses similar empirical research methods to theorize differences between the speech of men and women. In *Man Made Language* Spender shows how a change in language use might lead to a change in women's social position, and she makes an important step toward revaluing "feminine" speech rather than declaring it inferior to its masculine counter-part (Spender 1980). Spender's research is situated within a Marx-ist framework, and she thus interprets language as both a cause of oppression and a symptom of the greater material conditions of patriarchal capitalism.

Spender adheres to what is known as the Sapir-Whorf hypoth-esis, maintaining that language plays a powerful role in shaping human perceptions of reality.[7] She argues that language, rather than being a neutral vehicle that communicates already-formed ideas, works instead to shape our ideas about the world. Language is very influential in shaping the way we organize and understand reality, according to Spender: "Once certain categories are con-structed within the language, we proceed to organize the world according to those categories. We even fail to see evidence which is not consistent with those categories" (Spender 1980, 141). Lan-guage for Spender is therefore "both a creative and an inhibiting vehicle," organizing our experience of the world and discouraging change. Those who control language therefore also control percep-tions of reality—which puts them in a very powerful position, since for Spender there is nothing more to "reality" than our view of it.

According to Spender, men form a dominant group that has controlled language in its own interest, constructing sexist catego-ries and meanings through which all speakers of the language view the world.[8] The inhibiting nature of these categories makes it difficult to change the perception of women as "inferior" to men. Spender argues that the categories set up by male-dominated lan-guage make claims to objectivity and truth, as if they were simply "the way things are." Clearly, it is in the interest of the dominant group for their views to be regarded as transcendent truths, un-touchable and inalterable. Yet Spender maintains that there is a feminine alternative: she claims that women's language organizes the world differently than the dominant male one, because it does away with oppositional categories such as "masculine" and "femi-nine." This new, non-dualistic language, according to Spender, will help to usher in a new, non-dualistic way for us to view the world and each other. Spender therefore suggests that we dismantle our traditional, "man-made" language and articulate that of women instead.

Spender's analysis offers the advantage over those discussed above by explaining more precisely how and why a change in language use could lead to a change in the social status of women. If the categories of language do indeed shape our experience, then perhaps by changing language structures we could ultimately change social structures. Further, Spender attempts to valorize the speech of women, arguing that it is not, in itself, powerless and weak, but only appears so in the context of the dominant male language.[9]

A recent contribution to this debate has been made by the French feminist and psychoanalyst Luce Irigaray. Irigaray has also done empirical linguistic studies on the differences between men's and women's speech, and has published some of her findings in *I Love to You* (Irigaray 1996). There, she claims that women's use of language is directed toward a communicative function, while men's language use focuses on possession and manipulation of objects. Women, seeking dialogue, are frustrated in their linguistic exchanges with men, who concern themselves not with *who* is speaking, but rather with *what* is being spoken about. But such a focus on the objects spoken about draws attention away from the subject(s) involved in conversation, and therefore the subjectivity of the other tends to be ignored. In other words, the male language use, which emphasizes objective reality and truth, detracts from communication between subjects.

The problem cannot simply be remedied, however, by using a female language, emphasizing communication between subjects. According to Irigaray, communication can only take place if there is a recognized difference between subjects. *Recognition*, for Irigaray, requires an understanding of the irreducible difference between myself and another: "I recognize you goes hand in hand with: you are irreducible to me, just as I am to you. We may not be substituted for one another" (Irigaray 1996, 103). If I *recognize* another subject, this means that the other is never fully transparent to me. We can never fuse into a *one*, but will always remain separated by a mystery that incites dialogue. This irreducible difference is a necessary condition for communication between subjects—I can only talk *with* another if I *recognize* the other as separated from me by an insurmountable difference.

Irigaray locates the irreducible difference necessary for communication in sexual difference: "As for the opening up of this field [of communication], the relation between man and woman is paradigmatic" (Irigaray 1996, 46); and speaking of difference that is irreducible, Irigaray claims that "[o]nly the recognition of the other as sexed offers this possibility" (Irigaray 1996, 105). She argues that the "I," rather than being a neutral, all-encompassing "one," is always sexed, and ignoring this leads to a covering over of difference, an impossibility of "we." Irigaray suggests that we consider the otherwise gender-neutral "I" as rather "he" or "she," in order to bring out the otherness that is found within sexual difference. We can thereby avoid, she argues, the collapsing of this difference into a neutral oneness, an objective notion of subjectivity that can easily be used to exclude anyone who does not fit its parameters. This, of course, is what has happened to women: we have become the *other* of men, "the other of the Same." Women serve as mute exchange-value between men rather than as equal partners in exchanges, whether social, economic, political, or linguistic. Becoming an equal partner means having an equal, *female* and therefore *different* identity and subjectivity.[11]

Accomplishing this may require different strategies, but one way involves changing our language. Irigaray argues that a new kind of syntax may be required, a "syntax of communication" that facilitates and maintains links between subjects who see each other as different. The title of her book provides one example of such a syntax: "*I love to you* means I maintain a relation of indirection to you. I do not subjugate you or consume you. . . . I speak to you, not just about something; rather I speak *to* you" (Irigaray 1996, 109). Irigaray argues that such changes in language use could have important social and political effects. For example, she claims that simply using feminine pronouns more often (i.e., *she/they*, where the latter refers to a group of women—in French, *elles*) "alters our customs without our being aware of it . . ." (Irigaray 1996, 133). Irigaray maintains that a change in language use can contribute to a change in the social status of women, since "[l]anguage and its values reflect the social order and vice versa" (Irigaray 1996, 66).

Lakoff, Miller/Swift, Kramarae, Spender, and Irigaray each consider not only the possibility of a particularly female language use different from the dominant male one, but they also outline the terms for asking how changes in language use might lead to social and political changes for women. Their concerns remain prominent in feminist discussions of language today, which still include questions such as: Do differences in language use corresponding to gender exist, and if so, how important are they? Might such gender differences in language be a source of empowerment for women or could they lead to further oppression? How can changing our words lead to changes in the social order, and what linguistic changes ought we to seek? The essays in the first section of this anthology extend such discussions by considering new and important ways in which feminist words can lead to liberation.

Lynne Tirrell, in "Derogatory Terms: Racism, Sexism, and the Inferential Role Theory of Meaning," addresses a difficult yet important question for current feminist language theory: is it possible for a community that has been damaged by derogatory terms to reclaim such terms and use them in a positive, empowering fashion? This issue is of import to feminists, who must consider the possible effects of reclaiming not only terms such as "bitch," "whore," and "dyke," but even "girl," or "feminine," which may have taken on some derogatory force after centuries of patriarchy. It is necessary to ask whether feminists can reclaim such terms as their own without taking on their oppressive connotations. Tirrell considers this issue through an "inferential role theory of meaning" that locates meaning in a network of inferences licensed by a community of speakers. Arguing that it need not be necessary to refuse the use of derogatory terms altogether, Tirrell nevertheless points out that any project of reclamation will not be easy—what must be changed is not simply the connotation or denotation of such terms, but rather a set of discursive commitments supported by larger socioeconomic and legal factors. Tirrell concludes that though this issue is a difficult one to resolve, the discussion of it is helpful in itself because it makes explicit the unjust inferences and commitments these terms carry, and shows thereby the importance of paying attention to words.

Sara Mills, in "Discourse Competence: Or How to Theorize Strong Women Speakers," offers a means for women to use language without specifying a particularly "feminine" way of speaking. Addressing directly the concerns of theorists such as those discussed above, Mills criticizes the division of language use along gendered lines. She argues instead that differences in the way men and women speak is more a function of complex, social factors and power relations than simply a question of gender. Rather than advocating the replacement of a dominant, male language with a female one, Mills offers instead a theory of "discourse competence" that can apply to *any* speaker, providing women with a way to speak strongly without speaking "like men." Mills's view of discourse competence requires that speakers pay particular attention to the context of their language by exhibiting a concern for their audience and the response that is likely to ensue. It is a competence that recognizes and emphasizes the communicative aspect of language over its purely denotative or truth-naming aspect. Mills therefore brings feminist concerns into a view of language that does not fall prey to a potentially essentialist division along female/male lines.

In "Surviving to Speak New Language: Mary Daly and Adrienne Rich," Jane Hedley compares the changes in language use suggested by the writings of Daly and Rich. Both authors argue that word use is important and influential, and that feminists must therefore choose their words carefully in their efforts to repossess patriarchal language. But, Hedley argues, this repossession takes quite different forms in the work of these two feminists. Mary Daly creates a new lexicon for women that is separated from everyday speech and has the dubious effect of cutting off communication with anyone outside of the elect group who know the language. Rich, on the other hand, suggests an alternative means of speaking that works from within the context of the language already in use. Rather than building new words with radically new, metaphorical meanings as Daly does, Rich suggests revising already-common words to reflect feminist concerns. Rich keeps enough of language's traditional usage to maintain communication among women of varied backgrounds, while changing enough to promote societal transformation. She is therefore, according to Hedley, more successful than Daly at providing a transformative, feminist language that remains practical and open to many.

Georganna Ulary, in "From Revolution to Liberation: Transforming Hysterical Discourse into Analytic Discourse," considers the question of whether women can find a means for liberation within patriarchal language, or whether they can only be stifled by it. Ulary explains how feminists contending with this question have sometimes expressed only two, equally undesirable alternatives: women must either submit to the patriarchal symbolic order, or refuse it and speak hysterically instead. Looking to find a way of using language that does not merely *react* to the dominant discourse (leaving it intact) but rather goes beyond it in a revolutionary fashion, Ulary locates such a possibility in the work of Jacques Lacan. Ulary shows how it may be possible, under Lacan's view, for women to engage in a revolution over the patriarchal symbolic system from within. Specifically, she argues that merely *refusing* the symbolic through hysterical discourse is not truly *revolutionary* until it is transformed into the discourse of the analysand in psychoanalysis. Citing the work of Julia Kristeva, Ulary explains that analytic discourse may provide a way for women to experience liberation in language by allowing for the creation of a subject's own signifiers expressing unique experiences and desires.

Part II
The Power to Speak:
Who Is Speaking, from Where?

The authors in this section are concerned with identity, both that of the individual "I" that threatens to become normative, and the group "we" that threatens to obliterate difference among individuals. Elissa Marder, Susan David Bernstein, and Sangeeta Ray work to propose identities that do not do away with difference in favor of an oppressive unity. This is an especially important issue for feminism, which seems constantly in danger of reifying an exclusionary identity of "women." On one hand, there is assumed to be a group named by that term that grounds the existence of the feminist movement. And yet, "women" is a category whose employment too often has the effect of silencing those women who do not fit into its predetermined parameters. Feminism seems caught in the difficult position of having to work on behalf of a diverse group of individuals without eliminating their differences and alternative axes of identification, including race, class, ethnicity, sexual preference, age, etc.

Denise Riley addresses such concerns about identity in *Am I That Name?* (Riley 1988). Riley shows how the identity of "women" is a socially constructed category rather than a "natural" one. She presents a genealogy of the feminist movement in Britain from the late seventeenth century to the nineteenth, showing how "man" became more and more conceived as the objective, neutral individual, while "woman" became more and more associated with sex and gender. This was accompanied by an increasing need to "figure out" the female sex, and a resulting over-characterization of women. Over time, "women" became a distinct category, to which were attached various meanings at different points in history. These associations developed gradually, through a variety of religious, moral, scientific, economic, political, and other forces. Riley's work thus shows how "women" developed into a category through the various movements of power relations in British history, and is therefore a highly constructed identity rather than a biological or natural one. This means also that it is an identity that cannot be pinned down—feminists cannot say what "women" are, since we have been so many different things at different times.

Feminism, Riley argues, has always been ambiguous, a movement on behalf of an unstable identity called "women." This leaves feminists in a seemingly difficult position. On the one hand, the setting apart of "women" is what has allowed feminism to emerge and to make beneficial societal changes; yet an emphasis on any kind of fixed identity for "women" may tend to reinforce the oppressive power relations that earlier forced the division into separate sexes. Riley shows how "women" as a group is impossible: not only does this category purport to denote a unity of individuals too diverse to ever fit under one heading, but it has been discursively produced so variously that its meaning is vastly overdetermined. Yet it seems to be the task of feminism to work on behalf of all women, and if this is said to be impossible feminism leaves itself open to charges of injustice. Thus, while "women" is impossible, "some women" is inegalitarian, and feminism finds itself caught in the middle.

But this does not mean that feminists' efforts are ineffectual, or that the impossibility of the feminist task should be grounds for its dismissal. The instability of the category "women" is the *sine qua non* of feminism, Riley argues, and the feminist movement is the space of the fighting-out of that identity. For Riley, however, this is not a problem to be lamented. She doesn't advocate giving up on the identity of "women," but suggests instead that we embrace the constructedness and changeability that already characterize feminist identities and concerns. Riley proposes that feminists develop a political movement that accepts its lot of impossibility with a certain reflective and ironic spirit, using the fluidity of women's discursive identity to express multiple possibilities for achieving political goals. Pragmatically, this might mean suggesting that " 'women' don't exist—while maintaining a politics 'as if they existed'—since the world behaves as if they unambiguously did" (Riley 1988, 112). Redefining women continuously might help to overthrow what might otherwise be considered stable conceptions of female identity. Riley thus attempts to steer a middle ground between asserting an identity for women and clamoring for its dissolution.

Judith Butler, expressing similar concerns, shows how the insistence on a closed, unified identity is intimately linked to the use of power. For Butler, feminists must be wary of expressing a single, "female" identity, because doing so merely perpetuates the oppressive effects of power structures in society. In *Gender Trouble* Butler criticizes what she claims to be a general assumption within feminist theory, that there is a coherent identity called "women," which "not only initiates feminist interests and goals within discourse, but constitutes the subject for whom political representation is pursued" (Butler 1990, 1). One problem with this assumption, she argues, is that positing any particular identity for women is an exclusionary and coercive act that puts pressure on those who refuse it to either change their tune or submit to an "anti-feminist" label. Further, to seek representation for the interests of a category called "women" is to play into the hands of the power that produced such a category in the first place. Butler cites Foucault's critical analyses of identity and power, arguing that "perhaps a new sort of feminist politics is now desirable to *contest* the very reifications of gender and identity, one that will take the variable construction of identity as both a methodological and normative goal" (Butler 1990, 5, emphasis added). She claims that insisting on unity for the identity of "women" under feminism belies an assumption that a stable unity is necessary for political action—an assumption that need not necessarily be true. Instead, she promotes the idea of coalitions that accept their own internal contradictions, splittings, and fragmentations, and that can take action with these intact. Butler describes these groups as "provisional unities," identities that "come into being and dissolve depending on the concrete practices that constitute them" (Butler 1990, 16). Coalitions of women could come together to accomplish particular political goals without specifying an overall unity beforehand, and could then dissolve without regret.

Though identity carries with it the oppressive potential of exclusionary power, Butler does not advocate the rejection of identity altogether. She argues instead for the "contemporary task of rethinking subversive possibilities for sexuality and identity *within the terms of power itself*" (Butler 1990, 30, emphasis added). Butler seems to accept the Foucauldian assertion that one can never get "outside" power (and its attendant identity structures), and she suggests instead that feminist theorists *recirculate* identity in ways that will work to upset it.[14] She suggests parody and performative iteration as good strategies for exhibiting the constructedness of identity in order to "repeat and displace through hyperbole, dissonance, internal confusion, and proliferation the very constructs by which [gender is] mobilized" (Butler 1990, 31). If we can enact in language the constructedness of "women," this identity could be endlessly modified, resignified rather than being static and coercive.

In her essay "Subaltern Studies," Gayatri Spivak suggests the strategic use of identity in order to overcome oppression (Spivak 1987). Following Marx, Spivak describes a strategic deployment of a class or group identity for the sake of eliminating the very identity used as a political strategy. For example, workers may unite as workers in order to challenge capitalism and exploitation so that one day they will own the means of their own production and no longer be merely workers but also owners. Discussing the subaltern, Spivak maintains that group identity is necessary to come together in political struggle and change the very identity in question. If we apply Spivak's notion of "strategic essentialism" to women, we can acknowledge that it might be necessary for women to unite using the group identity that currently serves to keep them oppressed in order to challenge oppression and ultimately to challenge any notion of identity that essentializes *woman.*

The tensions in the debate over women's identity are becoming more apparent in recent feminist literature. As the variety and specificity of feminist concerns all over the world become more widely recognized within the movement itself, it is inevitable that any clear-cut identity of "women" or "feminists" be shaken by difference within. Theorists such as Riley, Butler, and Spivak try to find ways to balance the benefits and dangers of both emphasizing unity and recognizing its impossibility. The essays in the second section of this collection further such concerns while focusing on language use. They ask what can be done about identity—both the individual "I" and the group "we"—by considering what words can do.

Elissa Marder, in "Disarticulated Voices: Feminism and Philomela," considers the impossible necessity of "feminist" identity as well as the "we" invoked by those who adhere to it. Marder notes the political benefits of speaking performatively as feminists, of saying "we," while also recognizing the need to express the undecidability of such an identity. Because of its political value, Marder argues that the feminist "we" needs to be retained as a provisional, performative tool. But in order to avoid the exclusionary risks that go along with it, feminists must only speak "we" without asserting the existence of a knowable referent for it. In this context, Marder takes up the question of "reading as a feminist," asking what happens when feminists speak to and through literary texts. Suggesting a feminist reading of Ovid's Philomela story, Marder locates there a way for feminists to speak together, even through the silence that has been imposed upon them through patriarchy: a feminist "we" founded on a community of pain, a shared relationship to silence and alienation under patriarchy.

In "Confessional Feminisms: Rhetorical Dimensions of First-Person Theorizing," Susan David Bernstein considers the power of first-person theorizing in feminist theory, focusing on the potential for a confessional mode of writing to disrupt traditional notions of authority, objectivity, and truth in feminist scholarship. Bernstein argues that such confessional acts can be politically transformative, but only if they remain self-critical rather than becoming reified conventions. In other words, the confessional "I" can become a reified, authoritative entity if it is allowed to work as a unified source of truth and knowledge, as a ground for an unproblematized, unmediated "experience." After considering a taxonomy of confessional modes and illustrating them with examples from recent feminist writings, Bernstein argues that many feminist confessions are *reflective*—they simply mirror an "I" that is not self-critical, whose words are an unquestioned, authoritative account of a clear and coherent experience. As an alternative, Bernstein adds *reflexive* confession to her taxonomy, a mode that investigates its own process of subjectivity through a kind of Foucauldian genealogy.

Sangeeta Ray, in "The Postcolonial Critic: Shifting Subjects, Changing Paradigms," also considers the political efficacy of including autobiographical elements in feminist writing, with an emphasis on postcolonial criticism. She focuses especially on the designations of race, class, sexual orientation, and geographical location that are often used to indicate an author's position in the relations of power under discussion in postcolonial texts. Ray points out that while such "micro-narratives" are meant to challenge the impersonal, universal mode of critical discourse, they may also reproduce some of its problematic elements on a smaller scale.

Specifically, though seeking to question metaphysical notions of identity as presence, postcolonial critics may still use such notions to "present" themselves in their autobiographical statements. Ray argues that identity is implicated in a "social encounter" where cultural, political, sexual, and other factors affect the position of the subject vis-à-vis her interactions with others, and that personal narratives should work to express these relationships. Keeping these issues in mind, Ray considers the recent commodification of the voice of Gayatri Chakravorty Spivak as *the* postcolonial critic, and illustrates the need to avoid such a reification of Spivak's subject position. In a personal narrative of her own, Ray critically examines her own attempts to negotiate an identity through multiple, heterogenous subject positions and the reactions of those around her.

Part III
The Power of Masculinist Metaphors:
Words That Keep Women in Place

The essays in the last two sections of this volume consider the importance of metaphors, figures, and images in language through a focus on those used by particular philosophers. Natalie Alexander, Andrea Nye, and Roberta Weston each address the power of metaphor within the work of prominent figures in the history of philosophy: Immanuel Kant, Gottlob Frege, and Jacques Derrida, respectively. Their analyses rest on the assumption that metaphor is more than a mere flourish of style, an occasional poetic turn that beautifies, rather than being a necessary part of, the transmission of meaning in language. In this, they share the perspective of many feminist theorists that metaphor is not only a prevalent and indispensable part of language, it is also responsible for helping to shape our conceptions of the world. In other words, metaphor is capable of *doing* things, and doing *feminist* things with metaphor may be a function of criticizing and re-forming metaphors that have oppressive effects for women.

The prevalence of metaphor in language and its role in shaping concepts forms the subject of George Lakoff and Mark Johnson's highly influential work on metaphor, *Metaphors We Live By* (Lakoff and Johnson, 1980). Lakoff and Johnson argue that our concepts are largely formed by metaphor, meaning that "... the way we think, what we experience, and what we do every day is very much a matter of metaphor" (Lakoff and Johnson 1980, 3). Categorizing the various types of metaphors within language, they show how each fits into coherent, conceptual systems through which we categorize and understand our experience. These systems are grounded in groups of basic, central concepts that appear to arise more or less directly from experience, including "UP-DOWN, IN-OUT, FRONT-BACK, LIGHT-DARK, MALE-FEMALE" (Lakoff and Johnson 1980, 57). While admitting that there is no unmediated physical experience, that culture always intervenes in the way we experience the world, Lakoff and Johnson maintain nevertheless that concepts such as the above are based in experiences that are "more" physical and thus more basic than others. These then become the grounds for many of our metaphors, the bases upon which we build, metaphorically, connections to abstract, less-delineated concepts. How such connections are made is a matter of both physical and cultural experience—e.g., "rational is up, emotional is down" is based in our cultural view of humans as rational animals who are, on account of our rational capacity, in control (above) other animals.

According to Lakoff and Johnson, then, the particular metaphors we use arise in part from experience, both physical and cultural. But more importantly, perhaps, the relationship works the other way as well: metaphor also helps *create* our experience of the world. Lakoff and Johnson explain: "In allowing us to focus on one aspect of a concept ... a metaphorical concept can keep us from focusing on other aspects of the concept that are inconsistent with that metaphor" (Lakoff and Johnson 1980, 10). For example, in the metaphor "ARGUMENT IS WAR," the focus on the battling aspects of argument can hide other aspects of it, shaping our view of what an argument is or should be according to our understanding of war. This creative capacity of metaphor is especially evident when new metaphors come into usage, according to Lakoff and Johnson, who claim that much cultural change can be attributed to the introduction of new metaphors and the rejection of once-common ones.

What seems conspicuously missing from Lakoff and Johnson's analysis is a *critique* of the kinds of metaphors in use. If metaphor has the power to configure our conceptual picture of the world, it is clear that criticizing and especially changing our metaphors may be an important mechanism for social and political change. Lakoff and Johnson admit that culture always mediates physical experience, but they do not question or problematize the cultural structures and values that give rise to dichotomous concepts such as UP-DOWN, LIGHT-DARK, MALE-FEMALE, etc., or to their metaphorical connections such as RATIONALITY IS UP, EMOTION IS DOWN. It is clear that their task is almost exclusively descriptive: they seem concerned only to explain how metaphor works, so as to be able to categorize and summarize it.[15] They attempt to remain value-neutral, saying only that the choice of metaphors within a given language will vary with cultural values. The closest they come to criticism is in the assertion that ". . . each culture must define a social reality within which people have roles that make sense to them and in terms of which they can function socially" (Lakoff and Johnson 1980, 146). Arguably, some cultural values are better at accomplishing this goal than others (and thus some metaphors might be better at creating such a reality than others). Recognizing the power of metaphor to shape reality, Lakoff and Johnson do not criticize the reality we have created with our metaphors thus far.[16]

It is this critical task that is of interest to many feminists working on metaphor. For example, in *The Man of Reason*, Genevieve Lloyd criticizes metaphors and images within Western thought that work to exclude women from ideals of rationality (Lloyd 1984). Lloyd traces conceptions of reason throughout much of the history of Western philosophy, exposing therein a gender bias that is upheld and perpetuated through, among other things, metaphor. Lloyd shows that ideals of rationality have been conceived in part by excluding and transcending elements associated with femininity. Starting from Greek conceptions of reason, Lloyd explains how successive generations of philosophers have perpetuated and built upon such exclusions of the feminine from reason by their use of symbols, images, and metaphors.

According to Lloyd, Greek conceptions of reason centered upon a kind of master-slave relation, as knowledge is said to be gained through a process of controlling and transcending natural forces. The Pythagorean table of opposites exemplifies how clear, determinate reason is associated with maleness, while vague, indeterminate unreason is associated with femaleness. Pythagoras's table is made up of ten opposites, including male/female, light/dark, limit/unlimited, one/many, and straight/curved.[17] The principles in the table associated with clarity, regularity, and limit (and thus reason) are considered "good" while those associated with vagueness, ir-regularity, and the unlimited (and thus unreason) are considered "bad." The feminine thus becomes implicitly associated with that which must be left behind in order to exercise clear reason. This kind of dominance and exclusion resonates throughout the symbols and metaphors of Greek philosophers, according to Lloyd. Greek ideals of rationality were often conveyed through images of domi-nance, she argues: for example, Lloyd cites Plato's metaphor of the soul as a pair of winged horses driven by a charioteer to show how, in Greek thought, the unruly passions must be dominated in order to achieve reason. Lloyd argues that though such images are not explicitly associated with a male-female distinction, there is, as with the Pythagorean table, an implicit association of femininity with the matter, nature, or passion that must be dominated for the soul to participate in reason.

This theme, Lloyd argues, is perpetuated and reinforced through-out the history of Western thought, in the work of philosophers from Aristotle to Hegel and beyond. The images and metaphors associating gender with ideals of reason are more or less explicit, depending on the thinker. One of the most explicit is Francis Ba-con, whose metaphor of a marriage between mind and nature uses sexual dominance to illustrate and legitimize the dominance of reason over nature. Man must exercise control over nature in the same way he does over his wife—not completely or tyrannically, but with the same degree of force as is right and justified in nuptial relations. Later thinkers built upon such gendered associations, even if they were not explicitly aware of it. For example, Lloyd argues that Descartes's method of achieving right reason, even though it was meant to apply to women as well as men, perpetu-ated the earlier genderization of reason. The sharp division be-tween mind and body characterizing the Cartesian method was built upon earlier distinctions associated with gender (mind-male, body-female), making the latter even deeper and more polarized. Lloyd convincingly argues that the metaphors, symbols, and im-ages used by thinkers such as Hume, Kant, Rousseau, and Hegel also adhere to this kind of a gendered structure, regardless of their intentions.

Clearly, for Lloyd, the metaphors connecting gender bias with reason are not merely superficial embellishments. They are not just symptoms of past misogyny that we can do away with by eliminating the metaphors. Over the course of the history of Western thought, according to Lloyd, our ideals of reason have become "genderized" themselves. Lloyd maintains that our ideals of reason are "male," with the attendant consequence that femininity has been defined over centuries in terms of what has been excluded from reason. This puts feminists in a difficult position, since simply asserting women's capacity to conform to the ideals of reason leaves untouched the movement of exclusion inherent in the ideals themselves; and revaluing the "feminine" is little different, since it attempts emancipation within a space already defined by the conceptual model of dominance and exclusion it hopes to change. Leaving this model behind will not be an easy task, but Lloyd hopes that the recent contributions of women to the Western philosophical tradition, especially those of feminist theorists, will help spur Philosophy into self-criticism and a reevaluation of its ideals of reason.

Though Lloyd includes discussions of metaphor in *The Man of Reason*, she does not explicitly focus on it, and consequently does not explain in detail how metaphor affects conceptions of reality.[18] She does assert that metaphor and allegory can affect the way women are seen in terms of their rational capacity, since gendered symbolism exploits and reinforces already-existing views of women. In addition, she insists that gendered metaphors "do not merely express conceptual points about the relations between knowledge and its objects. They give a male content to what it is to be a good knower" (Lloyd 1984, 17). Clearly, metaphor has played an important role in reinforcing and perpetuating the maleness of reason, according to Lloyd. Thus, though she argues that our ideals of reason are too deeply gendered to be thoroughly transformed by simply changing our metaphors, the latter ought certainly to be *part* of such an endeavor.

Exposing gendered metaphors in language and analyzing the extent of their social and political effects is a theme shared by many feminists writing on metaphor. Such concerns have been especially prominent in feminist philosophy of science, where masculine metaphors of reason subduing and controlling nature have been well documented and criticized by theorists such as Sandra Harding (1986), Evelyn Fox Keller (1985), and Carolyn Merchant (1980). The work of theorists such as these, as well as Lakoff and Johnson and Lloyd, has focused attention on metaphor and its capacity to help shape our understanding of reality.[19] Recent feminist theorists have begun to look more carefully and critically at metaphor as harboring both oppressive and liberatory potential. The essays included in the third section of this anthology extend such concerns by considering both the prevalence and importance of figure and metaphor in language, as well as the effects of specific metaphors used by prominent philosophers in the history of Western thought.

In "Sublime Impersonation: the Rhetoric of Personification in Kant," Natalie Alexander points out that while in his moral theory, Kant insists on the universal dignity and intrinsic worth of all rational beings, he nevertheless sometimes characterizes men and women differently in his writings. Though Kant's views about women are often dismissed as reflections of his time, Alexander considers the issue of Kant's misogynism by exploring a number of rhetorical figures he uses as means of personification. For example, Kant uses "man" to personify human nature, "husband" and "wife" for specifically male and female characteristics, and "Adam and Eve" for the collective development of rationality in humanity. Focusing on the gendered figures in Kant's texts, and noting the characterizations of women that these reflect, Alexander argues that Kant uses such figures of personification in contexts where he wants to emphasize the difference between nature and reason. The gendered connotations of these tropes, according to Alexander, point to a female nature/male reason distinction that puts women in a different relation to the moral law than men, despite Kant's insistence on the universality of his ethical doctrine for all rational agents. Ultimately, Alexander argues, rational agency in Kant's moral theory is reserved for a masculine subject, since there is no place therein for women as subjects.

Andrea Nye, in "Frege's Metaphors," argues that Frege must resort to metaphor in order to explain his logical system of truth-bearing language, even though this system is meant to exclude metaphor. Frege argues that objective truth is best achieved through a logic that excludes imprecise elements such as personal feeling and metaphor, yet Nye shows how he must rely on metaphor in order to communicate his system of logic to others. Nye presents a series of metaphors to which Frege had to resort in order to illustrate the workings of his logic, prompting him to eventually admit an obstacle to logic within language, a kind of "essential inappropriateness" or metaphoricity of language where what is meant cannot be passed directly from "hand to hand" as would be the logical ideal. Instead, language requires a step forward on the part of one's audience, a meeting halfway in the murky waters of metaphor. Thus, according to Nye, Frege's authoritative account of truth relies on and covers over an alternative account that opens truth up to response—making it a function of a reciprocal relationship rather than something transcendent and oppressive. Nye concludes that this alternative account of truth can be of use to feminists who want to avoid notions of truth that set up an absolute authority and cut off responses from others.

In "Free Gift or Forced Figure? Derrida's Usage of Hymen in 'The Double Session,'" Roberta Weston criticizes Derrida's appropriation of "hymen" as a metaphor for undecidability. While Derrida presents the hymen, and its feminine associations, as a "beneficent figure" given freely as a "gift," Weston argues that its usage is forced, signalling instead a theft or a rape. Derrida forcibly appropriates the female figure through the metaphor of the hymen, according to Weston, and through it places her in a position of silence, lack, and self-sacrifice. Weston argues that Derrida's use of hymen requires a willful forgetting of the term's patriarchal history and associations, a forgetting that mirrors the term's effects on the figure of woman in his texts. Derrida's work, Weston contends, denies woman property rights to her body and to language, making of the hymen a blank page upon which the phallic instruments of writing are to leave their mark. Weston concludes that by covering over the violence of its appropriation through a catechresis, Derrida's use of "hymen" as metaphor insidiously perpetuates the very phallocentrism he means to deconstruct.

Part IV
The Power of Feminist Metaphors:
Words That Open Spaces for Women

The authors in this section discuss the power and pitfalls of feminist metaphors, considering along the way the liberatory potential of replacing masculinist metaphors with ones that empower women. Of central concern is making sure that any new metaphors we might endorse do not reinforce the divisions and power structures upheld by those we mean to replace. Ewa Płonowska Ziarek, Lisa

Walsh, and Cynthia Baker, addressing the work of French feminist theorists Julia Kristeva, Hélène Cixous, and Luce Irigaray, consider the theoretical and practical benefits of the maternal and other feminine metaphors used by these French theorists. Kristeva, Cixous, and Irigaray all work within a psychoanalytic framework, and their discussion of language and metaphor has been heavily influenced by Jacques Lacan. In order to adequately grasp the main concerns of these French feminists, it is necessary to be familiar with a portion of Lacanian psychoanalytic theory, especially as it touches on the role of language.

Lacan emphasized the significance of language in the development of individual identity. Identity, for Lacan, is constructed through difference—the self, the "I," exists for each individual only across a gap or a rift that signals what is "not-I." A description of Lacan's "mirror stage" may help illustrate this point. The mirror stage signals the beginning of individual identity development during childhood. Lacan argues that this occurs when the child learns to form an image of itself as a distinct and unified being by recognizing itself in a mirror (or in the reactions of others, who act as "mirrors"). What is important about the mirror stage is that the child comes to recognize itself in something that is *other* to it, in a reflection outside of itself. This means that the image it comes to call "I" or "myself" contains, and depends upon, what is *not* itself. This otherness is recognized in the difference between what the child experiences as a fragmented, uncontrolled body and the closed unity of the image with which it is faced as the "self."[20] Thus, the child gains a sense of identity through the mirror stage, but there is at the same time instituted within the psyche a gap that forever drives an unfulfillable desire for wholeness. For Lacan it is significant that the identity thus produced is never fully transparent to itself but is mediated by otherness. In other words, the self is necessarily *social*, shaped by its relationships to other persons, to various social and political factors, and to language.

The effects of language on the subject's identity are profound, since it is only by entering the "symbolic order" that the subject can become fully delineated as a subject. Entry into the symbolic order coincides, roughly, with the ability to use language and take on social and cultural identities. When the child begins to form its needs into words, or "demands" as Lacan calls them, language is inserted between the child and its mother. The symbolic order breaks into the mother-child dyad as a "third term," forcing the separation necessary for the child to develop a fully social identity. Through language the child learns to represent itself symbolically, widening the gap produced through the mirror stage. Language perpetuates and covers over this gap, substituting representations for the proximity and immediacy of the mother-child relationship. This means that in the Lacanian view all language works metaphorically to a certain extent, substituting symbolic elements for direct possession of objects.

An important issue for feminist theory is that for Lacan, the symbolic order is represented by a paternal metaphor—a disciplining father who breaks up the mother-child dyad, enacting the separation necessary for the full development of identity. In this process the child's relationship to the mother is lost in the gap of separation, setting up a *desire* for fullness that is forever sought after but never recovered. The father governs the development of identity and sociality through language, the symbolic order signified by the *phallus* he possesses and the mother does not. For Lacan, the phallus is the signifier *par excellence*. It signifies the process of signification as a whole, where signs both institute and attempt to fill the gap of absent objects—a movement akin to the above-mentioned *desire* since the gap remains forever unfilled. The phallus is thus never fully present, "it can play its role only when veiled" (Lacan 1977b, 288). It is "the signifier of the desire of the Other," and it therefore plays a pivotal role in instituting sexual difference (Lacan 1977b, 290). For Lacan, "[sexual] relations will turn around a 'to be' and a 'to have'" (Lacan 1977b, 289): the male *has* the phallus while the female *is* the phallus. In other words, the phallus possessed by the male signifies the desire of the Other, who "finds the signifier of her own desire in the body of him to whom she addresses her demand for love" (Lacan 1977b, 290). For the female, the phallus also signifies the desire of the Other, but being castrated like her mother, she does not *have* it. Instead, she *is* this signifier insofar as she strives to be desirable for the male through masquerade, through illusions meant to cover over her lack. Since the phallus is the signifier of signification, having it allows the male to wield the power of language, while the female, in Lacan's view, seems able to signify only through masquerade. This view puts women in the troublesome position of being unable to speak without pretending to be men, being capable only of playing at being the phallus, of imitating the male who has it. This is, on the face of it, clearly problematic from the standpoint of feminist theory, and later feminists theorists have criticized Lacan's view of sexual difference.[21]

The study of metaphor and of language in general has been very important in recent psychoanalytic theory, including the work of Luce Irigaray, Hélène Cixous, and Julia Kristeva. Each of these theorists emphasizes the importance of metaphor, suggesting in different ways a replacement of masculinist metaphors signifying homogeneity and rigidity with feminist ones signifying heterogeneity and fluidity.

Luce Irigaray's texts are filled with figures of multiplicity and fluidity, excess and overflow of boundaries. But it would not be legitimate to label these as metaphors in any traditional sense, since they express for Irigaray a *metonymic contiguity*, a touching of (at least) *two*, rather than a *metaphoric substitution* of *one* for *one*.[22] This is illustrated in the figure of touch as found in "When Our Lips Speak Together," where Irigaray uses *two lips*—those that speak, and those of the female genitalia—to portray a multiplicity within women (Irigaray 1985b).[23] Between the two lips there is a confusion of identity and boundaries: there is a multiplicity, but it is not separable into independent and coherent "ones." Within the figure of touch there are no sharp breaks, no gaps separating that which is touching from that which is being touched. "We are always one and the other, at the same time. . . . Without limits or borders . . ." (Irigaray 1985b, 217). With this figure Irigaray expresses a metonymic contiguity that may open a space within discourse for women to be able to symbolize their bodies, desires, and identities within language, through a symbolic economy different from the metaphoric, paternal one presented by Lacan.

In Lacan's view, entry into the symbolic order requires a substitution of the father for the mother, a sacrifice of the mother that makes of the symbolic an order of substitution, of replacement, of representation. It is an order of sameness that does not allow for *two*—the father *and* mother—but instead lets one fall into a gap for the sake of the unity of the other. Mothers and their daughters are left without access to discourse *as* women; they are either outside of the symbolic (in the realm of nature) or can enter it only as men. Irigaray's figures of contiguity, fluidity, and ambiguity seem designed to help shape a symbolic economy different from the singularity of the paternal one, an economy that allows for the coexistence, the touching of *two* who are irreducibly different. Irigaray does not put forward this economy to *replace* the other (since this would be another metaphoric substitution), but to allow for another kind of discourse, still symbolic and cultural, in which women can express their multiplicity: "If we don't invent a language, if we don't find our body's language . . . [we will] leave our desires unexpressed, unrealized. Asleep again, unsatisfied, we shall fall back upon the words of men . . ." (Irigaray 1985b, 214). This different discourse is not singular, not static, not representational, but fluid, ambiguous, multiple: "Between our lips . . . several voices, several ways of speaking resound endlessly, back and forth" (Irigaray 1985b, 209). Irigaray's figurative language presents images of a fluid, heterogeneous symbolic economy that may be able to shape new kinds of social, political, and economic relations for the benefit of women.[24] Perhaps through such figures as Irigaray's "two lips" we can envisage a culture and an ethics of difference, of (at least) two rather than one, of male *and* female.

Hélène Cixous also proposes changes in the metaphors of psychoanalytic theory. One of her main targets is Lacan's use of maternal and paternal metaphors in his story of identity development. Cixous counters Lacan's view that women speak only by masquerading as men with the notion of *écriture féminine*, or feminine writing. She argues that the Lacanian, phallic symbolic need not be the only medium through which to use language: it is "theirs," providing a place for "them," but "we" need not therefore remain silent. She urges women to write, to use the symbolic that has kept us silent to create new languages through our own, feminine, writing.

Cixous specifically criticizes the Lacanian assertion that the child must reject its mother in order to enter a "paternal" symbolic order. This story has several consequences, she argues, not the least of which is that language is thereafter characterized by lack, absence, and gaps. It makes of words mere substitutes for the "real" thing, never quite fulfilling enough, always tinged with nostalgia for the plenitude of the mother-child relationship. Cixous argues in "The Laugh of the Medusa" that it need not be necessary to suppress the mother in order to speak, to make of her a gaping hole for the sake of language (Cixous 1976). She suggests that it is really only men who do this anyway, that the story has been wrongly extended to include the childhood of women as well. She claims that women do not build up as many defenses against drives as men do, do not forego pleasure as they do; and in this sense, "[e]ven if phallic mystification has generally contaminated good relationships, a woman is never far from 'mother'. . ." (Cixous 1976, 881). Women have a privileged relationship to the mother, whose voice speaks closeness and plenitude within them: "In women there is always more or less of the mother who makes everything all right, who nourishes, and who stands up against separation" (Cixous 1976, 882). Cixous makes of this "mother" a metaphor for a closeness, a touching within women that counters lack.[25] She argues that we can counter "their" symbolic with our own, a symbolic that does not pine for the mother who is absent, but that speaks her voice from within. Cixous's feminine writing (*écriture féminine*) takes place within this new, female symbolic order.

Julia Kristeva also theorizes a space beyond language and connects it with the mother, but she does not claim any privileged link to it for women, nor does she argue for a particularly feminine language. Kristeva's work points to a destabilization of all identities, including the female. Still, she does adhere to the psychoanalytic framework that, metaphorically, makes of language a "paternal" order and labels the pre-linguistic stages "maternal." Like Cixous, Kristeva uses a maternal metaphor to criticize Lacan's insistence on the loss of the mother upon entering the symbolic order. She argues that the mother is never completely lost (for both men and women), that the relationship with her returns continually and plays a necessary role in the symbolic order. Kristeva calls the maternal element within symbolic language the "semiotic," referring to the rhythms and tones of language, its melodies and movements. But unlike Cixous, she does not use the return of the mother to ground a new kind of language for women. Rather, the maternal metaphor helps her to reassess the structure of the symbolic order generally and to theorize an otherness already present within it. For Kristeva, symbolic language transforms itself through its poetic, metaphoric, semiotic elements—which are indeed described in terms of a maternal metaphor, but which do not thereby constitute a specifically feminine language.

For Kristeva the semiotic order is rooted in the space of the mother-child relationship, a maternal space she describes in *Revolution in Poetic Language* as the *chora* (Kristeva 1984a).[26] The *chora* is ordered by the mother's authority over the child's drives, including her prohibitions and frustrations of the child's bodily needs. It is a rhythmic space regulated by divisions necessary to, yet different from, the later separations that occur through entry into the symbolic order and development of a clear personal identity. The semiotic order emerging from the *chora* is ordered by ambiguity, as it "effectuates discontinuities by temporarily articulating them and then starting over, again and again" (Kristeva 1984a, 26). The semiotic is not replaced by the symbolic after the mirror stage and the resolution of the Oedipus complex, but remains a necessary part of language. It is the material element of language, the rhythms, tones, and musicality of it. Moreover, for Kristeva it is the semiotic element of signification that makes metaphorical language transformative, even revolutionary, due to the influx of heterogeneity it brings into the symbolic order.[27]

Irigaray, Cixous, and Kristeva are each concerned in different ways with the power of figure and metaphor. Each agrees that language plays an important role in the life of the subject, since it is necessary for both the individual's identity and its social relations. For each of these three authors, metaphor can have powerful effects on both the subject and society. But whether or not such abstract changes in metaphor alone can change the world is a complex and controversial question. Even those feminists who subscribe to the view that language can have a creative role in shaping reality face a paradox: it seems political reality requires that women be empowered in language before they have a place from which to speak a new language, with new metaphors. There must be a dialectical movement between language use and women's social status—changes in language use produce changes in social positions which in turn produce changes in language use, and so on. In terms of women's oppression, sexual difference will not be liberating until it is no longer grounds for discrimination.

The authors in the last section of this collection provide important contributions to the debate over how to replace metaphors detrimental to a feminist agenda with ones that might help to empower women. They consider the ways in which we can use feminist metaphors to empower women while maintaining, even sustaining, differences between them.

Ewa Płonowska Ziarek, in "At the Limits of Discourse: Heterogeneity, Alterity, and the Maternal Body in Kristeva's Thought," considers Kristeva's controversial use of maternal metaphors in connection with the semiotic order and the chora. Kristeva has been criticized for locating the revolutionary potential of the semiotic in a prediscursive realm, which harbors the possibility of an essentialist biologism. Ziarek counters such criticisms by arguing that Kristeva's work presents an *infolding* of difference in language and culture that problematizes the very distinction between discursive and prediscursive realms. Ziarek shows how for Kristeva, the semiotic appears within the symbolic and is, in an important sense, *both* presymbolic and postsymbolic. The *chora* and the semiotic order are therefore not natural or biologistic, but cultural, symbolic strategies for discussing the heterogeneity that is a necessary, though often repressed, element of the symbolic order. The metaphor of the maternal body in Kristeva's work, according to Ziarek, is also characterized by an infolding of difference, an otherness within the same. Ziarek concludes by showing the value of Kristeva's work for feminists, including her notion of a subjectivity-in-process that could help shape an open, pliable feminist identity.

Lisa Walsh, in "Writing (into) the Symbolic: The Maternal Metaphor in Hélène Cixous," discusses in detail Cixous's use of a maternal metaphor. Criticizing the Lacanian view that the mother must be excluded, replaced by the father in order for the child to enter the symbolic order, Cixous brings her back into the Oedipal picture in a "metaphorical fourth to the Oedipal triad." According to Walsh, Cixous reestablishes a connection to the mother that disrupts the supremacy of the paternal position in the symbolic order, and makes possible the expression of a feminine imaginary within language through *écriture féminine*. This feminine writing privileges the rhythmic, lyrical elements of language associated with vocal expression, and provides evidence that the symbolic order need not be univocal, paternal only—the mother need not be silenced for the sake of language, but can instead provide a means for "us" to write in "our" symbolic. Walsh argues that Cixous's "maternal metaphor" is not really a metaphor at all, since it does not work according to the logic of substitution that governs metaphor—Cixous does not substitute a maternal symbolic for the paternal one. Instead, the maternal metaphor allows for what Walsh calls a renewed access to the symbolic in a "past future," a reconnection to the past maternal body which also provides for feminine writing within a symbolic future.

Cynthia Baker, in "Language and the Space of the Feminine: Julia Kristeva and Luce Irigaray," considers the differing ways in which Kristeva and Irigaray use "the feminine" as metaphor in their work. Baker is particularly concerned with showing that the two theorists need not be read against each other, as if to agree with one of them must require disagreeing with the other. She argues that this has often been the trend in the reception of French feminism on American shores, and that it reflects a movement of hierarchy and exclusion that Irigaray and Kristeva (as well as many American feminists) are trying to get beyond. Baker shows how the work of Irigaray and Kristeva can be read in a complementary fashion by emphasizing the similarities within the two theorists' views. They share, for example, the claim that the phallic symbolic exists only through the exclusion of women, and they use various images and metaphors of the feminine in order to bring it back into language and culture. Further, Baker argues, the methods of the two theorists complement each other: Irigaray's efforts to criticize contemporary aspects of Western culture as they reveal women's oppression are complemented, Baker suggests, by Kristeva's concerns to trace historical trends beyond their current manifestations in one culture at one time. Baker concludes that the work of Irigaray and Kristeva can be used together as an important contribution to feminist discourse.

Overall, the essays in this collection advance discussions of the relationship between language, oppression, and liberation. By addressing critical issues such as how changes in language use can have larger social and political effects, and how metaphor in particular may be especially effective in this regard, these authors present groundbreaking work in areas that are of significant concern for current feminist theories of language. Moving beyond past discussions into new regions of inquiry, the essays included here provide a valuable contribution to the important and often controversial discourse concerning the words of feminists, and what we can do with them.

NOTES

1. This title is a play on J. L. Austin's *How to Do Things With Words* (Austin 1962). There Austin breaks down his earlier distinction between "constatives" and "performatives" because various types of constatives also seem to be performatives. He develops a classificatory system for

"illocutionary forces" of which both constatives and performatives are sub-sets. One of the implications of Austin's analysis of language is that language use is not only action because we perform it but also because through language use we perform many other types of actions.

2. Elissa Marder, "Disarticulated Voices: Feminism and Philomela," chapter 5 of this volume.

3. There are, of course, feminists who reject this distinction, criticizing attempts to divide language along gendered lines. See, for example, Sara Mills's essay (Chapter 1 of this volume) for a detailed criticism of some of the views presented below.

4. Throughout this Introduction, terms such as "speech," "writing," and "language" (e.g., "female language" vs. "male language") will be used to designate various means of language use and will be used interchangeably rather than referring to differences between spoken and written language.

5. See also (Kramarae 1984) and (Kramarae 1983).

6. The work of Lakoff, Miller/Swift, and Kramarae can be criticized on several fronts. Linguists have criticized their research for methodological reasons, including the fact that they rely on small, unrepresentative samples as well as anecdotes and personal experience rather than engaging in comprehensive studies. In addition, counter-studies refute the findings cited above: e.g., a study by Dubois and Crouch concludes that men use more "tag" questions than women (Dubois and Crouch 1975). Also, the claim that there is a difference in language use that corresponds to gender difference is controversial. First of all, these theorists presuppose that which they are trying to find: they survey a particular group in order to demonstrate some characteristics that define the group, yet they have already defined the group in order to carry out their surveys. Secondly, male language use is taken as a norm against which feminine deviations are measured. As Deborah Cameron points out, these linguists are left to explain the female difference from the "norm" but not the male adherence to it (Cameron 1985, 45; see also Cameron 1992). Finally, there is a tension between the way these theorists view language when setting out the gender differences in its use (where they assume that language *reflects* social reality) as opposed to when they are making suggestions for change (when they seem to argue that language can *create* a new social reality). If women speak a certain way because of a social position that is powerless, how can they hope to gain power by changing the way they speak?

7. See (Whorf, 1976).

8. Important to Spender's view is the distinction between dominant and muted groups in societies. Here she is greatly influenced by the research of Edwin and Shirley Ardener (See Edwin Ardener 1971, Shirley

Ardener 1978, and Dube, et. al 1986). Like the Ardeners, Spender argues that in a society there will be dominant groups and muted groups, the former maintaining their power by silencing the latter. In our society men are one of the dominant groups, women one of those who are muted.

9. There are still important problems with her theory, many of which have been articulated by Maria Black and Rosalind Coward in their review of *Man Made Language* (Black and Coward 1990). Black and Coward argue that although Spender makes claims for the creative capacity of language, she still falls back on the view that language reproduces or expresses experience. Spender argues at times that male language reflects male experience, and female language, if it were to be voiced, would express the experience of women. Yet she also maintains that language shapes experience. This leads to some confusion as to what women can do to undermine man-made language. In some places Spender argues that women need to take control of their language and create a place for their alternative meanings (Spender 1980, 93, 101, 134, 162). Yet elsewhere she suggests that women's social status will not change as a result of a change in language (Spender 1980, 79); and further, women's meanings cannot even be articulated until women's status changes (77). It seems that Spender leaves us with a catch-22: we must change language *in order* to liberate women, yet we cannot change language *until* we liberate women.

10. Irigaray both refers to Hegel's notion of recognition and revises it. For Hegel, recognition of an "other" is what allows self-consciousness to emerge, i.e., consciousness of self is dependent upon consciousness of others *as* others, not as extensions of the self. This much Irigaray keeps. But for Hegel, the dual relation of self-consciousnesses involved is hierarchical at first, a "master-slave" relation that is eventually reversed through the recognition of each in the other. Irigaray argues for a kind of recognition that avoids hierarchy altogether, an understanding that the other is so irreducibly different that the self could never "master" it. As discussed below, she finds this kind of relationship in a view of the other as gendered, i.e., in recognition of sexual difference. See the section on "Lordship and Bondage" in Hegel's *Phenomenology of Spirit* (Hegel 1977, 111–119). See also (Irigaray 1996, 103–108).

11. Irigaray's emphasis on sexual difference has invited charges of essentialism. Critics have argued that she fails to adequately theorize the social construction of gender. See, e.g., (Moi 1985). Moi argues that Irigaray makes of the female gender a stable, unchanging and ahistorical identity, due to her characterization of patriarchal oppression as a monolithic power structure. Irigaray claims that her work leads to the opposite conclusion. For example, she claims that in her view "there is no more 'natural immediacy.' . . . to be born a girl in a male-dominated culture is not necessarily

to be born with a sensibility appropriate to my gender. No doubt female physiology is present but not identity, which remains to be constructed" (Irigaray 1996, 107). Irigaray argues that female identity is not stable or ahistorical, because it has never really existed as an equal to the male. It remains for us to make it. The debate over Irigaray's alleged essentialism is a very complex one, and continues in current feminist literature.

12. For an elaboration of Irigaray's views of language and women's position relative to it, see Cynthia Baker's essay in the last section of this volume.

13. Foucault argues that political resistance to power should take the form of resisting identity rather than reifying it. This is because for him, the notion of a closed identity is a function of power, and part of resisting power is resisting such an identity as well as the notion of transcendent truth that upholds it. For an elaboration of the relationship between power, truth and political resistance, see especially (Foucault 1980), (Foucault 1983), and (Foucault 1990, 92–96).

14. See (Foucault 1980, 141) for Foucault's assertion that power cannot be "gotten rid of."

15. There is one place where Lakoff and Johnson seem to move in a prescriptive direction: in their discussion of new metaphors, they do suggest a couple of new metaphors that might help us look at reality in what appears to be a *better* way (e.g., "LOVE IS A COLLABORATIVE WORK OF ART"). But they stop short of providing a strong interpretation of the value of such metaphors, saying only that they appear forceful to persons of a particular generation and culture, rather than that they are valuable metaphors in general (Lakoff and Johnson 1980, 139–146).

16. One might argue that such a discussion could have been left out by Lakoff and Johnson partly out of a concern for cultural pluralism, a fear of imposing one's own cultural values on the rest of the world by engaging in a kind of universal criticism of the kinds of metaphors in use. Criticizing "objective" notions of truth, they argue that truth is relative to conceptual systems, which means that it changes from culture to culture (Lakoff and Johnson 1980, 193). Still, recognizing this need not lead one into a crippling relativism that would disallow any criticism of metaphors and cultural values (within one's own culture, at least). In addition, there may be certain values that are arguably universal in an ethical sense, e.g., basic human rights; racial, ethnic, and gender equality and justice, etc., that could form the basis for critique.

17. These correspond in part with the pairs of opposites presented by Lakoff and Johnson, above. Clearly, Lloyd's work is aimed at criticizing objective assumptions about basic conceptual categories such as those they

present—i.e., up/down, front/back, light/dark, etc. may not be simple, in-nocent categories arising "more or less directly from experience," as Lakoff and Johnson argue. Instead, following Lloyd, we can easily see how they may harbor a gender bias that works to the detriment of women (espe-cially when one of the pairs is male/female!).

18. Phyllis Rooney takes up this task in "Gendered Reason: Sex Meta-phor and Conceptions of Reason" (Rooney 1991). Focusing exclusively on metaphor, Rooney extends Lloyd's discussion of gendered reason by adding a more detailed explanation of the workings of metaphor and its conse-quent effects on conceptions of reality and women's place therein.

19. See also Eva Feder Kittay, "Woman as Metaphor" (Kittay 1988). Drawing in part on her work on metaphor (see Kittay 1987), Kittay dis-cusses the motivations for and effects of men's use of woman as metaphor for their relations to and projects within the world.

20. See (Lacan 1977a).

21. The above criticism is taken primarily from Elizabeth Grosz, *Jacques Lacan: A Feminist Introduction* (Grosz 1990, 70–72, 121–134). See also (Gallop 1982), (Mitchell 1985) and (Rose 1985). In her essay included here, Georganna Ulary argues that Lacan's symbolic need not be a "prison-house of language" for women. Ulary explains that Lacan's view still leaves open a way for women to use language against the paternal symbolic from a position within it.

22. Irigaray mentions an "economy of metaphor" in "Plato's Hystera" see (Irigaray 1985a, 346), relating it to a "genealogy of sameness" that makes the male and female substitutable, the same, not in (contiguous) contact as different. See (Whitford 1991, 177–185) for an in-depth discus-sion of Irigaray's views on metaphor and metonymy (to which much of what follows is indebted).

23. See also (Irigaray 1985c).

24. How the figures of fluidity and touch can affect social and political circumstances for women is a complex question. Margaret Whitford sug-gests that Irigaray's figures are fictions or myths that may anticipate and therefore shape new kinds of social relations (Whitford 1991, 185–191). Elizabeth Grosz argues that Irigaray's images provide "new emblem[s] by which female sexuality can be positively *represented*," new models that can "construct women's experience of their corporeality and pleasures" outside of the models provided by the male-dominated culture (Grosz 1989, 116). Grosz points out that for Irigaray cultural change requires, among other things, changes in language and representational norms; so that changes in social circumstances for women may not come about without new ways

of symbolizing female sexuality (Grosz 1989, 109–110). This is not to say, however, that Irigaray's figures are meant to provide *the* models for female sexuality—Grosz argues that Irigaray uses these figures to expose the processes by which dominant discourses are produced, rather than to provide a feminine language for women to adopt (Grosz 1989, 127). New discourses, feminine languages, are possibilities that must be left open.

25. Lisa Walsh argues in chapter 12 of this volume that Cixous's "maternal metaphor" is not really a metaphor at all, since it does not work according to a movement of substitution.

26. See also (Kristeva 1982, 71–72) for further discussion of how the semiotic is ordered through maternal regulation of the child's bodily drives.

27. Kristeva's work has been criticized by feminists for several reasons. First, some feminists argue that by carrying over maternal and paternal metaphors from the psychoanalytic story of identity development, Kristeva may drag along much of the problematic baggage that goes along with them (see Grosz 1989, 65). Also, Kristeva's discussion of the semiotic *chora* as connected to the mother has led to charges of essentialism (see Ewa Płonowska Ziarek's essay, chapter 11 below for a discussion of these charges and some effective rebuttals). Another problem many feminists have with Kristeva's work is that she uses maternal metaphors such as the *chora* to upset all notions of identity, including female identity (see Grosz 1989, 66–68) for criticism of Kristeva's view on the grounds that it doesn't deal with the particular ways in which women are oppressed). The most obvious objection feminists can have to Kristeva's work, of course, is that she has at times rejected feminism outright. See especially (Kristeva 1984b, 273–275), where Kristeva discusses feminism in terms of "political perversion." Yet it may still be the case that Kristeva would support a feminism that respects radical, individual difference rather than covering it over. Overall, her warnings against adhering too closely to an identity that is coercive are important in terms of feminist theory, in order that we avoid turning our efforts into "the killer mechanism of individual difference" (Kristeva 1984b, 273).

--------------------- REFERENCES ---------------------

Ardener, Edwin, ed. 1971. *Social anthropology and language.* London and New York: Tavistock Publications.

Ardener, Shirley ed. 1978. *Defining females: The nature of women in society.* London: Croom Helm.

Austin, J. L. 1962. *How to do things with words.* New York: Oxford University Press.

Black, Maria, and Rosalind Coward. 1990. Linguistic, social and sexual relations: A review of Dale Spender's *Man made language.* In *The feminist critique of language,* ed. Deborah Cameron. London and New York: Routledge, 111–133.

Butler, Judith. 1990. *Gender trouble: Feminism and the subversion of identity.* New York: Routledge.

Cameron, Deborah. 1985. *Feminism and linguistic theory.* New York: Macmillan.

———. 1992. *Researching language: Issues of power and method.* New York: Routledge.

Cixous, Hélène. 1976. The laugh of the medusa. Trans. Keith Cohen and Paula Cohen. *Signs* 1, no. 4: 875–893.

Dube, Leela, Eleanor Leacock, and Shirley Ardener, eds. 1986. *Visibility and power: Essays on women in society and development.* New York: Oxford University Press.

Dubois, B. L., and I. Crouch. 1975. The question of tag questions in women's speech. *Language and Society* 4: 289–294.

Foucault, Michel. 1980. Two lectures. In *Power / Knowledge: Selected interviews and other writings 1972–1977,* ed. Colin Gordon. New York: Pantheon, 78–108.

———. 1983. The subject and power. In *Michel Foucault: Beyond structuralism and hermeneutics,* 2nd ed., ed. Hubert L. Dreyfus and Paul Rabinow. Chicago: University of Chicago Press, 208–226.

———. 1990. *The history of sexuality vol. I: An introduction.* Trans. Robert Hurley. New York: Vintage.

Gallop, Jane. 1982. *The daughter's seduction: Feminism and psychoanalysis.* Ithaca: Cornell University Press.

Grosz, Elizabeth. 1989. *Sexual subversions: Three French feminists.* Sydney: Allen and Unwin.

———. 1990. *Jacques Lacan: A feminist introduction.* New York: Routledge.

Harding, Sandra. 1986. *The science question in feminism.* Ithaca: Cornell University Press.

Hegel, G. W. F. 1977. *Phenomenology of spirit.* Trans. A. V. Miller. New York: Oxford University Press.

Irigaray, Luce. 1985a. *Speculum of the other woman.* Trans. Gillian C. Gill. Ithaca: Cornell University Press.

———. 1985b. When our lips speak together. In *This sex which is not one,* trans. Catherine Porter. Ithaca: Cornell University Press, 205–218.

———. 1985c. This sex which is not one. In *This sex which is not one,* trans. Catherine Porter. Ithaca: Cornell University Press, 23–33.

———. 1996. *I love to you: Sketch of a possible felicity in history.* Trans. Alison Martin. New York: Routledge.

Keller, Evelyn Fox. 1985. *Reflections on gender and science.* New Haven: Yale University Press.

Kittay, Eva Feder. 1987. *Metaphor: Its cognitive force and linguistic structure.* New York: Oxford University Press.

———. 1988. Woman as metaphor. *Hypatia* 3, no. 2 (Summer): 63–68.

Kramarae, Cheris. 1981. *Women and men speaking.* Rowley, Mass.: Newbury House Publishers.

Kramarae, Cheris, ed. 1983. *Language, gender and society.* Rowley, Mass.: Newbury House Publishers.

Kramarae, Cheris, ed. 1984. *Language and power.* Beverly Hills: Sage Press.

Kristeva, Julia. 1982. *Powers of horror: An essay on abjection.* Trans. Leon S. Roudiez. New York: Columbia University Press.

———. 1984a. *Revolution in poetic language.* Trans. Leon S. Roudiez. New York: Columbia University Press.

———. 1984b. [1997]. My memory's hyperbole. Trans. Athena Viscusi. *New York Literary Forum* 12/13: 261–276; reprinted in *The portable Kristeva,* 3–21, ed. Kelly Oliver. New York: Columbia University Press.

Lacan, Jacques. 1977a. The mirror stage as formative of the function of the I. In *Écrits: A selection,* trans. Alan Sheridan. New York: W. W. Norton, 1–7.

———. 1977b. The signification of the phallus. In *Écrits: A selection,* trans. Alan Sheridan. New York: W. W. Norton, 281–291.

Lakoff, George, and Mark Johnson. 1980. *Metaphors we live by.* Chicago: University of Chicago Press.

Lakoff, Robin. 1975. *Language and woman's place.* New York: Harper and Row.

Lloyd, Genevieve. 1984. *The man of reason: "Male" and "female" in Western philosophy.* Minneapolis: University of Minnesota Press.

Merchant, Carolyn. 1980. *The death of nature: Women, ecology and the scientific revolution.* New York: Harper and Row.

Miller, Casey, and Kate Swift. 1977. *Words and women: New language in new times.* Garden City, N.Y.: Anchor Books.

Mitchell, Juliet. 1985. Introduction—I. In *Feminine sexuality: Jacques Lacan and the école freudienne.* Ed. Juliet Mitchell and Jacqueline Rose, trans. Jacqueline Rose. New York: W. W. Norton and Pantheon Books, 1–26.

Moi, Toril. 1985. *Sexual/textual politics: Feminist literary theory.* New York: Routledge.

Riley, Denise. 1988. *Am I that name?: Feminism and the category of 'women' in history.* Minneapolis: University of Minnesota Press.

Rooney, Phyllis. 1991. Gendered reason: Sex metaphor and conceptions of reason. *Hypatia* 6, no. 2 (Summer): 77–103.

Rose, Jacqueline. 1985. Introduction—II. In *Feminine sexuality: Jacques Lacan and the école freudienne.* Ed. Juliet Mitchell and Jacqueline Rose, trans. Jacqueline Rose. New York: W. W. Norton and Pantheon Books, 27–57.

Spender, Dale. 1980. *Man made language.* London: Routledge and Kegan Paul.

Spivak, Gayatri Chakravorty. 1987. Subaltern studies: Deconstructing historiography. In *In other worlds.* New York: Methuen, 197–221.

Whitford, Margaret. 1991. *Luce Irigaray: Philosophy in the feminine.* London and New York: Routledge.

Whorf, Benjamin Lee. 1976. *Language, thought and reality,* ed. J. Carroll. Cambridge: MIT Press.

Part One

The Power of Words

Changing Meanings, Changing Social Spaces

Lynne Tirrell

1

Derogatory Terms

Racism, Sexism, and the
Inferential Role Theory of Meaning

"When *I* use a word," Humpty Dumpty said, in a rather scornful
tone, "it means just what I choose it to mean—neither more nor
less."
"The question is," said Alice, "whether you *can* make words mean so
many different things."
"The question is," said Humpty Dumpty, "which is to be master—
that's all." [1]

Mary Catherine Bateson recounts a conversation with Johnetta Cole,
president of Spelman College, who said " 'I found out about race very
early. I have a recollection from when I was three or four years old
of a kid calling me nigger.' I asked her how she knew 'nigger' was a
bad word. 'The tone of voice,' she retorted, provoked by the question,
'and the rocks that are being thrown—they tell you that "nigger" is
an insult.' " [2]

In the familiar debate between Humpty Dumpty and Alice, most
of us side with Alice, maintaining that speakers have little or no
power to change socially recognized meanings of words on our own.
This paper about derogatory terms is also about speaker meaning,
the role of community norms in establishing meaning, and more
generally, the question of which is to be master. An analysis of derogatory terms helps show why individual speakers cannot escape

41

the socially established meaning of their utterances, except occasionally by the grace of the communities in which they live and speak. Derogatory terms are rich with their own history and reflect (in some sense) the history of the community in which they have meaning, and they are profoundly normative. This chapter introduces a richer way of thinking about what is wrong with derogatory terms than simply labelling them as biased (citing problems with connotation, as some do) or saying they fail to refer (citing problems with denotation). Neither approach is satisfactory, for much more is at issue than bad attitudes and referential misfires. What is at issue between those who use the terms and those who attack their use is the legitimacy of the expressive commitment of the terms; what is at issue is a commitment to the viability and value of a particular mode of discourse or way of talking. Such modes of discourse are themselves social practices, and they are closely tied to other, nondiscursive social practices that give them their force. So, at issue is the legitimacy of a set of linguistic practices as well as the legitimacy of the social practices they support and by which they are supported.

After briefly presenting the framework of my analysis in terms of linguistic commitments, I shall offer a characterization of two opposing positions on the problem of derogatory terms. Both the Absolutist and the Reclaimer hold that such terms are undesirable, and both engage in active attempts to change the social practices in which these terms are embedded. The Absolutist thinks that the terms we are considering are ineradicably derogatory, and hence thinks that to undermine the social practices behind them (racism, sexism, homophobia) we must eradicate the terms from our available repertoires. The Reclaimer, on the other hand, thinks that the terms mark important features of the target group's social history, and that reclaiming the term—making it non-derogatory—is both possible and desirable. It is possible, she argues, because we can detach the semantic content of the term from its pragmatic role of derogation, and it is desirable because doing so would take a weapon away from those who would wield it and would empower those who had formerly been victims. The struggle between the Absolutist and the Reclaimer illustrates the importance of a focus on linguistic commitments to developing a social practice approach to derogatory terms. This chapter represents such an approach.

The Problem

Consider two true stories:

> While driving home from his office one evening, a dark-skinned African-American man, George, inadvertently irritates a neighboring car by staying within the speed limit despite the other driver's close tailgating and honking. Harry, the white man driving the other car, pulls up beside George and shouts, "GET OFF THE ROAD, NIGGER!"

> Ethel, Fred, and Lucy are summer help at a seaside resort. Fred admires Ethel's independence and assertiveness, and, knowing that Ethel and Lucy are friends, he asks Lucy whether she thinks Ethel would go out with him on a date. Lucy knows that Ethel despises Fred, so she gives him an emphatic "no." Convinced of his own worthiness, Fred is perplexed, and after finding out from Lucy that Ethel is not involved with another man, Fred finally says, "Oh, I get it—she's a dyke!"

These stories are nasty and their language is meant to be hostile and rude. The first case involves an insult hurled directly at its target. Both involve reductive classification.[3] Pragmatically, the perlocutionary effect of these utterances is clear: they are angry put-downs that attempt to reduce the person to one real or imagined feature of who they are. Sandra Bartky calls the catcalls men hurl at women on the street "rituals of subjugation"; something similar occurs in these stories.[4] This inquiry, in the borderland between semantics and pragmatics, asks how the semantics of derogatory terms contribute to these pragmatic effects, and how these pragmatic effects contribute to the very meanings of the terms.[5]

My concern is with a particular kind of derogatory term used to refer to people. To call someone tall or short seems to be straightforward description, but to call someone "a runt" is to use a derogatory term. Using "runt" to describe a person invokes stereotypes associated with being small, adding the hostile implication that this is someone who should not have been allowed to grow up. Even when used without hostility, there is still the associated inferential consequence that runts should be killed soon after birth. The derogatory terms used in our opening stories are even worse than "runt," for they are tied to frameworks of sexist and racist oppression. They have a rich and twisted history within American culture, and that history created a network of nasty inferences now associated with the terms. On the other hand, these two terms are also the subject of political reclamation projects; they are sometimes adopted as positive in-group terms by those at whom they have been hurled as epithets. Such reclamation projects defy any attempt to simplify the pragmatics of these terms. Because of this rich embeddedness, and because their social roles prohibit over simplification, I'm going to focus on these two deeply derogatory terms.

Philosophers may be inclined to think that I am adding another chapter to the discussion of the general significance of what have come to be called "thick" terms—terms or expressions that carry with them or convey an attitude, an approval or a disapproval. Thick terms are those in which the description and the attitude "form a compound or amalgam, rather than a mixture: the attitude and the description infuse each other, so that in the end, in the repertoire of the mature speaker, the two elements are no longer distinguishable."[6] Clearly derogatory terms are thick in an important sense, but the issue of attitude, the psychological states and stance of the actual speaker, is one that is best set aside. Attributions of attitude may be made on the basis of a speaker's use of such terms, among other things, but it is not simply because this particular speaker has this particular attitude that the term is offensive, insulting, or harmful. A speaker's attitude may be quite at odds with what he or she actually says on any given occasion, due to a variety of ways we can misfire, obfuscate, or dissimulate. The discussion that follows will have some significance for those who want a theory of thick terms in ethics, but I will not make such an application. Rather, I shall show that a proper understanding of derogatory terms illustrates the importance of a proper understanding of expressive and other linguistic commitments.

Contextualism: An Inferential Role Theory of Meaning

Trying to figure out what exactly "nigger" means, I turned to the *Oxford English Dictionary*, which lists "nigger" as synonymous with "Negro," "black," "African-American," and "third-world woman/man," noting that it is colloquial "and usually contemptuous."[7] The *OED* misses the mark here, for "nigger" is *not* synonymous with these terms. The racial designation is often taken to be central to the meaning of the term,[8] but in fact the heart of the expression is its designating the person as subordinate. Expressions like "white nigger," which was commonly used in the 1850s to denote "white workers in arduous unskilled jobs or subservient positions,"[9] show that the subservience aspect of the term is crucial and that the racial element may be less central than one might think.[10] The history of the term is tied to its consistent use against American blacks, but the term's extension has broadened and its intension has shifted since then. Historically, slavery in the United States established a dominance/subordination relation between Americans of European descent and those of African descent, marked most prominently by darkness of skin. As the term took hold, the roots set out in the ante-bellum period grew to support the development and maintenance of a black underclass that still exists. To call someone "a nigger" today is at minimum to attribute a second-class status to him or her, usually on the basis of race and, arguably, to take that lower status to be deserved.

So why, then, does the *OED* say that the term is "usually contemptuous" and not "always"? Perhaps its editors were considering a case like the following: When my elderly white neighbor said that she needed to find a "yard nigger," *she* did not think her words conveyed contempt for the black men in our North Carolina town who do yard work. (This was 1992.) What she intended was to let me know that she wanted someone to do her yard work who is, above all else, cheap labor. Her intention carried no explicit contempt, and when asked, she might reply that she sincerely shows respect to African Americans. What she does not think about, but what such words do convey and depend upon, is that the black man she seeks *is* cheap labor because of an oppressive racist social and economic structure that holds him in contempt. Her purportedly neutral intention in using the term is not sufficient for overcoming its socially and historically conferred derogatory power.[11] What both my former neighbor and the *OED* miss is that the term carries contempt even when the speaker does not.

Racism is often taken to be an attitude, a mental state, a matter of individuals harboring and acting upon prejudices. This characterization is consistent with racism's being primarily a matter of individual private judgments and preferences. In contrast, I take racism to be a structure of social practices that supports and enforces the subordination of the well-being of members of some races to the well-being of members other races.[12] Intentions, on this view, are derivative of these social practices.[13] Racist language is significant only within a context that sanctions wide varieties of disparate treatment of members of races deemed lesser, including social and economic isolation, harassment, violence, and even genocide. These practices are the core—the threat and the reality—of racism. Without their cultural and material "back-up," words like the derogatory terms we are considering would not have the force they do.[14] Taking just such a contextualist position, legal scholar Richard Delgado argues that racial slurs "conjure up the entire history of racial discrimination in this country."[15] This claim is too sweeping and too mentalisitic, but it is clear that derogatory terms for African Americans cannot be significantly distanced from the history of the enslavement of Africans in the United States and the mistreatment of blacks at the hands of whites since then. As Wittgensteinians are fond of reminding us: a language is a way of life. Without the way of life, the language is just so much wind.

This language/culture holism is nicely complemented by an inferential role theory of meaning, which offers a powerful conceptual framework for analyzing the social problems reflected in and the linguistic problems created by derogatory terms.[16] According to this view, the meaning of a sentence is a matter of its place in a pattern of inferences. The meaning of a word or expression is a matter of its various actual and possible sentential roles. These patterns of inference are governed by commitments, which are a matter of speakers issuing licenses and undertaking responsibilities. Which commitments a speaker may make depends on the speaker's social, cultural, and linguistic context. The speaker's social and linguistic community *licenses* or *entitles* nearly all its members to make certain kinds of basic linguistic commitments, such as "it's a sunny day today" or "if this is Roxbury, we must be in Boston." Specialization of labor and discrete distribution of authority in many communities results in those communities licensing only certain speakers to make certain kinds of commitments. Sometimes we give explicit licenses, as we do in allowing only certain people to prescribe and dispense drugs. Most linguistic licenses tend to be less explicit, but similarly effective.

The sorts of very basic linguistic commitments made by any speaker making an assertion can be seen by considering Lucy's assertion, "Ethel danced in the play but refused to dance at the party." Applying Robert Brandom's account of asserting, we find that Lucy undertakes two sorts of commitments in asserting this claim: an *identificatory* commitment and an *assertional* commitment.[17] Each commitment carries an associated *task-responsibility*. Here Lucy's identificatory commitment requires her to identify which Ethel, which play, or which party, if her audience is confused about them. Lucy's assertional commitment carries a responsibility to justify the claim if it should be challenged, and issues an inference license to her audience. Lucy's justification may be a matter of providing further claims that constitute evidence of her own (as in, "I saw Ethel dancing onstage, and I watched her the whole night at the party") or it may be a matter of deferring to another speaker (as in, "Fred told me"). An inference license entitles the audience to use the claim as a premise in arguments of their own while deferring justification for the claim back to the person who issued the license. When Lucy defers her justification back to Fred, she relies on a license Fred issued in saying what he did about Ethel. Then the listener in search of evidence has to go to Fred. When Lucy makes the claim about Ethel, she (*qua* asserter) must supply the antecedent inferential links (in justifying) and license others to use consequent inferential links.[18]

In addition to assertional and identificatory commitments, speakers undertake expressive commitments as well. An expressive commitment is a commitment to the viability and value of a particular way of talking. This concept was first developed to account for the way that metaphorical interpretation involves not only what is said but also how it is said and how that method of presentation influences both the assertional and the identificatory commitments associated with the expression.[19] When Romeo says, "But soft, what light through yonder window breaks/ It is the east, and Juliet is the sun," he undertakes a commitment to the viability and value of using sun-talk to talk about Juliet. The task-responsibility incurred by an expressive commitment is a matter of showing to the audience, if asked, that this way of talking really is viable and valuable. In the case of metaphors, we do this by extending the metaphor. Showing viability requires showing that the metaphor can be extended; showing value takes much more. Value is usually judged by assessing the utility of the extended metaphor to the goals of the discourse. In general, to judge whether a given mode of discourse is viable or valuable, one has to establish the goals of the discursive practice. Sometimes that goal will be seeking truth, sometimes it will be seeking power, and often it will be some species or combination of these.[20]

Ordinarily, one supports one's expressive commitment by supporting enough of the assertional commitments of the expression to show that the way of talking in which the expression fits is indeed viable and valuable. The assertional commitments of "nigger" are illustrated by Jerry Farber's attempt to make the case that "students are niggers."[21] Farber's contrast class is the faculty, and he cites segregated dining facilities, segregated lavatory facilities, segregated sleeping facilities, and anti-miscegenation rules between the classes as but partial evidence of his claim. He adds that "students . . . are politically disenfranchised" within the academic system and a good student, "like a good nigger," is "expected to know his place." Farber further suggests that students have "the slave mentality: obliging and ingratiating on the surface but hostile and resistant underneath." Each of these features represents one assertional commitment of the term. ("If X is a nigger, then there is a set of Ys such that Xs and Ys cannot sleep in the same facility"; similarly for each of the other features.) We now have a partial list of the elements in the inferential role of the term: the referent is a being defined in reference to others to whom she is considered subservient, from whom she must be kept separate, by whom she may be exploited, and so on.

Spelling out some of the assertional commitments here gives us a sketch of the inferential role of the term and shows its viability. Sometimes viability alone is enough to show value, since we may find some value in the term's power to communicate all that it does. In cases like this one, however, more needs to be said. Opponents to all uses of this term, Absolutists, would urge that simply showing us *some* of the semantic features of the term does not show *enough* value to overcome the devastating pragmatic force of the term. The Absolutist holds that the term's subordinating assertional commitments ultimately undermine the general value of the term. When expressive commitment is controversial, then a thorough exploration of the assertional commitments is in order.

While this example from Farber illustrates that the assertional commitments associated with the term supply what is usually called its semantic content, it also illustrates that this so-called "semantic" dimension cannot be separated from the pragmatic history and force of the term. Each specification of an associated trait here marks an inference licensed by the assertion of the term, and shows the central importance of the social practices in which the term took hold. The social, psychological, and economic practices of treating dark-skinned African Americans as less valuable than light-skinned European Americans give content and force to the term *nigger*. So, Harry's hurling this term at George on the highway *must* be considered in light of the social history of the term and the classes it has been used to maintain. Harry cannot hide behind the Humpty Dumpty defense: "When I use a term, . . . it means just what I choose it to mean—neither more nor less."[22]

With respect to the politics of discourse, attention to different aspects of a speaker's linguistic commitments raises the question of what the speaker endorses, and what those endorsements mean to the listener. Referential commitments made possible by the term show the term's extensional range. Assertional commitments made possible by the term show what can be said about and done to those in the extension of the term. Since the expressive commitment carried by the term is a rather global commitment to the viability and value of the assertional and referential commitments that constitute the mode of discourse, the expressive commitment, independent of any special contextual limitations, shows a range of what speakers *can* endorse with that term.

If I say nothing about her words when my neighbor says "nigger," then although I haven't explicitly sanctioned the term and its expressive commitment, I have done nothing explicit to challenge it either. Challenges have three basic types. Some deny that the referential commitment can be fulfilled: "There aren't any such folk."[23] Others address the assertional commitment by making undesirable inferential consequences apparent. Finally, some challenges make explicit the structure and function of the expressive commitment; I can ask my neighbor whether she means to be participating in linguistic conventions that at least mirror and reinforce and at worst *create* social inequalities and injustices. These latter challenges— which demand that the speaker show that the way of talking is viable and valuable on a very large scale—make most explicit what is at stake between those who engage in the mode of discourse and those who attack it.

It is worth noting that the derogatoriness of a term in its sentential context is not a function of whether the term is asserted. Embedding the term in the antecedent or consequent of a conditional does not take away the derogatoriness of the term. If my neighbor says, "If a nigger buys the house down the street I'll sell mine," she is as responsible for justifying the expressive commitment of the derogatory term (for justifying "nigger"-talk) as if she had said, "A nigger just bought the house down the street so I'm selling mine." Similarly, the logician's distinction between use and mention does not help us here. Consider a sentence that an academic David Dukes might utter: " 'Nigger' is a great word, for it keeps us all aware of who belongs where in the social order." The derogatory term is mentioned, not used, but the sentential context supports the derogatoriness of the term and so the mentioning does not wipe it away. Even though the term is not doing any specific referential work here, and even though its status as mentioned raises the question whether the speaker endorses its use, nevertheless the content of the rest of the sentence settles the question of speaker endorsement. Now consider, "Fred is wrong to call blacks 'niggers' because there are no niggers—only black citizens." The first instance of the derogatory term is mentioned, and the second is used. Despite this use of the derogatory term, we would not ordinarily call the claim racist or derogatory since the sentential context condemns the derogatory aspect of the term. We would, however, justly wonder about the felicity of the second occurrence of the derogatory term, for the speaker could just as well have said "there aren't any" without gratuitous repetition of the term.

Expressive commitment is neither attitude nor connotation, although it may enable us to make inferences about each.[24] Despite her self-described positive attitude toward African Americans, my neighbor's use of the derogatory term carries with it a commitment to the derogation thus effected. This commitment is not *acceptance* of the derogation, for she need not even recognize the derogation, much less accept it. Her psychological states are distinct from what the language presupposes and entails about the world and about itself. So, for example, whether one uses "dyke" pejoratively or admiringly, one undertakes an expressive commitment to the viability and value of "dyke"-talk. As we shall soon see, the detractor and the admirer may differ in their accounts of what the expressive commitment is a commitment to, but both are committed to showing any challenger the viability and especially the value of such talk. The arguments offered by activists who seek to eliminate or rehabilitate these terms, are, on my view, struggles over whether we as a community want to sanction expressive commitments like those associated with these terms. Their arguments show that we would do well to take a social practice view of fights over words in our community.

Social Context: An Absolutist Position Concerning Groups, Labels, and Power

The Absolutist begins with the empirical claim that derogatory terms are harmful to those whom they purport to denote. Motivated by a conviction that the harms done by derogatory terms are both avoidable and unjust, the Absolutist argues that such words should be eradicated from our available repertoire and often argues further that there should be sanctions against their use.[25] Richard Delgado claims, for example, that "words such as 'nigger' and 'spick' are badges of degradation even when used between friends; these words have no other connotation."[26] Taking such an Absolutist position is taking a stance toward the expressive commitment of the terms. The Absolutist position depends on the sort of holism, or contextualism, discussed in the previous section. For the holist, a sign design is a word only in the context of a language, and a language has significance only in the rich context of culture. Social context is especially important in the case of derogatory terms, so it is important to attend to the social dynamics that lend derogatory terms their power. These social dynamics also constitute in part the assertional commitments that make up what philosophers usually identify as the semantic content of the term.

Recognizing that harms may be done even where the victim is unaware of any hurt, social scientists have catalogued a long list of harms resulting from racial stigmatization.[27] Clearly, racist derogatory terms contribute to racial stigmatization, so they have some power to harm their victims. A derogatory term labels a person *qua* member of a group, bringing the person under any stereotypes associated with the group, and thus sanctions inferences about the person that ought not be so sanctioned.[28] So, one way that derogatory terms harm is through their association with stereotypes. Stereotypes oversimplify the diversity that exists within the group, they tend to concern behaviors or psychological traits, and, most importantly, they are difficult to empirically falsify.[29] Stereotypes are rigid, and their implication that the traits attributed are natural suggests that the possession of these traits by most members of the group is inevitable.[30] The assertional commitments associated with derogatory terms are *constituted* in large part by these stereotypes.

Articulating an important tenet of most versions of Absolutism, Greenberg, Kirkland and Pyszczynski claim that derogatory ethnic labels

> *come to symbolize all the negative stereotypic beliefs associated with the group.* Because DELs [derogatory ethnic labels] have the power to communicate *all* the negative beliefs about a given group in a single word, they are likely to be extremely potent communicative devices. Words have the power to make a concept seem like something that actually exists in the world. For example, there are negative beliefs about blacks in the United States, but *the term "nigger" crystallizes these beliefs into a concept or prototype* that has a sense of concrete reality to those who use the term. (my italics)[31]

The claim that the derogatory term has "the power to communicate *all* the negative beliefs about a given group in a single word" may just amount to saying that the association of a term with a stereotype is an all-or-nothing matter.[32] The Absolutist takes the assertional commitments of the derogatory term, which would be used to justify the expressive commitment, to be *nondetachable*. The Absolutist holds that a speaker who uses a derogatory term invokes the *entire* inferential role of the term and undertakes a global expressive commitment to that way of talking. That's a holist point. The Absolutist is a holist of a particular sort: she holds that specific inferential consequences are nondetachable from derogatory terms because of their social and historical embeddedness.[33]

The nondetachability of the assertional commitments of these derogatory terms, if indeed they are nondetachable, is due in part to the fact that they are constituted largely by stereotypes, which are notoriously rigid. This nondetachability may also be due to the covertly prescriptive nature of these concepts. The assertional commitments of these terms tell members of the target group how they *ought* to be, under the guise of describing how they *are*. Sarah Hoagland has argued that attributions of femininity to women function prescriptively rather than descriptively, since the claim that women are feminine is not, in practice, empirically falsified by the numerous unfeminine women among us. Instead, those women are labelled "deviant," "abnormal," or, even worse, it is said that they are "really men trapped in women's bodies."[34] When such conceptual and social gerrymandering goes on, one must ask what is at stake. Hoagland notes that the trappings of femininity are indeed traps, and argues that some of the behaviors classically labelled feminine are actually resistance to those traps. Similarly, Frantz Fanon argues that "the black man is supposed to be a good nigger; once this has been laid down the rest follows of itself."[35] Fanon's view, in my terms, is that the inferential role of the term *nigger* is prescriptive; its job is to prescribe a way of being for those to whom it is applied.

It is important to look at the function of the name calling on the level of social practices, not just on the level of what Fred is trying to do to Ethel. Fred's calling Ethel "a dyke" works between them only if there is a more general set of practices within which it fits. The rather obvious politics of name calling is neatly summed up by sociologist Irving Allen, who writes,

> Words are weapons; and "hurling" epithets is a universal feature of hostile intergroup relations. *Outgroup nicknames are preeminently a political vocabulary*. Name calling is a technique by which outgroups are defined as legitimate targets of aggression and is an effort to control outgroups by neutralizing their efforts to gain resources and influence values. (my italics)[36]

Pragmatically, a derogatory term: (1) may do the relatively external job of reminding the person of the social sanction of their status as lesser; (2) may do the more "internal" job of instilling psychological oppression, convincing the person that her socially sanctioned status is really deserved (as when it is suggested that it has biological roots, for instance); or (3) may accomplish both.[37]

Against such an explicitly political interpretation of derogatory terms, Richard Delgado argues that a racial insult "is not political speech" since "its perpetrator intends not to discover truth or advocate social action but to injure the victim."[38] Denying that the terms are political paves the way for the legal redress that Delgado seeks, but Delgado overlooks the fact that such terms serve to reinforce a political structure, a structure that settles who has power and who has resources. Although they may advocate no particular social action on a particular occasion, these terms advocate the division of society into separate and unequal classes according to skin color, sex, sexual preference, and the like. Only an excessively narrow construal of the political would rule these terms out. *These terms are enforcers of a system that keeps some people from full participation in their communities, that keeps some voices from being heard.*[39] Clearly, the derogatory terms under consideration are political speech. They don't convince by rational argument, but they do bully us into adopting or maintaining certain broadly political commitments and they support the social practices that support these commitments.

Delgado further argues that "the characteristic most significant in determining the value of racial insults is that they are not intended to inform or convince the listener. Racial insults invite no discourse, and no speech in response can cure the inflicted harm."[40] Although such expressions do not convince by rational argument, by giving and asking for reasons, we know that they do inform. As Johnetta Cole's early experience shows, they teach the targeted person about the social hierarchy and her designated place in it; they inform about the power structure.[41] Accordingly, I suggest that explicitly addressing particular uses of the term, making the expression itself the subject of rational discussion, goes some way toward ameliorating the harms of the term and toward weakening its potential to harm again. Making explicit the expressive commitment also makes explicit the political dimension of the term, both in its assertional commitments' being rife with rigid—perhaps nondetachable—prescriptive stereotypic traits and in the social function of the distinctions made therein.

Once the Absolutist claims that (in our terms) the expressive commitment of "nigger" is unacceptable because it carries with it an nondetachable commitment to assertions that depend on all the horrible elements of the history of the culture in which the term gained currency, he or she must explain and evaluate specific uses of the term and its associates. In a useful botanization of the philosophical literature, Simon Blackburn presents four different approaches relevant to questions about the meaning and value of areas of discourse, such as those being considered here. Against the background of the inferential role theory, these approaches can be seen as ways of challenging the expressive commitment of the term. Blackburn suggests that we could (1) reject the whole area of discourse "advocating that people no longer speak or think in the terms that seem problematic," or (2) give a reductive analysis of the objectionable area of discourse to an unobjectionable discourse, or (3) see the beliefs associated with that discourse as not carrying truth values at all but simply as expressions of attitude,[42] or (4) see them as "mind-dependent—not really describing a mind-independent reality at all, but as in some sense creating the reality they describe."[43] The Absolutist combines these strategies, for she seeks to reject the whole area of discourse on the grounds that there is no adequate reduction of the objectionable area of discourse to an unobjectionable area, and on the grounds that the beliefs do not carry truth values although they may be perceived as doing so. What the derogatory terms and their inferentially linked practices do is to create a social and material reality that oppresses those targeted by the terms.

Blackburn's characterization of the philosophical positions generally embraced is fair, but it, like the strategies it botanizes, it is importantly incomplete. The social and material reality created by commitment to and practice of the modes of discourse in which these derogatory terms gain their purchase is not captured here. That social reality is in some sense dependent (at least during some parts of its history) on the beliefs and attitudes of at least some of the members of the society. But the social reality outstrips the particular beliefs of particular individuals, and so cannot be considered mind-dependent in Blackburn's sense. Redlining neighborhoods may begin with perceptions on the parts of certain bank officers about property value depending on the racial makeup of the community, but it does not end there. The reality of the beliefs is cashed out in cold economic terms, which may then create policies that in turn are carried out by people who may not share the beliefs of those who instituted the policies. The fifth approach, missing from Blackburn's list, takes beliefs as creating and being created by social (and institutional) realities that can be evaluated independently of the intentions of those who participate in them. This fifth approach takes social practices seriously in its analysis of derogatory terms.

Challenges to the expressive commitments of these derogatory terms are challenges to the viability and value of the modes of discourse of which they are part. Such modes of discourse are specified in two ways: structurally by their inferential networks, and functionally by their goals and practices. Two major goals we adopt in our various social practices are the acquisition of truth and the acquisition of power. With derogatory terms, these goals clash, and the quest for power takes precedence over any pretense of seeking or speaking truth. The Absolutist demands that we make power serve truth, and not vice versa.

The Absolutist begins with the empirical claim that derogatory terms cause unjust and unnecessary harm to those they label. Since the assertional commitments of the term largely represent stereotypically assigned traits and relations, and since stereotypes are notoriously rigid, prescriptive, and difficult or impossible to undermine, the Absolutist holds that the assertional commitments of the derogatory terms are nondetachable. To stop the harms caused by the terms we would have to detach at least some of the stereo-typed assertional commitments, but since these are nondetachable, there is no rehabilitating the term. Without rehabilitation, any use of the term is racist, sexist, heterosexist, or whatever, and so promotes injustice. So the Absolutist holds that since we cannot drop the derogation from the term, we should drop the term.

The Reclamation Project: Reclaiming Labels, Regaining Power

Proponents of reclamation projects would be quick to deny Delgado's claim that the derogatory terms we are considering are always "badges of degradation even when used between friends." They say that sometimes when used by members of the in-group the term is a badge of pride that recognizes an important history of degradation without endorsing its continuation. Some African Americans say that they can use "nigger" as a term of endearment, and some lesbians now use "dyke" as a term of pride. Such reclamations are self-conscious attempts to change the meanings of these terms through subversive uses within the sub-community. The strategy is straightforward although far from simple: give the subcommunity jurisdiction over the expressive commitments of its own self-referring labels. Change the norms that settle the assertional commitments of the term within the subcommunity, and ultimately within the larger community, and in so doing you change the very meaning of the term.

Even within one linguistic and social community, even without reclamation, the pragmatic function of a derogatory term may vary depending on the speaker's relation to the target group. Irving Allen suggests that for members of the dominant group the use of derogatory terms helps to maintain their privilege and "justifies inequality and discrimination by sanctioning invidious cultural comparisons." On the other hand, for those derogated by the terms, their own use of such terms often redresses "social injustices and dignifies an imposed minority status and thus is sometimes," Allen writes, "a form of accommodation to conflict."[44] When, in Faulkner's short story "That Evening Sun," Nancy says over and over again, "I ain't nothin' but a nigger," we should not hear this as an *endorsement* of her situation but as an *accommodation* to it, a resignation to her assigned status,[45] which is underscored by her adding, "It ain't none of my fault."[46] Nancy's utterances are unreclaimed, and yet their pragmatic function is different from the uses of the term by whites in the story. Resignation like Nancy's is nowhere present in Johnetta Cole's account of the reclamation project. Cole says "the reason for taking such a term and making it a term of endearment is to soften the intensity of that pain [of others using it against you], so that 'my main nigger' becomes 'my best friend.' It's compensatory because it is so very powerful."[47] The reclamation project is linguistic aikido; it tries to use the power of the term to benefit those who were formerly harmed by it.

Reclamation depends upon the possibility of somehow severing the derogation from the term, although not upon the possibility of severing the history of the derogation *via* the term.[48] This flies in the face of the Absolutist's nondetachability thesis; some specific assertional commitments are dropped, others are relocated within the inferential network, and some stay the same but have different justifications or consequences. Made explicit, the Reclaimer's argument goes as follows: The *OED* is right—"Nigger" is just a word synonymous with "Negro," "colored person," "person of color," etc.

except that "nigger" captures a history of derogation that the others miss. When it is used to derogate, the derogation is a pragmatic effect, not a semantic aspect of the term. If the derogation were a semantic aspect of the term, then there could be no non-derogatory use of it. But there *is* a non-derogatory use: some African Americans use the term as an in-group term of endearment. So, the derogation is not built into the semantics. The pragmatic effect is a matter of the relation between the speaker's in-group and the referent's in-group, at least. When African Americans use the term among themselves it is *possible* for the term not to carry derogation, and this shows that group membership can enable disaffiliation from the common derogation.[49] Further, it may be that when others besides African Americans use the term it is *impossible* for the term *not* to carry derogation. If so, then if one is not a member of the group targeted by the term, one's use cannot disaffiliate. So, there are non-derogatory uses of the term, and pragmatic factors are the means by which the derogation is detached.

There is much that is right in the *spirit* of this argument, but it has several important weaknesses.[50] I will mention just three. The first two weaknesses work together: first, the argument treats the difference between the reclaimed and the unreclaimed term as merely pragmatic, and second, it erroneously takes this point to be shown by the presence of pragmatic triggers for detachment. Surely there are contextual features that trigger the audience to interpret the term as reclaimed or not, but these triggers do not *constitute* the difference between the terms. That difference is in the assertional commitments—in the inferential relations between claims made with this term and other claims. Writers on this topic like to think of the project as one of changing the connotation, but it is important to recognize that reclaiming the term results in changed assertional commitments, which bring with them changes in denotation.[51] Consider just one point: if it is a consequent of both reclaimed terms that the persons so labelled be resistant to the social system that defines them with the unreclaimed terms, then this changes who is included in the extension of each term. Unreclaimed "nigger↓" implies a kind of subservience, a recognized and resigned lower status, which reclaimed "nigger↑" overturns. So while pragmatic factors may trigger such detachments, we must ask what those detachments change in the assertional and referential commitments associated with the term.[52]

In addition, the argument depends upon, but does not argue for, the claim that the derogation has been successfully detached within the sub-group. Significantly, not all members of these sub-groups agree about the power of the sub-group to detach the derogation. There is considerable controversy among African Americans about which terms are appropriate group labels, and "nigger" is usually not even considered as a viable alternative. One might think that "dyke" has been more successfully reclaimed within its sub-group, but this is probably also false.[53] Consider a typical exchange from the pages of the journal *Lesbian Tide,* where a letter to the editors begins "I am not a dyke . . ."[54] The writer, Ginny Ray, does not deny being a lesbian but takes issue with the appropriateness of this term, even when uttered by lesbians. She continues,

> To me, the term "dyke," because of its common or street meaning, (which is that a dyke is a woman who is trying to act tough like a man) is on the consciousness level of "chick" or "nigger." People in the hippy [*sic*] and black subcultures told us that it was "correct" to use these terms and that we all knew that they were our words now. I never got it. I still don't. When Richard Pryor says nigger I don't laugh. When the hippy [*sic*] up the street calls her friend a chick I don't say cool. . . . I fought since 1969 to be called a woman and you are not going to stick some other dumb label on me in the name of politics.[55]

Ginny Ray joins the Absolutist in suggesting that the stereotype associated with the derogatory term is too powerful (perhaps too central) to be detached. Rejecting the stereotype, she rejects the term.

In response, the editors invoke the long history of using "dyke" to derogate mannish women—citing Radclyffe Hall and Gertrude Stein as but two examples—and they say that as a term of derogation there is more than an element of truth to it. Not only do they grant the term a truth-value, but they enlarge its scope beyond women who engage in lesbian sexual practices or who look unfeminine. Calling the term "a badge of honor" for women, to be "used for someone who refuses to be beaten down," the editors write that they "are proud to use the word 'dyke,' in loyalty and love for all the women who, in so many different and difficult ways, held strong."[56] They write,

The very power and destructiveness of the word "dyke" as
men use it comes from its connotations of aggressiveness and
independence—qualities men have always found ugly or threatening in women though highly valued in themselves. What
men have meant when they call us dykes is true: we ARE
uncompromising (where loving women is concerned), we
ARE ugly (when beauty is measured in rigid stereotypes or in
passivity), we ARE frightening (to those who fear independent
women), we ARE unpleasant (when silence and smiles are
pleasing).[57]

The editors' response shows that the reclamation project need
not deny the core assertional commitments of the term in order to
change the justifiability of the expressive commitment. The core
assertional commitments are the same, but the next layer out is
different. The first set of inferences licensed by "dyke" is still licensed: a dyke is aggressive, independent, uncompromising, ugly,
frightening, and unpleasant. The editors' parenthetical remarks
show that the next layer of assertional commitments, those that
support these stereotypical traits, has changed. Those second-layer
assertional commitments show the difference between the word's
role in the discursive practices of one community and its role in the
discursive practices of another community, the difference between
"dyke↓" and "dyke↑." Ultimately, "dyke↑," reclaimed, would no
longer sanction many of the inferences of "dyke↓." For instance,
because it is considered good to be a dyke, and because she is
uncompromising—with respect to loving women—then in the reclaimed scheme we would lose the inference, commonly associated
with "dyke↓," that somebody better find the dyke a good man so
that he can convert her to heterosexuality. We would not, however,
lose the inference that the dyke is a woman who does not serve
men.

Successful reclamation requires a reorganization of the inferential structure associated with the term. Some inferences will be
eliminated, some antecedents will be changed, and some conse-
quents will be changed.[58] This results in the rehabilitation of the
expressive commitment of the term; now, with the rehabilitated
term, what the expressive commitment is a commitment *to* has
changed. It is the same word, with the same history, but with a
new future. If, as I've been suggesting, the inferential role is what

marks the term's identity, then when a subcommunity reclaims a word, like "dyke," the new word "dyke↑" makes it clear that the old one must be recast explicitly as "dyke↓". Both "dyke↓" and "dyke↑" have the same past, but their present and their futures are significantly different. Their meanings overlap, but are not the same.

I said earlier that individual speakers cannot escape the socially established meaning of their utterances, except occasionally by the grace of the communities in which they live and speak. If it takes the grace of the community to let Humpty Dumpty mean "a nice knock-down argument" by "glory," then it would seem that Humpty Dumpty still hasn't escaped the social conferral of meaning, but has only been granted a temporary reprieve. In the cases of the derogatory terms we are considering, the truth of this caveat depends on marking a distinction between the broadly socially established meanings of expressions (which we may think of as *inter*-communal) and more narrowly socially established meanings (which we may think of as *intra*-communal). In American English generally the derogatory terms we have been considering are inescapably derogatory; that is, the social norms and practices that render them so are so prevalent across all our sub-communities that variations in contextual features usually do not and often cannot overturn the derogation. One speaker at one time cannot play the Humpty Dumpty game of making up a nonderogatory meaning and have it stick.

The rehabilitation of a term is not achieved by one speaker by fiat in an instant; it is a community-wide achievement that takes time to occur. For the reclaimed term to prevail, there must be community-wide agreement about the bulk of the assertional commitments. The problem for the members of a community as it moves from a derogatory inferential role to a laudatory one is epistemic. As interpreters of each other, we want, and sometimes need, to know who is committed to the old term, with its racist or heterosexist entrenchment, and who is committed to the new linguistic and social practices. Sometimes knowing is a matter of comfort or ease, and sometimes it is a matter of safety. Since "dyke↓" as we now understand it represents the common past of the two versions of the term, its inferential role serves as the default when there are no clear markers that the less common and more recent "dyke↑" is appropriate. Since there is so much at stake for those who have been targets, the default interpretation, in the absence of community-wide consensus and clear markers for community membership, will probably always be the unreclaimed term. Thus, the old bad word stays ever active.

Lesbianfeminist linguist Julia Penelope says that "dyke" is only acceptable if it is rehabilitated. This apparently sensible claim creates a problem. Either it condemns utterances of the term made during the process of rehabilitation, putting those who work to bring about the reclamation in an awkward Humpty Dumpty–like position, or it grants to speakers the power Humpty Dumpty claims to have, of changing word meaning almost by fiat. Usually in discussions about the reclamation project, "dyke↓" and "dyke↑" are treated as absolutes, but really these terms represent poles of a changing continuum. During the process of reclamation the assertional commitments of the new term, "dyke↑", undergo continual transformation as the community examines its inferential role.

Conclusion

There are many negative things we can say about someone that are virtually always negative but which do not play the categorizing and oppressive social function of the terms we've been considering. There is an important difference between the terms considered here and the wide range of more generic derogatory terms, such as "jerk," which also insult and belittle, but have none of the complexity of "nigger" and "dyke." They also have none of their power. The terms we have been considering are *deeply* derogatory; their power to derogate is not simply a matter of frequent and customary use as insults hurled at their targets.[59] Unreclaimed, "nigger" and "dyke" are deeply derogatory because of their complex sets of assertional commitments. "Jerk," like many other derogatory terms, is nearly purely derogatory, in that its semantic content is little more than "stupid" or "foolish person" (*Webster's New Collegiate Dictionary*). Calling someone "a jerk" is not tied to a rich structure of other social practices in the way that calling her "a whore" or labeling her with a racial or ethnic slur is. "Jerk" has little entrenched semantic content: from the fact that Jones called Smith "a jerk" we can't infer much, except that Jones has a bad attitude toward Smith's current behavior or perhaps toward Smith generally. Think, in contrast to "jerk," how much we can infer from Smith's calling Jones "nigger" or "dyke." The reductive categorization achieved by these terms and their service in support of the oppression of their targets is a significant part of their ontological force and is a source of their pragmatic force.

Absolutists and Reclaimers agree that the assertional commitments of the unreclaimed term are unacceptable. Absolutists want to reject the whole mode of discourse. Reclaimers think we can reject some (the bad stuff) while keeping some (good stuff), while Absolutists argue that either it is not really clear how to sort them out (an epistemic problem) or it is impossible to detach them (a metaphysical problem). In this case, it is pretty clear how to sort them out: the bad stuff tends to the detriment of the people derogated. Calling blacks "niggers↓" is different in kind from celebrating Kwanzaa, even though both are tied to a history of racial difference and discrimination. One serves to maintain the discrimination; the other serves to empower those who have suffered the discrimination to overcome it. Solving the epistemic problem, in this case, helps set the metaphysical solution in motion. The Absolutist's claim that there is no way to detach the undesirable commitments from those that are acceptable is usually grounded on the strength of the stereotype that partially constitutes the inferential role and on the power of the social practices in which the term is embedded. What the practical failures of actual reclamation projects emphasize is that their success requires concomitant changes in the social practices that support the undesirable linguistic practices. Otherwise, the (old bad) default kicks in. Perhaps ironically, when the Absolutist argues for sanctions against the use of such terms, she is arguing for at least some of the kinds of social changes that would back up the goals of the reclamation project.

Absolutists and Reclaimers both tend to be holists, but they differ about how to break the particular language/culture cycle that both want broken. Absolutists think that with terms like these, the expressive commitment, ranging as it does over the whole mode of discourse, is so powerful that it cannot be dismantled piecemeal but must be jettisoned. Reclaimers, on the other hand, think that we can change the structure of the assertional commitments and so change the very nature of the expressive commitment. Perhaps the most important issue between them is whether the speaker who uses the derogatory term may, through creative use of context, narrow down the elements of the term that are operative in that context. If so, then the reclamation project is underway. Unfortunately, the social norms and practices that generate the assertional commitments of these terms are so prevalent across all our subcommunities that variations in contextual features have had little success in overturning the derogation. That does not prove that the reclamation project is doomed; it just suggests that it is not easy.

Even if one doubts that the reclamation project can succeed, it is clear that the Absolutist's brand of holism is too strong. Undertaking an expressive commitment does not require adhering to every possible element in the inferential role of the term. In general, we often quite carefully limit our endorsement of the inferential roles with which we work. We can narrow the scope of the endorsement, but if we reject something very central to the inferential role, then there is a real question about whether we are undertaking the expressive commitment at all. Without its central assertional commitments, the viability and value of the discursive practice that supports the term becomes questionable. Exploiting the metaphor of viability, the Reclaimer urges that just as careful pruning enhances the health of real trees, so too with "inferential trees." The Reclaimer's project shows us that we can reject Greenberg's claim that a derogatory term communicates *all* the negative beliefs a community endorses about its target, while still accepting the point that these expressions are "extremely potent communicative devices." They communicate more than they justify, and they invoke a system of nasty claims, which is embedded in a system of unjust behaviors.[60]

The problem with derogatory terms is not primarily or exclusively a matter of their pragmatics. Not all uses of derogatory terms can be subsumed under what the courts have labelled "fighting words," i.e., words "which by their very utterance inflict injury or tend to incite an immediate breach of the peace."[61] Fighting words are defined primarily by their pragmatic effects, not by their semantic content. Unreclaimed, "nigger↓" and "dyke↓" are not really fighting words as legally understood, simply because immediate breach of the peace is usually not forthcoming when these terms are used against their targets. Too much is at stake for the targeted person to be free to fight back. They tend not to provoke a fight because the match is rigged and everyone knows it. Instead, we should think of these terms as *bully-words*. They depend for their force and for their content upon a system that favors those not taken to be denotable by the terms, and they use that force to threaten and control persons taken to be so denotable. "Nigger↓" is a bully-word, whether or not it is uttered in a speech act that we would ordinarily call bullying. "Dyke↓" is a bully-word used to keep lesbians in the closet and to keep heterosexual women from knowing their own strength. Bully-words are a degree stronger, a degree more effective than fighting words. Their strength is in the social and linguistic practices that back them up.

Seeing these terms as bully-words, whose enforcement power is so great that they tend not to provoke any response that would render them fighting words, enables me to agree with part of the Supreme Court's claim that "the reason why fighting words are categorically excluded from the protection of the First Amendment is not that their content communicates any particular idea, but that their content embodies a particularly intolerable (and socially unnecessary) mode of expressing whatever idea the speaker wishes to convey."[62] The Absolutist argues that this sort of derogatory term ought not to be protected by the First Amendment, and the position set out here helps to keep the Absolutist safe from the typical slippery-slope worries that arise from content-based abridgments. The Absolutist shows, however, that one serious problem with these terms *is* that "their content communicates [a] particular idea," namely, the idea of dominance and subordination on the basis of race or sex or sexual preference (and more). Even more impor- tantly, the Court blurs the distinction between content and mode of presentation, saying that "their content embodies a particularly intolerable . . . mode of expressing whatever idea the speaker wishes to convey." There is a significant difference between saying, "I think I'm better than you because I'm an Anglo and you're not," and saying, "You're just a nigger." The challenge is to articulate what is intolerable about the mode of expression, and the inferential role theory of meaning helps us with that task.

Derogatory terms are political discourse on three counts. First, they inform about the power structure; they tell both those who are their targets and those who are not where their place is in the social hierarchy. Second, they function prescriptively; their assertional commitments are constituted by inferences that set out norms (parading as descriptions) by which the target group is supposed to live. And third, they are bully-words, which are significantly worse than fighting words. While fighting words may breach the public peace, bully-words corrupt the public morality. They do not convince by rational argument, by giving and asking for reasons; instead they bully their targets into compliance with the norms they represent. When those norms oppress and exploit, justifying untold abuses, there are grounds for addressing the very mode of discourse in which these terms occur.

Addressing the use of these terms explicitly, making the expressions themselves the subject of rational discussion, has the potential to help ameliorate some of the harms of the terms and may help weaken their potential to harm again. We need to call the bully out. Making explicit the expressive commitment of a derogatory term makes explicit the political dimension of the term, both in its assertional commitments being rife with expressions that depict rigidly ascribed stereotypic traits and in the social function of the distinctions made therein. Making explicit the structure of these commitments enables us to demand of those who would use these terms that they justify the expressive commitments undertaken in the process. It enables us to demand that they *show* us that the mode of discourse of which the term is part is both viable and valuable. That requires showing that the mode of discourse serves a valuable end—and that is the hard thing to do with these terms.

This chapter is the beginning of an exposition of the structure by which such words become what they are. An inferential role theory of meaning is helpful for moving us away from thinking about the harms of derogatory terms as being located in their connotation (representing the mere bias of the speaker) or in their denotation (saying that they fail to refer since the descriptive content of the terms is inaccurate). According to the inferential role theory developed here, these terms license inferences about those they are used to denote which we think ought not be licensed.

In the end, what's wrong with derogatory terms? Surely a simple answer is "the harm they cause." It is bad when they reflect the hate and the prejudice of the speaker, and it is bad that they serve to denote by way of prejudice, falsehood, and stereotype. Even worse, however, is their rigid codification of stereotypes into assertional commitments, licensing inferences that have no legitimate grounds.

The derogatory terms we have been considering are bully-words with ontological force: they serve to establish and maintain a corrupt social system fuelled by distinctions designed to justify relations of dominance and subordination. Despite their differences, both the Absolutist and the Reclaimer are fighting this phenomenon. Both show us that the central issue in fighting these words is undermining the viability and value of the particular mode of discourse, that is, undermining a meta-level commitment to a bulk of the assertional commitments associated with the term. What is wrong with derogatory terms is that they are part of a set of unjust discursive practices that support and are supported by a set of unjust social, economic, and legal practices. Derogatory terms such as those considered here may not be fighting words, but they set in bold relief the importance of fighting over words.

 NOTES

I would like to thank Robert B. Brandom and William G. Lycan for helpful comments on an earlier draft of this paper. Thanks also to the members of the Five Colleges Philosophy Group for their insightful discussion of the paper with me at Smith College. I would also like to thank Bijan Parsia for help with documentation.

1. Lewis Carroll, *Through the Looking Glass* (New York: St. Martin's, 1977), 131.

2. Mary Catherine Bateson, *Composing a Life* (New York: Penguin, 1989), 43.

3. A reductive classification is one that purports to reduce the person's rich and complex identity to the category that is applied.

4. Sandra Lee Bartky. "On Psychological Oppression," in her *Femininity and Domination: Studies in the Phenomenology of Oppression* (New York: Routledge, 1990), 27.

5. Here I am disagreeing sharply with Davidson, who in "A Nice Derangement of Epitaphs" claims that "nothing should be allowed to obliterate or even blur the distinction between speaker's meaning and literal meaning," and that "we must pry apart what is literal in language from what is conventional or established" (in Ernest LePore, ed., *Truth and Interpretation: Perspectives on the Philosophy of Donald Davidson* [New York: Blackwell, 1986], 434.) In what follows, I hope it becomes clearer

that the literal is what it is by convention and that ignoring this is a distortion of literal meaning and meaning more generally.

6. Simon Blackburn, "Through Thick and Thin," ms p. 13.

7. Of its eight quotations listed at that entry, three make a distinction between "niggers" and "blacks" or "colored" persons.

8. The *OED* is separating the denotation of the term from its connotation (here, the attitudes one can "read off" it), not treating the term as an amalgam but as a mixture with separable elements. Distinguishing between the denotation and connotation can be helpful, but it is not helpful to take the connotation to be a matter of what the speaker's attitude is, or even what a reasonable person might take the speaker's attitude to be.

9. David Roediger, pp. 144–145. Roediger is concerned with explaining the relation between African Americans held as slaves and Irish immigrants whose lives also were considered of little social value.

10. Betty Rundle, an Irish Catholic woman who lives in Chicago, told Studs Terkel: "My Father's family came here to get away from the potato famine, 1840. They worked on the Erie Canal. So much Irish history suppressed. We were the niggers of the time." In Studs Terkel, *Race: How Blacks and Whites Think and Feel About the American Obsession* (New York: The New Press, 1992), 113. Similarly, Delgado cites *Johnson v. Hackett*, a case in which a police officer called a citizen "a Chinese nigger" (284 F. Supp 93 [E.D. Pa 1968]); *contra* Delgado's insistence, it seems that this case shows that to some extent the racial status of the object of reference *can* be divorced from the derogatory term. Richard Delgado, "A Tort Action for Racial Insults, Epithets, and Name-Calling," *Harvard Civil Rights—Civil Liberties Law Review* 17 (Spring 1982), and in Mari Matsuda, Charles R. Lawrence III, Richard Delgado, and Kimberlé Williams Crenshaw, *Words that Wound* (Boulder: Westview Press, 1993), 101–102. Also, sailors sometimes use the term "deck nigger" as a designation of position, not race.

11. Frantz Fanon argues that far from excusing whites, their use of such expressions *without* any intention to insult and degrade is worse than an intentional slight: "it is just this absence of wish, this lack of interest, this indifference, this automatic manner of classifying him, imprisoning him, primitivizing him, decivilizing him, that makes him angry," in *Black Skin White Masks*, (New York: Grove Press, 1967), 32. The force behind our words is our social practices, which in turn make possible many of our affective states, so our analysis need not invoke intentions, although it can accommodate them. See Naomi Scheman, "Individualism and the Objects of Psychology," in *Discovering Reality*, ed. Sandra Harding and Merrill B. Hintikka (Dordrecht: D. Reidel, 1983), 225–244.

12. There's a problem speaking about races as if they exist independently of these structures of subordination. See, for example, Anthony Appiah, "Racisms," in *Anatomy of Racism*, ed. David Theo Goldberg (Minneapolis: U. of Minnesota Press, 1990), 3–17; "The Uncompleted Argument: DuBois and the Illusion of Race," *Critical Inquiry* 12 (Autumn 1985) (reprinted in Henry Louis Gates Jr., *"Race," Writing and Difference* [Chicago: U. Chicago Press, 1986], 21–37); and " 'But Would that Still Be Me?': Notes on Gender, 'Race,' Ethnicity, as Sources of Identity," *The Journal of Philosophy* LXXXVII, No. 10 (Oct. 1990): 493–499. See also Ashley Montagu, *Man's Most Dangerous Myth: The Fallacy of Race* (New York: Oxford University Press, 1974).

13. Smith's intention to slur Jones with a particular racial epithet cannot be formulated, much less coherently understood prior to the onset of the practices that establish the subordination of the races and the linguistic practices that render this particular term a slur. A more complete argument would simply be a fairly straightforward application of the arguments given by Scheman, *op cit.*

14. Consider the difference between invoking the history of slavery by saying, "She is the great granddaughter of a freed slave," versus saying, "She's a nigger." Both invoke the history of slavery, but one carries a default endorsement of that history and the other doesn't. For more on the importance of social back-up, see Lynne Tirrell, "Definition and Power," *Hypatia* 8, no. 4 (Fall 1993): 1–34.

15. Delgado, in Matsuda *et al.*, p.100.

16. An inferential role theory of meaning is holistic, for it emphasizes the place of the expression in relation to its context and it emphasizes the significance of the relation of that context to other contexts (similar and dissimilar).This sort of view is played out on many different fields: it is seen in Hempel's discussion of the importance of non-black non-ravens for understanding verificationism, in Quine's holism, and in Saussure's structuralism, to name but a few variations. For more on holism, see Jerry Fodor and Ernest LePore, *Holism: A Shopper's Guide* (Cambridge, Mass.: Basil Blackwell, 1992).

17. Robert B. Brandom, "Asserting," *Nous* IV (November 1983): 637–650. This account is clearest in the case of assertion, although it can easily accommodate other sorts of speech acts.

18. This language of undertaking the commitment is not meant to preclude the possibility that someone might categorically refuse to ever justify anything she asserts, might never actually be forthcoming with an identification, and so on. These commitments represent a reconstruction of our social practices, and it is a well-known fact about all social practices

that there are normally a few free riders and general non-cooperators. When someone generally shirks her linguistic responsibilities, we tend to treat her as an unreliable interlocutor.

19. See Lynne Tirrell, "Extending: The Structure of Metaphor," *Nous* XXIII (March 1989): 17–34.

20. The Supreme Court has a history of deciding the value of modes of discourse, and particular bits of speech, almost exclusively in terms of their utility in promoting truth. I say "almost exclusively" because the tendency to decide on these grounds is very strong, but can be overridden by considerations of threats to the public peace.

21. Jerry Farber, "The Student as Nigger," from *The Student as Nigger* (New York: Pocket Books, 1969); all the quotes in this paragraph are from pages 90 and 91. Farber is not asserting that students are blacks, but rather that they are second-class citizens if citizens at all. I don't think this claim requires metaphorical interpretation, as the rest of the paragraph should illustrate. The claim is literally interpretable and literally supported (or not).

22. Lewis Carroll, *Alice's Adventures in Wonderland and Through the Looking Glass* (New York: Collier, 1962), 247.

23. In explaining what is wrong with the sentence, "The niggers and broads in this town will benefit from improvements in medicine," which she labels "(4)," Kriste Taylor maintains that "it is the use of the referring expression 'niggers and broads' that makes any utterance of (4) somehow sexist and racist." See K. Taylor, "Reference and Truth: The Case of Sexist and Racist Utterances," in *Sexist Language*, ed. Mary Vetterling-Braggin (Totowa, N.J.: Littlefield Adams Inc., 1981), 311. Taylor says that such use fails because the derogatory terms fail to refer.

24. The expressive commitment of a derogatory term is independent of the psychological states of the person who utters it, and is independent of whether the term is used as a direct insult, hurled like a rock, or used as a casual term of reference. As an insult, it is irrelevant whether the term is directed against oneself or against others in one's presence; when a speaker utters the word, an endorsement of the expressive commitment is generally concomitantly undertaken, and that expressive commitment carries a general endorsement of the derogation. This point is nicely illustrated in the following story, told by Joseph Robinson, president of the Chicago local of the United Steel Workers of America, to social historian Studs Terkel. Robinson says: "Some of the guys on the picket line have his [the owner's] concept [of race hate], but I think they're growing up. They're learning who their enemy really is. It's not the black man, it's not the Hispanic. It's this guy, the owner. Some of these guys voted for me as

president. They treat me with respect. I can be standing there and they will forget that I am a black man. A black man will walk down the street and they holler, 'Hey nigger.' I'm standing right beside them. It's like I blend right in with them for a minute. [*Laughs.*] They forget I'm black. The other guy, passing by, is a nigger. When I hear these guys calling, 'Nigger,' my head roars up inside me but I can't let it defeat me. I've learned to live with it. Sure, it disturbs me when somebody calls a black man a nigger. It disturbs me when somebody calls an Italian a wop. Some of them will still be racists when this strike is over, but I feel good about a couple of them. They've been raised in that environment but they're growing out of it. If I can save one or two . . ." Robinson may be right that these men who yell at the passers-by intend no insult to him. Surely they are not hurling the term at him. Still, unless they can find a way to change the default extension of the term, they are derogating him just the same, no matter what their intentions. Studs Terkel, *op cit.*, p. 74.

25. I do not think that the Absolutist has in mind the burning of every book and essay and letter that uses or mentions the term, but simply that the term not be used and that it be scorned when it is. In fact, I have not seen any clarifications of this point by Absolutists.

26. Richard Delgado, in Matsuda et. al., p. 107; see also p. 94 and pp. 109–110. As we shall see below, expressive commitment of the term is at issue, not the connotation. Delgado's use of "connotation" here and elsewhere in his article is the ordinary language use, so I take him to mean something like "attitudes conveyed or associated with the expression." (In contrast, the logician's use of "connotation" refers to the sort of thing that has been collected in the dictionary, while "denotation" refers to the objects of reference for the term.)

27. See for example Ari Kiev, "Psychiatric Disorders in Minority Groups," in *Psychology and Race*, ed. Peter Watson, (Chicago: Aldine Publishing, 1974), 416–431. Summing up the literature, Richard Delgado lists: diminished sense of self-worth, lowered sense of dignity, sense of failing to meet social standards, mental illness, psychosomatic diseases, drug abuse, hypertension, diminished ability to form attachments, diminished ability to pursue a career, etc. See Delgado, op cit., pp. 90–96.

28. Charles Lawrence argues, "Stereotypes are cultural symbols. They constitute our contemporary interpretation of past and present meaningful behavior." See Charles R. Lawrence III, "The Id, the Ego, and Equal Protection: Reckoning with Unconscious Racism" *Stanford Law Review*, 39, No. 2 (Jan. 1987): 372.

29. The fact that we all know fat people who aren't jolly, blacks who lack rhythm, Latinos who are not passionate, inarticulate Irish people,

and so on, doesn't undermine the power of those stereotypically assigned traits. Because stereotypes have this kind of power, members of the stereo-typed group who do not fit the stereotype are seen as rare exceptions, and lose their power to undermine the force of the stereotype. Historian David Roediger points out, for example, that the stereotype of blacks as shiftless and lazy is incommensurate with another stereotype that blacks do all the hardest, lowest, dirtiest work our society needs. It is important to note that these stereotypes are commonly held by the same individuals, not just by different individuals within the same community. See David R. Roediger, *The Wages of Whiteness: Race and the Making of the American Working Class* (London: Verso, 1991).

30. See Judith Andre, "Stereotypes: Conceptual and Normative Considerations" in *Racism and Sexism: An Integrated Study*, ed. Paula S. Rothenberg (New York: St. Martin's Press, 1988), 256–262.

31. Jeff Greenberg, S. L. Kirkland, and Tom Pyszczynski, "Derogatory Ethnic Labels," in *Discourse and Discrimination*, ed. Geneva Smitherman-Donaldson and Teun A. van Dijk (Detroit: Wayne State University Press 1988), 77.

32. Similarly, Joseph Hayes claims that "*dyke* is not just a label, but calls to mind all past stories about dykes: the label as a short, running narrative history." Joseph J. Hayes, "Lesbians, Gay Men, and their 'Languages,'" in *Gayspeak: Gay Male and Lesbian Communication,* ed. James W. Cheseboro (New York: The Pilgrim Press, 1981), 33.

33. In general, simply undertaking the expressive commitment does not require adherence to *all* the elements of the term's inferential network—just most. See my "Extending: The Structure of Metaphor" for a discussion of the ways of restricting, augmenting, or even overturning expressive commitment (*Nous* XXIII [March 1989]).

34. John Money used this locution of one sex being trapped in the body of another during an interview on *The Oprah Winfrey Show,* and is cited by Jan Raymond for similar statements in *The Transsexual Empire: The Making of the She-Male* (Boston: Beacon Press, 1979).

35. Frantz Fanon. *Black Skin, White Masks,* 35. See also Sarah L. Hoagland, " 'Femininity,' Resistance, and Sabotage," in *Women and Values*, ed. Marilyn Pearsall (Belmont, Cal.: Wadsworth, 1986), 78–85.

36. Irving Lewis Allen. *The Language of Ethnic Conflict: Social Organization and Lexical Culture* (New York: Columbia University Press, 1983), 15. In many contexts, there is a distinction to be made between using derogatory terms as what our legal tradition calls "fighting words"—hurling them at a person who is targeted for linguistic (and perhaps other)

assault—on the one hand, and using such terms casually to denote, as my neighbor did. For the purposes of this inquiry, the difference between direct and indirect derogation is not at issue. What matters here are the grounds for the charges that such talk is undesirable and settling what is at issue between those who accept it and those who do not. Both direct and indirect derogation achieve the same political end of dividing insiders and outsiders, and seeing to it that members of one group have more access to power and resources than members of the other.

37. For more on psychological oppression, see Frantz Fanon, *Black Skin, White Masks*, and Sandra Lee Bartky, "On Psychological Oppression," in *Femininity and Domination*, 22–32.

38. Delgado, in Matsuda et al., p. 107. Delgado's strategy here is to argue in a legal context that these terms and expressions are not political speech because political speech is so clearly protected by the First Amendment; this strategy is misguided. The expressions are political; what his considerations show is that not all political speech ought to be protected. In fact, the Court's maintaining a strict public space/captive audience criterion for application of restrictions of speech suggests that the political arena is precisely where the restrictions may apply. (Perhaps what matters just as much is its rhetorical mode, or that the expressions function as bullying tools.)

39. In fairness to Delgado, he recognizes this harm of racism, even as he argues that such speech is not political. At issue between us is the scope of what counts as political.

40. Delgado, in Matsuda et al., p. 108.

41. In his opinion on R.A.V. v. City of St. Paul, Justice White writes, "fighting words are not a means of exchanging views, rallying supporters, or registering a protest; they are directed against individuals to provoke violence or inflict injury" (Lexus, p.13). There is no conversation (speaking *with*) when fighting words are used, and racial epithets are of this sort. Just the same, there is a talking *to*, and that talking to is informative and political.

42. Within the community it is obvious that the beliefs have truth values (as Blackburn notes). What is important to see, however, is that claims made with derogatory terms carry their place in a social and historical context nearly on their sleeves. For an interesting discussion of this, see Simone de Beauvoir's introduction to *The Second Sex*, trans. H. M. Parshley (New York: Vintage, 1989).

43. Simon Blackburn. *Spreading the Word: Groundings in the Philosophy of Language* (Oxford: Oxford University Press, 1984), 146.

44. Allen, p. 15.

45. William Faulkner. "That Evening Sun," in *Major American Short Stories*, ed. A. Walton Litz (New York: Oxford University Press, 1975), 576–590. Also in *These 13* (1931) and *The Collected Stories of William Faulkner*. This story provides an interesting case of both blacks and whites using "nigger" clearly as a derogatory term but none seeming to mind the linguistic derogation. (It simply is not the case that any use of the term to one's face constitutes fighting words, in the legal sense.)

46. Ibid., p. 578. Other instances: "I ain't nothin' but a nigger," Nancy said, "God knows. God knows." (p. 581); "I just a nigger. It ain't no fault of mine" (p. 590).

47. In Mary Catherine Bateson, *Composing a Life*, 44.

48. One argument for the possibility of reclaiming derogatory terms like "nigger" and "dyke" depends on *not* taking the terms to be what Blackburn, McDowell, Gibbard, Williams, and others call "thick." "Thick" terms are terms or expressions that carry with them or convey an attitude, an approval or a disapproval, in which the description and the attitude "form a compound or amalgam, rather than a mixture: the attitude and the description infuse each other, so that in the end, in the repertoire of the mature speaker, the two elements are no longer distinguishable" (Simon Blackburn, "Through Thick and Thin," ms p. 13).

49. Not all uses of the term by African Americans will effect the detachment.

50. One weakness I will not go into in the text: The argument relies on a false premise in its attempt to show that the derogation is not built into the semantics. Generally, many semantic features of our utterances can be overturned or cancelled by the pragmatic effects of particular uses, and so it would take a special argument to support the premise that claims that if the derogation were a semantic aspect of the term, then there could be no nonderogatory use of it. Certain kinds of pragmatic effects, like irony, for example, can cancel or overturn semantic meanings; what is less clear is that they can radically change semantic meanings. Would a continued ironic use of "he's a real prince," in a community that no longer spoke non-ironically about princes, ultimately change the meaning of "prince," losing the irony along the way while retaining the ironized meaning? Perhaps, but to assume so here is to beg the question. Thanks to Bob Brandom for pointing this out.

51. I'm using Blackburn's notation, in "Through Thick and Thin," for my own purposes here. As I am using them, "dyke↓" represents the unreclaimed derogatory term, in all its derogatoriness, while "dyke↑" rep-

resents the reclaimed term. What is missing from this denotation, and from discussion of the reclamation, is attention to the term-in-transition.

52. At this point it would be interesting to see whether the assertional commitments of "nigger↑ " are the same as for the so-called synonymous terms.

53. According to Julia Penelope, a lesbianfeminist linguist who is concerned with this question in her *Call Me Lesbian: Lesbian Lives, Lesbian Theory* (Freedom, Cal.: The Crossing Press, 1992), 90. Penelope makes a point in her earlier book that may help to explain why "dyke" has generally been more widely accepted amongst lesbians than "nigger" has amongst African Americans. She argues that if an oppressed group is to reclaim a derogatory term, it must be one that results from a strength-building noncompliant stance. It must be a term with some assertional commitments worth saving: "I would argue, for example, that we can reclaim words like *dyke* and *bitch*, but not *slut* or *fuck*. The first two have been used as insults because the idea that we are out of our place inheres in their meaning. We can take the strength and defiance of such words for ourselves and be proud of our refusal to stay within the confines of behavior assigned to us by men. *Dyke* and *bitch* label things we do that break patriarchal rules and place us outside men's control. Slut, whore, slit, and gash all refer to us as objects of male predation and, like men's compliments, are fetters that hold us within their conceptual framework. They are names whose meanings and values exist only because we live in a patriarchy." For women, Penelope argues, "the words we decide to reclaim should be those that name a behavior or attitude that enables us to move outside the world as men have named it." (*Speaking Freely: Unlearning the Lies of the Father's Tongues* [New York: Pergamon Press, 1990], 215–216.) In spite of the heroic resistance of Africans brought to the United States in slavery and African Americans since, there is reason to doubt that "nigger ↓" meets this condition, and this may be a factor in the only moderate success of the reclamation of that term, even within the subcommunity.

54. Ginny Ray, " 'Niggers,' 'chicks,' and 'dykes' " (letter), *The Lesbian Tide* 8, no.6 (May/June 1979), 20.

55. Ibid.

56. "Dyke: A History of Resistance" (Editorial), *The Lesbian Tide* 8, no. 6 (May/June 1979), 21.

57. Ibid.

58. Consider the difference between rehabilitating these derogatory terms and changing the so-called generic "man." What we did in the latter

case was substitution, not rehabilitation. We did not make "man" truly generic, but argued that it *never was* generic, and then offered alternative constructions, such as "person . . . he or she," "person . . . she," or "people . . . they." Recognizing that "man" is not truly generic did not force a reorganization of the inferential role of the term, but it did diminish the number and scope of the inferences licensed by the term. In particular, it made explicit that the central inferences in its inferential role are about males and cut off broader application to women. Substituting generic for nongeneric terms left the inferential structures associated with these nongeneric expressions nearly intact.

59. In fact, it may not be true that this is the commonest use of these terms, for the terms may just as often be used as third-person terms of reference (as when one white man says to another, "that nigger over there," or when heterosexuals say, "Let's go to Provincetown and watch the dykes and faggots"). These terms do not depend on the form of the speech act in which they occur for their derogation, and their content not only specifies that the terms are derogatory, as "jerk" and "weirdo" do, but also conveys specific grounds for the derogation.

60. The issue is the speaker during the transition period (a sort of limbo, or perhaps purgatory). Once the reclamation is achieved within the subcommunity, then that subcommunity takes on the speaker role *vis-à-vis* the broader community and the same sort of problem arises.

61. *Chaplinsky v. New Hampshire,* 315 U.S. 146 (1942).

62. Scalia for the majority (Lexus/Nexus, p. 9). I disagree with the parenthetical "socially unnecessary" claim in that I think these kinds of modes are necessary to maintaining certain kinds of societies. Of course, they are not necessary to the maintenance of society per se, but it is important to see how they are intertwined with certain social structures and it is important to consider the possibility that they may be inextricable from those particular social structures. If so, then changing or eradicating the mode would ultimately undermine the social order.

REFERENCES

Allen, Irving Lewis. 1983. *The language of ethnic conflict: Social organization and lexical culture.* New York: Columbia University Press.

Andre, Judith. 1988. Stereotypes: Conceptual and normative considerations. In *Racism and sexism: An integrated study,* ed. Paula S. Rothenburg. New York: St. Martin's Press.

Appiah, Anthony. [1985] 1986. The uncompleted arguments: Du Bois and the illusion of race. *Critical Inquiry* 12 (Autumn 1985); reprinted in *"Race," writing and difference,* 21–37, ed. Henry Louis Gates Jr. Chicago: University of Chicago Press.

———. 1990. "But would that still be me?": Notes on gender, 'race,' ethnicity, as sources of identity. *The Journal of Philosophy* LXXXVII, no. 10 (October): 493–499.

———. 1990. Racisms. In *Anatomy of racism,* ed. David Theo Goldberg. Minneapolis: University of Minnesota Press.

Bartky, Sandra Lee. 1990. On psychological oppression. In *Femininity and domination: Studies in the phenomenology of oppression.* New York: Routledge.

Bateson, Mary Catherine. 1989. *Composing a life.* New York: Penguin.

Blackburn, Simon. 1984. *Spreading the word: Groundings in the philosophy of language.* Oxford: Oxford University Press.

———. Through thick and thin. (unpublished manuscript)

Brandom, Robert B. 1983. Asserting. *Nous* IV (November): 637–650.

Carroll, Lewis. 1962. *Alice's adventures in wonderland* and *Through the looking glass.* New York: Collier.

———. 1977. *Through the looking glass.* New York: St. Martin's Press.

Chaplinsky v. New Hampshire, 315 U.S. 146 (1942).

Davidson, Donald. 1986. A nice derangement of epitaphs. In *Truth and interpretation: Perspectives on the philosophy of Donald Davidson,* ed. Ernest LePore. New York: Blackwell.

de Beauvoir, Simone. 1989. *The second sex.* Trans. H. M. Parshley. New York: Vintage.

Delgado, Richard. 1982. A tort action for racial insults, epithets, and name-calling. *Harvard Civil Rights—Civil Liberties Law Review* 17 (Spring).

Dyke: A history of resistance (Editorial) *The Lesbian Tide* 8, no. 6 (May/June 1979): 21.

Fanon, Frantz. 1967. *Black skin white masks.* New York: Grove Press.

Farber, Jerry. 1969. The student as nigger. In *The student as nigger.* New York: Pocket Books.

Faulkner, William. 1975. That evening sun. In *Major American short stories,* ed. A. Walton Litz. New York: Oxford University Press.

Fodor, Jerry, and Ernest LePore. 1992. *Holism: A shopper's guide.* Cambridge, Mass.: Basil Blackwell.

Greenberg, Jeff, S. L. Kirkland, and Tom Pyszczynski. 1988. Derogatory ethnic labels. In *Discourse and discrimination,* ed. Geneva Smitherman-Donaldson and Teun A. van Dijk. Detroit: Wayne State University Press.

Hayes, Joseph J. 1981. Lesbians, gay men, and their "languages." In *Gayspeak: Gay male and lesbian communication,* ed. James W. Cheseboro. New York: The Pilgrim Press.

Hoagland, Sarah L. 1986. "Femininity," resistance, and sabotage. In *Women and values,* ed. Marilyn Pearsall. Belmont, Cal.: Wadsworth.

Johnson v. Hackett, 284 F. Supp 93 (E.D. Pa 1968).

Kiev, Ari. 1974. Psychiatric disorders in minority groups. In *Psychology and race,* ed. Peter Watson. Chicago: Aldine Publishing.

Lawrence, Charles R. III. 1987. The Id, the Ego, and equal protection: Reckoning with unconscious racism. *Stanford Law Review* 39, no. 2 (January).

Matsuda, Mari, Charles R. Lawrence III, Richard Delgado, and Kimberlé Williams Crenshaw. 1993. *Words that wound: Critical race theory, assaultive speech, and the First Amendment.* Boulder: Westview Press.

Montagu, Ashley. 1974. *Man's most dangerous myth: The fallacy of race.* New York: Oxford University Press.

The Oxford English Dictionary. 1974. Vol. N. Oxford: Oxford University Press.

Penelope, Julia. 1990. *Speaking freely: Unlearning the lies of the father's tongues.* New York: Pergamon Press.

———. 1992. *Call me lesbian: Lesbian lives, lesbian theory.* Freedom, Cal.: The Crossing Press.

R.A.V. v. City of St. Paul, 505 U.S. 377 (1992).

Ray, Ginny. 1979. "Niggers," "chicks," and "dykes" (letter). *The Lesbian Tide* 8, no. 6 (May/June).

Raymond, Janice G. 1979. *The transsexual empire: The making of the she-male.* Boston: Beacon Press.

Roediger, David R. 1991. *The wages of whiteness: Race and the making of the American working class.* London: Verso.

Scheman, Naomi. 1983. Individualism and the objects of psychology. In *Discovering reality,* ed. Sandra Harding and Merrill B. Hintikka. Dordrecht: D. Reidel.

Taylor, Kriste. 1981. Reference and truth: The case of sexist and racist utterances. In *Sexist language,* ed. Mary Vetterling-Braggin. Totowa, N.J.: Littlefield Adams Inc.

Terkel, Studs. 1992. *Race: How blacks and whites think and feel about the American obsession.* New York: The New Press.

Tirrell, Lynne. 1989. Extending: The structure of metaphor. *Nous* XXIII (March): 17–34.

———. 1993. Definition and power. *Hypatia* 8, no. 4 (Fall): 1–34.

Sara Mills

2

Discourse Competence

Or How to Theorize Strong Women Speakers

In feminist linguistic analysis, women's speech has often been characterized as "powerless" or as "over-polite"; this paper aims to challenge this notion and to question the eliding of a feminine speech style with femaleness. In order to move beyond a position which judges speech as masculine or feminine, which are stereotypes of behavior, I propose the term "discourse competence" to describe speech where cooperative and competitive strategies are used appropriately.

The aims of this article are twofold: to contest some of the theoretical and empirical work undertaken on women's language that has portrayed women as disabled in speech and to describe how it is possible for women to be strong, competent speakers despite social and discursive constraints. Rather than assuming that strong women speakers are in some ways interacting according to masculine norms, I propose to use the term "discourse competence" to describe speech that is both assertive (concerned with speaker needs) and cooperative (concerned with group needs). In this way, it is possible to theorize strong women speakers without reference to a system of masculine/feminine opposition.

I. Women and Powerless Speech

Since Robin Lakoff's influential *Language and Woman's Place* (1975) and Dale Spender's *Man-made Language* (1979) many feminists

81

have described women's language in terms of powerlessness. Males have been viewed as oppressors who "ruled" language, forcing women into submissive speech or even into silence. Following Lakoff and Spender's analyses, early feminist sociolinguists focused on certain features that were asserted to be found in greater quantities in women's speech than in men's. These features constituted a sex-preferential usage, that is, a style used by women which included features, to a statistically significant degree, in comparison to the style used by men. Women's speech was thus characterized as, for example, more inclined to over-politeness, mitigating the force of requests and statements, in order to avoid threatening the face of the co-participant in talk, by the use of epistemic modality and tag questions (Mills 1982; see also Tannen 1991). This early feminist work represented women as being concerned not to offend anyone, for example, in general women were shown to avoid taboo and offensive language, such as swear words. Thus women's speech was characterized as deviant in relation to a male norm which, by implication, was characterized as being direct, confident and straight-talking (see Mills 1987).

For many early feminist theorists, women's conversational role was that of a listener rather than a speaker. For example, women were shown to use more minimal responses (such as, "uhuh," "mmm," "yeh," "right") than men use, to attempt to initiate more opening moves in conversation and to do more "repair-work," for example, when there were awkward silences or when difficult subjects were broached (Fishman 1983). This was viewed as an illustration that women did not intervene in conversation so much as ensure that the conversation went well for other participants.[1] In a similar way, women were seen to be interrupted more frequently by men, than they interrupted back, and when they were interrupted by men, they were more likely to cede, than to continue talking (Zimmerman and West 1975). Thus, women were presented as being more concerned with the interactional welfare of the group as a whole than with their own contribution. Much of this work implicitly or explicitly characterized women's speech as necessarily different from men's, and also as akin to housework, with all the negative connotations that the term is accorded in Western society.

However, there are two important factors that must be considered. Firstly, many of these features, particularly those associated with women's over-politeness and deference, are in fact characteristic of feminine rather than female speech, that is, a stereotype of what women's speech is supposed to be. Although femininity is a determinant and a constraint on women's behavior, it is not the only one (see Mills 1991a and 1991b; and Smith 1990).[2] By focusing on stereotypical features of femininity, which is itself classified as weak in comparison to masculine strength, theorists have described women's speech as if it only contained these powerless and self-effacing elements. The second factor that must be considered when we are analyzing women's speech is whether it is perhaps features of what has been termed "powerless speech" that we are discovering. O'Barr and Atkins (1980) have shown that powerless men also employ features of over-politeness and deference in their speech. They claim that "the tendency for women to speak powerless language and for men to speak less of it is due, at least in part, to the greater tendency of women to occupy relatively powerless social positions" (O'Barr and Atkins 1980, 104). This view presents women, in general, as powerless because of social status, but it still allows for the possibility of women not using powerless speech.[3]

II. Women and Power

There are more factors involved in the attainment of a powerful interactional position than a simple correlation with social status, although this must be acknowledged as an important factor in Western society (Fairclough 1989). Socioeconomic power relations are often enacted, reflected, and reaffirmed in language, but factors (both actual and perceived) such as education, family background, age, gender, race, general self-confidence, knowledge base, voice quality, past interactive experience, and others can lead to a person being interactionally in a position of power.[4] For example, a woman who has had consistently patronizing and derogatory interactional relations with her male partner may produce hesitant and deferent language, if other factors affirm her perceived power position. However, if other factors do not in her perception confirm her partner's linguistic behavior toward her, her response may not display deference. For example, despite a difference in socioeconomic power and status, in the following interaction between a male manager and two female secretaries, the secretaries do not display the expected deference:[5]

The participants are J and D, secretaries who are discussing a report that the manager K would like altered slightly. Instances of interruption, or two persons in simultaneous speech, are indicated by a slash (/); pause is indicated by an ellipsis (. . .).

J: I was really mad . . . cause it took me ages to do
D: Yes
K: Um I'll tell
    you what I was going to say Education Act, etc. . . . could
    you just add here you can start with a capital letter for
    session one 15 September I I should have put that
J: /For session one 15 September
K: /of September 1981
J: /session one 15 September
K: /comma 15 September
J: 1981
K: If
    you would do that for me then I'll run them off
J: I'll do it this
    second then you can take them
K: /Er do we have an afternoon post today?
J: [to D]   Uh,
    goes at what time?
D: Usually about . . . you mean incoming or ?
J: /Incoming
D: About
    1 o'clock Janet usually brings it 'round
K: I'm hoping there won't
    be anything in it
                                        [data tape 31.1]

In this interaction, the manager K displays hesitation and deference while the secretary, especially J, displays a great deal of interactive power. For example, K is the only consistent user of false starts ("I'll tell you what I was going to say . . . ," "could you just add here . . ."), hesitation ("er," "um," "oh"), epistemic modality ("if you would do that," "I should have"), hedging ("just," "you know"), and he makes one unsuccessful attempt at a conversation initiation, ("I'm hoping there won't be anything in it"). This linguistic behavior is due at least in part to his requesting something; still this cannot wholly explain his deference, since it is his job to request the secretary to type reports for him and to alter them if necessary. While he does attempt to assert himself by insisting on the secretary putting a comma before September, the secretary largely ignores this move, simply continuing to read out the words that she has typed, not indicating whether she has inserted a comma or not. She also ignores his interactive gambit, when he states that he hopes he will have no incoming mail; this lack of cooperation is normally considered to be behavior indicative of a difference in power relations, but in quite the opposite direction than that demonstrated in the present example. The secretary J interrupts more than her manager, and talks more to the other secretary than to him, displaying little hesitation or deference in relation to K, and performing face-threatening acts (Brown, and Levinson, 1978).[6] It is impossible to generalize about J's linguistic behavior from this short interaction; however, a simple opposition of women's speech = powerless and men's speech = powerful, even when there is a clear socioeconomic power difference at work, is evidently inadequate to describe J's behavior.

A person's power relations in language are constantly the subject of negotiation. Thus, rather than seeing, as Spender does, language as "man-made," as a system in which and by which a speaker is subjected, it is possible to view women's roles in interaction in terms of positions that are largely socially determined but within which there are possibilities of negotiation. Thus, in this model, men as well as women can be disadvantaged in language, though clearly not to the same extent or degree, nor for the same reasons. It is important to separate out the variables of power and gender, although this is almost impossible to do in practice, since gender roles and power relations are so inextricably mixed (see Butler 1990). We need to be aware of factors other than gender that are important in the analysis of interactional power.

While O'Barr and Atkin's work is important in drawing our attention to the possible confusion of variables, it fails to analyze two important elements. The first is the fact that there is a relatively high proportion of women using these seeming "powerless" markers in situations in which power differences do not appear to be the most salient variable, and therefore there cannot be a simple homology between gender and power. Nor for that matter can we be sure that these "powerless" markers are the simple markers of powerlessness as has been claimed. And second, as O'Barr and Atkins admit, even when women do not use these markers of deference, they are often judged to be speaking in a powerless way. They argue, "It could well be that to speak like the powerless is not only typical of women because of the all-too-frequent powerless social position of many . . . women, but is also part of the cultural meaning of speaking 'like a woman'" (O'Barr and Atkins 1980, 110). If it is enough that a woman speak "like a woman" to be considered to be speaking in a "powerless" way, then a more complex model of the production and particularly the reception of women's speech is necessary.

III. A Different Way to Analyze Gender, Power, and Language

It is now no longer possible to make large-scale generalizations about women's speech as has been done before. While acknowledging that women as a group are oppressed within Western societies, feminist analysts now are more attuned to the diversity within the term "woman" and are therefore less willing to assume that women are a homogeneous grouping (see for a discussion, *Feminist Review* 1989; Black and Coward 1990). Recent work by theorists such as Deborah Cameron and Jennifer Coates has shown that it is necessary to move away from such monolithic analyses of women's language (Coates and Cameron 1988).[7] There has also been a significant shift in feminist theory in general toward a different form of analysis of power, stressing power as a relation rather than as a quality or an imposition (Smith 1990). If power is seen as a process, resistance to it is easier to consider than has been the case so far with feminist theorizing, which has run the risk of depicting women as passive victims (see Diamond and Quinby 1988, for a feminist Foucauldian analysis of power and resistance).

Individual women do not necessarily have a single speech style; that is, they do not use one form of speech in all situations. Instead, analysis now focuses on the context of the speech setting and the participants within it. For example, in an article entitled "Gossip Revisited: Language in All Female Groups," Coates analyzes the way that women in an informal group use cooperative strate-

gies rather than the competitive strategies used by men in similar single-sex groups (Coates 1988). She suggests that when using cooperative strategies, participants tend to forego their personal aims in the interaction for the benefit of the group or particular group members and produce text jointly by finishing each other's utterances, rather than staking a claim to individual turns at talk. Thus, Coates makes several important contributions to the debate. Instead of assuming that female speech and male speech are globally different, she isolates a particular context (single-sex, informal speech among close friends) and analyzes one feature of the interaction (speech style). Furthermore, she takes features of women's speech that had previously been labeled as signs of weakness and deference, and she relabels them as positive attributes of a larger concern for the smooth running of the group's interaction. While this analysis is flawed by not being adequately contrasted with a similar male interaction, it nevertheless permits us to generalize about tendencies in styles within particular contexts, allowing for the possibility that not all women will use this style all of the time.

Deborah Cameron, Fiona McAlinden, and Kathy O'Leary have also made an important departure from previous theorizing in the stress they lay on the multifunctionality of linguistic elements (Cameron, McAlinden, and O'Leary 1988). In their analysis of tag-questions, they argue that it is not possible to assume, as has been done in the past, that tag-questions have one function; rather, drawing on Holmes's work (1984), they show that there are at least two uses of tag-questions: modal tag-questions which request information, show uncertainty, and are speaker-oriented (for example, "But you've been in Reading longer than that, haven't you?") and affective tag-questions which do not show uncertainty, indicate concern for the addressee and are thus addressee-oriented (for example, "Open the door for me, could you?" and "Quite a nice room to sit in, isn't it?"). A linguistic element is not simply indicative of deference, solidarity, power, or other factors; rather, it is necessary to analyze the multiple possible uses of each element in a range of different contexts.

We must also consider the possibility that even when women are using certain linguistic elements in a particular way, they may be open to misinterpretation in certain contexts, because of this multivalence of items. For example, if a female states at the beginning of her presentation of an academic paper to a mixed audience at a conference that her paper is to be considered as work-in-progress and very provisional, she may intend to be understood to be stating that her interest lies with the group as a whole rather than with taking up a power-position in relation to the group (i.e., cooperative rather than competitive). However, members of the audience may interpret her statement as a form of incompetence, deference, and self-denigration. In a similar way, strategic use of hesitation and hedging may be used by female speakers in all-female groups to indicate that they are not intending to silence other contributions, but they may be interpreted as displaying uncertainty or low self-esteem. Thus, it is important to consider both speaker intention, however difficult that is to isolate, and hearer interpretation in order to come to an analysis of the way that women speak and are heard to speak.

Stereotypes of feminine behavior and male interactional behavior may determine that, in certain situations, women produce language that seems to accord with a notion of "women's language." However, a more complex form of analysis will allow for a range of possible speech styles—from deferent to assertive—that, because of context, power relations, personal preference and so on, women decide to adopt. Many theorists argue that there are certain women who do not use the features that have been described as "women's language," or who speak in a seemingly aberrant way (for example, drawing on features of "women's language" while performing in a seemingly "masculine" way). I would like to clear a theoretical space for these speakers. Rather than strong female speakers being seen as deviant or as "masculine," their behavior can be classified as discursively competent. At the same time, I am fully aware that most women suffer some form of oppression in language, both through the conditioning of femininity, which tries to instill into them that they should speak in particular "lady-like" ways, and through the interactional work of certain males whose behavior is apparently sanctioned by society's gender norms. However, rather than seeing patriarchy as a global system of oppression whereby women are reduced to passive victims, I prefer a more productive form of theorizing of power, where women negotiate and resist the social and discursive systems that attempt to oppress them (see Diamond and Quinby 1988).

IV. Beyond Masculinity and Femininity:
Discourse Competence

By accepting the theorizing of femininity and masculinity as opposite poles of a stereotyping of male and female behavior, with femininity aligned with weakness and masculinity aligned with strength,
we accept a system in which there is no space for women to speak
in a strong way, except by adopting that position which is normally
reserved for males; (nor for that matter, is there a space for men
to behave in a "feminine" way). If we consider what the characteristics of masculinity in speech are generally taken to be, we will see
that they are complex; there are very negative features—for example, aggression, competition and self-orientation—alongside the
seemingly more positive ones, such as strength and self-confidence.[8]
Both femininity and masculinity in speech are a stereotypical form
of interactive excess, in that they form the extreme ends of a cline.
However, it is not possible to view them as homogeneous groupings
of elements. The term "femininity" covers both those elements that
are disabling, such as hesitation and deference, as well as those
elements that show concern for the group, such as refraining from
interrupting, asking leading questions, and so on. Femininity, in
fact, is contrasted not to masculinity, but to a notion of discourse
competence—that is, an ability to perform adequately in speech,
being assertive enough to ensure that the speaker's face is maintained while at the same time displaying sufficient care for
the maintenance of the interlocutor's face (for a full discussion of
face in interaction, see Brown and Levinson 1978; and Goffman
1972).[9] Male speakers, by contrast, are often assumed to be discursively competent, even when their behavior does not accord with
the above definition, simply because of an eliding of masculinity
and competence.

Thus, there must be a position outside this system of sexual
difference where it is possible to describe women and men speakers
who are displaying features of neither feminine nor masculine speech
behavior, but who are simply competent speakers. By this, I mean
those speakers who are able to speak fluently, with the appropriate
amount of cooperative and competitive markers, with a due amount
of care for both the group and the individual speaker's own needs.
Discourse competent speakers have a range of speech strategies

available to them, and are able to adopt them at will; they are aware of the effect that their use of language has on others and can modify their speech according to the situation.

Someone who is discourse competent is not simply an assertive speaker (which would seem to accord with notions of masculine, competitive speech behavior) but is assertive as well as being aware of the needs of the group and the general functioning of the conversation.[10] I am not suggesting a form of androgyny as an ideal, since androgyny almost inevitably involves women in performing in both masculine and feminine ways, while men are still restricted to only masculine behavior (see Palmer 1989; Grabrucker 1988; Mills 1991a and 1991b). What I am attempting is to wrest away from the masculine pole of the cline the notion of strength and competence, since I would argue that discourse competence comes only from a combination of cooperative and competitive strategies. For example, Margaret Thatcher is often considered to be a very aggressive, "masculine" speaker who drew on the markers of femininity to temper that possibly face-threatening behavior. In fact, on many occasions, Thatcher can be considered a discourse competent speaker in that, at the same time that she used appropriately assertive interactive behavior (appropriate, that is, for a prime minister), she also employed elements that signaled to her interlocutors that she was still behaving as a "feminine" woman, a strategy she adopted on the assumption that this was the only tactic available for a female prime minister to be taken seriously. The following extracts illustrate Thatcher's ability to tailor her speech style to what she perceived to be the discourse constraints of the situation. In this first extract, Thatcher is speaking in an interview with the TV presenter, Pete Murray about her son Mark when he was missing in the desert in 1982:

> [T]he relief when he was found was just indescribable . . . and just, I just felt on top of the world and I don't worry so much now about little things. . . . I know how anyone feels if their son is missing, if a child is missing, and then you know there are some terrible cruelties and personal tragedies in life . . . but how fortunate we were, and Mark knows too. (Quoted in Webster 1990, 99)

She is discussing an emotional and very personal experience, and here she uses hesitation, pausing, hedging, and false starts. The context is a one-to-one interview which is fairly informal. In other contexts, she changes this rather meandering style for a direct one; in answer to a question in 1986 about whether her Iron Lady image was out of date she replied:

> No, no, no, no, no. There's still so much to be done. Let me say this. If you want someone weak you don't want me. There are plenty of others to choose from. (Quoted in Webster 1989, 87)

In other situations, she uses extremely direct, assertive language, but she tempers it by addressing and including her interlocutor. For example, in an interview with Miriam Stoppard in 1985, she constantly uses "you" and "one" in an inclusive way, and uses phrases like "Do you see what I mean" (Quoted in Webster 1990). Thatcher could have used other strategies to modify the force of her utterances, or to give the impression of being a caring person, but in a public arena this combination is an obvious one. Not all women public speakers adopt an aggressive pose and temper it with markers of femininity, such as breathiness, softness, or constant smiling, as Thatcher did. Since discourse competence is not the same as masculine speech, we do not need to assume that low voice tone is indicative of competence. However, that may be an element chosen as part of a woman's presentation of herself as competent, combined with other elements, according to the constraints of a situation. It is possible for a woman to maintain her voice tone, for example, if she speaks with a fairly highpitched voice, which may be interpreted stereotypically by her interlocutors as displaying femininity and hence powerlessness, but she may couple this with speech markers of a more powerful nature, such as lack of modification, thus achieving discourse competence.

One speech style for all encounters marks discourse incompetence; thus, a man who uses stereotypically masculine language and is assertive or aggressive in all interactions is not competent, nor is a woman who uses feminine language all of the time. Many people become attached to one particular speech style, and it is often the case that a speech style that is overly powerful or overly deferent often carries over into other inappropriate speech contexts. There are clearly different pressures on women and men. For example, public speaking for many women is very difficult, because of constraints of femininity (see Kaplan 1986 for a discussion of public language). As Cameron states: "Even secular social rituals—wedding receptions, for example—allot the role of speaker specifically to men, and for women to challenge this (for a bride to speak at her own reception, say) is still a daring move" (Cameron 1990, 5). However, while there are constraints on women's speech in the public sphere, women have always challenged and negotiated these limitations. Despite the constraints of femininity, many women express themselves competently in speech: that is, they judge the type of language behavior that is appropriate to a context, varying their speech in terms of their audience and in terms of their own needs. There are many women who do speak strongly, for example, women in positions of easily recognizable authority (politicians, trade unionists, businesswomen, mothers, teachers, and so on) and also women who are in positions of lesser socioeconomic power, as in the example of the secretaries cited earlier. But to be considered discourse competent, these women need to display concern for their interlocutors and for the smooth running of the conversation or speech. Those who simply speak assertively or aggressively are conforming to competitive or masculine speech norms, which may be effective in achieving the aims of the speaker, but usually only at the cost of the group or the conversation itself.

The conventional view is that women's speech is powerless or not to be taken seriously. One way to explain the possibility of women's strength in speech is to be aware of the heterogeneity of "women" as a group and to pay special attention to factors such as class, education, knowledge, skills, and age, which may give speakers a space from which to speak. Discourse competence is a practice that is acquired through exposure to a wide range of speech situations and learning to alter speech patterns accordingly. Women who have had access to a range of speech situations, or who are in positions of power (however that is defined) are more likely to be able to combine cooperative and competitive strategies in speech in order to achieve their aims without putting the conversation or group dynamics at risk. Thus, women who have had access to education, particularly higher education, are often called upon to speak in public, and in a range of group settings (seminars, tutorials, conferences, etc.), and this skill often carries over to other settings in which they speak.

There are clearly many cases of women and men who are not competent speakers, either because they are too deferent or too aggressive in speech, but that does not mean that this is solely their fault. Most of the ways in which we speak are determined by factors beyond our control, such as the way we were brought up, the type of education we have had, the sort of job we hold, the exposure we have to different speech styles—all of which are largely related to socioeconomic factors. We need to be aware that women and men have been brought up to consider certain types of speech as more appropriate to each gender, but the fact remains that many men and women do not conform to these stereotypical norms. It is possible to learn different speech styles that are more empowering for both ourselves and the groups within which we speak. The notion of discourse competence locates ability in language very much in the learned arena of people's language, rather than locating deference and aggression within the biological sphere. This competence can be learned, and it is not a reflection of a fixed state in a person's language, but rather as a stage in a process. Both women and men can change their speech styles in order to interact more effectively.

Because of the more complex analysis of women's and men's speech that is currently developing, feminist theorists will now be able to concentrate on the analysis of a full range of women's and men's speech, analyzing the factors that lead to a person speaking in a particular way in a specific situation, and analyzing gender as a complex term that contains within it variables such as socioeconomic status, educational background, knowledge and so on. Feminist theorists will have to pay as much attention to factors of context as to factors of gender, and to factors of reception as to production. This does not mean that men and women will be analyzed as if they were the same, but rather that gender itself will become a more multilayered term. The analysis will be far more complex and potentially cumbersome, since it will no longer be possible to make simple generalizations about women and men as a whole. A combination of quantitative and qualitative research methods is probably more useful in this context; for example, a sociolinguistic empirical piece of research could possibly isolate the most important variables, and come to some general tentative conclusions about an interaction. However, the next stage might involve following it up with a questionnaire or series of interviews with the participants of the interaction, in order to find out what factors entered into their production of certain types of speech, or which factors led them to judging others to be using certain forms of speech. In this way, it will be possible to give "thick descriptions" of interactions that will yield a space for strong, competent women speakers within feminist theorizing, so that we can analyze women who are not over polite, for example, without suggesting that they are not women. Rather, we will analyze their aims in the conversation, their perceived and actual power position, the reception given to their speech by some of the other participants in speech, and we will then try to analyze some of the strategies that they have employed. In this way, we will no longer have to describe women as weak, nor will we have to reclaim feminine qualities as positive (although that may be involved); rather, we will be aware of the way that women as speakers negotiate with a range of potentially disabling constraints and yet very often manage to achieve discourse competence in speech.

NOTES

1. Even recent work on women's and men's speech, such as Deborah Tannen's, still characterizes women as, in general, more likely to concern themselves with the maintenance of conversation.

2. At the same time, it is important to remember that many people still do confuse femininity with femaleness—that is, the social construct with the biological essence. This may lead them to interpret women's speech in particular ways, for example, a woman who does not use "feminine" markers may be analyzed as trying to speak like a man. Consider Wendy Webster's analysis of Margaret Thatcher's speech (Webster 1990).

3. The term "powerless language" is in itself problematic, because it assumes that there is a binary opposition between powerful and powerless, with speakers fitting into one of these categories. Completely powerless speakers do not exist; thus, a term that denotes a range of positions within power should be adopted instead.

4. These factors are generally not considered in analysis of women's speech for the simple reason that they are extremely difficult to quantify; however, there are large numbers of women who, despite being relatively powerless on a socioeconomic scale are, nevertheless, powerful interactionally.

5. This data was collected as a part of a larger project on women and politeness in 1986. The two secretaries share an office in an educational department in a county council building, in Suffolk, England.

6. Also see Tannen (1991) for a discussion of politeness. It is difficult to classify interruption simply as powerful speech, especially since Coates's

(1988) work has shown that simultaneous speech need not necessarily be classified as interruption. However, in this interaction, J's simultaneous speech with K on two occasions does not iterate or reiterate K's statements, whereas when there is simultaneous speech with D, there is reiteration.

7. However, some linguists such as Deborah Tannen (1991) still maintain that women's speech and men's speech is radically different, and that this has evolved due to different subcultures and social conditioning.

8. It is interesting that the characteristics of male speech or masculine speech are rarely considered; it is simply assumed that all male speakers are in fact competent speakers. For a discussion of this see Mills (1987).

9. I am aware that I am using "discourse competence" in a different way from the general usage of the term "competence" in linguistics, where, for example, competence is used to mean an ideal, abstract knowledge of the system of the language, in opposition to performance in the language.

10. I am using "discourse competence" rather than, say, the term "assertiveness," since the latter can occasionally appear to manifest itself solely in a concern to fulfill one's individual needs; while this may involve signaling a concern for others, it is usually only when this furthers one's own aims. Discourse competence, in contrast, is concerned both with being assertive and with displaying concern for others' interactional welfare. In this way, Coates's notion that women are more likely than men to draw on cooperative strategies is also questioned.

REFERENCES

Black, Maria, and Rosalind Coward. 1990. Linguistic, social and sexual relations: A review of Dale Spender's *Man made language*. In *The feminist critique of language,* ed. Deborah Cameron. London and New York: Routledge.

Brown, Penelope, and Stephen Levinson. 1978. Universals in language usage: Politeness phenomena. In *Questions and politeness,* ed. Esther N. Goody. Cambridge and New York: Cambridge University Press.

Butler, Judith. 1990. *Gender trouble.* London and New York: Routledge.

Cameron, Deborah. 1985. *Feminism and linguistic theory.* London and New York: Macmillan.

Cameron, Deborah, Fiona McAlinden, and Kathy O'Leary. 1988. Lakoff in context: The social and linguistic functions of tag-questions. In *Women in their speech communities,* ed. Jennifer Coates and Deborah Cameron. London and New York: Longman.

Cameron, Deborah, ed. 1990. *The feminist critique of language.* London and New York: Routledge.

Coates, Jennifer. 1986. *Women, men, and language.* London and New York: Longman.

———. 1988. Gossip revisited: Language in all-female groups. In *Women in their speech communities,* ed. Jennifer Coates and Deborah Cameron. London and New York: Longman.

Coates, Jennifer, and Deborah Cameron, eds. 1988. *Women in their speech communities.* London and New York: Longman.

Coward, Rosalind. 1983. *Patriarchal precedents: Sexuality and social relations.* London and Boston: Routledge & Kegan Paul.

Diamond, Irene, and Lee Quinby, eds. 1988. *Feminism and Foucault: Reflections on resistance.* Boston: Northeastern University Press.

Fairclough, Norman. 1989. *Language and power.* London and New York: Longman.

Feminist Review. 1989. The past before us: Twenty years of feminism. No. 31.

Fishman, Pamela. 1983. Interaction: The work women do. In *Language gender and society,* ed. Barrie Thorne, Nancy Henley, and Cheris Kramarae. Rowley, MA: Newbury House.

Goffman, Erving. 1972. On face work: An analysis of ritual elements in social interaction. In *Communication in face to face interaction,* ed. John Laver and Sandy Hutcheson. Harmondsworth: Penguin.

Grabrucker, Marianne. 1988. *There's a good girl.* London: Women's Press.

Holmes, J. 1984. Hedging your bets and sitting on the fence: Some evidence for hedges as support structures. In *Te Reo* 27: 47–62.

Kaplan, Cora. 1986. *Sea changes: Culture and Feminism.* London: Verso.

Kramarae, Cheris, ed. 1980. *The voices and words of women and men.* Oxford: Pergamon.

Kramarae, Cheris, and Paula Treichler. 1985. *A feminist dictionary.* London and Boston: Pandora.

Lakoff, Robin. 1975. *Language and woman's place.* New York: Harper Colophon.

McConnell-Ginet, Sally, ed. 1980. *Women and language in literature and society.* New York: Praeger.

Mills, Jane. 1989. *Womanwords.* London and New York: Longman.

Mills, Sara. 1982. Woman and politeness. Master's thesis, University of Birmingham.

———. 1987. The male sentence. *Language and communication* 7.

———. 1991a. Negotiating discourses of femininity. Paper presented at Centre for Women's Studies. York University, York, UK.

———. 1991b. *Discourses of difference: Women's travel writing and colonialism.* London and New York: Routledge.

Mills, Sara, et al. 1989. *Feminist readings/Feminists reading.* Charlottesville: University Press of Virginia.

O'Barr, William, and B. Atkins. 1980. 'Women's language' or 'powerless language.' In *Women and language in literature and society,* ed. Sally McConnell-Ginet, Ruth Borker, and Nelly Furman. New York: Praeger.

Palmer, Paulina. 1989. *Contemporary women's fiction: Narrative practice and feminist theory.* Jackson: University of Mississippi Press.

Smith, Dorothy. 1990. *Text, facts, and femininity: Exploring the relations of ruling.* London and New York: Routledge.

Smith, Philip. 1985. *Language, the sexes and society.* Oxford and New York: Blackwell.

Spender, Dale. 1979. *Man-made language.* London and Boston: Routledge & Kegan Paul.

Tannen, Deborah. 1991. *You just don't understand: Women and men in conversation.* London: Virago; New York: Morrow.

Walby, Sylvia. 1991. *Theorizing patriarchy.* Oxford: Blackwell.

Webster, Wendy. 1990. *Not a man to match her.* London: Women's Press.

Zimmerman, Don, and Candace West. 1975. Sex roles, interruptions and silence in conversation. In *Language and sex: Difference and dominance,* ed. Barrie Thorne and Nancy Henley. Rowley, MA: Newbury House.

3

Surviving to Speak New Language

Mary Daly and Adrienne Rich

As radical feminists seeking to overcome the linguistic oppression of women, Rich and Daly apparently shared the same agenda in the late 1970s; but they approached the problem differently, and their paths have increasingly diverged. Whereas Daly's approach to the repossession of language has been code-oriented and totalizing, Rich's approach is open-ended and context-oriented. Thus Rich has addressed more successfully than Daly the problem of language in use.

"For many women," Adrienne Rich explained in 1977, in her introduction to the collected poetry of Judy Grahn, "the commonest words are having to be sifted through, rejected, laid aside for a long time, or turned to the light for new colors and flashes of meaning: *power, love, control, violence, political, personal, private, friendship, community, sexual, work, pain, pleasure, self, integrity. . . .* When we become acutely, disturbingly aware of the language we are using and that is using us, we begin to grasp a material resource that women have never before collectively attempted to repossess" (*LSS,* 247).[1] Beginning in the 1970s, the attempt to repossess language was an important dimension of second-wave feminism in the United States. For many feminists, what this attempt came down to was "the great he/she battle" (Nilsen 1984): the struggle to discredit "generic he," along with a large set of nouns that are officially gender neutral but have installed masculine gender as normative for entire categories of persons, and indeed for the human species as a whole. The he/she battle was for "equal opportunity," with an emphasis on the ways in which standard usage interferes with women's efforts to hold their own in public life and in the world of work.[2] Meanwhile, however, radical feminists found it more important to stress that "the oppressor's language" interferes with women's ability to communicate and bond with one another. Thus, for example, in a poem called "Natural Resources" (1977), Rich announced:

> There are words I cannot choose again:
> *humanism   androgyny*
>
> Such words have no shame in them, no diffidence
> before the raging stoic grandmothers:
>
> Their glint is too shallow, like a dye
> that does not permeate
>
> the fibers of actual life
> as we live it, now: (*FD*, 262–263)

Here Rich expresses the conviction that an equal-opportunity agenda is not radical enough: gender-neutral usage cannot grasp the specificity of women's experience in the present, and it short-circuits the attempt to rescue a collective past from the oblivion to which the history of "mankind" has largely consigned women's lives.

In 1978, Mary Daly spoke in very similar terms of being engaged in an ongoing collective process of sifting and winnowing the words that feminist women would use to speak of important matters: "There are some words which appeared to be adequate in the early seventies, which feminists later discovered to be false words. Three such words . . . which I cannot use again are God, androgyny, and homosexuality" (Daly 1978, xi). Thus in 1977–78 Rich and Daly apparently shared the same agenda, as lesbian feminists whose "dream of a common language"—Rich's phrase, originally—gave direct expression to a politics of woman bonding and woman identification. "The crucible of a new language," Rich asserted in the Grahn introduction (1977), is *that primary presence of women to ourselves and each other* first described in prose by Mary Daly" (*LSS*, 250); meanwhile in *Gyn/Ecology* Daly hailed Rich as a "boundary breaking poet and warrior" with whom she shared in an "uncommon quest for 'a common language'" (Daly 1978, xvii). Daly's "uncommon quest" would culminate ten years later in *Websters' First New Intergalactic Wickedary of the English Language*. Meanwhile, however, Rich would come to understand her own relationship to language differently, and she would "survive to speak new language"[3] on very different terms.

The Australian feminist critic Meaghan Morris has suggested that there are two different ways of construing radical feminism: as "a *politics* which works on whatever all women have in common" or as "a *theory* of the determining role played by sex over class, economic and cultural factors in the oppression of women" (Morris [1982] 1988, 46).[4] Ever since *Gyn/Ecology,* Daly's commitment to radical feminism in Morris's second sense has been unequivocal and unwavering: it was, if anything, strengthened by opposition from both inside and outside the feminist movement. In the 1970s Rich apparently shared this commitment: in "Compulsory Heterosexuality and Lesbian Existence" (1978), she argued that "the power men everywhere wield over women . . . has become a model for every other form of exploitation and illegitimate control" (*BBP*, 68). But Rich explicitly distanced herself from this position during the 1980s: in "Notes toward a Politics of Location" (1984), she is outspokenly critical of "a form of [American] feminism so focused on male evil and female victimization that it . . . allows for no differences among women, men, places, times, cultures, conditions, classes, movements" (*BBP*, 221). The approach she favored by 1984 was one that would shelve the whole primacy question and broaden the feminist agenda by acknowledging that "most women in the world must fight for their lives on many fronts at once" (*BBP*, 218).

In one of Rich's earliest formulations of the problem both she and Daly sought to address, we can begin to see how Rich's language radicalism would also come to differ from Daly's:

> This is the oppressor's language
> yet I need it to talk to you (*FD*, 117)

In this pair of lines from a poem dated 1968, the boldly totalizing generalization about language is very much in the spirit of Daly's project; yet Rich has framed that generalization as a particular instance of discourse. She has used the deictic words *This, I,* and *you* to stage the subjective experience of a particular woman, at a particular historical juncture, who is actively trying to communicate with someone else.[5] Rich's formulation thus calls attention to the two different modes in which language exists for us simultaneously: as a system of already encoded meanings and as ongoing, open-ended meaning-making activity.

From the outset, Daly's effort to repossess language was code-oriented: "the oppressor's language" presented itself to her as a totalizing system that must be modelled as such and completely dismantled. Her priorities were those of a systematic theologian, for whom the power of words belongs primarily to their "cosmic" function—their power to name reality into being. Meanwhile Rich, though by no means indifferent to the cosmic power of words, was even more obsessed with their communicative function: in her foreword to *The Fact of a Doorframe,* a comprehensive selection of her poems from 1950 to 1984, she confessed that her worst fear as a poet had always been "that these words will fail to enter another soul" (*FD*, xv). Rich's approach to the repossession of language therefore was—and still is—context- or usage-oriented. And whereas Daly's "master trope"[6] is metaphor, the trope that uses the code against itself to produce semantic novelty through deviant predication, Rich favors metonymy, the trope of contexture, as she struggles to keep the language of her poetry grounded in "the actual world."[7]

Both Daly's code-oriented, "metaphoric" approach to the repossession of language and Rich's context-oriented, "metonymic" approach are "radical," in the sense that language itself is what they have sought to change.[8] Their difference exposes a tension that belongs to language itself in its dual existence as *langue* and *parole*—a code whose structures we internalize, but also the changing, context-sensitive medium of our dealings with one another.

Wielding Our Labryses:
Mary Daly and the Deep Spinning Power of Metaphor

Derived from the Greek *meta* (meaning after, behind, transformative of, beyond) and *pherein* (meaning to bear, carry), *metaphor* in the deepest sense suggests the power of words to carry us into a Time/Space that is after, behind, transformative of, and beyond static being—the status maintained by phallocracy. (Daly 1973, xix)

Daly begins *Websters' First New Intergalactic Wickedary of the English Language* by explaining that "the word *webster*, according to *Webster's Third New International Dictionary of the English Language,* is derived from the Old English *webbestre*, meaning female weaver" (Daly and Caputi 1987, xiii). Under the entry for *Webster,* she credits Judy Grahn with this Dis-covery and cites *The Queen of Wands*, where Grahn engages in speculative etymology:

> The word-weavers of recent centuries who have given us the oration of Daniel Webster and the dictionary listings of Merriam-Webster stem from English family names that once descended through the female line. Some great-grandmother gave them her last name, *Webster*, she-who-weaves. (Quoted in Daly and Caputi 1987, 178)

This meta-etymology models both the process whereby words can be said to have been stolen from women and the strategy Daly uses to repossess them: "a process of freeing words from the cages and prisons of patriarchal patterns" (Daly and Caputi 1987, 3).

In the *Wickedary*, weaving becomes the prototypical strategy of feminist lexicography. The book consists of a series of "Word-Webs"— "according to *Webster's* [Third International], the first meaning of web is 'a fabric as it is being woven on a loom. . . .' "(Daly and Caputi 1987, xvii)—and Daly invites her readers to conceive of language itself as a fabric that was originally woven by women in conversation with one another. She cites conversations with other women as sources for some of her entries, to convey that she and her Cronies are once again actively engaged in language making; and she stresses that the *Wickedary* itself is not, and could not be, finished. In the preface she explains that she has intended to model a certain "tension between incompletion and completion" (Daly and Caputi 1987, xviii)—between language as meaning-making activity and language as system of signs.[9]

Daly's understanding of language is close to that of sociologist Peter Berger,[10] who treats language as the primary agent of what he calls "world-building." Human society, as theorized by Berger, is a "world-building enterprise," and language is the means by which the social world is constituted for its members as a meaningful order, or "nomos": "Every empirical language may be said to constitute a nomos in the making, or, with equal validity, as the historical consequence of the nomizing activity of generations of men [*sic*]" (Berger 1967, 20). From the perspective of nomos in the making, language is an ongoing, open-ended activity that expresses the human craving for meaning; but as the product of this activity, language "acts back upon" its producers and their descendants, imposing its conventions upon them as their patrimony. "The original nomizing act is to say that an item is *this*, and thus *not that*. As this original incorporation of the item into an order that includes other items is followed by sharper linguistic designations (the item is male and not female, singular and not plural, a noun and not a verb, and so forth), the nomizing act intends a comprehensive order of *all* items that may be linguistically objectivated" (Berger 1967, 20–21). Berger emphasizes that although the nomizing act is totalizing in its intention, in fact it never attains to totality: "just as there can be no totally socialized individual, so there will always be individual meanings that remain outside of or marginal to the common nomos" (Berger 1967, 20).

Like Berger, Daly regards language as the objectified consequence of an activity, but for Daly "the nomizing activity of generations of men" has been a conspiracy to uproot and stultify language. Dictionaries epitomize for Daly a whole set of cultural activities—including theology, metaphysics, gynecology, as well as lexicography—that have codified, in order to fix and perpetuate, the patriarchal status quo (otherwise known in Daly's writings as Stag-nation, or the State of the Living Dead). They have sought to legitimate pseudorealities—"civilization," "history," "God"—that alienate women from their own world-making powers. Dictionaries make a pretense of establishing the true senses of words by tracing them back to their earliest forms, but these etymologies have "no Originality in them": "appearing capable of taking us back to our roots or to first principles or sources, they in fact block access to Origins" (Daly and Caputi 1987, 244). Fortunately, however, this work of deracination has not entirely succeeded: thus *Webster's*, the *American Heritage Dictionary*, and the *O.E.D.* "contain fragments of and clues to our own stolen heritage" (Daly and Caputi 1987, xxiii).

The *Wickedary* situates itself on the boundary of what Berger calls "the common nomos"; but whereas for Berger all that can be glimpsed beyond that boundary are individual meanings and the terrifying specter of "anomie," for Daly the boundary is a vantage point from which women, collectively, can begin to Activize Original

Be-ing. A Witch or Hag—Daly has used the *O.E.D.* to trace *Hag* back to a "prehistoric" West-Germanic compound with components akin to Old English *haga* "hedge" and Old German *dus* "devil"—is one who "haunts the Hedges/Boundaries of patriarchy, frightening fools and summoning Weird Wandering Women into the Wild" (Daly and Caputi 1987, 137). "Sitting on the Fence between the worlds," she "is engaged not only in Boundary Living but also in Boundary Breaking" (Daly and Caputi 1987, 267). The way that language can be enlisted for Boundary Living and Boundary Breaking is through the power of metaphor. "To a large extent," Daly explains, "metaphors are the language and the vessels of metapatriarchal Spiraling, that is, of Be-Witching" (Daly 1984, 404).

In her *Wickedary* entry under *Metaphors, Metapatriarchal*, Daly dissociates herself from the ornamental or figures-of-speech view of metaphor,[11] defining it in a way that is consistent with Suzanne Langer's account of metaphor and its role in language and with the work of more recent theorists of metaphor such as Max Black and Paul Ricoeur. According to Ricoeur, for example, metaphor produces semantic innovation through "deviant predication." We make a metaphor when we combine a subject and a predicate whose common or usual meanings clash in some important way. The predication thus produced is deviant, but if the metaphor succeeds it is also acceptable: its impertinence does not disappear, but is overcome by our having recourse to connotations or secondary semantic features of its crucial words. Metaphors thereby have the potential for enlarging the domain of what seems possible or can be thought: "*new* predicative meaning emerges from the collapse of . . . the meaning which obtains if we rely only on the common or usual lexical values of our words" (Ricoeur [1978] 1981, 232).

Metaphors thus live on the boundaries of conventional usage. When we speak of a dead or faded metaphor, we are citing a process whereby those boundaries have shifted: the conventional range of application of a particular expression has been extended through the assimilation of what had once been deviant, metaphorical applications. Suzanne Langer suggests that every new idea "evokes first of all some metaphoric expression. As the idea becomes familiar, this expression 'fades' to a new literal sense of the once metaphorical predicate, a more general use than it had before." This, Langer argues, is how language grows: metaphor is "the power whereby . . . new words are born and merely analogical meanings become stereotyped into literal definitions" (Langer 1942, 141). Langer's theory of language is based on a speculative account of its origins in a prediscursive human capacity for symbolic thinking: metaphor is for Langer not only the power whereby new words are born, but also the power of abstraction by which words as such were born in the first place, out of the sounds our prelinguistic forebears must have used to greet significant events.[12]

The process Langer treats as a positive or at least necessary one, insofar as it is central to the elaboration and maturation of languages, is assimilated by Daly to a process linguists call "pejoration," whereby words associated with women and their activities have, over time, become negatively stereotyped. "Like Langer, Shrews are aware of apparently faded metaphors, but . . . Shrewish analysis dis-covers a sexual politics of fading" (Daly 1984, 28). Daly is especially interested in words still used to denote women and their activities whose etymologies connect them with the elemental symbols of prediscursive thought, so that they seem to be etymologically linked to collective intuitions of Original Be-ing. Thus, for example, she reclaims the meaning of the word *spinster* not only by challenging the negative stereotype of the unmarried woman and restoring primacy to the word's original meaning, "a woman whose occupation is to spin" (Daly and Caputi 1987, 167), but also by attaching to that occupation a mythic dimension of meaning. She reminds us that in mythology the Fates are Spinsters (Daly 1978, 176): thus she discovers in this woman's occupation a presentational symbol for elemental cosmic process. *Spinning* becomes, in Daly's lexicon, a woman-identified synonym for world making: "Gyn/Ecological creation; Dis-covering the lost thread of connectedness within the cosmos . . ." (Daly 1978, 96). She regards the fading of the word's symbolic resonance as a semantic impoverishment and as evidence of a patriarchal conspiracy to divest language of its cosmic power. Restoring that power is a metaphoric process that gives the word *Spinster* several dimensions or levels of meaning: "When, for example, I say 'Spinsters Spin,' multileveled images of creation and change are evoked" (Daly 1984, 404).

In other instances, the work that metaphor does for Daly is critical rather than "cosmic." Thus, for example, she explains in the preface to her fourth book, *Pure Lust*, that its title has a double meaning. In lowercase, this phrase invokes the current, conventional meaning of *lust* and is used to name the "life-hating lechery" that "assails women and nature on all levels"; at the same time, however, Daly reclaims a more positive definition, now obsolete, of lust—"intense longing or eagerness"—so that in uppercase, the phrase can be used to mean "simple sheer striving for abundance of be-ing" (Daly 1984, 2–4). The phrase *Pure Lust* thus becomes a double-edged "labrys": it refers to both the problem and its solution, the State of Bondage and the energy that will launch Wild Women into freedom. Just as with *Spinster*, the woman-identified definition of *Pure Lust* cites its more archaic, "original" meaning. In this case, however, Daly's strategy is to put the word's two meanings in conflict: she uses deviant predication to overcome the conventional, current meaning of *lust*; and deviance, as a feminist survival strategy, is thematized by the double definition.

Language can only do the consciousness-altering work Daly wants it to do insofar as words are used disruptively, jarringly, deconstructively: "Websters are aware that new words are new in the sense they are heard in an Other semantic context" (Daly 1984, 404). Thus many of Daly's neologisms are self-contextualizing compounds (*Nag-Gnosticism*, *Pure Lust*) that have metaphoric deviance built right into them, and she often mixes her metaphors, to keep them fade-resistant. In *Pure Lust* she explains that metaphoric predication is a safeguard against building a new prisonhouse on the ruins of the old one, which is what will happen if radical feminists begin "accepting Hag-identified new words as taken-for-granted labels" (Daly 1984, 404).

Long before Daly's linguistic project had emerged full-blown in the *Wickedary*, Meaghan Morris made a telling criticism of her whole approach to language. Writing for the Marxist journal *Intervention* after Daly had made a controversial appearance in Sydney, Australia, in 1981, Morris accused her of using language to create a self-enclosed speech community of the elect, and thereby largely ignoring the problem of *"language in use"* (Morris [1982] 1988, 30). Daly, Morris argued, appears to subscribe to the view that "there is a strength-potential in isolated signs which is sufficient to overcome the histories of their use":

> The word *race*, for example, can be cheerfully put to "new" political purposes by reviving the dictionary "meanings" of rushing onwards, or of two tides meeting in a choppy sea— while the function of *race* in certain particular discourses, the

history of those discourses, and the histories which those discourses have made and still make possible, remains . . . entirely beside the point. (Morris [1982] 1988, 42)

Morris took issue with this position in no uncertain terms: "Unlike Mary Daly," she wrote, "I do not believe that 'meanings' are in 'words,' but that meaning is produced in specific contexts of discourse" (Morris [1982] 1988, 32).

Daly was not so naive about how language works or how meaning is produced as Morris seems to be suggesting here: as we have seen, Daly's metaphoric feats involve and indeed rely upon adroit manipulation of context. But her discourse is *self*-contextualizing and autotelic to a quite remarkable degree. This tendency is not nearly so pronounced in *Beyond God the Father* (1973), the first book she wrote after her conversion to radical feminism, as it is in *Gyn/Ecology*, where she undertook to expose and denounce "the totality of the lie which is patriarchy" (Daly 1978, 20), and in *Pure Lust*, which is structured to model an "Otherworld Journey of Exorcism and Ecstasy" (Daly 1984, x). In *Beyond God the Father* Daly was still making arguments. Here is a sample paragraph from that work, with italics added to highlight its discursive framework to the extent that Daly has made that framework explicit:

> *A qualitatively different understanding* of justice also *emerges when* the peculiar rigidities of the stereotypic male no longer dominate the scene. *Tillich has written* of transforming or creative justice, which goes beyond calculating in fixed proportions. *Unfortunately, he tries to uphold the idea that* "the religious symbol for this is the kingdom of God." *I suggest that* as long as we are under the shadow of a kingdom, real or symbolic, there will be no creative justice. The transforming and creative element in justice *has been intuited and dimly expressed by the term* "equity." *Aristotle defined this as* a correction of law where it is "defective owing to its universality." *What this leaves out is* the dynamic and changing quality of justice which does not presuppose that there are fixed and universal essences, but which is open to new data of experience. (Daly 1973, 128)

In this paragraph, Daly's linguistic usage is neither transgressive nor uncommon, and neither is her discursive procedure. The "qualitatively different understanding of justice" she seeks to establish is played off against classic formulations with which she disagrees but which afford a discursive context for her own. If the effort to redefine justice presages her growing interest in total renovation of the lexicon of "first philosophy," it nevertheless acknowledges and connects with the ways this concept has been understood within the tradition of Western metaphysics.

In *Pure Lust* Daly again cites Tillich's notion of "creative justice." Instead of paraphrasing Tillich, this time she quotes him directly, after declaring that his formulation is "so alien to Pyrosophical awareness and analysis . . . that it will make a feminist's flesh crawl" (Daly 1984, 276). She sets up her quotation from Tillich as a separate block of text, suggesting that the reader try imagining a priest, rabbi, or minister reciting it to a woman who has been repeatedly battered by her husband. "What happens in such a case," Daly explains, is that "the woman is morally bullied [by Tillich's notion of creative justice] into forfeiting her right to judge . . . [and] breaking her own Naming process." We conclude that "Tillich's moral verbiage . . . is worse than useless" and that "*justice* is not an adequate name for that which Canny, Raging women create." Daly has already proposed that we substitute the woman-identified term *Nemesis*, and she now proceeds to explain why this would be desirable:

> The new psychic alignment of gynergy patterns associated with Nemesis is not merely rectifying of a situation which the term *unjust* could adequately describe. Nemesis is Passionate Spinning/Spiraling of new/ancient forms and connections of gynergy. It is an E-motional habit acquired/required in the Pyrospheres. It demands Shrewd as well as Fiery judgment and is therefore a Nag-Gnostic Pyrognostic Virtue. Nemesis is a habit built up by inspired acts of Righteous Fury, which move the victims of gynocidal oppression into Pyrospheric changes unheard of in patriarchal lore. (Daly 1984, 277)

What we should notice about this entire passage is not only that Daly is now unwilling to engage in dialogue with Tillich, but that her text's relationship to its hypothetical readers has also changed. Both Tillich's account of "creative justice" and her own celebration of Nemesis are proffered to the reader not as arguments, but as rival incantations. We are to imagine a priest or a rabbi reciting Tillich's text, and then, having repudiated his "moral verbiage," we are to enter into a "new psychic alignment of gynergy patterns" as Daly's verbal Pyro-technics burst upon us. In repudiating the moral verbiage of Tillich and his ilk, we not only disagree with him and reject his approach to the definition of justice, we leave his world for another—the world Daly's discourse weaves around us.[13]

Daly relies on what Roman Jakobson calls the "poetic function" of language (Jakobson [1960a] 1987) to set her discourse apart from the ordinary language of patriarchy and to strengthen its internal cohesiveness. The rhythms of her prose are often incantatory, and she makes lavish use of alliteration to "conjure the Chorus of Wild Racing Words" (Daly and Caputi 1987, xvii). These are poetic strategies that promote an iconic relation between sound and meaning, signifier and signified. Her neologizing compounds, her hyphenations and capitalizations, likewise call attention to the process of signification, forcing us to attend very carefully to the shapes of words. All of these strategies work together to foster the illusion that words do indeed possess their meanings intrinsically—that they have an inherent power or life of their own.[14] But this is only an illusion, one that Daly has had to work very hard to create. In the preface to *Gyn/Ecology* she betrays this by claiming, with Humpty Dumpty–ish bravado,[15] that the word she has coined for her title "says exactly what I want it to say"—and then taking three pages to explain what she wants it to say, in explicit defiance of the standard definition of *gynecology*, which she quotes from the *O.E.D.* The prominence and frequency of this kind of explicit word definition is much greater in *Gyn/Ecology* than in Daly's earlier writings, and greater still in *Pure Lust*, the work that immediately predates the *Wickedary*. In *Pure Lust* it begins to seem as if word redefinition had become the primary task of Elemental Feminist Philosophy.

As we proceed through Daly's writings chronologically we can thus, as it were, see the *Wickedary* coming. Despite her intention to model an open-ended, ongoing process of community building through language, and despite the commitment to dialogue with other women that she often professed, Daly's "uncommon quest" developed according to an inner logic of its own.[16] The *Wickedary* is full of "we"-statements, but the collectivity or community they invoke is internally generated by a proliferating series of epithets that reinforce one another in a circular fashion within the work itself: "*Websters* do not use words, *we* Muse words"; "*Wild women* recognize *our* Guide Words . . ."(42); "*Wise women* . . . find here clues to *our* own liberation"; "*Wicked women* Announce *our* Departure from the State of Patriarchal Paralysis" (Daly and Caputi 1987, 24, 42, 284; italics added).[17] The women's community whose Naming process Daly champions in the *Wickedary* is an abstraction—not the agent but the figment of its prophetic exhortations.

Toward a Politics of Location: The Metonymic Poetry of Adrienne Rich

> When language fails us, when we fail each other
> there is no exorcism.
>
> ("Rift," 1980; *WP*,49)

In her foreword (1984) to *The Fact of a Doorframe*, Rich acknowledged that for her "the learning of poetic craft was much easier than knowing what to do with it—with the powers, temptations, privileges, potential deceptions, and two-edged weapons of language." Her strongest imperative as a poet, she suggests, has always been communication, and increasingly "this has meant hearing and listening to others" (*FD*, 15). It has also meant grappling with the problem Meaghan Morris accused Mary Daly of failing to deal with— the problem of language in use.

In 1981 Rich published an editorial in *Sinister Wisdom*, the lesbian feminist journal of which she was then coeditor, in the form of a series of "Notes" with the title "What Does Separatism Mean?" She raised the question because, as she explained, "I hear discussions, dialogues, confrontations in which the lack of agreed-upon meaning of separatist or separatism leads to needless confusion and gaps in understanding, therefore needless and wasteful failures to connect, at a time when we feel all our connections threatened" (Rich 1981, 83). Interestingly enough, however, she did not propose a definition of *separatism* to fill this lack. Instead, she offered a series of quotations from feminist manifestos over a twenty-year period, as if to construct a comprehensive microhistory of all the ways the word had been used by different feminist groups—feminists of the New Left in the 1960s, members of a lesbian-separatist collective in New York City in the 1970s, women of the Combahee River Collective, and so on. "Can the complexity and courage of each position be honored," she wondered, "its radicalism understood?" (Rich 1981, 87). Far from answering the question "What does Separatism Mean?" with a definition-proposal, these "Notes" seem to be trying to convince their readers not to try for any such thing. Insofar as women who are differently "located" may use the same word differently, communication is fragile and problematic; nevertheless Rich appears to be committed to the premise that the word *separatism* means no more *and no less* than what it has been used to mean in particular contexts.

One of the contexts she cites is *Gyn/Ecology*, a text she had welcomed in 1977 as one that would help lesbians/feminists conceive of "a separatism which is neither simplistic or rigid" (*LSS*, 229–230). In 1977 she admired Daly's definition of separatism in that it gave priority to an internal process of "separating ourselves from the patriarchal elements in our own thinking" (*LLS*, 229). "Crone-logically prior to all discussion of political separatism from or within groups," Daly had insisted, is "the basic task of paring away the layers of false Selves from the Self" (Daly 1978, 381). By defining *separatism* in this way Rich hoped to foster a separatist politics within the lesbian community that would overcome the stereotype of man-hating defensiveness that was keeping many feminists from fully understanding the issues involved. In "What Does Separatism Mean?" Rich was still trying to give this kind of leadership, but she was also ready to take issue with Daly's political priorities. In the passage Rich quotes from *Gyn/Ecology*, Daly goes on to suggest that "since each Self is unique," there are bound to be "chasms of difference among sister Voyagers"—"deep differences," for instance, "in temperament and abilities" (Daly 1978, 381). Rich was uncomfortable, in 1981, with a tendency she detected here to privilege ahistorical categories of difference[18]; "and surely," she remarks, "difference means not just differences in 'temperament and abilities' (which tend to sound like inborn qualities) but all the historical, material differences which are the contexts of all our choices" (Rich 1981, 88).

Rich's commitment to honoring these historical, material differences, along with her commitment to what she calls "poetry of the actual world" in her 1984 essay "The Location of the Poet," put her out of sympathy, finally, with Daly's linguistic program. And in fact her own approach to the repossession of language had always had a different emphasis. The common language Rich was dreaming of in the 1970s was to be "common" not only in the sense of enabling women to "re-member" a common heritage but also in the sense of being an ordinary language, a language of everyday use. Thus, while Daly set out to dismantle and replace the patriarchal "dicktionary," Rich was using her poems to engage in a subtler process of contextual reorientation—one that would acknowledge as fully as possible the lives her words had already lived in other contexts. And whereas philosopher Daly uses poetic devices in her prose to flout the discursive norms of philosophical writing, Rich is a poet who has always mistrusted the poetic function of language.

Rich was talking about the poetic function of language when she explained in her introduction (1977) to the poems of Judy Grahn that poetry is "above all a concentration of the *power* of language": "in setting words together in new configurations, . . . in the relationships between words created through echo, repetition, rhythm, it lets us hear and see our words in a new dimension" (*LSS*, 248). But in "North American Time," dated 1983 (*FD*, 324–328), she focused on an aspect of this power that troubled her, soberly reminding her sister poets that "whether we like it or not" the words of a poem "stand in a time of their own":

> We move   but our words stand
> become responsible
> for more than we intended
>
> and this is verbal privilege

A poem enables us to see and hear our words "in a new dimension" by detaching them from the circumstances to which they originally spoke.[19] This is a high price to pay for its "concentration of the power of language," because of the risk that this power will later "be used against us/ or against those we love"—that the poem's words may deliver, under other circumstances, a message the poet would never have wished to send:

> No use protesting *I wrote that*
> *before Kollontai was exiled*
> *Rosa Luxembourg, Malcolm,*
> *Anna Mae Aquash, murdered,*
> *Before Treblinka, Birkenau,*
> *Hiroshima . . .*

By dating all of her poems, Rich resists the tendency poems have to float free of the context in which they were originally written. In "The Location of the Poet" (1984) she explains that this practice, which she began as early as 1956, "was an oblique political statement—a rejection of the dominant critical idea that the poem's text should be read as separate from the poet's everyday life in the world" (*BBP*, 180).

To keep her poems firmly grounded in everyday life, Rich sets them up for the reader as discourse events in particular contexts. She does this by using deictic words and background detail to give each poem's speaker a situation or vantage point that is quite specific:

> The thirtieth of November.
> Snow is starting to fall.

> My body opens over San Francisco like the day-
> light raining down   each pore crying the change of light

> Today I was reading about Marie Curie:

> Your silence today is a pond where drowned things live . . .

> This August evening I've been driving
> over backroads fringed with queen anne's lace

Each of these sentences occurs at or near the beginning of a different poem in *The Dream of a Common Language*.[20] Much of the work the language of each passage is doing is deictic: time and place adverbials, definite articles, proper names, personal pronouns, and demonstratives all gesture toward a specific temporal, geographical, and/or interpersonal context for the poem's utterance or "message."[21] The context is not fully spelled out, but we are encouraged—indeed to some extent we are forced—to produce it hypothetically, in order to make sense of what the speaker is saying. In one instance, she must be in an airplane over San Francisco; in another, she is with someone whose silence is making her uncomfortable; in a third, she is perhaps on vacation in Vermont. It is appropriate to call this strategy "metonymy," because it is a way of making the part stand for a larger whole: the speaker's utterance presupposes external circumstances that are not fully explained but which her deictic references invite her readers to produce.

Whereas Daly privileges metaphor, metonymy is the poetic figure Rich most often uses in her poetry to concentrate the power of language. In a more extended example, from a poem titled "Upper Broadway" and dated 1975, we can also begin to see how metonymy helps her shape the meanings of important words. Like the poems I have already cited, this one is firmly "located" by its title and its opening lines:

> The leafbud straggles forth
> toward the frigid light of the airshaft   this is faith
> this pale extension of a day
> when looking up   you know   something is changing
> winter has turned   though the wind is colder (*FD*, 247)

It is late in the afternoon in the heart of the city, at the far edge of winter. The season is sharply epitomized, through strategic use of detail, as an external context for the poet's wintry reflections. As those reflections unfold, "the leafbud"—a small, specific instance of the way in which life persists and renews itself against the odds—becomes a kind of talisman for the poet as she experiences her own inner survival imperative. If "this is faith," then she herself can be faithful without believing in miracles; she need not profess allegiance to any truth beyond a personal intuition that "something is changing." By focusing on the leafbud, the poet gives a meaning to "faith" that helps her keep faith with herself:

> I look at my hands and see   they are still unfinished
> I look at the vine and see the leafbud
> inching towards life
>
> I look at my face in the glass   and see halfborn woman
> (*FD*, 247)

In the Grahn introduction (1977), Rich highlighted "the mere, immense shift from male to female pronouns" (*LSS*, 248) as an important contribution a feminist poet could make to the repossession of language; and the politics of the personal pronoun was an important dimension of her own linguistic activism. In English, of course, first-person pronouns are not marked for gender: thus, in a poem the use of the pronoun "I" will not, by itself, disclose the gender of the poetic persona or "speaker." But the poetic "I" is generically masculine.[22] When Rich first began writing poetry, as she explained in the autobiographical essay "When We Dead Awaken: Writing as Re-vision" (1971), she "tried very much *not* to identify myself as a female poet" (*LSS*, 44) because she "had been taught that poetry should be 'universal,' which meant, of course, nonfemale." As late as 1961, she still resorted to a masculine persona to "universalize" personal material.[23] For Rich personally, then, the decision to speak from a female subject-position was an immense shift, one that highlighted for her the way in which discourse-deixis can be enlisted to situate or locate poetic utterance.

In two of the poems she continued to republish from the 1960s, we find her using personal pronouns strategically to highlight the way in which a "generic masculine" subject position has functioned historically, either to forestall or to marginalize women's contributions to Western civilization. In her 1964 poem to Emily Dickinson, "I Am in Danger—Sir—" (*FD*, 70–71), she uses the second-person pronoun to address Dickinson directly, avoiding the use of "I" for self-reference: the first-person pronoun appears only in the poem's title, which is quoted from one of Dickinson's letters to her "mentor," Thomas Wentworth Higginson. "I am in danger—Sir—" is what Dickinson wrote to Higginson after he had urged her to straighten out her rhythms and punctuate her poems in a more conventional way to render them publishable. As the title of Rich's poem, Dickinson's words epitomize the predicament of the woman artist, but at the same time they are unmistakably, idiosyncratically, Dickinson's words—the words of a woman who "chose to have it out at last / on your own premises."

In "Planetarium," dated 1968 (*FD*, 114–116), Rich uses "I"-reference to identify more explicitly with her subject, the astronomer Caroline Herschel: she noted in 1972 that "the woman in the poem and the woman writing the poem become the same person" (*LSS*, 47).[24] But she begins her account of Herschel's career in the third person, citing what looks like a standard encyclopedia entry: *"Thinking of Caroline Herschel (1750–1848) astronomer, sister of William; and others."* Caroline Herschel's "I" is also the "virile" eye of the scientist: thus her discoveries have been incorporated by the historical record into her brother's career.[25] Rich depicts Herschel seeing her own reflection, every time she looks through her telescope, in a sky that has been configured into constellations by mythological stories of women whose boldness angered the gods:

> A woman in the shape of a monster
> a monster in the shape of a woman
> the skies are full of them.

In the middle of the poem she begins to use the first-person plural pronoun, "we," to sponsor a vision of the heavens in which the subject and the object of knowledge knowingly interpenetrate:

> What we see, we see
> and seeing is changing

In the final section she resorts, at last, to the pronoun "I," in order to produce the complex, layered subject position of a woman who struggles to reenvision herself:

> I am an instrument in the shape
> of a woman trying to translate pulsations
> into images   for the relief of the body
> and the reconstruction of the mind.

In both of these poems, the "mere immense shift" to a poetic vantage point that is woman centered involves more than just the first- and second-person pronouns: "new colors and flashes of meaning" are elicited from other words also by the woman-centered context Rich creates for them. In "Planetarium," the language of science acquires a new dimension when the scientist's "eye/I" is located in a woman's body: throughout the poem Rich assimilates the abstract terminology of space physics—its pulsars and light waves and radio impulses—to intimate bodily experience. In this way she overcomes the dichotomy between objectivity and subjectivity, physical and mental experience, science and myth, that she holds implicitly responsible for women's exclusion from science. "I

Am in Danger—Sir—" begins with a piece of language quoted from the famous letter Thomas Higginson wrote to his wife after he visited the poet for the first time: " 'Half-cracked' to Higginson . . ." But Dickinson gets the last word: the poem's last word, *premises*, creates a double entendre that thematizes the relationship between Dickinson's "location" and her ownership of language.

"Transcendental Etude," a poem that epitomized Rich's vision of art as feminist practice in 1977, suggests that the restoration of meanings that have been obscured by patriarchal usage is a crucial dimension of the feminist repossession of language. The poem includes some experiments in transgressive archaism that testify to Rich's interest at that time in the linguistic archaeology that Daly had already begun to practice. Even here, however, Rich's approach was conspicuously different from Daly's, and in line with the commitment I have already elicited from her editorial notes on separatism—to the premise that words mean no more, and no less, than what they have been used to mean in particular contexts.[26]

The poem's culminating image is of a pioneer woman sitting down in her kitchen and beginning to "turn in her lap"

> bits of yarn, calico and velvet scraps,
> laying them out absently on the scrubbed boards
> in the lamplight, with small rainbow-colored shells
> sent in cotton-wool from somewhere far away,
> and skeins of milkweed from the nearest meadow—(*FD*, 268)

Is she making a quilt? Perhaps, but as Rich's description becomes increasingly abstract, her pioneer woman takes on the quasi-mythic status of a wisewoman or female demiurge. This woman "quietly walked away," we are told, from a room full of "argument and jargon": sitting in her kitchen, with "experienced fingers quietly pushing / dark against bright, silk against roughness," she is

> pulling the tenets of a life together
> with no mere will to mastery,
> only care for the many-lived unending
> forms in which she finds herself . . . (*FD*, 269)

The word *tenets* in this passage seems oddly chosen,[27] until we recognize that it does here mean, more concretely or literally than usual, "things that one holds." In "the oppressor's language" *tenet* is used to refer to religious beliefs, abstract principles, "truths we hold to be self-evident"; here it seems to have had an older, simpler meaning restored, by "experienced fingers." Something similar, though a bit more complicated, happens with the word *musing*, as the poet explains that the process of "composition" this woman is engaged in

> has nothing to do with eternity,
> the striving for greatness, brilliance—
> only with the musing of a mind
> one with her body... (*FD*, 268–269)

The English verb *muse* is derived from a verb that in Old French meant "sniff the air" or "cast about for a scent," which derives in turn from the medieval Latin word for an animal's snout or muzzle. However, the synonyms the *American Heritage Dictionary* uses to define the verb *muse* are all words that befit a more conscious and exclusively cerebral activity: "to ponder or meditate; consider or deliberate." The *O.E.D.* suggests that *muse* came to have this inflection under the influence of the etymologically unrelated homonym *Muse*—the being to whom musicians and poets have traditionally prayed to be given more than human powers of memory and imagination.[28]

In these examples, words that have functioned in "the oppressor's language" to give world-building or "nomizing" activities a generically masculine inflection are used in such a way that older meanings are recovered for them in the context of the traditionally female activity of world maintenance and world repair. Rich's pioneer woman is a figure for the woman artist, whose artistic creativity is in no way separate from her capacity for everyday living, and whose "musing" is an activity that needs no higher sanction and seeks no deliverance from "actual life."

Like the pioneer woman she depicts in this passage, Rich is "care"-ful of the words for which she has furnished "an other semantic context"; and this is not an accidental or unimportant difference between her strategy and Daly's. Whereas Daly characterizes her own project as one of "freeing" words by wrenching them from their patriarchal contexts,[29] Rich has been concerned to demonstrate that we can begin to use words differently without repudiating their American heritage. Her usage relieves the words *tenets* and *musing* of some of the metaphysical baggage they have accumulated, but is not so transgressive as to force the issue of who they really belong to, as Daly insists on doing. Neologism is also quite alien to Rich's linguistic practice: rehabilitation of "the commonest words" is her objective, and she does this by enlisting connotations that have not completely disappeared and can therefore be revived without extraordinary measures by the context in which a word is set. The etymological information I have cited may sharpen our awareness of what the word *musing* does and does not mean in "Transcendental Etude," but we do not need that information to understand what Rich has used the word to mean in this context. It is important, however, that a word like *musing* or *tenets* brings a history of usage with it into Rich's poem, because it is by virtue of that history, which gives it a range of possible meanings, that the "same" word can be used to mean different things in different contexts. Relocation would be a better rubric than repossession for what happens to these words in Rich's hands, because it is not a question for Rich, as it characteristically is for Daly, of "who is to be master?"

In *A Wild Patience Has Taken Me This Far*, the volume of poems that covers the period from 1978 through 1981, Rich continued to engage in feminist relocation of important words: *freedom* in "For Memory"; *protection* in "Coast to Coast"; *integrity* in the poem "Integrity"; in "Culture and Anarchy," not only the title words but also *escape, emancipation, suffrage*; *matrices* in "For Julia in Nebraska"; *exceptional* in "Heroines"; and so on. Each of these poems models a process that is both critical and constructive, one that is set in the context of everyday living—of housecleaning, preparing meals, reading, typing, collaborating, and arguing with a beloved other woman. The poem "Rift" (1980) stages a lovers' quarrel that is focused on a disagreement about language, and here we find Rich suggesting that the price of an outright rejection of standard usage is unacceptably high:

> *Politics,*
> you'd say, *is an unworthy name*
> *for what we're after.*
> What we're after
> is not all that clear to me, if politics
> is an unworthy name. (*WP*, 49)

This example presages the tendency of both her poems and her prose writing in recent years to be less concerned with the repossession of language than they were in the 1970s, and more accepting of standard usage.

Whereas Daly's "uncommon quest" resulted in a language that is so uncommon as to have no general currency, Rich's recent writings suggest that she is no longer dreaming of a common language at all. Where she does call attention to particular words and their meanings, she emphasizes that a particular word has meant different things to the same person at different points in her life, or stages encounters in which differently located usages need to be respected. Her 1986 poem "Negotiations," for example, is addressed to a sister poet with whom, it seems, she has often angrily disagreed:

> Someday if someday comes we will agree
> that trust is not about safety
> that keeping faith is not about deciding
> to clip our fingernails exactly
> to the same length or wearing
> a uniform that boasts our unanimity (*TP*, 9)

Their hypothetical truce day will not come, the speaker is suggesting, until she and her interlocutor have become more comfortable with their differences: thus, with respect to the words *truth* and *faith* her strategy here is not to formulate positive definitions, but by means of negative definitions to forestall premature closure.

Rich's career can thus be seen to have followed a trajectory that is more or less the opposite of Daly's. Even as Daly's project of code renovation disclosed its totalizing intention more and more clearly, Rich tried—more valuably, I think—to keep faith with the historical, material conditions of language in use. Perhaps the most important lesson her poetry has for us is that there is no question of getting any word's meaning finally "right." Meanings are not "in" words, and the kind of usage-oriented change that Rich has consistently modelled for feminist readers is open toward the future as well as the past.

────────── *NOTES* ──────────

1. Where possible, in quoting from Rich's poems and prose writings, I will use abbreviations to refer the reader to three collections:

LSS for *On Lies, Secrets, and Silence: Selected Prose 1966–1978*;
BBP for *Blood, Bread, and Poetry: Selected Prose 1979–1985*;
FD for *The Fact of a Doorframe: Poems Selected and New 1950–1984*.

Poems from *The Dream of a Common Language* (1978) and *A Wild Patience Has Taken Me This Far* (1981) that were not reprinted in *FD* are referred to *DCL* and *WP*. Poems written after 1984 and published in *Time's Power* (1989) are referred to *TP*. The date that appears in my text will always, however, be the date Rich provides to establish when she wrote the poem or when she delivered or published the prose piece originally.

2. On the whole, American feminists have been more pragmatically interventionist than feminists working in the French intellectual tradition have been, as Betsy Draine (1989) points out. Their efforts have resulted in the adoption of guidelines for nonsexist usage by most of the major educational publishers in this country and by many organizations concerned with the teaching of English. For a bibliography of these guidelines, see Frank and Treichler (1989, 310–314).

3. This phrase is taken from "Transcendental Etude" (*FD*, 267), a 1977 poem I will be using later on to illustrate Rich's approach to the repossession of language.

4. For a brief account of the origins and development of radical feminism, see Eisenstein (1983, 125–135).

5. The gender of her interlocutor is not specified, but in view of the poem's date and her references to lovemaking between them I infer that Rich in this poem is still "trying to talk to a man."

6. This phrase was coined by Kenneth Burke (1941), whose suggestive discussion of metaphor and metonymy predated Jakobson's more precise linguistic analysis.

7. The classic discussion of metaphor and metonymy as opposed, complementary radicals of language is Jakobson ([1960b] 1987).

8. Within the British feminist movement, which took its bearings from a Marxist tradition of social and political analysis, the radical feminist approach was criticized for paying too little attention to the history of sexist usage within particular "discursive formations"; see, for example, Black and Coward ([1981] 1990).

9. I will argue later that the *Wickedary* cannot do this successfully. Because of its emphasis on code refashioning, Daly's project is implicitly totalizing in its intention, despite her professed intention to model an ongoing communal process.

10. See Fiorenza (1983, 23), for whom Daly's writings afford a classic example of a "sociology of knowledge" approach to theology. Daly was apparently reading Berger in the early 1970s: she uses many of his key formulations in *Beyond God the Father* (1973), while calling attention to Berger's androcentrism. In *Gyn/Ecology* (1978), although she does not cite Berger, she uses his notion of "legitimation" to explain that the purpose of all major world religions is to shelter the male against anomie, and suggests that the symbolic message of all of them is "Women are the dreaded anomie" (Daly 1978, 39).

11. See Daly (1984, 25), where she approvingly cites Julian Jaynes's assertion in *The Origin of Consciousness in the Breakdown of the Bicameral Mind* that "metaphor is not a mere extra trick of language, as it is so often slighted in the old schoolbooks on composition; it is the very constitutive ground of language."

12. See Cassirer (1946), especially chapters 3 and 6. Langer is the English translator of *Language and Myth* and has built upon Cassirer's account of the origins of language.

13. Morris uses the "Dissembly of Exorcism" from *Gyn/Ecology* to make a similar point (Morris [1982] 1988, 40). My own example is chosen to highlight the way in which Daly's discursive posture has changed over time.

14. See Jakobson ([1976] 1987, 378): "Poeticity is present when the word is felt as a word and not a mere representation of the object being named or the outburst of emotion, when words and their composition, their meaning, their external and internal form, acquire a weight and value of their own instead of referring indifferently to reality." The *Wickedary* is full of explicit claims that words are living creatures or can be made to "come alive" (Daly and Caputi 1987, xvii).

15. On the subject of "feminist Humpty-Dumpties," see Cameron (1990, 11–12).

16. Morris recalls a telling moment from Daly's address in Sydney, when "the *we*-ness of the address was ruptured . . . by a woman who called out 'Mary, you're not speaking to *me* . . .'" (Morris 1988, 39).

17. I do not mean to accuse Daly of lying when she claims that her "we" in the *Wickedary* refers to other women who have helped her with the project in various ways (Daly and Caputi 1987, xxii), but rather to point out that the pronoun is manipulated in such a way as to take on a life of its own within the discursive system of the work itself.

18. This tendency of Daly's becomes even more explicit in *Pure Lust*, where she argues that "the deep connections that are rooted in one's

individuality as an intentional creator of her be-ing are more significant than are accidental connections in space and time....more radical even than familial, ethnic, and class ties, and ties of religious and educational 'background'" (Daly 1984, 353).

19. For an elaboration of this same idea in prose, see Rich's 1984 essay "Blood, Bread, and Poetry: The Location of the Poet" (*BBP*, 167–187).

20. "Toward the Solstice," 1977 (*DCL*, 68–71); "Splittings," 1974 (*DCL*, 10-11; *FD*, 228-29); "Power," 1974 (*DCL*, 3; *FD*, 225); "Twenty-One Love Poems," IX, 1974–76 (*DCL*, 29; *FD* 240); "Transcendental Etude," 1977 (*DCL*, 72; *FD* 264).

21. Deictics, also known as "shifters," are all of those elements of a verbal message that refer to its speaker and orient the message from its speaker's vantage point: thus "I" always means "the one who is saying 'I,'" and "here" designates the place from which "I" am speaking, wherever that happens to be. Benveniste (1966) explains that the function of deictic words is to produce "a conversion that one could call the conversion of language into discourse" (Benveniste [1966] 1971, 219–220).

22. See Gilbert and Gubar (1979, xxii) for a persuasive explanation of why the lyric "I" has been historically difficult for women to assume, in contrast to the novelist's posture of self-effacing social critic: "the lyric poet must be . . . assertive, authoritative, radiant with powerful feelings while at the same time absorbed in her own consciousness—and hence, by definition, profoundly 'unwomanly,' even freakish."

23. See, for example, "The Roofwalker," 1961 (*FD*, 49-50).

24. In the essay I am quoting, Rich suggests that this poem marks a turning point in her personal journey toward a female subject position: "*at last* the woman in the poem and the woman writing the poem become the same person" (italics added).

25. Rich explains (*LSS*, 47) that the poem was written after a visit to a planetarium where she had "read an account of the work of Caroline Herschel, the astronomer, who worked with her brother William, but whose name remained obscure, as his did not." In the poem the word *virile* is quoted from a description of the scientific genius of Tycho Brahe, whose world view this woman scientist is depicted as challenging.

26. I have discussed this poem at greater length, making some of these same points about its language, in my *Genre* article of 1995.

27. The English word *tenet* comes from Latin, where it was the form taken by the verb *tenere*, "to hold," in the third-person singular. According to the *American Heritage Dictionary*, a *tenet* is an "opinion, doctrine, principle, or dogma held by a person or, more especially, an organization."

28. Far from seeking to relieve the word *muse* of this accumulated baggage, Daly welcomes the *muse-Muse* connection, even while remarking upon its etymological spuriousness. Thus in *Pure Lust* she finds it to be "a happy circumstance that the verb *muse*, although it is apparently not etymologically related to the noun *Muse*, so aptly describes the activity of a woman who meets her Muse" (Daly 1984, 301–302).

29. Words like *wrenching* and *snatching* are frequently part of Daly's characterization of Websters' activity: in the *Wickedary* (Daly and Caputi 1987, xxiii) she explains that "our" Meta-etymologies transform the meanings of ordinary etymologies, "wrenching them out of their old contexts and making them visible and audible in a New/Archaic context"; see also page 14, where she argues that changing the spelling of a word like *gyn / ecology* "wrenches back Weird Wordpower."

REFERENCES

The American Heritage dictionary of the English language: New college edition. 1976. Ed. William Morris. Boston: Houghton Mifflin.

Benveniste, Emile. [1966] 1970. *Problems in general linguistics*. Trans. Mary Elizabeth Meek. Florida: University of Miami Press.

Berger, Peter. 1967. *The sacred canopy: Elements of a sociological theory of religion*. New York: Doubleday.

Black, Maria, and Rosalind Coward. [1981] 1990. Linguistic, social and sexual relations: A review of Dale Spender's *Man made language*. *Screen Education* 39 (Summer); reprinted in *The feminist critique of language: A reader*, 111–133, ed. Deborah Cameron. London: Routledge.

Black, Max. [1954–55] 1981. Metaphor. *Proceedings of the Aristotelian Society*, n.s. 55 (1954–55), 273–294; reprinted in *Philosophical perspectives on metaphor*, 63–82, ed. Mark Johnson. Minneapolis: University of Minnesota Press.

Burke, Kenneth. 1941. Four master tropes. *Kenyon Review* 3: 421–438.

Cameron, Deborah. 1990. Introduction: Why is language a feminist issue? In *The feminist critique of language: A reader*, 1–28, ed. D. Cameron. London: Routledge.

Cassirer, Ernst. 1946. *Language and myth*. Trans. Suzanne K. Langer. New York: Dover.

Daly, Mary. 1973. *Beyond God the father: Toward a philosophy of women's liberation*. Boston: Beacon Press.

———. 1978. *Gyn/Ecology: The metaethics of radical feminism*. Boston: Beacon Press.

———. 1984. *Pure lust: Elemental feminist philosophy*. Boston: Beacon Press.

Daly, Mary, and Jane Caputi. 1987. *Websters' first new intergalactic wickedary of the English language*. Boston: Beacon Press.

Draine, Betsy. 1989. Refusing the wisdom of Solomon: Some recent feminist literary theory. *Signs* 15: 144–170.

Eisenstein, Hester. 1983. *Contemporary feminist thought*. Boston: G. K. Hall.

Fiorenza, Elizabeth Schussler. 1983. *In memory of her: A feminist theological reconstruction of Christian origins*. New York: Crossroad Press.

Frank, Francine Wattman, and Paula A. Treichler. 1989. *Language, gender, and professional writing: Theoretical approaches and guidelines for nonsexist usage*. New York: Modern Language Association.

Gilbert, Sandra, and Susan Gubar. 1979. *Shakespeare's sisters: Feminist essays on women poets*. Bloomington: Indiana University Press.

Hedley, Jane. 1995. Re-forming the cradle: Adrienne Rich's "Transcendental Etude." *Genre* 28: 339–370.

Jakobson, Roman. [1960a] 1987. Linguistics and poetics. In *Style in language*, ed. Thomas A. Sebeok. Cambridge Mass.: MIT Press; reprinted in *Language in literature*, 62–94, ed. Krystyna Pomorska and Stephen Rudy. Cambridge, Mass.: Belknap Press.

———. [1960b] 1987. Two aspects of language and two types of aphasic disturbances. In *Fundamentals of language* [with Morris Halle], part 2. The Hague: Mouton; reprinted in *Language in literature*, 95–119. See Jakobson [1960a].

———. [1976] 1987. What is poetry? Trans. Michael Heim. In *Semiotics of art: Prague school contributions*, ed. Ladislav Matejka and Irwin Titunik. Cambridge, Mass.: MIT Press, 1976; reprinted in *Language in literature*, 368–378. See Jakobson [1960a].

Langer, Suzanne K. 1942. *Philosophy in a new key*. Cambridge, Mass: Harvard University Press.

Morris, Meaghan. [1982] 1988. A-mazing grace: Notes on Mary Daly's poetics. *Intervention* 16; reprinted in Morris, *The pirate's fiancee: Feminism, reading, postmodernism*, 27-50. London: Verso.

Nilsen, Alleen Pace. 1984. Winning the great he/she battle. *College English* 46: 151–157.

The Oxford English dictionary, 2d ed. 1989. Ed. J. A. Simpson and E. S. C. Weiner. Oxford: Clarendon Press.

Rich, Adrienne. 1978. *The dream of a common language: Poems 1974–1977*. New York: Norton.

———. 1979. *On lies, secrets, and silence: Selected prose 1966–1978*. New York: Norton.

———. 1981a. What does separatism mean? *Sinister Wisdom* 18 (Fall): 83–91.

———. 1981b. *A wild patience has taken me this far: Poems 1978–1981*. New York: Norton.

———. 1985. *The fact of a doorframe: Poems selected and new 1950–1984*. New York: Norton.

———. 1986. *Blood, bread and poetry: Selected prose 1979–1985*. New York: Norton.

———. 1989. *Time's power: Poems 1985–1988*. New York: Norton.

Ricoeur, Paul. [1978] 1981. The metaphorical process as cognition, imagination, and feeling. *Critical Inquiry* 5 (1978), 143–159; reprinted in *Philosophical perspectives on metaphor*, 228–247, ed. Mark Johnson. Minneapolis: University of Minnesota Press.

Georganna Ulary

4

From Revolution to Liberation

Transforming Hysterical Discourse into Analytic Discourse

Were there no analytic discourse, you would continue to speak like birdbrains.

—Lacan (Sem. XX)

With the increasing desire of several contemporary philosophers to formulate an adequate discursive politics and ethics comes the perennial question of the role and function of language, especially in the form of discourse.[1] The problem beckoning us is whether language, especially discourse, is only that which represses and stifles us with its imperatives and laws or whether there is a chance for liberation within discourse. Is discursive language no more than the oppressive tyrant ruling over the way we manifest our human subjectivity? Can we only ever fail in our attempts to express ourselves and communicate ourselves within the symbolic system that defines language? Such concerns are of particular interest to feminist theories of language precisely because women typically have been the ones stifled by patriarchal discourse. That is, to a large extent, women's desires and sexuality are repressed within our culture. To some degree then, all women "suffer" from hysteria in their attempts to find a language of their own. Many current theorists argue that the subjective experience of women resists the logical and grammatical structure of normal, symbolic

129

signification. Consequently, there has been an attempt to posit something like a feminine language, which would have a radically different structure than the patriarchal, symbolic structure of language.[2] The motivation for adopting such a position rests in the argument that "women feel rejected from language and the social bond"[3] that discourse supposedly gives birth to. The symbolic realm, where one comes into language and social relations, is cast in the phallic mold and as such it assumes the "values promulgated by patriarchal society and culture."[4] As a result of this patriarchal mastery, women are left with no voice of their own. They are forced to conform to the "law" that has been instituted by male subjects.

We might be tempted to assert that women don't really want to escape; that they *desire* to remain within the confines of an oppressive discourse. After all, aren't we all living in the "prison-house of language"? What this assertion obscures, however, is that as long as women continue to desire what the other (man) desires, they lack subjective autonomy and freedom; they lack the very thing that humans, as self-conscious subjects, *should* want. That is, they fall short of becoming autonomous, free subjects. From the influx of patients to the analyst's couch it is becoming evident that many subjects—particularly women—are seeking refuge from the stultifying effects of this "home life." They are looking for ways to more e(a)ffectively change their position with respect to patriarchal language and symbolic discourse. Under such constricting laws women are left with little to no hope for escape: "their exclusion is *internal* to an order from which nothing escapes: the order of (man's) discourse."[5] Many forms of this other, "feminine" language (that is, opposed to the masculine, symbolic language) take shape *only* by protesting against, and inevitably giving up all remnants of the symbolic realm, thereby leaving the female subject in a position of incommunicado and reticence. There appears to be an unbridgeable gap between the rational, representational, logical structure of language (i.e., the symbolic or masculine structure) and the expressive, affective, drive-related experience of human subjectivity (i.e., the real or feminine structure). By accepting this unmitigating gap, a common result of such judgments is that one is left with an either/or position: *either* the subject—especially the female subject—can remain submissive to the symbolic, *or* the subject can become psychotic or hysterical, thereby leaving no possibility for a subject position between these two extremes. As Kristeva points out: "consequently, it is difficult, if not impossible, for women to adhere to the sacrificial logic of separation and syntactic links upon which language and the social code are based, and this can eventually lead to a rejection of the symbolic that is experienced as a rejection of the paternal function and may result in psychosis."[6] Neither of these two options yields the hoped-for liberation that language and discourse might provide. So, can this desired liberation ever be realized? The question that must be asked is, "how linguistics and learned discourse, as symbolic systems, are able to capture an object in principle beyond any symbolic system."[7]

It is becoming more and more evident that the hope for social and political change can only be embodied in and through discursive practices. What is called for is a *revolution*[8] which would liberate the human subject—especially the subject as woman—from the constraints of repressive master signifiers (which tend to be both phallic and logocentric) that seem to have her programmed according to their own desire rather than her own; signifiers that are restraining subjects not only from the very act of *speaking and desiring for themselves* but also from the act of feeling pleasure, from satisfying their *jouissance*. Within the traditional symbolic mode, women's desires are not their own, but their desire is only ever the desire of/for the other, or men's desire: that is, women either desire the other (men), or they desire what the other (man) desires. Because of this, they lack both autonomy and self-recognition. Consequently, "if women are defined [and desire] according to masculine interests, given no place as active, self-defined subjects and no language to speak their specificity, then how is change possible?"[9] In their efforts to resist the patriarchal symbolic (what Lacan calls the master's discourse), women are prone to adopt the hysteric's discourse both somatically and verbally, as their only defense: "within patriarchal cultures and representational systems there is no space and few resources women may utilize in order to speak, desire and create *as women*."[10] Moreover, it is becoming equally apparent that these new methods of political action must be preceded by revolutions within the subject herself.[11] Rather than merely positing an autonomous subject who, as an agent, uses language, there must be an accounting of how the subject comes into—literally, is born into—language and how the body is always already overwritten with signifiers (albeit signifiers which are not her own, but are the other's).

My question is, is Irigaray's miming hysteric revolutionary and liberatory enough to produce the changes called for by feminist theory? Is it liberating enough only to *revolt* against the oppressor (patriarchy) in some *reactive* way, or must we *actively subvert* the tyrannical system itself? In examining these questions, I wish to propose that there is a discourse that women, and other marginal subjects, can employ that would shatter the commanding gaze of the symbolic Other—an Other that is progressively becoming more and more uncomfortable for us to surrender to. It is not the case that all discourse—because it is a symbolic system—is doomed to failure in its liberatory potential. It is not the case that we must simply resign ourselves to the fact and fate that as speaking beings we must learn to adapt to and live within the symbolic, accepting the limitations therein, accepting the fact that we will always be subordinate to the patriarchal, and at times misogynistic/matricidal, symbolic Other.

A response to most of these concerns can be found through an examination of the subject's relation to and constitution within language. Discourse seems to be the necessary (but not sufficient) condition for liberating the human subject from both psycholinguistic and material oppression. Only when we tell our stories, talk out our maladies, does the possibility of freedom exist. Silence leads us nowhere. Moreover, we only adequately express our demands and desires once we've entered into the realm of language (the symbolic). Prior to coming into language, all our attempts to satisfy or fill up our lack are only inarticulate cries. We begin to fill the lack we experience by coming into language, through demanding and desiring certain things from others. In return for those things given, the Other places certain demands and restrictions on us. The Other can adopt many faces, such as another human being, or God, or society at large, or our parent(s), or the laws, customs, and traditions of a culture. However, for the most part, this Other is related to the patriarchal, social, symbolic realm that we all inhabit as speaking beings. We are immediately dwellers within the symbolic as soon as we come into language. The symbolic sets down the law. It gives us the *gift*[12] of structure and order in our psychic and material lives. As Lacan formulates it, the *Nom /Non -du-père* or Law of the Father is that signifier which bars the desire of the mother (woman) thus instituting primal repression. This is the law that sets the parameters outlining what is communicable and what is non-sense. As patriarchal and phallo-logocentric, the law is pro-grammed to restrict women's free play of language, while men "have the law on their side and they don't hesitate, when the occasion arises, to use force,"[13] to lay down the law to women.

At one point in *Seminar XX* Lacan claims that women are not worth listening to, implying that their speech is filled with utter non-sense or stupidities. He adds that women utter the most stu-pidities when asked to describe their pleasure. In her criticism of Lacan, Irigaray highlights that the question of "whether, in his logic, they [women] can articulate anything at all, whether they can be heard, is not even raised. For raising it would mean grant-ing that there may be some other logic, and one that upsets his own. That is, a logic that challenges mastery."[14] Just as there is no law governing or describing women's pleasure, there is no discourse of their own either: "if women—according to him—can say nothing, can know nothing, of their own pleasure, it is because they cannot in any way order themselves within and through a language that would be on some basis their own."[15] Although Irigaray hits at the heart of the feminist issue with Lacan, there may be a way of reading or interpreting him that might allow for more liberation than is otherwise apparent. The question I am posing is, can Lacan adequately respond to Irigaray's criticisms? Are there spaces within symbolic language and discourse where women can speak their desires and speak their bodies or must women resort to hysterical or poetic language? In the remainder of this chapter I will attempt to formulate such a Lacanian response, arguing that there are such spaces of liberation within discourse. Similar to Irigaray's mimetic strategy insofar as it is a strategy that works from within the "prison" of language, there is another strategy that women, as prisoners, can employ to foster their freedom. It is strategy that first entails adopting the discourse of the hysteric and then trans-forming this discourse into analytic discourse.[16]

Both the hysteric's discourse and the analyst's discourse can be seen as representing possible ways in which the subject is struc-tured in relation to its jouissance and to others—including the Other. As such, these different formulations present different modes or strategies of how the subject can be either inhibited by the Other or liberated from the Other. The transformation that is called for is one that reveals the "analytic" progression that an analysand undergoes in moving from one type of discourse to another and

back again: a progressive movement from being in a subject position that is hampered by or constrained by the Other (the patriarchal, symbolic Other, or the law) toward a subject position that
frees the analysand from the condemning gaze and *word* (signifier)
of the Other. I will first elucidate the differences and characteristics of hysterical and analytic discourses, after which I will argue
that although the hysteric's discourse goes further than other types
of discourse, it still falls short of the task of a liberatory discourse.
More specifically, I hope to reveal the "revolutionary" character
imbedded within hysterical discourse, but only to say that such a
revolution does not go far enough. It is a revolution without liberation. In arguing this point I will make use of Irigaray's depiction of
the hysteric to dramatize my position. Finally, relying on Lacan's
formulation of analytic discourse and Kristeva's plea for analysis,
I argue that only *analytic* discourse is able to answer the question
of discursive liberation effectively. Only therein can the subject
truly transform her position in relation to her jouissance and in
relation to the other. Through this analysis of discourse I hope to
show the implications of it for feminist theories of language.

> Discourse always aims at the least stupidity, at sublime stupidity. . . .
> Stupidity nevertheless has to be nourished.
>
> —Lacan *(Sem. XX)*

The problem of being "stuck" in language gives rise to a variety
of "new maladies of the soul." Maladies that result from the inability to symbolize, to represent, to "mean"—where discourse is cut
off, castrated, from all affect. Kristeva claims that in such states,
"expression is standardized . . . discourse becomes normalized. For
that matter, do you really have a discourse of your own?"[17]

Different discourses can be seen to produce certain psychological
effects in the subject. If we extend these effects beyond the individual subject to culture or society at large, perhaps they might
have more wide-ranging social implications. In her own plea for
analysis, Kristeva writes:

> The current transformations of psychic life may foreshadow a
> new humanity, one whose psychological conveniences will be

able to overcome metaphysical anxiety and the need for meaning. Wouldn't it be great to be satisfied with just a pill and a television screen? [However, the problem lies in the fact that] the path of such a superman is strewn with traps. A wide variety of troubles can bring new patients to the analyst's couch: sexual and relationship difficulties, somatic symptoms, a difficulty expressing oneself, and a general malaise caused by a language experienced as "artificial," "empty," or "mechanical."[18]

If different discourses can produce certain psychological effects in individual subjects, what is to prevent them from producing similar effects on the social and political level? As Lacan presents it, it seems quite evident that one such discourse, namely the "master's" discourse, has far exceeded the others in producing pronounced psychological effects on society. The master's discourse appears to dominate the realm of all discourses much as the queen bee dominates her hive. In general, the master's discourse is one that completely dominates and subordinates the subject (particularly the subject as woman), producing in her a sense of servitude and submission to the commands of the governing authority.[19] The "university" discourse, which amounts to not much more than a slave to the discourse of the master, seeks to provide rational justification for the master's signifiers. Consequently, the subject is indoctrinated or educated to believe such reasons without question. By means of inculcation, the university discourse, working in the service of the master discourse, aims at "legitimizing" the subject's subordination to the law of the master signifier (the symbolic Other). Hysterical discourse reveals the subject as rebelling or revolting against this symbolic Other, but reveals not much more than a desiring voice of protest. Finally, only in analytic discourse (or the discourse *between* the analyst and the analysand) is it possible for the subject to truly transform her position in relation to her jouissance and in relation to the Other.[20] Here is where the hysteric's revolutionary power becomes actualized and reconfigured into a liberatory power.

Perhaps the one common denominator among all discourses is that in every discourse there is a loss of jouissance; at the same time, however, language is a jouissance apparatus where the subject finds pleasure (*jouis-*) in meaning (*sens-*). In other words, there is something lost to language; at the same time, however, language helps fill our loss or lack, it helps satisfy our desires. Lacan writes, "the fact that one *says* remains forgotten behind what is *said* in what is *heard*. Yet it is in the consequences of what is *said* that the act of *saying* is judged."[21] This "saying" is what Lacan also refers to as the function of the "written," which corresponds to the level of the "real" (while the function of the "read" and "said" correspond to the level of the symbolic). As such, this "real" dimension is beyond the "law(s)" of language and "is not in the same register as the signifier."[22] The essence of law, says Lacan, is "to divide up, distribute, or 'retribute' everything that counts as jouissance."[23] The "real" is characteristic of the speaking being insofar as it is that which is lost or not understood, or repressed, in what is said. As structures, both language and the unconscious must be *talked out* or *said* in order for the advent of the subject to emerge; that is, for the subject to emerge where there hadn't been a subject. The analyst can only deal with and interpret the subject's unconscious based on what is said by the analysand.

I mentioned that one of the common denominators in all forms of discourse is the fact that in every discourse there is a loss of, or a sacrificing of, jouissance on the part of the subject. Consequently, one *speaks* in order to "master" her loss, or to go beyond her loss, or to satisfy her loss. Discourse, then, not only represents the way in which a subject is related to *jouissance* and others, but more specifically, it represents the peculiar way in which language is used as an apparatus of jouissance. This point becomes even more striking in the discourse of the hysteric.

We are all hysterics, at least intermittently.

—Kristeva (*New Maladies of the Soul*)

In the hysteric's discourse we see the split subject move into the position of agency or domination rather than be that which is always repressed. Rather than positing a completely autonomous subject, hysterical discourse discloses the subject as split or divided. The subject now becomes the agent who interrogates the master signifiers that she has been programmed to speak and value. Instead of working in the service of the master, we now see the hysterical subject in the dominant position of questioner. The subject of the hysteric's discourse complains and protests, asking the master signifier to prove why he should be, or why he *is*, "master." She now commands the master to "show what he is made of," to "prove his merit" so to speak; to produce something "serious" by way of his knowledge. In her role as interrogator, the hysteric speaks about being "logically repressed . . . about contempt for form as such, about mistrust for understanding as an obstacle along the path of jouissance and mistrust for the dry desolation of reason."[24] Reason inhibits her. She has something more to say than can be said "reasonably." The hysteric's problem or challenge is to:

[B]reak down the walls around the (male) one who speaks. . . . [Her] task is to go back through the house of confinement and the darkness of the night until once again [s]he feels the light that forms and other speculative veils had shrouded from [her] gaze.[25]

The subject within the hysteric's discourse experiences her jouissance through acquiring knowledge. She "gets off" on knowledge. Lacan writes, "the discourse of the hysteric reveals the relation between the discourse of the master and jouissance in this, that knowledge comes in/to the place of jouissance."[26] The subject involved here is one who desires: and her desire involves the questioning of master signifiers in an attempt to move beyond them—in an attempt to acquire more knowledge. Yet she tries to "abstain from all discourse, to keep quiet, or else utter only a sound so inarticulate that it barely forms a *song*"[27]—all the while waiting for an opportune moment to interrogate the master, to put his back up against the wall. The subject *challenges* the very notions that ground systematic knowledge because she refuses to embody the master signifiers: "hysteria can be seen as the woman's rebellion against and rejection of femininity—a refusal."[28] The old master signifiers don't speak to or about her situation. They no longer satisfy her. The hysteric refuses or revolts not only verbally but also bodily, where "hysterical symptoms can be seen as a refusal rather than the expression of desire. . . . She articulates a corporeal discourse; her symptoms 'speak' on her behalf."[29] In her revolution, the war wounds are exhibited in her flesh: "she is torn apart in pain, fear, cries, tears, and blood that go beyond any other feeling. But already, there is delight and longing in this torment"[30]—already there is pleasure and pain (jouissance) in this torment. Underlying her *desire* is its "true" driving force: *objet a*. We now begin to see that the hidden, repressed fire of her discourse is the thrust of the real—her unconscious drives. Moreover, the force of her discourse is dominated by her symptom where "the symptom is an act of (unconscious) defiance."[31] In other words, "the hysteric's symptom is a response to her annihilation as active subject . . . ; she lives out and uses her passivity in an active defiance of her social position. She (psychically) mutilates herself in order to prevent her brutalisation at the hands of others—hence the tragic self-defeat entailed by hysterical resistance."[32]

In her self-destructive revolution she continues to give herself up to others. She is judged as possessed or mad by her confessors, who

> are horrified to see or hear her fall stricken to the ground, toss and turn, shriek, grunt, groan convulsively, stiffen, and then fall into a strange sleep. They are scandalized or anxious at the idea of her striking herself . . . , thrusting sharp points into her stomach, burning her body to put out the fire of lust, searing her whole frame, using these extreme actions both to calm and to arouse her sleeping passions. . . . These violent attacks go through her, though alien to her. Sometimes they shake her, at other times they leave her prostrate, pale, like a dead woman. . . . In the dark. Always without consciousness.[33]

In light of her discourse, the question we must ask the hysteric is, do you genuinely find such torment and violence liberating, "can life go on in such violence? Swooning, fainting, bones and flesh torn apart with a crack that covers up the sound of all words of remission."[34] What her discourse fails to do is to completely move beyond the realm of the conscious symbolic into the unconscious real. She fails to articulate her unconscious drives but instead continues to repress them. What is still being repressed or barred is the real, the *objet a*—that *thing* which would satisfy her desire. Because of this, the hysterical subject only succeeds in protesting against the master signifiers, rather than moving beyond them. Indeed, "she is already caught, enveloped in various representations, in different configurations and chains that lead her, bit by bit, back to her unity. To resembling what she would ideally be in her own form. . . . And her eye has become accustomed to obvious 'truths' that actually hide what she is seeking."[35]

These "obvious" truths, however, are merely the truths and desires of the other rather than her own. These "obvious" truths hide what she is really seeking: her own desire, her own jouissance, the truth that her unconscious is painfully trying to express. Consequently, the subject remains in solidarity with the function of the master.[36] She is still merely *reacting* against the master. She is still *demanding and desiring* the master signifier *from* the other—that the other *give* her this signifier—rather than producing it herself. Yet still, "she cannot specify exactly what she wants. Words begin to fail her. She senses something *remains to be said* that resists all speech, that can at best be stammered out. All the words are weak, worn out, unfit to translate anything sensibly."[37] Here we can see that her language has become a jouissance apparatus at the same time, however, it fails her. This hysterical subject seeks "a maximal symbolic and psychic jouissance while simultaneously postulating the impossibility and the futility of this desire."[38] This desire is futile because it is not her own. She will receive no satisfaction in desiring this type of "symbolic" jouissance. She will remain only at the level of protest and still her voice will not be heard. Paralyzing her own desire, the subject fails to overpower or "bar" the symbolic Other and instead relies on that other for her own desire and satisfaction. In some sense, then, the hysteric's discourse succeeds in being a type of revolution but only a revolution that is still identified with the Other's (master's) desire. It is not a discourse in which she authentically finds liberation and autonomy despite all her trials and torments. As Irigaray explains, the hysteric's "soul cannot prevent herself from being buried and sealed off in her crypt. Hidden away, she waits for the rapture to return, the ecstasy, the lightning flash, the penetration of the divine touch."[39] The "divine touch" she is waiting for can only come about in analytic discourse, where she can engage the buried language of her unconscious; where she is free to roam through the prison and utter as many "stupidities" as she desires. But "this most private chamber opens only to one who is indebted to no possession for potency. It is wedded only in the abolition of all power, all having, all being;"[40] it opens only in analytic discourse wherein she, as analysand, can speak and be heard by the other, as analyst. It is not enough merely to speak hysterically. She must also be heard and interpreted. The hysteric is still preoccupied with recognition of/from the other. She becomes truly revolutionary by moving beyond this preliminary stage of recognition to the stage of recognizing herself via the other; where the other (analyst) provides the discursive avenue by means of which the hysteric gains self-recognition. Only then is discourse no longer dominated by her symptom. She continues her "nocturnal wandering . . . onward into a touch that opens the 'soul' again to contact with divine force, to the impact of searing light. She is cut to the quick within this shimmering underground fabric that she had always been herself, though she did not know it."[41] Analytic discourse reveals this underground, unconscious surface that has always been repressed. In revealing it to her, she then *speaks* it and becomes the cause of her own desire.

The subject must progress beyond the mastery of the *Other's* signifier to the point or position where she creates or produces her *own* signifiers and consequently becomes the cause of her own desire. This position can only be achieved in analytic discourse. In advocating this Lacanian answer, I support the idea that the only hope for liberation in/from language comes through the analysand's engagement in something like analytic discourse.[42]

> What is at stake in analytic discourse is always the following—you give a different reading to the signifiers that are enunciated than what they signify.
>
> —Lacan *(Sem. XX)*

The method employed by the analyst is to get the analysand—the hysteric—to "utter stupidities,"[43] the same type of non-sense and stupidities we originally thought Lacan was berating her for. He writes:

> [T]he subject is precisely the one we encourage to utter stupidities. . . . For it is with those stupidities that we do analysis and that we enter into the new subject—that of the unconscious; to draw consequences from [her]words—words that cannot be taken back, for that is the rule of the game.[44]

What the analyst strives for, is to get the analysand to utter stupidities that will reveal the subject's own master signifiers: signifiers that have not, as yet, been brought into relation with other signifiers, signifiers that have been repressed by the structure of phallologocentric discourse. According to Lacan, "analysis came to announce to us that there is knowledge that is not known, knowledge that is based on the signifier as such."[45] A successful interrogation of the subject aims at those precise moments, words, slips of the tongue, and dreams where the subject is most definitely divided between conscious and unconscious. The analysand will most likely call such utterances accidents or "utter" nonsense. There ensues a combat between discourses which succeeds in liberating the split subject from the oppressive symbolic master signifiers imposed on her by the Other: the analyst adopts analytic discourse, while the analysand is forced into a hysterical discourse where she demands that the analyst *give* her knowledge. The hysterical subject demands that the analyst produce knowledge; i.e., the hysteric asks the analyst to tell her about herself, to tell her what her problem is. She does this in order to discern the Other's desire so that she will know how to position herself in order to become what the Other lacks. The analyst, however, refuses to supply her with what she wants. The analyst refuses to answer her demands and instead "puts the hysterical subject to work," forcing her to produce her own knowledge. It is in this way that the analyst must listen to the *letter* (i.e., word and grammar), the *dit-mension*,[46] rather than the spirit or intention of the analysand's words. The letter is that which cannot be understood, it is "stupid," yet it is the voice of the unconscious. It is in this discourse that the most "revolutionary" and liberatory potential lays for effectively removing the tyranny wielded by the patriarchal other through language. For feminist theories of language, this type of discourse provides an alternative to the either/or situation that I presented earlier. That is, women are no longer forced to choose strictly between the patriarchal symbolic and the psychotic or hysterical types of discourses. Instead, they are invited, urged, to develop their own discourse based on their own desires, and to experience liberation from within the dynamic structure of discursive language. They no longer have to give up all remnants of the symbolic in order to speak their bodies. Consequently, such discourses cannot be accused of being exclusionary or merely the reverse of the patriarchal language. Analytic discourse is "open" to anyone who desires to speak.

As I mentioned earlier, Lacan does not get rid of master signifiers, and because of this, even analytic discourse takes on some of the characteristics of the master's discourse but with one major difference: in analytic discourse, the subject is no longer *given* the master signifier by the other who imposes it, but she creates her own signifiers and continues to dialectize them. This new, self-designated signifier is not imposed from outside in some absolute, rigid way which mandates the subject's identity. Instead, the subject now creates her own "identity" through the process of subjectivization. But this production also involves a dialectization, whereby the subject learns how to dialectize her own master signifiers much as she has learned to dialectize the master signifiers of the other. That which has always been repressed and beyond symbolization (*objet a*) is now in the commanding position, and "where it speaks, it enjoys."[47] In terms of feminist analyses, this means that women are then able to *speak* and *enjoy* their bodies and their desires rather than be tormented and tortured by them in hysterical symptoms. That which has always been oppressed is now free to speak and move according to its own "laws" and desires. According to Lacan, it is by taking up this position, and by failing to "give in" to the demands made on him/her by the subject, that the analyst promotes psycholinguistic changes in the analysand. In so doing, the analyst reveals the fundamental fantasy ($S \diamond a$) that is the *cause* of the subject's desire. The analyst's purpose is to

> analyze psychic life, that is, to break it down and to start over . . . [and] to discover a *new malady of the soul* in each of his/her patients; to revitalize grammar and rhetoric, and enrich the style of those who wish to speak with us because they can no longer remain silent and brushed aside.[48]

Analytic discourse implores women and other boundary subjects, who typically have been silenced or reduced to inarticulate cries, to become part of the *fluid* dynamics of discourse. The analysand, in dialogue with the analyst, answers the call for liberation by *producing* her own signifiers and satisfaction rather than merely submitting to the Other's. For Kristeva, as well as Lacan, "the linguistic mechanism remains at the core of treatment: as a signifying construct, the speech of both the analysand and the analyst incorporating different series of representations."[49] Thus, the "revolution" that analytic discourse advances is one that is *not* fought by anarchists or hysterics who are merely *reactionary* forces against the Other, but one that employs "analysts" and productive "analysands" who actively take on the position of liberating the speaking subject. Analytic discourses investigate and interpret how subjects, and society at large, participate in and constitute themselves in relation to the position of mastery. They investigate and interpret how women have been constituted in relation to the other's [man's] mastery and provide an efficacious response to women's call for liberation. Through this discursive method, the speaking subject is encouraged to work through her oppression by the Other; to dialectize the systematic knowledge that works in the service of this Other; and finally, to recognize herself as a split subject who has been forbidden a certain jouissance by the Other. By engaging in analytic discourse, the subject's primary task is to free up this forbidden jouissance in order to liberate herself from the Other's masterful discourse.

--- *NOTES* ---

1. The terms language and discourse are often used synonymously, however, there is somewhat of a distinction I wish to make between these two terms. For my purposes here, I am using language to mean the fixed structure of signification, including grammar and logic. It might help to think of language as the static structure, while thinking of discourse as the more lived, dynamic, fluid aspect of language. That is, discourse corresponds to the reflective act engaged in by speaking whereas language corresponds to the rules governing this act. Discourse also encompasses both linguistic and non-linguistic activities, such as gesturing, art, and semiotics.

2. See, for example, Cixous's notion of *écriture féminine* and Irigaray's notion of *parler femme*.

3. Julia Kristeva, *New Maladies of the Soul*, trans. Ross Guberman (New York: Columbia University Press, 1995), 213. Hereafter cited as *NMS*.

4. Luce Irigarary, *This Sex Which Is Not One*, trans. Catherine Porter (Ithaca: Cornell University Press, 1985), 86. Hereafter cited as *TS*.

5. Ibid., 88.

6. Kristeva, *NMS*, 213.

7. Andrea Nye, "Woman Clothed with the Sun: Julia Kristeva and the Escape from/to Language," *Signs* 12(1987): 677.

8. I have italicized this notion because Lacan employs it in a somewhat different sense than it is commonly used.

9. Elizabeth Grosz, *Sexual Subversions: Three French Feminists* (Sydney: Allen and Unwin, 1989), 132. Hereafter cited as *SS*.

10. Ibid., 133.

11. See Kristeva's *Strangers to Ourselves*, trans. Leon S. Roudiez (New York: Columbia University Press, 1991).

12. I am playing on the notion of *das Gift* in German, as well as the Greek notion of *pharmakon*. That is, I want to say that the symbolic law is both the poison and the cure for speaking beings.

13. Irigaray, *TS*, 95.

14. Ibid., 90.

15. Ibid., 95.

16. Although I will be making a distinction between the hysteric's discourse and the analyst's discourse, it should always be kept in mind that both are "discourses," and as such, are symbolic articulations. I am not suggesting that hysterical discourse falls outside symbolic articulations, only that it does not go far enough in liberating the subject from the desire of the other. I will elucidate this in greater detail when I explain Lacan's "four discourses."

17. Kristeva, *NMS*, 8.

18. Ibid., 8–9.

19. All of Lacan's algorithms follow the same pattern:

$$\frac{\text{agent}}{\text{truth}} \longrightarrow \frac{\text{other}}{\text{loss, product, jouissance}}$$

In his formula for the master's discourse, the master signifier is in the position of agent which interrogates the other. The result or product of this interrogation is systematic knowledge. What is repressed or barred in the master's discourse is the truth of the split subject and the *objet a*.

20. It is important to keep in mind that not all analysts and analysands adopt the analytic discourse just as not all hysterics adopt the hysteric's discourse. The hysteric, for example, may adopt any one of the discourses depending on his or her relation to jouissance and the other.

21. Lacan, *Seminar XX*, p. 2.2 in translated manuscript by Bruce Fink.

22. Ibid., 3.3.

23. Ibid., 1.2.

24. Luce Irigaray, *Speculum of the Other Woman,* trans. Gillian C. Gill (Ithaca: Cornell University Press, 1985), 191. Hereafter cited as *SOW*.

25. Ibid., 192.

26. Lacan, *Seminar XVII*, 107. All English translations from Lacan's *Seminar XVII* are mine.

27. Irigaray, *SOW*, 193.

28. Grosz, *SS*, 134.

29. Ibid.

30. Irigaray, *SOW*, 193.

31. Grosz, *SS*, 137.

32. Ibid., 138.

33. Irigaray, *SOW*, 198–199.

34. Ibid., 196.

35. Ibid., 192–193.

36. Lacan, *XVII*, 107.

37. Irigaray, *SOW*, 193.

38. Kristeva, *NMS*, 70.

39. Irigaray, *SOW*, 195.

40. Ibid., 196.

41. Ibid., 193.

42. Although the hysteric's discourse is most certainly effective, insofar as it is a voice of protest, it is only the first step toward real liberation.

43. Lacan, *XX*, 2.7.

44. Ibid.

45. Ibid., 8.6.

46. Lacan offers an explanation of this term in *Seminar XX*.

47. Ibid., 9.10.

48. Kristeva, *NMS*, 6, 9–10.

49. Ibid., 5.

REFERENCES

Grosz, Elizabeth. 1989. *Sexual subversions: Three French feminists.* Sydney: Allen and Unwin.

Irigaray, Luce. 1985. *Speculum of the other woman.* Trans. Gillian C. Gill. Ithaca: Cornell University Press.

———. 1985. *This sex which is not one.* Trans. Catherine Porter. Ithaca: Cornell University Press.

Kristeva, Julia. 1991. *Strangers to ourselves.* Trans. Leon S. Roudiez. New York: Columbia University Press.

———. 1995. *New maladies of the soul.* Trans. Ross Guberman. New York: Columbia University Press.

Lacan, Jacques. 1991. *Seminar XVII L'envers de la psychanalyse (1969–70).* Paris: Seuil.

———. forthcoming. *Seminar XX Encore.* Trans. Bruce Fink. New York: Norton.

Nye, Andrea. 1987. Woman clothed with the sun: Julia Kristeva and the escape from/to language. *Signs* 12, no. 4: 664–86.

Part Two

The Power to Speak

Who Is Speaking, from Where?

Elissa Marder

5

Disarticulated Voices

Feminism and Philomela

By juxtaposing readings of selected feminist critics with a reading of
Ovid's account of Philomela's rape and silencing, this essay interrogates the rhetorical, political, and epistemological implications of the
feminist "we." As a political intervention that comes into being as a
response to women's oppression, feminism must posit a collective
"we." But this feminist "we" is best understood as an impersonal,
performative pronoun whose political force is not derived from a
knowable referent.

I. Articulating Silence

If feminism comes into being discursively as a political response
to "women's oppression," the rhetorical figure most commonly
invoked to express that oppression is that of being silenced. But in
what language can one speak the effect of being silenced? How does
feminist discourse situate itself in relation to patriarchal law, institutions, and discourse? As a collective speech act that often begins
by saying both "we are oppressed" and "our voices are suppressed
by patriarchal discourses," feminist discourse can never not examine the parameters of its own possibility of speaking. How does a
speech act that posits a politicized "we" determine both who is
designated by that "we" and what that "we" can say? In what ways
does the political necessity of speaking as a collective "we" determine and affect the ways in which that collectivity can be thought?

149

If, as Teresa de Lauretis has proposed, "the relation of experience to discourse, finally, is what is at issue in the definition of feminism" (de Lauretis 1986, 5), how does feminist discourse articulate this relation? If there is no experience "outside" of patriarchal structures and no discrete language "outside" of patriarchal discourse, in what terms can this experience be spoken? I propose to address these questions through two sets of readings, beginning with an examination of some punctual moments in feminist discourse in which the language of feminism is explicitly interrogated and ending with a feminist reading of a classical literary text, Ovid's Philomela story. This text stages a scene of a woman's "experience" of violation and the relationship between that violation and the language of its articulation. By juxtaposing these two different textual articulations of women's relationship to discourse, I hope to raise questions concerning the impact of rhetorical figures on political language as well as the place of politics within a feminist reading practice.

II. The "Feminist" Label and the
Dream of a Common Tongue

The term "feminist" is not a proper name. It denotes no precise group, race, class, or even gender. It is a peculiar label—one that is seemingly personally conferred (I declare myself a feminist) and collectively confirmed (I am acknowledged by others as participating in feminism). While the field of feminism has flourished in the space that is left undefined by the term, the word "feminist" has remained a site of perpetual conflict and controversy. Even those feminists who declare with absolute certainty their commitment to feminist politics cannot say with any precision *who* is named by the term or *what* such a naming implies. To state that "one cannot *know*" who or what is named by the name "feminist" is not at all to say that it has no meaning. On the contrary—each moment of feminist thinking has paradoxically defined itself *in response* to the resoundingly open-ended echo of these insistent questions: "who" or "what" is implied by my/our use of the term?

In *Gynesis,* Alice Jardine describes a moment of high tension in the audience when she presented an early version of a paper that engaged French theories of the "feminine":

During a discussion following the presentation of an early version of "Gynesis" at an MLA conference in New York City, a lot of energy was expended over the words "feminist" and "antifeminist." It was as if the problems of translation foregrounded here could be resolved if everyone in the room could just come to an *agreement* about what feminism is or is not. The problems with that (primarily Anglo-American) approach to interpretation are, of course, made abundantly clear by many of the French theorists we will be concerned with here. What is important, they might say, is not to decide who is or is not a feminist, but rather to examine how and why feminism may itself be problematic; is itself connected to larger theoretical issues; is not a natural given but a construction like all others. This kind of questioning does not have to be undertaken from a conservative position; it can in fact provide feminism's most radical moments. (Jardine 1985, 21)

One does not have to have been present in that audience to reconstruct from Jardine's brief description that the debate was no doubt extremely heated and to realize that even if the particular terms of the debate are now, in 1991, somewhat outdated in feminist writing, the *anxieties* that fuelled this debate are very much alive. Ultimately, it would seem, it boiled down to a question of name-calling. Some women, probably trained in the Anglo-American tradition, must have passionately proposed that French theories of the "feminine," written by women who were proud to say both that they were not feminists and that they were influenced largely by French male theorists, were consequently *not* feminist—they were antifeminist. To refer to this as name-calling is not, I believe, to trivialize the terms of the debate. Far from it: name-calling is never a neutral act—politically, ontologically, or epistemologically. Jardine's observation that "it was as if the problems of translation foregrounded here could be resolved if everyone in the room could just come to an *agreement* about what feminism is or is not" is perhaps feminism's central dream—its necessity (as a collective speech act) as well as its constituting impossibility. If, as I imagine, the women in Jardine's audience were, as we say, reduced to name-calling, this reduction was rendered necessary by the troubling difficulties of "translating" the epistemological interrogation of feminism by French theories of the feminine into a discourse of American political intervention. What Jardine calls "energy"—the friction between the terms "feminist" and "anti-feminist" has as much to say about the peculiar epistemological challenge that the field of feminism poses as it does about the different political agendas that were undoubtedly represented in that audience. As Jardine points out, the French theorists *refuse* to enter into debates concerning who is or is not a "feminist" and choose, instead, to interrogate the philosophical ramifications and methodological difficulties implied by the term "feminist" itself. Read in this context, the issue of name-calling becomes the site of a political/epistemological chasm that, acknowledged or not, is spoken by every feminist intervention.

If I am insisting upon retelling a rather familiar scenario, it is because I think that the aporia at work here—the peculiar undecidability that the name "feminist" names—has a variety of very specific consequences and implications for feminist scholarship that remain to be thought through and explored carefully. Jardine's thematization of the problem of Franco/American "translation" (the fact that "feminists" do not all speak "feminism" in a common tongue) is not merely a function of national or linguistic differences but a problem within any feminist collectivity. Because feminism has no one discourse or language, translation is always an issue. Even though aporia names the site of an undecidability, feminist scholarship—as political intervention—has always decided to decide, provisionally and in specifically telling ways what it means to speak or for that matter to read "as a feminist."

One of the most powerful of these decisions is to dream feminism as a kind of utopic metalanguage. This desire to a universal language that could comprehend all the possible referents designated by the term "feminist" can be heard in the cadences of Elaine Showalter's mapping of feminist theory in "Feminist Criticism in the Wilderness":

> English feminist criticism, essentially Marxist, stresses oppression; French feminist criticism, essentially psychoanalytic, stresses repression; American feminist criticism, essentially textual, stresses expression. All, however, have become gynocentric. All are struggling to find to terminology that can rescue the feminine from its stereotypical associations with inferiority. (Showalter 1982, 16)

This text dates from the same general period as Jardine's text; the difference lies in its rhetoric. Where Jardine's text is largely concerned with the difficulty of importing French texts to an American context, Showalter's text marks the moment when traditional American academic feminism attempts to incorporate the French infiltration into a larger, general, universal Feminist project. It is no accident if, at this moment in her essay, Showalter's map of theoretical advances looks very much like a map of the First World, a world where all feminist critics speak rhyming dialects of one basic, feminist Esperanto—"oppression," "repression," "expression." Paradoxically, in her attempt to find a common tongue for all forms of feminist expression that would speak in harmony and unison, Showalter has effectively silenced the force of the specific contributions of those voices she mentions while excluding other voices from her map.[1] Despite her obvious intention to invoke the diversity of this collectivity, she has muted the productive discord of specific speech acts. The collective "we" implied by Showalter's chorus is one that monotonizes feminist language by minimizing, among other things, the incompatibility of different sorts of discourses.

III. Saying "We" Epistemologically and Politically

If feminism cannot speak without positing a "we," the question "to whom does this *we* refer?" has generated enormous discussion. Most feminist theorists have long been concerned with the implications and consequences of invoking a collective "we." For the purposes of this essay, I have chosen to focus on two discrete examples of how this "we" has been thoughtfully invoked. In her 1982 article "Replacing Feminist Criticism," Peggy Kamuf calls attention to the dangers of conflating the invocation of a "we" with a critical approach that would presume to know who that "we" is. Reading a passage from an anthology of essays on feminist literary theory, Kamuf claims that the appeal to a "we" usually engages an attempt to uncover something specific to "women" that patriarchy has veiled:

> What is striking about this passage, I think, is first the combined appeal to a specific "we" and to a certain method of defining who that "we" is. The "we," in other words, is constituted by a shared faith in its consolidation at the end of an

empirical process which has codified its patterns of consciousness. Secondly, there is an implicit assumption in such programs that this knowledge about women can be produced in
and of itself without seeking any support within those very
structures of power which—or so it is implied—have prevented
knowledge of the feminine in the past. Yet what is it about
those structures which could have succeeded until now in
excluding such knowledge if it is not a similar appeal to a
"we" that has had a similar faith in its own eventual constitution as a delimited and totalizable object? (Kamuf 1982, 45)

For Kamuf, following both Foucault and Derrida, this sort of appeal to a "we" recalls the traditional (invisibly masculine) humanist's
blindness in assuming that a human "we" speaks for all humanity.
But if feminism begins by understanding that women have always
been erased by the traditional humanist's claim that his "we" speaks
for everyone, then why, Kamuf asks, do feminists believe that their
use of the same "we" will not result in similar sorts of blindness?
She argues that in order for this feminist "we" to believe in the
truth of its own consolidation, it employs the very strategies of
exclusion to which women have always been subjected. In the act
of establishing an aim, an end, or a telos to the question "who are
we?" that end has already been subverted. Feminism subverts its
own power to subvert when it refuses to acknowledge its negative
debt to the inheritance of patriarchy. The language of feminism is
not outside the language of patriarchy. For Kamuf, feminist politics
would seemingly follow from, and not precede, an attention to problems of epistemology. Ultimately, Kamuf proposes that the one thing
that feminism cannot afford *not* to do is to leave "its own undecidable margins of indeterminacy visible" (Kamuf 1982, 47). While I
agree with Kamuf's general concern, her insistence on the necessity of constantly dislocating the grounds of feminist discourse does
not account for the possibility that punctual, political interventions
can function *formatively* and that they must be provisionally
"grounded." I most emphatically share, however, her conviction that
feminism must leave its own undecidable margins visible. Feminism's performative power retains its force only by acknowledging
its ultimate difficulty in speaking. And the specific effects of patriarchal structures are often rendered visible where "feminism" has
difficulty articulating its own terms.

More recently, Teresa de Lauretis has suggested that the feminist "we" is a political construction that emerges as both product and function of women's historical and material conditions. For de Lauretis, feminism defines itself as it turns around to look at the material history of its own production. "Feminists" are therefore constructed out of what "women" have produced:

> Women have written books, to say nothing of diaries and letters and drawersful of words, about how much it takes to be able to write, at best, and how many other women do not even have that much. We have written books about our writing and the suppression of our writing; we have written about silence and madness, marginality and invisibility, negativity and difference. But we have also written of femininity and feminine writing, of identities, differences, and commonalities. (de Lauretis 1986, 5)

De Lauretis implies that the "we" of the second sentence is produced by the history recounted in the first sentence. Only after having posited a historical and institutional relationship between "women" and "writing" does de Lauretis finally invoke the "we." Although she is careful not to conflate the feminist "we" with the term "women" it is clear that for her the two are linked. "Feminism" is a possible aftereffect that can only come into being in the wake of a certain critical mass of writings by women. The category of "women," however, is invoked through the *institution* of writing. The power in this description lies in the fact that the "we" is constructed through a kind of dialectic between affirmation and negation. It posits itself and negates itself simultaneously, incorporating moments of failure to produce within the history of its own production. Furthermore, this "we" is a function of that history and not a representation of it; it does not coincide with the term women that engenders it. This "we" neither names a coherent identity nor does it speak with one voice. De Lauretis's invocation of this kind of feminist "we" suggests that feminists can say "we" without positing identically constructed subjects that speak in harmony or unison. I would argue that the feminist "we" can and paradoxically must continue to speak as a "we" as long as that "we" does not believe its own concrete identity. Our collective "we" only has force as long as we collectively refuse to accord that "we" status as a knowable, identifiable category.

IV. Reading (and) the "Experience of Real Women"

But are there limits to what this political, collective "we" can mean-ingfully say? What, for example, is at stake when the politicized voice speaks to and through a literary text? What is involved in reading "as a feminist?"[2] Can politically motivated terms such as "experience" or "power" be deployed in order to ground feminist readings?

Speaking in the name of a collective "we" in "Feminism and the Power of Interpretation: Some Critical Readings," Tania Modleski (1986, 121–38) argues that the categories of "experience" and "power" are essential to a feminist reading practice. Modleski begins her essay by positing a narrative of literary history that is essentially one of monolithic male oppression accompanied by monolithic female enslavement: "Recognizing that women have long been prisoners of male texts, genres, canons, many feminist critics have argued for the necessity of constructing a theory of the female reader and have offered a variety of strategies by which she may elude her captors" (Modleski 1986, 121). The three most slippery terms that circulate in her essay are "power," "real women," and "experience." The word "power" is invoked as a universal, monolithic thing that one either does or does not possess. Toward the end of her essay she writes:

> Interpretation is, as I have insisted throughout this essay, crucially bound up with power. For feminism, power is the stake of the critical enterprise, and each and every interpre-tative act involves an exercise of power over a text, whether we like to admit it or not . . . In any case the ultimate goal of feminist criticism and theory is female empowerment. My particular concern here has been to empower female readers of texts, in part by rescuing them from the oblivion to which some critics would consign them. . . . By working on a variety of fronts for the survival and empowerment of women, femi-nist criticism performs an escape act dedicated to freeing women from *all* male captivity narratives, whether these be found in literature, criticism, or theory. (Modleski 1986, 136)

In her overarching deployment of the notion of power (which is articulated variously as "truth," "domination," and "mastery,") Modleski fails to make distinctions between limited and largely privileged academic institutional power relations and the act of reading a literary text. Under the umbrella of the word "power," Modleski conflates two different and incommesurable sorts of relations: a reader with her text and the positions that particular male and female professors hold within the American (largely white and middle-class) academic institution.

In this text, Modleski's strategy for "empowering" female readers turns out to be a critique of the work of two feminist readers who, she believes, betray the feminist cause by selling out to the enemy. Their crime is their refusal to understand the task of reading as one of mastery and power:

> To my mind there is something profoundly depressing in the spectacle of female critics' avowing their eagerness to relinquish a mastery that they have never possessed. Since when have women been granted the power of interpretation or our readings accorded the status of interpretative truth by the male critical establishment? For a woman to proclaim an end to critical mastery, then, is quite different from a male critic's repudiation of the textual dominance he in fact possesses. (Modleski 1986, 127)

To read is not to dominate: male critics do not "dominate" texts. They do occupy certain pivotal positions within academic institutions where certain reading practices are ideologically valorized and others are not. A relationship to a literary text that proclaims the "power" of its own interpretive truth by asserting textual domination is, quite simply, not a reading at all, whether performed by a male or by a female critic.

The feminist reading that "depresses" Modleski is a reading of Ovid's Echo and Narcissus myth. Ovid's *Metamorphoses* is a classical Latin text about gods, nymphs, men, and women, all of whom are magically transformed into animals or inanimate beings. There are no "real women" in Ovid's text—only allegories of representations of gendered subject positions. A reading of Ovid can have no direct, mimetic applicability to the plight of particular oppressed "real women." Ironically, it is Modleski, and not the readers she criticizes, who transforms the woman named Peggy Kamuf into a mythological figure: "In depicting a situation in which real women and their experience are superfluous to the process she describes (since beginnings are arbitrary and all notions of identity negated) Kamuf plays the role of Juno condemning Echo to a repetition that ultimately leads to her physical annihilation" (Modleski 1986, 134). While this is clearly meant as some sort of parody of Kamuf's position, one is struck by Modleski's use of these mythological figures in order to make her point about the suppressed "experience" of "real women." Invoked throughout the essay, the "experience" of "real women" finds a dubious voice through this sort of unexamined reliance upon mythological models of representation. A feminist reading practice that reads mythological figures as if they are "real women" is also a reading practice that, conversely, mythologizes the notion of "real women." To condemn a reading because it betrays a political agenda is to betray politics as well as reading.[3]

Modleski's ideal feminist reader would be engaged in a narcissistic endeavor: the reader constructs the text as a mirror in which she reads an emancipated or enslaved image of herself as an analogy of "real women" in "real-world" situations. This gesture insists upon reading images of a *hypothetical* "real world" in mythological allegories while simultaneously constructing a mythologized image of a "real world." As interpretive practice it does not allow the literary text to speak in its own literary language. It reduces that text to a transparent field of resemblances where literary figures confirm political positions that need to be grounded. But to use literature as the stable anchor for political intervention is to misrecognize the specific function and power of literary figures. Succumbing to the seduction of analogy, this sort of reading conflates text and world; it deflates literary texts by using them to construct a myth of a real world. If the primary concern of a reading is its applicability to political interventions "in the world," that reading is grounded on the notion that the relationship between text and world is reducible to analogic resemblance. Such a reading can only confirm what is already known before the text is read. Feminists cannot explore the possibilities of speaking differently from texts they dictate and manhandle. If to read "as a feminist" is to look for traces of real women in allegorical texts, then that reading practice ultimately fails to the extent that it succeeds in mastering its text. A literary text is not an object to be mastered or beaten into submission. A reading occurs only to the degree that the text is allowed to speak in terms that are foreign to its reader. Where a reading's primary function is its applicability as exemplum of a particular political agenda, it ceases to be a reading. It might function as discursive example—but then the text is ultimately silenced and rendered superfluous to the ends to which it is put.

The task of reading "as a feminist" is a demanding challenge. For a feminist reading to fulfill this challenge, it must go beyond reading for the plot of male oppression and female victimization, even and especially when that plot seemingly dominates the text. A feminist reading cannot dictate specific political action. But by opening up the fabric of a literary text, feminist readings can examine the discursive structure of patriarchy in order to help formulate an effective language of response. Some feminist readings might provide women with new means of expression; others might provide an articulation of why, how, and where feminist discourse stutters. In any case, the discourse of patriarchy is neither seamless nor univocal—feminist readings can puncture and punctuate the dominant discourse only by forcing its texts to unfold.

V. Reading "Philomela" as a Feminist

While one could dispute the value of reading Ovid's Echo and Narcissus story as a paradigm of patriarchy and the oppression of "real" women, Ovid's account of the Philomela story seems to beg for such a reading.[4] Unlike the Echo and Narcissus story, where gender positions, bodies, and identities are destabilized and interrogated by the narrative, and where the main characters are not human and are condemned to their respective fates because of divine intervention, divine presence is strikingly absent from the story of Philomela. While most of the preceding Ovidian tales depict conflicts between human and divine figures, present confusions of animal and inanimate worlds, and involve magical or supernatural operations, the story of Philomela is presented as a human drama among characters who are endowed solely with human powers, proper names, and social positions. In this story it would seem that figures of men and women correspond mimetically to stable gender positions and that they can be read accordingly. Furthermore, the story recounted in this "human" textual hiatus is a horrific and violent tale of a woman's rape, mutilation, and silencing. In the context of both this discussion of feminist discourse and Ovid's general project in the *Metamorphoses,* the story of

Philomela occupies a unique and privileged position. This story thematizes a woman's experience of violation and rhetorically enacts her inability to speak that experience. While Philomela does ultimately find a discourse for her rage, her experience is expressed in disarticulated speech—by a language that has no "tongue."

The story goes roughly as follows: Tereus, a Thracian king, marries a woman named Procne, and brings her to Thrace to live with him.[5] After some time, Procne desperately misses her sister Philomela and begs her husband to return to her father's house and bring Philomela back with him. Tereus agrees, travels to Procne's father's house, and sees Philomela. Burning with a sudden desire for her, he convinces the father to let her leave with him to visit her sister. He takes Philomela to his country, drags her into a forest, where he tells her that he is going to rape her, and then he rapes her. When she threatens to tell the world what happened to her, he cuts out her tongue and rapes her again. He leaves her locked in a cottage in the woods where, unable to speak, she finds a loom and weaves the story of the rape in violent thread against a white background. She manages to send the weaving to her sister Procne. Using a Bacchic festival as a pretext for finding her sister, Procne dances in frenzy to where Philomela is locked up. Procne releases her sister, brings her back to the palace, and there plots the proper medium of her revenge. After consideration, she decides not to cut off Tereus's tongue or his penis. Instead, struck by the resemblance between her husband and her son, Procne takes a knife, stabs her son, decapitates and dismembers him, and puts the pieces of his body in a stew, which she serves to Tereus. While he is eating, he asks to see his son. Procne informs Tereus that his son is in his belly. Philomela bursts in, gleefully holding the head of the dead son. As Tereus draws his sword to kill the sisters, all three are transformed into birds and fly away.

This text invites a feminist reading not only because it recounts the story of a woman's rape, but also because it establishes a relationship between the experience of the violation and access to language. Unable to speak, Philomela weaves the story of her rape. Only after she has been raped and mutilated does Philomela attempt to write. Through weaving, she writes her story because she cannot speak, and the only story she has to tell is that she has lost her voice. She writes out of necessity and in response to violation, but that writing is bound by the terms of violation.

Although Tereus cuts out Philomela's tongue *so that* she cannot bear witness to the rape, the rhetorical link that binds the terms "rape" and "silencing" exceeds the justification provided by the narrative's logic. The textual relationship established between these two acts (the rape and the severed tongue) interrogates the significance and readability of the term "rape" itself. The severed tongue does not merely function as a narrative consequence of the rape, but rather becomes a figurative representation of it. The act of cutting off the tongue reads that rape and gives it a figurative meaning. The rape itself does not become either fully figured or fully meaningful until it is repeated by the mutilation that ostensibly functions to cover it up. Rather than suppressing the rape, Tereus's act of cutting off Philomela's tongue both represents and repeats it. Philomela's rape accrues meaning through multiple repetitions and varied representation.

The text appears to stage two "rapes": one "literal" and the other "symbolic." While one might assume that the literal rape rapes the body and the figurative rape violates access to speech, the text reverses these two registers. The first actual rape is accompanied and preceded by a speech act that announces the crime. The act of speaking rape is supplemented by the act of "raping" speech—the cutting off of the tongue—that occurs later. Between these two acts comes the physical act of sexual domination. The Latin text insists on the convergence between speaking the crime and doing the deed: *"fassusque nefas et virginem et numa vi supererat . . .* [the crime having been spoken, he overwhelmed the virgin, by force, all alone]" (1.524, pp. 324–25). One cannot speak "rape," or speak about rape, merely in terms of a physical body. The sexual violation of the woman's body is itself embedded in discursive and symbolic structures. The description of the impact of the rape is worth noting:

vi superat frustra clamato saepe parente, saepe sorore sua,
magnis super omnia divis. illa tremit velut agna pavens, quae
saucia cani ore excussa lupi nondum sibi tuta videtur, utque
columba suo madefactis sanguine plumis horret adhunc
avidosque timet, quibus haeserat, ungues, mox ubi mens
rediit . . . [he violates her, just a weak girl and all alone, vainly
calling, often on her father, often on her sister, but most often
on the great gods. She trembled like a frightened lamb, which,
torn and cast aside by a grey wolf, cannot yet believe that it

is safe; and like a dove which, with its own blood smeared over its plumage, still palpitates with fright, still fears those greedy claws that have pierced it. Soon, when her senses came back . . .] (ll. 525–31, pp. 324–25)

After the rape is announced, instead of describing the raped body, the narrative voice substitutes comparisons to animal predator/ prey relations. While one might be tempted to read these descriptions as an attempt to naturalize the violation that has occurred (since between animals there is no crime involved, only natural predator/prey power relations), one might also read this comparison as a stutter in the narrative voice. The rape of Philomela's body is represented as unspeakable in human terms. There is no human, symbolic description of rape, because the rape violates human powers of description along with Philomela's body. The animal comparisons serve to figure the symbolic silencing that is initiated by the rape. To the extent that the rape is represented by animal figures, the limits and necessity of such a comparison only further testify to Philomela's violation. The final line of the passage, *"mox ubi mens rediit* [when her senses came back]" underscores that the rape has violated the boundaries of Philomela's consciousness as well as her humanity. Neither narrator, nor reader nor Philomela has access to the experience of the raped body. At the moment of the rape, because of the rape, Philomela is outside herself and beside herself; she cannot be present to herself as body or as human form.

When she returns to her senses, Philomela accuses Tereus of violating the symbolic boundaries of law and family. This actual or literal rape is presented as a symbolic crime more than a physical one:

Soon, when her senses came back, she dragged at her loosened hair, and like one in mourning, beating and tearing her arms, with outstretched arms she cried: "Oh, what a horrible thing you have done, barbarous cruel wretch! Do you care nothing about my father's orders, his affectionate tears, my sister's love, my own virginity, the laws of marriage? You have confounded everything; I have become a concubine, my sister's rival; you, a husband to both. Now Procne must be my enemy. Why do you not take my life, that no crime may be left undone, you traitor?" (ll. 531–40, pp. 324–27)

Once again, where we might have expected to find a referential trace of Philomela's body, at this juncture the meaning of the rape is defined by violations of law as place. In raping Philomela, Tereus has "confounded everything." Philomela's physical violation is depicted as a violation of social and familial positions. This rape is incestuous not only because Tereus is Philomela's brother-in-law, but also because it "confounds" the boundaries by which the social order of the family are constructed and sustained. In violating this family structure, Tereus has violated the grounds of the patriarchal social order.[6]

But the horror of this tale and of the rape that is recounted is not primarily located in this first, literal rape. Tereus's act of cutting off Philomela's tongue horrifies not only because it prevents Philomela from speaking, but also because it repeats metaphorically the literal rape that has just occurred. In the description of this figurative or metaphorical rape, the effects of rape are most clearly represented. Rape is both symbolic violation and physical mutilation; it "confounds" the distinctions between the literal, physical body and the metaphorical or symbolic structures through which that body can be represented.[7] The tongue is a privileged site for this representation of rape because it incarnates this confusion between literal and figurative, referential and symbolic registers. The Latin word *lingua,* even more than its English counterpart "tongue," refers both to the physical body part as well as to the totality of language. While the first, literal rape produces a linguistic, articulate, and articulated response from Philomela, this second rape—the cutting off of the tongue—violates the possibility of discourse both literally and figuratively. In other words, to be raped is also to be deprived of a language with which to speak the rape. This ultimate symbolic violation—the stripping of a language of violation—is accomplished through a peculiar physical mutilation. Once severed from the body, the tongue becomes strangely animated; it loses its status as body part and becomes a symbolic locus of Philomela's lost voice. Her empty body bears silent witness to the inarticulate stutter of the severed tongue, which speaks for her. In one of the most lyrical passages of this text, when Philomela can no longer speak, the severed tongue—irrevocably cut off from the body—speaks in her place:

> But he seized her tongue with pincers, as it protested against the outrage, calling ever the name of father [*et nomen patris*

usque vocantem] and struggling to speak, and he cut if off with merciless blade. The mangled root quivers, while the severed tongue lies palpitating on the dark earth, faintly murmuring; and, as the severed tail of a mangled snake is wont to writhe, it twitches convulsively, and with its last dying movement it seeks its mistress's feet. (ll. 555–60, pp. 326–27)

The stuttering murmur of the voice of the tongue calls out, in vain, for the *nomen patris,* the "name of the father." If Philomela's tongue, in its last dying gasp, calls for the name of the father, it is perhaps because the invocation of patriarchal law, the stability of place within the patriarchal law, is the only language that this tongue can speak. Philomela has been doubly silenced, first by the rapist who transgresses the father's law and then by the paternal law itself. Philomela's tongue speaks only the language of the law: the name of the father. While the horror of the rape violates the paternal order, the effects of the rape disclose the implicit violation *by* the paternal order.[8]

After this double moment of silencing, the language that is engendered by this outrage is one of disarticulation. Once Philomela no longer speaks through her body, her new form of expression paradoxically speaks of and for the body. The language with which she communicates her body's silence is a language that is no longer bound to the body. Beside herself with rage, she tells of her violation and mutilation through weaving. Curiously, the text does not specify whether the weaving describes the rape through pictures or words; it simply states that she weaves purple signs in threads on a white background. The Latin word *notas,* translated as "signs," can mean marks of writing on a page, punctuation, perforation, as well as marks on a body, such as a brand or tattoo and, by extension, a distinguishing mark of shame and disgrace. In a sense then, the Latin text implies that the story of Philomela's mutilation and rape is communicated by neither words nor pictures. The purple threads on the white background figure the bloody writing as tattoo marks on a branded body. Although alienated from her body, this form of writing through weaving represents and writes the mutilated body. The writing is one of outrage and necessity; the text explains that "great pain is inventive, and cunning comes from wretched things [*grande doloris ingenium est, miserisque venit sollertia rebus*]" (ll. 574–75, pp. 328–29). This is a form of writing born from a violation of speech; its clarity and urgency derive from marks of pain. But the language that is derived from pain and mutilation can say nothing outside a discourse of pain and mutilation.

The weaving that writes of outrage and silencing produces outrage and silence in its reader. When Procne receives the weaving, she too is rendered speechless; she loses her voice, and her tongue can find no expression for her outrage. Although Procne still has a literal tongue, that tongue has no language with which she can speak her rage: "she reads the wretched fate of her sister (a miracle that she is able to) and she is silent. Grief represses her mouth and her questing tongue fails to find words equal to her rage" (p. 329 ll. 582–85). Like Philomela, Procne can no longer speak with the tongue. To refuse the language of the tongue is also to refuse to speak the tongue of the "name of the father." Searching for the proper medium of revenge, Procne vents her rage on her husband by violating the terms of paternity She says:

> This is no time for tears, but for the sword, for something stronger than the sword. . . . I am prepared for any crime, sister; either to fire this place with a torch, and to cast Tereus, the author of our wrongs, into the flaming ruins, or to cut out his tongue and his eyes, to cut off the parts which brought shame to you, and drive his guilty soul out through a thousand wounds. (p. 331, ll. 611–18)

Procne rejects a logic of symmetry or exchange. She refuses to take a tongue for a tongue or even a penis for a tongue. The weapon that is stronger than the sword is a language fuelled by excess instead of loss. She stuffs his mouth and belly with the body of his son, leaving Tereus no room for words. Procne violates her husband by making him gag on the law of the father; she arrests the progression of paternity by feeding him his own child through the mouth. Procne thus uses her own child as a substitute for a tongue. She speaks through her child, forcing the child into her husband's mouth and belly. In the body of the father, the belly becomes the place of a tomb instead of a womb. Rather than relying on a logic of exchange and a discourse of loss, Procne transgresses the boundaries of the male body by forcing it to assume the presence of another. Metaphorically, Procne turns Tereus into a pathetic mimicry of a sterile, masculine maternity.

After Tereus has been sterilized and feminized through the incorporation of his dead son, Tereus, Procne, and Philomela are transformed into birds. In the *Metamorphoses,* transformation is often substituted for death. Characters rarely die; they fall out of human forms into animal or inanimate shapes. To fall from human shape is also to fall out of the relationship between gender and language. The Ovidian transformation that ends every story (and takes the place of death) figures death as a world indifferent to gender, a world in which things and beings coincide and speak their identity transparently through naturalized forms. These transformed figures dream a world in which gender and sexuality are no longer constitutive of discourse. But the transformations that end each Ovidian narrative only further underscore the complex relationship between language and gender positions figured of sexed bodies that are written and read; the experience of the body never transcends linguistically determined social relations. Even the raped body is named and constructed by language.

Although Philomela and Procne begin the story united as biological sisters, they end up being drawn together through a different and painful form of "sisterhood." The rape ruptures the natural bond between the two women joined through their common relationship to the father. In place of this natural relation, the two women now speak together through the language of rage. It is significant that Procne rescues Philomela by taking advantage of a Bacchic festival. She conceals both her own identity and that of her sister by donning the Bacchic garb, and the two women escape via a communal dance of frenzied women. The women who participate in this dance are "beside themselves" in rage and ecstacy. They form a collectivity through their particular relation to this celebration of madness. They are not alike, but they are joined through their common alienation from patriarchal reason. When the two sisters are reunited through this community, they speak together through a discourse of rage. The language of rage is a language without a tongue, a language of disarticulation. To speak in rage is to be "beside oneself"—it is to abandon the possibility that one's speech coincides with the place of one's experience. Under such conditions, that experience is spoken perversely and becomes legible in part through the *notas* or "punctures" in the fabric of its discourse.

VI. Painful Politics and the Performative "We"

Like the story of Philomela, which articulates the difficulty of speaking the experience of being silenced, the discourse of feminism constantly struggles to find a discursive vocabulary for experiences both produced and silenced by patriarchy. Such experiences cannot be spoken directly, but their effects infiltrate all discursive activity. Searching for a way of identifying the specificity of feminist texts, Alice Jardine has recently written:

> Struggle. The *inscription* of struggle. When members of the ... feminist theory group ... tried to articulate how we can recognize a feminist text—whether written by a man or a woman—it was this that was found to be necessary. The *inscription of struggle*—even of pain. (Jardine 1987, 58)

Responding to this description, Cary Nelson adds the following analysis:

> What I find as a credible referent for Jardine's claim is something different: the shock of recognition that feminism often provokes—the sudden recognition that one's prior experience has been reread, reinterpreted, rendered intelligible by feminist knowledge. For feminism at its core is nothing less than a recasting of one's world view, a collectivizing of experience that may until then have seemed only individually painful ... for it constructs a community—reaching back through history—of comparable pain and comparable achievement. (Nelson 1987, 159)

For me, Nelson's most telling point finds its expression through his use of the word "shock." The recognition inspired by a community founded by pain is not the recognition of shared identity but the shocking recognition that such a community is unthinkable through models of shared identity. If women become a collectivity through their communal articulation of pain, it is a language of pain that mediates between those women and each other. Pain cannot provide the basis for unmediated identification: pain cannot be shared. No one can feel another's pain: what is shared is a relationship to pain. This description establishes a basis for a necessary but painful feminist community; it opens a space for a "we" that is not based upon an illusory, but comfortable, model of identification. Women may not be alike in their pain, but when we speak together, "as feminists," we speak through the disarticulated voice of pain.

In speaking "as a feminist," I am beside myself. The term "feminism" always speaks in the plural; not only is feminism itself plural (there are many different "feminisms" under the name "feminism") but when one speaks "as a feminist," in the name of the feminist project, one must say "we." If feminism posits this "we," it is because its necessity, its reason for being as discursive praxis, is as political response. As Diana Fuss has recently noted, "politics is precisely the self-evident category in feminist discourse— that which is most irreducible and most indispensable. As feminism's *essential* component, it tenaciously resists definition; it is both the most transparent and elusive of terms" (Fuss 1989, 36). What is at stake is to read how politics, this most transparent and elusive of terms, inflects feminist language and, in particular, how it constitutes the peculiar power and status of the feminist "we." I have argued that the feminist "we" is best understood and read not as the collective voice of a community based on a notion of experience or identity, but rather as an impersonal, performative pronoun whose political force is neither dependent on, nor derived from a knowable link to a particular referent.[9] To the extent that this "we" coheres, coalesces, and is consolidated as a political intervention, it undergoes a disarticulation from its multiple sites of issue. It is, paradoxically, this disarticulation that allows the "we" to perforate what is referred to as "the dominant social discourse." To intervene politically is to speak punctually, performatively, and strategically. Thus the first moment of the feminist "we" cannot really ask "who are we?" or even "what do we mean?" but rather, "what does our 'we' *do*?" or "what are the effects of our speaking together?" It is only in a syncopated second moment—a moment that never coincides with the preceding one, but that haunts it like a shadow— that feminism turns around to look at itself, as it were, and asks its "we" those troubling impertinent epistemological questions ("who are we?" "what do we mean?" "how do we speak?") that were initially suspended. The challenge of feminism, and one of its greatest difficulties, is that it is always limping—precariously perched on the divide between two discursive terrains, one political and the other epistemological. Where there have been attempts to negotiate this unavoidable slippage (which is not reducible to a theory/practice division), feminism has retained both its power to excite as well as incite; where this slippage is denied or conflated, feminism risks cutting off its tongue—to reduce its means of expression to a vocabulary of self-recognition wherein the fact of patriarchal oppression serves to stabilize the discourse rather than to challenge its modes of expression.

NOTES

I would like to thank Lalitha Gopalan, Tom Keenan, Sean Miller, Claire Nouvet, and Sharon Willis for their generous help in thinking through these issues with me.

1. Showalter's rhetoric of universalized inclusion runs counter to her stated intention to account for racial and cultural differences in women's voices in the latter parts of her essay. I remain unsatisfied, however, by her description of "the black American woman poet's" literary identity. She writes: "A black American woman poet, for example, would have her literary identity formed by the dominant (white male) tradition, by a muted women's culture, and by a muted black culture. She would be affected by both sexual and racial politics in a combination unique to her case . . ." (1982, 32). The "black American woman poet" is invoked as a marginalized "example" of overdetermined "literary" identity rather than as theoretical intervention and voice; after all, the black American woman poet was nowhere present in the earlier invocations of national British, French, American feminisms. I am not at all sure that racial and sexual "literary" identities can be layered in this sort of schematic manner.

2. There are, of course, many prominent feminist *readers* whose work has been a sustained response to this question. I am thinking in particular of the work of Nancy K. Miller, Naomi Schor, and Mary Jacobus. For the purposes of this discussion, however, I highlight some of the problematic implicit methodological assumptions and effects common to many feminist readings. The feminist reader often bases her readings on unspoken models of identification between readers and literary figures and makes political claims based on these models. In this essay, I emphasize the risks (in relation to politics as well as reading) inherent to such an approach.

3. It is most unfortunate that in her introduction to the collection, Teresa de Lauretis (1986, 16) chooses to describe this attack on deconstruction as itself a "deconstructive" reading. It might be useful to remind

feminist readers that the term "deconstruction" is not synonymous with negative affect or vitriol. In this context, see Gayatri Spivak's important discussion (1989, 207–20) of the relationship between feminist politics and deconstruction, in particular the passages about deconstruction and love. For an excellent discussion of the necessary but problematic relationship between politics and deconstruction see Thomas Keenan (1990).

4. For an astute and convincing analysis of the sociohistorical political subtext of the erotic conflict in the Philomela myth, see Joplin (1984: 25–53). Among other things, Joplin argues that Philomela and her sister Procne function as objects of exchange in the conflict between Pandion, Greek king of Athens, and Tereus, "barbarian" king of Thrace.

5. I will only be treating Ovid's version of the Philomela story as it appears in the *Metamorphoses,* book VI. I have consulted both Rolfe Humphries's (1955) translation (Bloomington: Indiana University Press) and Frank Justus Miller's (1977) translation in the Loeb Classical Library edition. All page and line references are to the Loeb edition; the translations have sometimes been modified by me.

6. Joplin reads the effect of the rape on the social order as follows: "If marriage uses the woman's body as good money and unequivocal speech, rape transforms her into a counterfeit coin, contradictory word that threatens the whole system" (1984, 42).

7. The issue of the woman's body as referential, literal or figurative in literary texts is a very thorny one, particularly in relation to the question of rape. Feminist critics often have a stake in attempting to read a "real" referential body in texts that engage representations of the raped body. Jane Gallop (1982, 287) observes that in matters concerning representations of the body, the "feminist critic cannot help but to produce metaphors . . . in reaching for some non-rhetorical body, some referential body to ground sexual difference outside of writing, the critic produces a rhetorical use of the body as metaphor for the nonrhetorical."

8. This reading has been influenced and guided (in the use of the term "law of the father," the insistence on the role of the tongue and the discussion on the rejection of a law of symmetry) by Hélène Cixous's writings. See Cixous (1988).

9. This argument runs parallel to recent work by Judith Butler (1990), Denise Riley (1988), and Joan W. Scott (1991). Butler aptly describes the problem of the feminist "we" as follows: "The feminist 'we' is always and only a phantasmatic construction, one that has its purposes, but which denies the internal complexity and indeterminacy of the term and constitutes itself only through the exclusion of some part of the constituency that it simultaneously seeks to represent" (Butler 1990, 142).

———————————— *REFERENCES* ————————————

Butler, Judith. 1990. *Gender trouble: Feminism and the subversion of identity*. New York: Routledge.

Cixous, Hélène. 1988. *The newly born woman*. Trans. Betsy Wing. Minneapolis: University of Minnesota Press.

de Lauretis, Teresa. 1986. Feminist studies/Critical studies: Issues, terms and context. In *Feminist studies/Critical studies*, ed. Teresa de Lauretis. Bloomington: Indiana University Press.

Fuss, Diana. 1989. *Essentially speaking: Feminism, nature, and difference*. New York: Routledge.

Gallop, Jane. 1982. Writing and sexual difference: The difference within. In *Writing and sexual difference*, ed. Elizabeth Abel. Chicago: University of Chicago Press.

Jardine, Alice. 1985. *Gynesis: Configurations of woman and modernity*. Ithaca: Cornell University Press.

———. 1987. Men in feminism: Odor di uomo or compagnons de route? In *Men in feminism*, eds. Alice Jardine and Paul Smith. New York: Methuen.

Joplin, Patricia K. 1984. The voice of the shuttle is ours. *Stanford Literature Review* 1(1): 25–53.

Kamuf, Peggy. 1982. Replacing feminist criticism. *Diacritics* 12: 42–47.

Keenan, Thomas, 1990. Deconstruction and the impossibility of justice. *Cardoza Law Review* 11(5–6): 1675–86.

Modleski, Tania. 1986. Feminism and the power of interpretation: Some critical readings. In *Feminist studies/Critical studies*, ed. Teresa de Lauretis. Bloomington: Indiana University Press.

Nelson, Cary. 1987. Men, feminism: The materiality of discourse. In *Men in feminism*, eds. Alice Jardine and Paul Smith. New York: Methuen.

Ovid. 1977. *The metamorphoses*. Trans. Frank Justus Miller. The Loeb Classical Library, vol. 1. Cambridge: Harvard University Press.

Riley, Denise. 1988. *Am I that name?: Feminism and the category of 'women' in history*. Minneapolis: University of Minnesota Press.

Scott, Joan W. 1991. The evidence of experience. *Critical Inquiry* 17(4): 773–97.

Showalter, Elaine. 1982. Feminist criticism in the wilderness. In *Writing and sexual difference*, ed. Elizabeth Abel. Chicago: The University of Chicago Press.

Spivak, Gayatri C. 1989. A response to the difference within: Feminism and critical theory. In *The difference within: Feminism and critical theory*, eds. Elizabeth Meese and Alice Parker. Amsterdam and Philadelphia: John Benjamins Publishing Company.

Susan David Bernstein

—————————— *6* ——————————

Confessional Feminisms

Rhetorical Dimensions of First-Person Theorizing

I offer this frame around an essay that I wrote in 1991 to position better my reading of autobiographical feminist criticism as it first appeared in the 1980s. Since 1991, confessing feminist theory, as I originally titled this essay, has become more prevalent as well as, at least in many instances, more self-vigilant. In addition to the increasing numbers of intellectual memoirs by feminist academics, many are tackling this question of **why now** and in **what ways** does this persistence of the personal thicken theorizing across different academic disciplines, those tagged "feminist" and elsewhere. A salient example of this kind of "disciplining" of the personal—that is, its regularized and predictable appearances in academic writing—is the October 1996 *PMLA* issue devoted to "The Place of the Personal in Scholarship." At the same time, recent perspectives on performance, identity, and culture provide theoretical fulcrums—such as Leigh Gilmore's "autobiographics"—for reading the autobiographical interludes that I describe below. When I return to this frame of my earlier essay, I will elaborate briefly on how identity studies, cultural studies, and performance studies have each enlarged and rearticulated this interest in the personal in the 1990s. I introduce here my assessment six years ago of a particular scene of confessional feminisms as I also recognize that today such modes are more frequent, more varied, and in some cases more attentive to their own suggestive contradictions. Rather than overhaul this essay, I leave it largely as I wrote it then as a reception study of sorts on a history of first-person rhetoric in contemporary feminist literary scholarship.

Embattled Subjects of Personal Disclosure:
What's "I" Got to Do with "It"?

The eruption of first-person voices in critical discourse in recent years has been limited neither to feminists nor to literary theory, although these are the parameters that frame my interest here. For instance, the February 1991 issue of *Lingua Franca* boasts on its front page an article titled, "True Confessions: Feminist Scholars in the First Person," which surveys a host of feminist academics who are doing confessional theory. Nancy Miller's *Getting Personal: Feminist Occasions and Other Autobiographical Acts* is an impressive reckoning of what she calls and practices "personal criticism." This new confessionalism marks a struggle between the subject—or the subjective—or the personal—and theory. In the wake of either the poststructuralist death or feminist and materialist transfiguration of the author has dawned an increasing fascination with the relationship between "I" and "it," that is, theory in its various guises as the intellectual, the ineluctably abstract, the flip side of a real-world personal. Confessional feminisms interest me not as a panacea for estrangements induced by theoretical discourse or as a corrective for the disingenuous stance of objective authority, but precisely for the way they dramatize entanglements between "I" and "it," between rhetorical subjectivity and critical attention to its very construction.

One recent example of personal scholarship beyond literary studies is Patricia Williams's *Alchemy of Race and Rights*, a study of law that incorporates a variety of firsthand disclosures.[1] This "inside" perspective is registered on the jacket cover, which sports, beneath a photo insert of the author, the caption "diary of a law professor." In the scene of academic writing, these first-person anecdotes transgress disciplinary boundaries; although Williams is a law professor, the back jacket copy promotes her book through endorsements of two professors of literature.[2] Similarly, deploying the confessional mode raises questions of genre and discourse. Williams's book is both theoretical and autobiographical; its style is analytical, colloquial, and literary. Of her project "to write in my own voice," Williams claims, "I am trying to challenge the usual limits of commercial discourse by using an intentionally double-voiced and relational, rather than a traditionally legal black-letter, vocabulary" (Williams 1991, 6). This discursive virtuosity of the "double-voiced and relational" has attracted a range of designations including first-person theorizing, anecdotal individualism, and the new personalism, all approximating what I label the confessional mode.[3]

I prefer "confessional" here to "autobiographical" or "personal" because of the implication of transgression encoded in the first term. I am interested in the intrusive "I" as a rhetorical event; this textual moment carries the capacity to accentuate and overturn conventions of authority, particularly the pretense of objectivity as an ideological cover for masculine privilege. Along with this challenge of discursive authority and the motivated interests that inscribe it, the confessional mode contests and redesigns what constitutes legitimate "truth." In this way, first-person theorizing has been crucial to feminist epistemologies that seek to broaden and contextualize what counts as knowledge, a vector in constructions of truth. However, as confessional acts become more prevalent across academic writing—with increasing appearances in an array of disciplines from anthropology to women's studies—so do they cease to confront the structuring of authority and knowledge; this crucial transgression of conventions becomes instead a convention that loses its inquisitive and unsettling edginess. Although the confessional mode continues to offer politically transformative potential, its interrogative effect is often undermined by critical neglect of the very categories it employs. Often taken as transparent truths, untroubled concepts of confessional feminist theory like "identity" and "experience" perpetuate a mystification of "women's experience" by rendering their representations self-evident, continuous with and reflective of an essential self and real world.

Because subjectivity is the cornerstone of feminist inquiry, it is no wonder that first-person theorizing, with its insistence on the "I," has garnered so many practitioners. Elizabeth Young-Bruehl suggests that recent theories of subjectivity provide "a rhetorical space for identity assertion" (Young-Bruehl 1991, 16) with confessional feminisms as both product and process of this discursive trend. Confessing feminist theory offers a stylistic instance from which to complicate and address questions of subject positioning, yet personalizing feminist theory also provides an expedient frame for mere identity assertion. Miller rightly notes that "positional" and "personal" modes of authority in confessional feminisms are not synonymous (Miller 1991, 16–17). I would further qualify "positional" as the use of the personal that attends critically to the politics of its own construction.

I focus my discussion of confessing feminisms on a sometimes neglected distinction between "subject" and "self," between the process and the product of representation. Without attending to the varied implications of a particular verbal display of subjectivity, confessional modes often reclaim a coherent, unmediated self, a universalizing source of knowledge whose identity rests squarely on her gendered experiences. Because "experience" is an interpretation and, as such, demands interpretation, Joan Scott notes that when experience simply bespeaks empirical evidence, it "reproduces rather than contests given ideological systems" (Scott 1991, 778). For Teresa de Lauretis, "experience" is "a constellation of meaning effects . . . [that] shift and is reformed continually" (de Lauretis 1987, 10). In other words, "experience" is an interpretive process of identity production, coded with assumptions about power, privilege, and legitimacy. By the same token, "experience" in confessional feminisms often acts as an integrative device that interpellates a subject into a gendered identity that absorbs other subject-positions like class, race, sexuality, each with multiple and contradictory claims.

I am not suggesting that "experience" should be discounted in feminist scholarship. What I am calling attention to in this examination of confessional feminisms is the tendency to advocate experience as the reigning authority on feminist knowledge while overlooking contexts and contingencies. For a depiction of experience is an alloy of both attribution and imposition. Recounting experience encompasses qualities culturally ascribed to a particular phenomenon as well as the excess or latitude of meaning entailed in its representation.[4] The persuasions of real-life testimonies compel promiscuous identification, the promotion of a correspondence between textual and historical subjects that champions an uncomplicated resemblance disguising in turn a vexed non-resemblance. I am using "promiscuous" here not as a moral pronouncement against identification between readers and first-person voices, or between a textual performance of identity and the writer, or between representation and history. Surely the social import of the capacity of this rhetoric of personal voice deserves special attention of its own. For my purposes here, "promiscuous" highlights mixing or overstepping boundaries without due notice. To some extent, confessional feminism is motivated by an anxiety of pluralism and a desire to domesticate identity difference through the exchange of personal experience without attending to the limits of identification. I maintain that confessional modes furnish a strategy to explore the discursive and social constructions of subject positioning that any act of identification suggests.[5]

To what follows I bring this series of questions: Do confessional modes enrich theory, or does theory legitimate confessing? To what extent can confessing provide a suggestive staging of theoretical speculations on the rhetorical forms and consequences of personal voice? Are confessional modes, as Michel Foucault would have it, part of repression's work of subjection? Rather than the emancipation of an imprisoned personal (or identity-specific) "I," do confessional feminisms enforce the production of a privatized discourse to uncover the truth of gender? Has personal disclosure become an obligatory gesture to impress feminists with a remarkably unified different voice, one adopted by a broadening range of academics in recent years? What kinds of claims about identity, experience, agency, and signification underwrite this discourse?

Anatomizing Confession

To begin to answer these questions, I present a taxonomy of confessional modes, a variety of descriptive categories for viewing textual moments where the first person intrudes as a rhetorical performance. I do not offer them as mutually exclusive and monolithic categories, nor do I presume an intentional "I" that masters the specific rhetorical effects of a given confessional passage. These modes sketch a heuristic for apprehending the way first-person theorizing constructs subjectivity. I am especially interested in how these modes repeatedly cohere around the subject (in both senses) of violence, whether construed as texual violation or sexual domination.

Let me quickly cover the terrain of five confessional modes in feminist theory. *Contestatory confession* deploys excursions into the first person as a theoretical device to redress limitations of critical (or "academic") discourse. All confessional maneuvers begin here; that is, every confession in the context of feminist theory stages a challenge to customs of voice in scholarship. In its most common form, confession as dissension brandishes the familiar "I" to defamiliarize the subject/object dialectic undergirding the tradition of Western epistemology. As part of its critique of power and knowledge, this first-person subject takes a close-up stance to interrupt conventions of discursive authority predicated on detached distance. To this end, confessing feminist theory invokes representations of personal experience as a structure and source of knowledge. As confession, this disputatious voice is transgressive insofar as it unsettles the rhetorical sovereignty of supposed objectivity in academic language, although as first-person theorizing becomes more frequent, this transformative potential also diminishes. At the same time, this confessional "I" reinforces discursive power relations where an organizing personal voice masters the others in its discourse. Where all confessional modes in the framework of feminist theory embark with some implication of protest, their varying contexts, tone, and substance suggest a few descriptive subcategories of contestatory confession.

Expressionist confession relies on the articulation of emotions to contest the precedent of objective authority in critical language. Inspired by "the personal is political" rhetoric, this confessional mode celebrates self-identity by imparting feelings. A kind of politics of sentiment, expressionist confession values affective discourse as a way to build solidarity among women academics aliented by both the distance of an objective stance as well as the abstractions of a theoretical lexicon. In this politics of sentiment, emotions and the experiences from which they arise redefine power relations in critical discourse and replace knowledge as the source of truth.[6] The articulation of this confessional "I" qualifies as a liberating gesture, sometimes without due attention to the contingencies of its very construction. *Exhibitionist confession* uses personal disclosure as rhetorical striptease to entice readers with juicy tidbits flaunting a mutuality of body and mind beneath this audacious "I." Although this showwomanship contests prescriptions of authority and detachment that structure an opposition between critic and text, exhibitionist confession runs the risk of reinscribing a hegemonic subject position through the force of its sensational revelations.

If the intrusive voice of the confessional "I" assumes a local rhetorical force, *hypertheorized confession* exploits theory to sanitize a troubling personal disclosure. A pretext rather than a context, the surrounding theory attentuates through intellectual somersaults the substance of the confession. While this confessional mode attempts to rectify the untheorized use of identity and experience that mark expeditions into the first-person, in this case theory supplants any notion of political struggle prompting the disclosure in the first place. A related strain of first-person theorizing, *aestheticized confession* signifies a genre of American feminist work informed by French feminisms in which personal voices, in the form of anecdotes, diary entries, meandering meditations, along with theoretical speculations, attempt to dissolve divisions between poetic and critical discourses.[7] In offering these intersecting categories of first-person feminist theory, I want to call attention to Miller's capacious definition, what she terms "a typology, a poetics of 'egodocuments' that constitute personal criticism: confessional, locational, academic personal, narrative, anecdotal, biographematic, etc." (Miller 1991, 2–3). While both our inventories address the contextual bearings of personal disclosure, I attend to the rhetorical intonations of specific confessional acts.

Personal Subjects in Contestatory and Expressive Confessional Modes

With this taxonomy as a descriptive device, I now turn to particular instances of confessing feminist literary theory in the United States from the mid-1980s to the early 1990s. Ellen Messer-Davidow's "Philosophical Bases of Feminist Literary Criticism" in the Autumn 1987 issue of *New Literary History* is a landmark event in the recent history of feminist confessional modes, one that generated many such replies in kind, both within and beyond the volume of its first appearance.[8] As the title suggests, Messer-Davidow explores the nature of feminist knowledge, one distinguished by allusions to "lived experiences." The essay seeks "a rehumanized epistemology" of literature that conjoins "our female selves" with "a critical self" through the corrective methodology of self-reflection in scholarship. Messer-Davidow implies that knowledge qualifies as feminist if it is informed by "perspicacity," a term for self-awareness, in which literary critics are "knowers" defined by "their experiences, self-reflection, and contingent standpoints" (Messer-Davidow 1989, 88). This "perspicacity" bears resemblance to Foucault's notion of effective history which recognizes "knowledge as perspective." Yet the two perspectives diverge. For Foucault, "effective history . . . shortens its vision to those things nearest it," thus rendering knowledge partial and provisional (Foucault 1988, 155). For Messer-Davidow, the shortsighted view constitutes a unified and self-evident awareness rather than a fragmented, decontextualized particle.

Just as Messer-Davidow promotes a feminist epistemology that incorporates self-reflection in order to remedy the pretense of objectivity, confessional voices question oppositions between subject and object, intellect and emotion, the abstract and the particular, theory and practice. In this scheme, the twin foundations of self and experience fortify feminist discourse, something Jane Tompkins claims in her reply to Messer-Davidow in which she locates: "The female subject *par excellence*, which is her self and her experiences, has once more been elided by literary criticism" (Tompkins 1989, 135).

Conflating subject and self, Tompkins's first-person theorizing attempts to heal the rift between two voices, "the critic" and "this person." Marianna Torgovnick transposes this distinction from self to style as she bridges a gap between critical and creative writing (and critic versus creative writer) with her genre of "experimental critical writing" (Torgovnick 1990, 25). Similarly, Olivia Frey opposes two methods of critical discourse used in writing as well as in the classroom: the "adversarial" and the "personal," the first aligned with male critics, the second with women academics who yearn to speak in a "personal feminist voice" (Frey 1990, 511). The oppositional logic that structures these three accounts replays Messer-Davidow's division between "a critical self" and "our female selves," despite the fact that such a dichotomy does not hold steadfast in critical discourse.

This notion of a beleaguered voice and style, one that must be held in check in order to pass muster as an accomplished critic, describes in many instances the position of academic women who entered the profession in literature departments well stocked with white men in the 1960s and early 1970s, and whom feminism politicized in the 1970s through the early 1980s. At the same time, confessing oneself into scholarly work is also a prerogative that some academic feminists, established in their careers, can afford better than those at the outset of their professional lives. When do readers tolerate this journey into confessional feminism and what motivates its acceptance? In part, this tolerance accommodates a desire to make academic work incorporate its own criticism, that is, to register the limitations of any interpretive enterprise. In some instances, confessional modes function as a rhetorical design where the intrusive "I" highlights the provisional nature of its representation and the institutional forces that govern it. In other cases, personalizing academic work builds a self-indulgent obstacle to the project of reflexive scrutiny when such methodology becomes more absorbed in autobiographical details and less attentive to the wider implications of its own rhetoric.

While contestatory confession assumes that the convention of objectivity and distance must be countered, it has become a truism in interpretive theories that "objectivity," or the exlusion of the subjective, describes a style of presentation rather than even a remote possibility. Tompkins and Frey wage their confessions to battle the tradition of impersonal academic discourse. For example, Tompkins's "Me and My Shadow" advertises the virtues of "a new personalism," one that distills an essence of "Me" from "My Shadow," or the discourse of "the critic." If this critic is a feminist or a woman, then she suffers from discursive oppression, from the disciplinary mandate that she adhere to "a male standard of rationality that militates against women's being recognized as culturally legitimate sources of knowledge" (Tompkins 1989, 124). To describe this gendered division between her two writing voices, Tompkins likens academic prose to "wearing men's jeans." This clothing metaphor for a style of writing encourages a comparison between confessional feminisms and *écriture féminine*. Tompkins wishes to outfit her prose with discursive garments that fit a uniformly gendered body type.

Progenitor of *écriture féminine*, Hélène Cixous celebrates the female body as revolutionary confession, as transgressive language that threatens to unhinge patriarchal hegemony: "Women must write through their bodies, they must invent the impregnable language that will wreck partitions, classes, and rhetorics, regulations and codes" (Cixous 1981, 256). Unlike the dispersed and multivoiced "I" in *écriture féminine*, this expressive mode of confessional feminisms recuperates a unified "I" where personal voice recuperates a core truth of self. The discursive clothing of first-person theorizing marks the wrapper of authenticity rather than the critical abstractions of "men's jeans."

Just as this new personalism presumes that representation amounts to forthright transcriptions with the confessional "I" as purveyor of this truth, Tompkins describes a discourse rooted in experience: "The criticism I would like to write would always take off from personal experience. Would always be in some way a chronicle of my hours and days. Would speak in a voice which can talk about everything, would reach out to a reader like me and touch me where I want to be touched" (Tompkins 1989, 126). Tompkins's sloganeering of the personal captures in tone and syntax the language of consumerism resounding in advertising formulas such as AT & T's "reach out and touch someone." Similar to the ploy of commercials, Tompkins rehearses a retreat into sameness— "a reader like me"—and by implication an aversion to difference, where others are absorbed into this mirroring scheme as counterparts of "I," and identity functions through figures of unity and similarity. This campaign for "a reader like me" typifies what Lauren Berlant calls "the scene of monstrous doubling, or narcissistic horror that reproduces the dominating fantasy of female self-identity" (Berlant 1988, 253). Instead of perpetuating an uncontested notion of identity "like me," Berlant urges feminists to pursue "a policy of female disidentification at the level of female essence." In other words, by mapping out contingencies of difference in the very process of enacting promiscuous identification, it is possible to trouble even updated versions of universal selfhood.

Expressionist confessions, such as Tompkins's, are also embedded within an ideology of capitalism that acclaims and perpetuates the sanctity of private property. Tompkins offers the following profile of herself: "This person talks on the telephone a lot to her friends, has seen psychiatrists, likes cappuccino, worries about the state of her soul" (Tompkins 1989, 122). Details of fashion construe a particular kind of subjectivity that domesticates the potential of difference in a confessing "I" into a homogeneity manifesting the "self"-importance of traditional humanism. More a renovation than a reformation, this confessional mode is a matter of style.

Transgressive Acts: Violence of Confessions and Confessions of Violence

Redressing the domination of "impersonal" disinterested authority in academic discourse, many of these confessional anecdotes intimate scenes of violence. On the level of rhetoric, these first-person feminisms contest a violation of personal voice scholarly language belittles, marginalizes, or occludes. On the level of autobiographical anecdote, however, confession transfers political struggle into the realm of the material and the everyday, where sexual difference is not only a matter of the semiotics of gender but also the threat of superior bodily force. Rita Felski notes that feminist confession "is marked by a tension between a focus upon subjectivity and a construction of identity which is communal rather than individualistic" (Felski 1989, 115). This vacillation between a narcissistic self and an "I" of political advocacy surfaces in many confessional instances. Attempting to link intellectual work to activism, confessing feminist theory often rivets attention on physical, sometimes sexual, transgressions.

Catharine Stimpson incorporates a scene of sexual assault to close her essay "Feminism and Feminist Criticism," which aims to forge a political bond between academic and political feminisms. She does so by converting a "woman colleague" into an object for feminist advocacy: "I wish to end with a difficult anecdote. I was thinking about feminist criticism one night as I was driving home from my university work. On either side of the highway's twelve lanes were oil refineries, with great curved pipes and round towers. I smelled industrial fumes. I saw no green, except for paint and neon signs. Earlier that day, after a meeting, a woman colleague had told me about an experience. She had been raped, at knifepoint, in her car, with her son watching. She was in her late twenties, her son only six. She was no Leda, the rapist no swan. To remember the story, to keep it as a fire within consciousness and political will, is the feminism in feminist criticism" (Stimpson 1990, 28–29).

In this appropriated confession, Stimpson exhibits a voiceless unquoted "woman colleague" who has sustained violent sexual domination in order to illuminate a political accent in Stimpson's academic writing. After warning that "a difficult anecdote" is on the horizon of this passage, Stimpson veers off into the commonplace scenery of a highway embellished with the signposts of industrial life. Following this associative chain of thought, she then moves back in time from the "personal" realm of a drive home to the "professional" realm when her colleague "told me about an experience." The word "experience" is strikingly mundane in contrast to the sensation of words that follow: "She had been raped, at knifepoint, in her car, with her son watching."

Stimpson's point here is to conjoin seemingly segregated languages and spheres of knowledge together, in a sense to heal the fracture between Tompkins's "critic" and "person." Helena Michie qualifies Stimpson's "integrative 'I'" as rhetorical evidence of a commitment to "a systematic dialectical pluralism." Encompassing personal, academic, and political voices, this "integrative 'I,' " Michie maintains, "refus[es] to see any rupture between them" (Michie 1989, 20). But the synthesizing impulse of this "difficult anecdote" also carries a troublesome contradiction. For Stimpson insinuates the violence of aestheticizing sexual crime in her epigrammatic contrast between this real-life rape and Yeats's poetic imagery: "She was no Leda, the rapist no swan." Even so, this recounted incident is subject to the way Stimpson's sensationalizing language as well as the ultimate placement of the passage in her essay manage its representation; this contestatory confession also operates as exhibitionism to accentuate the argument's rhetorical force. While Stimpson invokes a literary reference to make evident that rape survivors and their assailants are not mythological characters and poetic phrases, the passage also uncovers a fraught relationship between experience and text, between the personal and the academic, between a quotidian story of sexual violence and an aestheticized counterpart. It might be productive to explore how knowledge of real rape invigorates a feminist reading of a poem. Nevertheless, by enlivening feminist criticism with this jolt of political advocacy, Stimpson likewise renders the incident a rhetorical flourish.

Where Stimpson's appropriated confession of sexual violence works as an anecdotal copula to yoke feminist theory to political struggle, Gerald MacLean uses theory to justify and displace an equally disturbing personal disclosure of domestic violence. In a response to Tompkins's "Me and My Shadow," MacLean construes his essay "Citing the Subject" as a heterogeneous genre with personal letters addressed "Dear Jane" interspersed with dated reflections. MacLean contends that Tompkins's confessional "I" uncritically endorses an ideology of presence, unique individuality, and free choice that bolsters her "commitment to self-improvement [that] substitutes for a commitment to more radical transformations in a social order that exploits people because of their race, class, or gender" (MacLean 1989, 141). Rather than a personal voice that, like Tompkins's, lapses into solipsism, MacLean calls for "the figure of the politicized personality" in order to promote "a collective practice toward social justice" (MacLean 1989, 142, 147).

How does MacLean go about politicizing his personality in the interests of this "collective practice toward social justice"? Indeed, he turns this critical scrutiny toward himself and concedes that he is a "white, heterosexual, first-world male" who does "what I was trained to do, telling 'women' what to do, how to think and behave" (MacLean 1989, 148). This disclaimer seems fairly doctrinaire self-criticism, an instance of male grandstanding on the feminist band-wagon.[9] The rhetorical meaning of "white, heterosexual, first-world male" in MacLean's reply behaves like an act of contrition about his socially privileged position. He can't help himself because he is a subject subjected to the rules of dominant culture. While Tompkins neglects to theorize her "personal" voice, MacLean resorts to theory to sanitize and displace the "person"—and any sense of agency or responsibility that a commitment to social justice presumably entails—in the disturbing disclosure he makes toward the end of the essay.

MacLean's hypertheorized confessions gather momentum as the essay proceeds. First, he describes himself as someone who teaches "from a 'feminist' stance" as he flirts with both women and men students and talks about sex "a good deal." When MacLean observes that no one has "begun to examine fully the range of erotic interactions that go on between students and teachers," he then retreats from this examination by resorting to the personal: "I need to be liked" (MacLean 1989, 150). Oddly, this confessional foray into classroom erotics troubles the meaning of his "collective" commitment to "social justice." With this pedagogical scene of erotic domination, MacLean frames his confessional crescendo of domestic violence. Launching into a narrative that collects various auto-biographical details, including the economic and familial privations of his British working-class childhood, his mother's recent death, and the complications of his two-career academic marriage, MacLean delivers this revelation: "That winter, during a period of gloom which reading [Alice] Miller led me to associate with guilt over Mother's death, I had hit Donna during an argument over nothing that important. This must not happen again" (MacLean 1989, 151).

Through its allusion to a historical event as a rhetorical disruption, the violence of this disclosure operates on two levels. The syntax of the last sentence transposes a confession of domestic assault into an agentless abstraction. MacLean deflects his personal agency in relation to this incident by displacing "the problem of my violence" onto a generalized social phenomenon of "male violence" constituted by unspecified "institutional privileges and pressures." One might well wonder why MacLean chooses to place on exhibition, in the context of an academic article, painful details of his marriage, something he encourages Tompkins to do as well. Does this confession narrow or widen the alleged gap between personal and political, subjective and theoretical? As macho exhibitionism, MacLean's confessional mode demonstrates the gulf between his theorizing and his individual practices at work and at home. What MacLean construes as an overdetermined cultural problem of violence against women absolves him in this specific instance. Not unlike the oblique pun in the essay's title "Citing the Subject," these suggestions or provocative glimpses of self-confessed infraction dissolve repeatedly into theoretical language.[10]

One might question whether first-person theorizing perpetuates an opposition between the personal and the intellectual despite an articulated interest in complicating and undoing this dichotomy. Inevitably, autobiography and theory motivate each other. But how does one assess this relationship between first-person disclosures and theory in a given text? It is likewise important to ask whether the theoretical becomes a justification for confessional displays that upstage the theory billed as the main attraction. To some extent, I am questioning the usefulness of genre boundaries. Are distinctions between intellectual memoir and feminist literary theory a valuable way to forecast something to readers? Or is it perhaps more productive, that is, more unsettling and thus more provocative, to read theory and autobiography sewn together in a rhetoric that incorporates both?[11]

The double feature of Jane Gallop's confessional mode in *Thinking Through the Body* is this intrication of the theoretical and the personal, or mind and matter, as her title indicates. The Madonna of the exhibitionist confession, Gallop wields first-person theorizing as a "Truth or Dare" proposition that fetishizes the life of the authorial body from infancy to childbirth, including professional landmarks along the way. These sensational excursions into the life of Gallop's sexualized corpus promise a personal truth as the origins of her theoretical reading of a given text.

In collecting the series of articles first written and published between 1977 and 1986, Gallop contextualizes *Thinking Through the Body* within confessional frames that situate her essays as byproducts of her perverse (in the best postmodernist sense) desires. Like the title and the confessions themselves that seek to suture the gap between the intellectual and the material, the table of contents records Gallop's concerted effort to embody theoretical analysis: "The Bodily Enigma," "The Anal Body," "The Student Body," "The Female Body," "The Body Politic." Accentuated by confessional blurbs, this somatic discourse suggests Gallop's particular practice of *écriture féminine* by writing her body into her text. Personal disclosures advertise Gallop's daring style of self-representation from the cover photograph that spreads out her body at the moment of childbirth to the divulgences of love affairs. Clearly, Gallop wants to complicate the status of "author" by placing each essay within a confessional context that centers on the specific personal and professional occasions from which she writes. Yet these "autobiographical bits," as Gallop terms them, install the reader into the position of voyeuristic confessor, as unwitting analyst of these striptease revelations that unfold Gallop's scenes of delivery.[12]

The theory that motivates Gallop's confessional flamboyance is the psychoanalytic concept of transference, something Jacques Lacan qualifies as "the subject presumed to know," which structures any cathexis to an object of desire, whether a sexual body or a textual source of knowledge. More broadly, "transference" means any carryover or affiliation. In this manner, Gallop's confessional feminism takes up the challenge of transference that undermines divisions between, say, the personal and the intellectual, the desiring body and the inquiring mind.

In her previous book, *Reading Lacan*, Gallop acknowledges her transference onto Lacan and onto the discourse of psychoanalysis that undergirds her own interpretive practice.[13] In *Thinking Through the Body*, Gallop explores not "*the* Body," as the title announces, but *her* body as the privileged site of knowledge that shapes her own critical "thinking." The confessional portions map out a transferential link between Gallop's sexualized body and her intellectual pursuits. At the same time, these first-person exposés suggest an authorized, exclusive access to the writer's transference and, by association, a genuine, unexpurgated story of authorial motivation, without explicitly allowing for the limitations posed by such a methodology. In one confessional instance Gallop explains: "I wrote 'The Student Body,' my reading of [Sade's] *Philosophy of the Bedroom* and my attempt to understand 'the sexuality that underlies' my chosen profession" (Gallop 1988, 3). A related blip appears in the "Prelims" preface to "The Student Body": "The series [of love affairs with thirty-six-year-old men] began while I was at graduate school. The first member was a professor on whom I developed a crush. . . . This paper tries to think through the place of the female student in the pederastic institution" (Gallop 1988, 41).

Like fast-paced news clips from the confessional tabloids, Gallop's "autobiographical bits" titillate uneasy speculation.[14] Do these exhibitionist disclosures impart knowledge that transforms a reader's apprehension of Gallop's close readings of Sade, for instance? Do Gallop's intellectual, institutional, and embodied struggles with sadomasochistic desires necessarily inform other readers's appreciation of her analysis? Or does her transference methodology furnish a rhetorical stage on which Gallop can uncurtain real-life experiences of this writer "thinking through the body"? Gallop's confessional scholarship demonstrates that no interpretation, no intellectual endeavor, can be wholly disinterested, that a mind is never truncated from a body, and from social and historical conditions. This insistence on materializing literary criticism, on making academic writing matter, justifies such acts of confessing as a crucial component in Gallop's feminist practice. Yet the confessions belie this political project by substituting a narcissistic body exploring the reaches of individual power for a collective body promoting equity for a particular social group.

The confessional scenes of transference that fetishize Gallop's representational body reveal a fascination with erotic domination, with a transgressively violating or violated body. Citing a passage about motherhood and the mind-body problem from Adrienne Rich's *Of Woman Born*, Gallop takes up this opposition as a figure of violence: "If we think physically rather than metaphysically, if we think the mind-body split *through the body*, it becomes an image of shocking violence" (Gallop 1988, 1). While this invitation to "think physically" is enticing if never altogether comprehensible as an analytic method, the "image of shocking violence" that Gallop introduces here forecasts the nature of the confessions she inserts around her essays in the volume.

The first such image comes not from the considerable arsenal of Gallop's own autobiography but from a sensational news story of infanticide quoted in Rich's study of maternal ambivalence. This criminal case violently literalizes the mind-body split upon which Gallop's volume meditates. Situating the maternal body as the perpetrator of domestic violence, the news clipping reports that "Joan Michulski, thirty-eight, the mother of eight children . . . took a butcher knife, decapitated and chopped up the bodies of her two youngest on the neatly kept lawn of the suburban house where the family lived outside Chicago" (Gallop 1988, 1). Not unlike Stimpson's concluding confession of her woman's colleague's rape, Gallop frames the collection of essays with an appalling example to remind her readers that violence is uncomfortably familiar.

Gallop situates the present volume more explicitly, more autobiographically, in the context of maternal violence both produced by and reproducing the mind-body split. Theorizing the confessional, Gallop declares that she incorporates "autobiographical bits, not only, I hope, because I tend toward exhibitionism," but also because she reads associatively, that is, "through things that happened to me" (Gallop 1988, 4). With this speculative introduction, Gallop confesses one of these "things": "At the age of eleven months I was strangled and left for dead by a woman who cared for me. I have no memory of the event, of course, but learned about it years later from a newspaper clipping my mother gave me to read" (Gallop 1988, 4–5). Gallop "hope[s]" the "exhibitionism" of her confessional mode is secondary to the more esteemed intellectual project of thinking, reading, interpreting "through things that happened to me," a variation on the interest proposed in the title, despite her assertion that in this initial instance she has "no memory of the event, of course." In addition, Gallop's startling revelation places her in the position approximate to the nameless victims of infanticide in Rich's book. Are readers thus encouraged to use this frame to understand Gallop's other confessions of embodied indiscretions as somehow shaped by this early event, inaccessible to the memory of the mind but nevertheless tatooed on the memory of the body?

This brief reference to an autobiographical clipping typifies Gallop's confessional style in which she knocks off her "bits" like commercial sound bites to captivate the reader, to turn her audience's attention—for interspersed spectacular moments—toward the history of an authorial body implicated in the violent physical or erotic encounters that qualify the essays that follow each quick glimpse at "things that happened to me." Collecting these confessional tidbits together, readers encounter the author alluding to the embodied acts of crying, masturbating, and fornicating.

Interestingly, Gallop expresses her discomfort with the "celebration of self" as a problematic feature of American feminism that also retreats from embodied experiences like sexuality. Gallop maintains that she has improved this practice precisely because she theorizes "self" through the body: "I had not only overcome my own sense of illegitimacy but had moved the body (my body?) from an embarrassment to a source of power" (Gallop 1988, 92). The parenthetical and interrogative accidentals encasing "(my body?)" constitute what Gallop would elsewhere label a symptomatic moment where the text reveals a vested interest, one the writer does not explicitly recognize. Gallop's confessions privilege the body as the source of knowledge, but "(my body?)" doubly encodes a hermeneutic uncertainty. Instead of incorporating a discussion of this interpretive struggle around the status of her authorized and authorial, textualized and textual bodies, Gallop tends to wield her confessional blurbs as "a source of power" that both provokes and reproduces promiscuous—that is, uncontested, untheorized— identifications between a historical Jane Gallop and the rhetorical performance of her subjectivity here.[15]

Toward a Confessional Mode of Reflexivity

Confessing feminisms, in its various tones, betokens both a stylistic contagion worth reconsideration and a rhetorical ploy useful for the way it opens up spaces for renegotiating the status of the subject in feminist theory. Recognizing the resourcefulness of first-person theorizing, I would like to add *reflexive confessions* to the taxonomy I am delineating. In the modes I have already surveyed, that is, in contestatory, expressionist, exhibitionist, aestheticized, and hypertheorized personal disclosures, confession is often *reflective*, the product of an uncomplicated "I" whose unveiling of experience provides a shunt to an intrinsic truth of female selfhood, society, and sexism. In contrast to the mirroring gesture of reflective intrusions of the first person, reflexive confession is primarily a questioning mode, one that carefully theorizes the process of subject positioning through particular discourses and at a historical moment within a specific cultural space.

This reflexive mode of confession approaches signification as a genealogical process after Foucault.[16] Judith Butler describes the genealogical critique that "refuses to search for the origins of gender, the inner truth of female desire, a genuine or authentic sexual identity that repression has kept from view; rather genealogy investigates the political stakes in designating as an *origin* and *cause* those identity categories that are in fact the *effects* of institutions, practices, discourses, with multiple and diffuse points of origin" (Butler 1990, viii–ix). Where reflective confessions depend on such foundationalist concepts as "inner truth" and "authentic . . . identity," reflexive confession views these ideas not as the basis of selfhood, or as the genesis of an interpretive act, but as the consequence of a web of representational forces. Rather than the naive scrutiny of power that frequently marks reflective confessions, reflexive confession as a genealogical critique registers its complicity with the institutions and discourses that structure its very appearance in feminist theory.

Critically punctuating theory with autobiographical material, many feminists do interrogate not only citations of their experiences but also the identity politics that foster how they position themselves as subjects in their own arguments. Reflexive uses of confessional feminism, then, complicate and defamiliarize the "I" and selfhood of first-person infiltrations. A provocative example of a text that establishes a dialogue between materialist feminist theory and autobiography is Carolyn Steedman's *Landscape for a Good Woman*. One might argue that Steedman's attention to the imbricated narratives of her/her mother's lives is far too extensive to be considered a contained rhetorical mode. Yet the way Steedman explicitly structures autobiography through cultural materialism and in relation to other "official interpretive devices of a culture" (psychoanalysis, Marxism) renders the personal as interventions on the theoretical, much like the confessional intrusions I have been discussing (Steedman 1987, 6). Steedman repeatedly questions narratives of personal histories—her own, her construction of her mother's, and various "official" discourses. To this end, she allows for the vagaries of memory, she questions the truth status of life documents such as birth certificates, and she stresses how autobiography, like other narratives of personal history, is a "story" that also taken for history and interpretation (Steedman 1987, 143).

In keeping with the examples of confessional modes I have tended to pursue, let me turn to Gayatri Chakravorty Spivak's essay "French Feminism in an International Frame," where her reflexive confessing facilitates both a probe of subjectivity formation based on identity categories and an analysis of the global politics of theoretical discourse. Deploying a personal anecdote to introduce the term "ideological victimage," Spivak profiles the cultural hegemony that First World (in this case French) theories cast over intellectual work from "other worlds." For instance, Spivak relays a conversation with a Sudanese woman sociologist who has written " 'a structural functionalist dissertation on female circumcision in the Sudan' " (Spivak 1988, 135). Picking up on the abstractions of "Structural Functionalism," as well as the sexism encoded in "female circumcision," Spivak questions the sovereignty of Western theoretical persuasions that displace or occlude political struggles particular to the work of "so-called Third World women" (Spivak 1988, 135). Like other confessing feminists, Spivak addresses textual and sexual violence in the two registers of theory and practice, that is, the imperialism of (First World) theories and the ritualized brutality of clitoridectomy. The erotic domination that "fascinates" Tompkins assumes a collective political urgency in Spivak's context that materializes male sexual privilege. Thus "ideological victimage" works on two planes. To bring the term into close range, Spivak recites her own interpellation in this system of intellectual domination:

> The "choice" of English Honors by an upper-class young woman in the Calcutta of the fifties was itself highly over-determined. Becoming a professor of English in the U.S. fitted in with the "brain drain." In due course, a commitment to feminism was the best of a collection of accessible scenarios. . . . Predictably, I began by identifying the "female academic" and feminism as such. . . . When one attempted to think of so-called Third World women in a broader scope [than the restricted sense behind "International Feminism"], one found oneself caught, as my Sudanese colleague was caught and held by Structural Functionalism, in a web of information retrieval inspired at best by: "what can I do *for* them?" (Spivak 1988, 134–135).

The shift from third-person to first-person voice in the course of the passage exemplifies Spivak's reflexivity. The grammar dramatizes the discursive construction of this female Third World subject as excentric, the product and process of multiple mediations, with ruptures within and between her assorted and fluctuating identities. Spivak uses the example of her professional training to consider the way dominant cultural ideologies shape the meaning of a "female academic" from an "International Frame."

This condensed academic bildungsroman renders Spivak's career "choices" not a matter of some mythologized free will, but constituted through the supremacy of Western ideology over a woman of color with ambitious aspirations shaped by her own "upper-class" upbringing. Spivak's interest in writing herself into the essay has less to do with expressing or exhibiting personal truths as the foundation for her theorizing; rather, she provides her story as a way to underscore the precarious positions of an academic feminist, of theories (whether French feminism or Structural Functionalism), of identity politics, each speaking *for* an "other"— in this case, for "so-called Third World Women" with whom Spivak unevenly identifies. As a "westernized Easterner," by virtue of her professional training, itself a part of a broader cultural imperialism, Spivak questions her own ability to "know her own world," to know whether or how to utilize French feminist theory to "do" something *"for"* nonwestern women. Tentatively positioning herself alongside, but not identical with, subaltern Indian women, Spivak explores the possibilities of speaking for/as/of "them." At the same time, she notes her associative identity with First World women who presume a knowledge of exclusion and oppression based on a homogenized notion of "woman," a subject position that overlooks cultural and historical specificities.

Spivak's reflexive confession offers an incisive tool for feminist inquiry. Rather than a plaintive quest for a genuine female voice reflecting some internal and external truth, confessing feminist theory—used with reflexive analytic caution—can explore the politics of rhetorical subject construction. While subjectivity is not simply reducible to linguistic performance, the dimensions of language mold the representation of any epistemological claims about an "I," at once discursive, ideological, historical, and institutional. I also think that critical attention to the positioning of subjectivity revitalizes the author function that feminists have recently tried to overhaul.[17] Because of confession's attention to a transgressive "I," this rhetorical strategy exposes the process and product of subjectivity as both contradictory and irregular, textual and contextual. In other words, "I" does have a lot to do with "it"; any constitution of subjectivity through personal voice is also a theory that confessional feminisms might usefully explicate.

Updating Confessing Feminist Theory

In returning to this topic briefly some five years later, I want to redesign the rough edges between productive—or reflexive—and insufficiently politicized—or reflective—critical uses of the personal in feminist theory. My critique has been joined by others such as Linda Kauffman's "The Long Goodbye: Against Personal Testimony, or An Infant Grifter Grows Up," in which the writer cautions against specious claims of political activism by virtue of practicing confessional feminism: "Writing about yourself does not liberate you, it just shows how ingrained the ideology of freedom through self-expression is in our thinking" (Kauffman 1993, 269). Yet Kauffman resorts to personal experience in framing her essay as if to demonstrate the correct way to do first-person theorizing. With this attention to so-called self-expression and ideological domination, questions arise: how does anyone decide which instances of confession obscure and which contest existing power relations?[18] Given the logic of interested criticism (that is, the demise of objectivity), how does one judge the relevance of the critic's confessed investments? What about interests that inevitably remain occluded? Are specific kinds of personal revelations more politically effective in an academic context, such as Stimpson's yoking of Yeatsian imagery and a colleague's rape with the significance of feminism in the academy? Finally, what is at stake in such hybrid crossings between autobiography and theory?

In their introduction to a collection of essays on autobiographical storytelling in American popular culture, Sidonie Smith and Julia Watson acknowledge a current "obsessive desire to create and authenticate individual identity," a desire fuelled by a postmodern skepticism of traditional autobiography and its celebration of radical individualism (Smith and Watson 1996, 6). Karl Kroeber likewise diagnoses the current "autobiographical impulse" as a panacea for this postmodernist "loss of meaningful subjectivity" (Guest Column and Forum, *PMLA* October 1996, 1163). At the same time,

Smith and Watson observe the proliferation of the autobiographical today as a function of American commodity culture that produces and circulates discrete narratives of identity. Such hypotheses are useful for placing this style in feminist criticism and theory at a specific time and in a particular culture. The onslaught of the personal, by this assessment, is contradictory both as an effect of market forces that tell us who we are and as an anxious response to the current crisis over representation that teases apart essential, reflective alliances between language and experience, identification and rhetoric.

Rather than refurbishing my taxonomy of confessional modes with an updated catalogue of examples, I offer a retrospective on the subject in light of different arenas of feminist inquiry that have shaped theorizing the personal. For instance, feminist autobiography studies attempts to encompass various disciplinary and methodological ways of reading the autobiographical and the theoretical as inextricably mixed. Leigh Gilmore's "autobiographics" dislodges self-represenation from the Augustinian (or masculine, Christian, Western) literary tradition. Instead of a narrative of origins, conversion, and self-discovery, "autobiographics" is both a feminist writing and reading practice that illuminates modes of self-invention: "there are not so much autobiograph*ies* as autobiograph*ics*, those changing elements of the contradictory discourses and practices of truth and identity which represent the subject of autobiography" (Gilmore 1994, 13). With an emphasis on the complex uses of truth and identity as constitutive of writing and reading an autobiographical subject, Gilmore scrutinizes identification as a primary mode of encountering the personal, a form of precritical interpretation similar to promiscuous identification that participates in naturalizing ideology, stabilizing truth, and establishing authenticity.

More recent explorations of identity studies bring a range of theoretical and disciplinary persuasions to bear on interpreting identity and identification, including poststructuralism, anthropology and sociology, postcolonial, materialist, and queer theories. Identity studies, as a conglomerate of theories about self-construction, assumes that identity is both materially and historically situated; that identity is fluid, shaped by geographical, cultural, and special social locations; that identity is always an intricate negotiation of sameness and difference, one that problematizes easy identification between readers and autobiographical subjects.[19] In contrast to this critique of identification, identity *politics* furnishes a platform for asserting one's intrinsic experience of a social world, a position that forestalls the questioning of this lived reality from anyone who doesn't inhabit it. Where identity politics tends to legitimize solipsism, identity studies recognizes the contingencies and vagaries of any geography of subjectivity.

Although not invoking a lexicon of identity studies, Spivak's reflexive confession is consistent with this stripe of theorizing subjectivity as she considers markers of class, gender, culture, history, and profession as ways of constituting the skewed alliances of her wardrobe of identifications as "upper-class," "Third World," "woman," "academic," "Calcutta of the fifties." The intersection of a first-person voice and an ambivalent Third World identity of the Indian honors student trained in the First World subject of English exposes the difficulties of any process of identification.

Where identity studies has provided an array of useful concepts to interrogate occasions of personal voice, permutations on cultural studies have encouraged interdisciplinary methodologies in this arena of first-person theorizing. In *Getting Personal*, Miller justifies autobiographical criticism as a species of cultural criticism where narratives of self are also descriptions of culture. In a similar turn, feminist interventions in autobiography studies have retooled ethnography as an interpretive device called "autoethnography": a "'figural anthropology' of the self" that takes into account "the defining of one's subjective ethnicity as mediated through language, history, and ethnographical analysis" (Lionnet 1989, 99).[20] At the same time, anthropologist Ruth Behar cushions her defense of the personal in feminist ethnography with references to the work of autobiographical literary scholars including Tompkins. No longer an objective investigator, Behar's version of the ethnographer is a "vulnerable observer" whose "emotions" and personal history must be rehearsed in order to appreciate the value of a particular study of another culture. Like parallel modes in feminist literary criticism, Behar's hybrid genre of "writing vulnerably" means to "locate oneself in one's own text," not simply as a narcissistic flourish, but as a way to highlight an engagement with "serious social issues" (Behar 1996, 13–14).

I mention Behar's intention to personalize "social facts" as transformative because her argument defends this use of the autobiographical as resistance to an academic tradition of a distanced, objective, and abstract style. As I maintain earlier, this opposition between objectivity and subjectivity has been significantly and widely questioned in recent decades. While I have said that touting such uses of the personal as protest approaches the gratuitous, I also appreciate the value of redundancy given the entrenchment of an impersonal pretense in literary criticism. However, I continue to question the styling of reflective confessions as political resistance. In contrast, reflexive confessional modes would complement this cultural studies version of "resistance" with the psychoanalytic concept that defines "resistance" as a complex and contradictory obstacle to analytic work. This doubleness of the meaning of "resistance" also squares with the different resonances of "confession" that I have been interrogating here, from the transgressive and disruptive to the institutionalized and recuperative exercise of personal voice in academic writing.[21]

Perhaps the most suggestive trope for a rhetorical analysis of confessional feminisms is performativity.[22] Sylvia Molloy regards "the necessary, intrusive, and discontinuous uses of the first-person narrative" as a kind of scene, an effect or pose that ranges from an expedient performance "to root the universal" to an ineffectual spectacle of narcissism (*PMLA* October 1996, 1073). This figure of performance underlines what Molloy calls "the necessary duplicity of all texts and discourses." Rather than reading first-person intrusions as the appearance of an authentic self on an abstract plane of academic criticism, attention to the performative spotlights the rhetorical dimensions of any argument.[23] Performativity also allows for elements of staging, that is, the blocking out or literary shaping of narrative for effect.[24] Stimpson's culminating exercise of appropriated confession functions as a rhetorical finale, a climactic tableau of poetry, professional women, and sexual violence that is a set piece for the necessity of feminism within the academy.

Like cultural studies approaches, the idea of performativity draws on the importance of audience encoded in any rhetorical act. For even the most seemingly privatized genres of personal writing such as the diary betray some sense of a listening other.[25] What kinds of reader responses are anticipated in poses of personal voice in feminist academic writing? While Tompkins and Frey call for sympathetic readers who promiscuously identify with their pirouettes of the personal, Gallop and MacLean deploy confessional modes for shock effects that disrupt any regularized reading of academic arguments. Whether informed by cultural or performance studies, this attention to audience resonates with the formal structure of confession that accentuates the power of an interlocutor who interprets the transgressive disclosure and prescribes penance.[26]

From a different angle, performance highlights process over product, as "an activity which generates transformations, as the reintegration of art with what is 'outside' it, an 'opening up' of the field" (quoted in Chasnoff 1996, 109). In this way, performativity negotiates boundaries between text and context, between rhetoric and referent. Salome Chasnoff considers autobiographical performance as a way to investigate the construction of identity: "Current feminist and performance theories bid us view all performance—the quotidian, the ritual, and the theatrical—as constitutive of identity and thus inherently political. Autobiographical performances, or the making of representations of the 'self,' because they are self-conscious, heightened, and shared, are paramount moments of performance as identity construction" (Chasnoff 1996, 110). Inflected by identity and cultural studies, this vantage on performing autobiography forges connections between rhetorical posture and power, between the representational stage and a representative social world where roles are consequential. How might confessional interventions signify a dramatic staging of identity construction, a reflexive theatrics attendant to the power dynamics that bear on categories of subjectivity?

With this plethora of first-person theorizing, I must question whether the transgressive that defines my sense of "confessional modes" continues to carry any weight. Yet I would preserve this connotation, if for different reasons. The stylistic blend of personal voice and academic feminist critique opens up rhetorical spaces for exploring the stakes involved in distinctions of genre and categories of subjectivity. Where do we draw boundaries between the autobiographical and the theoretical, between personal voice and authorized critique? Although Audre Lorde's *Zami*, for instance, has been marketed and consumed as autobiography, the text is replete with theorized performances of identity that pursue relationships between narrative and subjectivity, between power and social categories of selfhood, and between memory and truth in what Lorde calls "a biomythography." Lyn Hejinian's *My Life* likewise investigates the uses of different genres and discourses as constitutive of notions of selfness as she brings poetics and poststructuralist theory to bear on this rhetorical envisioning of a personal-pronoun "life." And Mary Karr's *The Liars' Club* conceptualizes autobiography around a porous partition between verifiable fact and narrative fiction. There are also many recent examples of intellectual memoirs by feminist literary critics who commingle in various ways the theoretical and the autobiographical; for one example, Marianna Torgovnick divides *Crossing Ocean Parkway* into two kinds of essays—one where the autobiographical prevails and the cultural critique operates as an undertone and another style that reverses this juxtaposition. While I may appear to be drifting from confessional feminisms, I make reference to more protracted autobiographical texts to cite instances of first-person compositions that trouble the illusion of this construction as simple reflection from an originary experience and self. My agenda here isn't to provide a quick survey, but to urge, once again, for a reflexive reading of any theory, which is also an autobiography, and of any autobiography—whether a brief intervention or a larger narrative display—which also signifies a theory of subjectivity.

 NOTES

1. Williams has more recently published *The Rooster's Egg: On the Persistence of Prejudice,* in which she continues this style of interspersing her personal history with theoretical analyses of contemporary issues of race, politics, and the law.

2. Barbara E. Johnson and Houston A. Baker Jr. are the previewers from literature departments.

3. Some other terms used to describe this mode in academic writing include: autobiographical criticism, egodocuments, testimonial writing, narrative criticism, and personal materialism (See Miller 1991 for a lengthy lexicon on the subject).

4. See Scott (1991, 787).

5. Linda Alcoff (1988) devises "positionality" as a way to draw together the most politically productive features of poststructuralist and cultural feminist theories. Alcoff's positionality signifies the foregrounding of a particular subject position from which a feminist theorist might speak. I am interested in the way this positioning of the subject of the confessional

mode is limited by the operations of language, by the surrounding discursive and ideological contexts that complicate the way this subject position gets read. For Gayatri Spivak (1988, 55–56), unveiling one's positionality becomes closed proposition, framed as it is within specific discourses and their particular "communities of power."

6. For a concept related to "politics of sentiment," see Ann Cvetkovich's "politics of affect" (Cvetkovich 1992, 1–12).

7. For examples of the aestheticized confessional mode, see DuPlessis (1978), Jardine (1989), and Sedgwick (1987, 1992).

8. This issue of *New Literary History* contains nine replies to Messer-Davidow's essay. As many as six of the respondents (Joan E. Hartman, Ruth Hubbard, Patricia Clark Smith, Amy Ling, Nellie McKay, and Jane Tompkins) employ personal (invoking experiences) or positional (underscoring the act of "speaking as") modes. *Gender and Theory: Dialogues on Feminist Criticism*, edited by Linda Kauffman, includes both Messer-Davidow's and Tompkins's contributions and adds the following essays by men that incorporate confessional acts, some brief, others protracted: David Shumway, "Solidarity or Perspectivity?," Gerald MacLean, "Citing the Subject," and Joseph Allen Boone, "Of Me(n) and Feminism: Who(se) is the Sex that Writes?" Miller also analyzes the articles by Tompkins and MacLean in the first chapter of *Getting Personal*.

9. Miller (1991, 17–18) says of MacLean's obvious condescension toward women, "The challenges, therefore, for me writing about this in my turn is not simply to condescend *as a feminist* to him *as a man* . . . without sounding like the feminist police." Condescension and positionalities notwithstanding, I am pointing out the contradictions between MacLean's professed politics and his rhetorical use of confession and related personal modes like his "Dear Jane" addresses.

10. Although Miller (1991, 17–19) devotes attention to what she calls the "personal criticism" of MacLean's essay, she submerges a bracketed allusion to this confession of domestic violence in an explanatory note: "I am also not taking into account the self-narrative MacLean produces . . . which leads to the confession of having struck his wife during an argument" (Miller 1991, 28). Miller doesn't explain why she forecloses this confession from her discussion despite the fact that MacLean's revelation offers an extreme example of "getting personal" in academic discourse.

11. I have in mind the recent spate of intellectual memoirs by feminists. Here is an abbreviated list of book-length memoirs by American academic feminists who also write literary criticism: Davidson (1993), Kaplan (1993), Tompkins (1996), Torgovnick (1994). All of these writers are

professors at Duke University and have participated in an "experimental writing" group (see Torgovnick 1990). Because of their length, these texts do not qualify as the confessional interruptions that I examine here.

12. I owe this insight to an illuminating discussion of Gallop's book by Ellen Michel who notes Gallop's vexed attention to her own institution subject positions: "Gallop is, after all, a 'woman scholar' who frequently plays the part of the seductive daughter, the call girl who can turn an intellectual trick" (Michel n.d., 20).

13. For an examination of Gallop's confessional mode in *Reading Lacan*, see Bernstein (1989, 195–213).

14. My allusion here to "confessional tabloids" anticipates the style and content of Gallop's most recent publication, *Feminist Accused of Sexual Harassment*, which offers Gallop's version on the case in which she was accused of sexual harassment by two female graduate students at the University of Wisconsin-Milwaukee.

15. Toril Moi (1988, 16) makes some observations about Gallop's textual antics in *Reading Lacan* that are relevant to my reading here. She argues that "the relentlessly self-subversive strategies of [Gallop's] writing unwittingly come to reproduce the very monological monotony they set out to deconstruct." Moi construes Gallopian criticism as a "postfeminist" enterprise attempting "to replace feminist politics with feminine stylistics," which produces "a marvellously shrewd, brilliant, and witty text which somehow has nothing to say" about "the material and ideological bases for women's oppression."

16. See Foucault (1988) and Ferguson (1990).

17. See Walker (1990, 558–560) for a discussion of the embattled author position as a source of power and an instance of contradictions. Walker suggests many useful connections with my treatment of confessional feminism that pursues the function of author in a particular discursive formation.

18. Several of the responses to the *PMLA* invitation for commentary on the "place, nature, or limits (if any) of the personal in scholarship" (*PMLA* October 1996, 1146) call attention to the institutional politics of academic confessional writing. Ruth Perry cautions that personal criticism often bolsters "the cult of personality, the emerging star system in university life" as "grist for the feature-story mill in a media-saturated culture" (*PMLA* October 1996, 1166). Celebrity professors seem to confess with impunity, but does this hold true for untenured or non-tenure-track academics? Also see Terry Caesar's remarks on how institutional authority determines when the use of the personal is "too personal" (*PMLA* October 1996, 1168).

19. See Friedman (1996) for her six discourses of positional identity that trace an interdisciplinary variety of ways of looking at subject construction. Friedman focuses in particular on spatial rhetoric in theorizing identity, hence such terms as positionality, locationality, situational, nomadic, migratory, relational identities.

20. The term "autoethnography" is often attributed to Mary Louise Pratt although Lionnet's usage predates Pratt's. For Pratt, autoethnography refers to "instances in which colonized subjects undertake to represent themselves in ways that *engage with* the colonizer's own terms" (Pratt 1992, 7).

21. A related point is Stephanie Sandler's angle on how contemporary uses of "self" replace "sex" in an updated version of Foucault's repressive hypothesis where discursive prohibitions against talking sex have the contradictory effect of inciting sex talk elsewhere (Guest Column and Forum, *PMLA* October 1996, 1162).

22. For a collection of essays on performance studies, see Parker and Sedgwick (1995).

23. In a similar vein, Joseph Boone likens invoking the personal in written scholarship and in the classroom as a performance "in efforts to forge new avenues of thinking about and transmitting knowledge (Guest Column and Forum, *PMLA* October 1996, 1153).

24. See Cathy N. Davidson's "Critical Fictions" for an account of the fictionalizing dimensions of personal writing (Guest Column and Forum, *PMLA* October 1996, 1069–1072).

25. See Davidson's discussion of an intriguing entry in an early nineteenth-century American diary which brings forth "complexities and inconsistencies in a historical model of scholarship that is based on personal writing" (Guest Column and Forum, *PMLA* October 1996, 1069).

26. See Bernstein (1997, 17–18) for a discussion of the role of the confessor where confession, by definition, is an act of power.

REFERENCES

Alcoff, Linda. 1988. Cultural feminism versus post-structuralism: The identity crisis in feminist theory. *Signs* 13 (3): 405–436.

Behar, Ruth. 1996. *The vulnerable observer.* Boston: Beacon Press.

Berlant, Lauren. 1988. The female complaint. *Social Text* 19/20 (Fall): 237–259.

Bernstein, Susan David. 1989. Confessing Lacan. In *Seduction and theory*, ed. Dianne Hunter. Urbana: University of Illinois Press.

———. 1997. *Confessional subjects*. Chapel Hill: University of North Carolina Press.

Butler, Judith. 1990. *Gender trouble*. New York: Routledge.

Chasnoff, Salome. 1996. Performing teen motherhood on video: Autoethnography as counterdiscourse. In *Getting a life: Everyday uses of autobiography*, ed. Sidonie Smith and Julia Watson. Minneapolis: University of Minnesota Press.

Cixous, Hélène. 1981. The laugh of the medusa. In *New French feminisms*, ed. Elaine Marks and Isabelle de Courtivron. New York: Schocken Books.

Cvetkovich, Ann. 1992. *Mixed feelings: Feminism, mass culture, and Victorian sensationalism*. New Brunswick, N.J.: Rutgers University Press.

Davidson, Cathy N. 1993. *Thirty-six views of Mount Fuji: On finding myself in Japan*. New York: Dutton.

De Lauretis, Teresa. 1987. *Technologies of gender*. Bloomington: Indiana University Press.

DuBois, Page. 1986. Antigone and the feminist critic. *Genre* 19 (Winter): 371–383.

DuPlessis, Rachel Blau. 1978. Washing blood. *Feminist Studies* 4(2): 1–12.

Felski, Rita. 1989. *Beyond feminist aesthetics*. Cambridge: Harvard University Press.

Ferguson, Kathy. 1990. Interpretation and genealogy in feminism. *Signs* 16(2): 322–339.

Foucault, Michel. 1988. Nietzsche, genealogy, history. In *Language, counter-memory, practice,* ed. Donald F. Bouchard. Trans. Bouchard and Sherry Simon. Ithaca: Cornell University Press.

Freedman, Diane P., Olivia Frey, and Frances Murphy Zauhar, eds. 1993. *The Intimate critique: Autobiographical literary criticism*. Durham: Duke University Press.

Frey, Olivia. 1990. Beyond literary Darwinism. *College English* 52(5): 507–526.

Friedman, Susan Stanford. 1996. "Beyond" gynocriticism and gynesis: the geographics of identity and the future of feminist criticism. *Tulsa Studies* 15(1): 13–40.

Gallop, Jane. 1988. *Thinking through the body*. New York: Columbia University Press.

———. 1997. *Feminist accused of sexual harassment*. Durham: Duke University Press.

Gilmore, Leigh. 1994. *Autobiographics: A feminist theory of women's self-representation*. Ithaca: Cornell University Press.

Guest Column and Forum. 1996. *PMLA* 111, 5 (October): 1063–1169.

Hejinian, Lyn. 1991. *My Life*. Los Angeles: Sun and Moon Press

Jardine, Alice. 1989. Notes for an analysis. In *Between feminism and psychoanalysis*, ed. Teresa Benjamin. New York: Routledge, 73–85.

Kaplan, Alice. 1993. *French lessons*. Chicago: University of Chicago Press.

Karr, Mary. 1995. *The Liars' Club*. New York: Viking.

Kauffman, Linda S. 1993. The long goodbye: Against personal testimony, or an infant grifter grows up. In *American feminist thought at century's end*, ed. Linda S. Kauffman. New York: Basil Blackwell.

Lionnet, Françoise. 1989. *Autobiographical voices: Gender, race, self-portraiture*. Ithaca: Cornell University Press.

Lorde, Audre. 1982. *Zami: A new spelling of my name*. Freedom, Cal.: The Crossing Press.

MacLean, Gerald. 1989. Citing the subject. In *Gender and theory: Dialogues on feminist criticism*, ed. Linda Kauffman. New York: Basil Blackwell.

Messer-Davidow, Ellen. 1989. The philosophical bases of feminist literary criticisms. In *Gender and theory: Dialogues on feminist criticism*, ed. Linda Kauffman. New York: Basil Blackwell. First published in *New Literary History* 19, 1 (1987): 65–103.

Michel, Ellen. n.d. Jane Gallop's cryptogrammatic discourse: Rebuses of elation and violation in *Thinking through the body*. Unpublished ms.

Michie, Helena. 1989. Not one of the family: The repression of the other woman in feminist theory. In *Discontented discourses*, ed. Marleen S. Barr and Richard Feldstein. Urbana: University of Illinois Press.

Miller, Nancy K. 1991. *Getting personal: Feminist occasions and other autobiographical acts*. New York: Routledge.

Moi, Toril. 1988. Feminism, postmodernism, and style. *Cultural Critique* 9: 3–22.

Parker, Andrew, and Eve Kosofsky Sedgwick, eds. 1995. *Performativity and Performance*. New York: Routledge.

Pratt, Mary Louise. 1992. *Imperial eyes: Travel writing and transculturation.* New York: Routledge.

Scott, Joan W. 1991. The evidence of experience. *Cultural Inquiry* 17(2): 773–797.

Sedgwick, Eve K. 1987. A poem is being written. *Representations* 17 (Winter): 110–143.

———. 1992. White glasses. *The Yale Journal of Criticism* 5(3): 193–208.

Smith, Sidonie, and Julia Watson, eds. 1996. *Getting a life: Everyday uses of autobiography.* Minneapolis: University of Minnesota Press.

Spivak, Gayatri Chakravorty. 1988. French feminism in an international frame. In *In other worlds.* New York: Routledge.

Steedman, Carolyn. 1987. *Landscape for a good woman: The story of two lives.* New Brunswick, N.J.: Rutgers University Press.

Stimpson, Catharine R. 1990. Feminism and feminist criticism. In *Where the meanings are.* New York: Routledge.

Tompkins, Jane. 1989. Me and my shadow. In *Gender and theory: Dialogues on feminist criticism,* ed. Linda Kauffman. New York: Basil Blackwell.

———. 1996. *A life in school: What the teacher learned.* Reading, Mass.: Addison-Wesley Pub. Co.

Torgovnick, Marianna. 1990. Experimental critical writing. In *Profession 90* (MLA, New York): 25–27.

———. 1994. *Crossing Ocean Parkway.* Chicago: University of Chicago Press.

Veeser, H. Aram, ed. 1996. *Confessions of the critics.* New York: Routledge.

Walker, Cheryl. 1990. Feminist literary criticism and the author. *Critical Inquiry* 16(1): 551–571.

Williams, Patricia J. 1991. *The alchemy of race and rights.* Cambridge: Harvard University Press.

———. 1996. *The rooster's egg: On the persistence of prejudice.* Cambridge: Harvard University Press.

Young-Bruehl, Elizabeth. 1991. Pride and prejudice: Feminist scholars reclaim the first person. *Lingua Franca* (February): 15–18.

Sangeeta Ray

———————— 7 ————————

The Postcolonial Critic

Shifting Subjects, Changing Paradigms

M any recent feminist and postcolonial critical essays contain a
recurring sentence that foregrounds the critic's subject positions *vis-à-vis* the text that she is attempting to read and or critique.[1] A characteristic sentence may read something like this: I am
a postcolonial feminist critic educated in a former British colony
(this would automatically indicate that the critic's education was
highly Anglicized and that she comes from a privileged neo-colonial
background) who now teaches in an American academic institution
(this would imply that she either teaches in the English, Comparative Literature, Philosophy, or perhaps Women's Studies department and occupies a marginal position) and therefore intimately
implicated in my reading of "this text." One can substitute heterosexual white woman, disenfranchised African-American, Chicana,
American Indian, Asian-American, lesbian/white, lesbian/non-white
woman, and so on for variations within the above structure. On the
one hand, the insistence on the heterogeneity of one's subject position prevents indulging in any utopic desire that one can exist
outside relations of power; it is a methodological trope, evoking an
involvement in the dynamics of the very discourses of power we
seek to alter or dismantle. On the other hand, in the uncritical
appropriation of this methodological trope lies the danger of its
becoming yet another "buzz-sentence" (to coin a phrase) that
unproblematically situates one's personal history as yet another
instance of the heterogenous, heteronomous, and discursively dis-
placed status of identities. This could in turn lead to a facile and

207

often comfortable praxis in the analysis of difference/s, which in the last decade feminist theorists from the margins have struggled to prevent.[2] The autobiographical preamble that foregrounds the critic's subject positions in terms of race, class, sexual orientation, and geographic location/displacement, instead of ratifying and reinforcing the political significances of her reading, is transformed into a series of nouns and adjectives that produces a renewable symbolic economy with the addition of yet another denomination.[3] In one's desire to argue for multiple mediations in a heterogenous and highly politicized academic and social landscape, one can seemingly more and more easily dip into the well of terminologies, unproblematically contextualize oneself, and come up barely wet.

I am extremely sympathetic to the critical use of the autobiographical trope;[4] however, the ratification of difference via an unquestioned and unexamined appropriation of the various signifiers that indicate one's race, gender, national and cultural heritage does not reinforce the strategic deployment of "situated knowledges" against the constraining power of an imperialistic center. In the effort to make one's positionality explicit, one could end up claiming an unmediated, "privileged" status for the voices of the oppressed. The efficacy of the strategy identified broadly as "identity politics" necessarily challenges the apparently impersonal paradigm of critical presentation where the narrative voice of the critic is postulated as universal in its effect. However, the shift in emphasis from macro-narratives to the proliferation of micronarratives that insist on the local, the contingent, the contextual, and the personal does raise problems for its practitioners.

The underlining of the axioms of self-representation, reminding both critic and reader of the temporal, spatial, and subjective nature of every social and critical inscription, generates what Laura Kipnis has called the "hypervisibility" of the "ideological category of the subject" (Kipnis 1993, 158). This "hypervisibility" has its flip side where the fractured voices seeking simultaneously to speak *for* and *as* cannot double back to address the gaps occasioned by the omissions produced precisely because of such self-conscious practices of representation. The conundrum for such a critic then is not only how to interrupt the constructed reality of "fictionally unmarked subjectivities" that grow out of the disparate experiences of the "oppositional consciousness" of the diverse oppressed voices of the world with the "epistemologies of marked subjectivities"

(Hartsock 1989–90, 24), but how to address the internal imbalance produced in the narrative voice that seeks to present itself even as it challenges the metaphysical impossibility of the representation of identity in and as presence. In this postmodern moment of identity crisis, if we wish to go beyond the mere cataloging of other voices and other scenes and break out of an "institutionally authorized personalism" (Miller 1991, 25) we can but try to write a social performance where the "personal is at odds with the hierarchies of the positional—working more like a relay between positions to create critical fluency" (Miller 1991, 25). One of the crucial terms in the critical vocabulary of writers/critics seeking to clarify and problematize the history of difference through the invocation of autobiographical moments is "experience." The subject's own account of what s/he has lived through often becomes an irrefutable point of departure for an analysis of the epistemology of the "other." However, if one fails to interrogate the very construction of experience as experience, if one fails to recognize the "truth" value traditionally bestowed on the category of experience in the annals of orthodox history, if one's project is solely concerned with making visible what has hitherto been rendered invisible then, despite the shift from the universal to the personal, the parameters of the structures of address for the critical argument remain unchanged and unchallenged. As Joan Scott puts it, "[w]hen experience is taken as the origin of knowledge, the vision of the individual subject . . . becomes the bedrock of evidence upon which explanation is built. . . . [T]he evidence of experience . . . reproduces rather than contests given ideological systems . . . [it] precludes analysis of the workings of [the] system and of its historicity: instead it reproduces its terms" (Scott 1992, 25).[5]

My realization of the problems underlying the recent commodification of the critical vocabulary generated by the successful voices of hitherto marginalized groups has never been so blatantly obvious and discomforting as during my four-week visit to Calcutta after a gap of five years. The categories that I used to define myself against the majority or those used to position me as the "other" in the United States alienated me from myself and from those around me in India. I will return to this autobiographical account later. For now I wish to suggest that my experiences at home revealed not only the inadequacy of certain subject positionalities but also the problems involved in the availability of previously inadmissible and powerless discursive spaces that are at present overloaded with politically charged epistemological markers. Chandra Talpade Mohanty separates feminist scholarship from traditional modes of knowledge by visualizing it as a force of interference. Mohanty argues that the best kind of feminist scholarship is one that is absolutely dedicated to both resisting the "imperatives of age-old 'legitimate' and 'scientific' bodies of knowledge" as well as producing a counter discourse that interjects and subverts certain dominant discursive practices (1984, 334). I believe this definition is valid for other discursive practices that inhabit the margins as well. However, the definition carries weight only when one constantly reminds oneself, as Abena Busia does in positioning herself as a black African woman, that when she speaks she does so by "deliberately invoking all the significances of race, gender, and national and cultural heritage and history that those three terms call up without privileging either gender or race and without distilling gender or race from origins" (1989, 83). Those of us who struggle to negotiate between cultures, languages, and complex configurations of meaning and power must be constantly aware that every time we speak or write we participate in "a social encounter [that] generates and is generated by complex sets of negotiations between externally produced meanings and internally created subjectivities, between the ways we see and hear and the ways in which we are seen and heard" (Busia 1989, 82).

In this chapter I will use my visit back to India to analyze one of the many social encounters that has enabled me to recognize more clearly the multivalent trajectory that my own multiple negotiations between "internally created subjectivities" and "externally produced meanings" continue to traverse. To this I will juxtapose the consolidation of a species of the "Postcolonial Critic" by briefly looking at the collection of interviews of Gayatri Chakravorty Spivak published by Routledge under the title *The Post-Colonial Critic: Interviews, Strategies, Dialogues* and edited by Sarah Harasym. My interest here lies not so much in the interviews themselves, which more often than not are brilliant expositions of some of the most cogent and intelligent theories postulated by one of the leading theorists of our times, but in the commodification and marketing of a self-designated postcolonial intellectual by another critic who except in the voice of one of the many interviewers does not in any visible measure inhabit the one hundred and sixty-eight pages of the text that she has undertaken to edit.

Gayatri Chakravorty Spivak, one of the dominant feminist, postcolonial critics on the U.S. academic scene today, has insisted on the need to foreground the constructions of one's identities in order to resist the homogenizing tendency predicated by the Western epistemological predilection for a universal subject. The "I" that investigates and interrogates as a postcolonial subject within the U.S. academy has to be constantly aware of the direct relationship of domination and exploitation between the United States and other Third World countries. Moreover, as a Third World woman moving up in the First World committed to cross-cultural exchanges, Spivak has also to "consider the historical (rather than romantic or nostalgic) constitution of geography—how the world (geo) was written (graphy) in the last few centuries. Such considerations would not rule out the desire to cross cultures, but would reveal the difficulty of the task" (Spivak 1988, 115). In my critique of the book titled *The Post-Colonial Critic: Interviews, Strategies, Dialogues,* I will consider Spivak's success in interrogating her own position as a leading postcolonial critic as she engages in dialogues with various people. I am primarily interested in those moments in the interviews where Spivak's undeniable commitment to cross-cultural exchanges is undermined by the resurgence of her authoritative subject position. This dominant voice then deflects productive tensions generated by critical scrutiny of the category postcolonial as one that is, to use Teresa de Lauretis's words in a different context, "multiply organized across positionalities along several axes and across mutually contradictory discourses" (de Lauretis 1988, 136).

In "A Literary Representation of the Subaltern: A Woman's Text from the Third World," Spivak is extremely successful in analyzing the multiple positionalities of the postcolonial subaltern woman Jasodha, the main character of Mahashweta Devi's story "The Breast Giver" (Spivak 1987). Spivak provides different, contradictory, and opposed readings of the condition of Jasodha by interweaving the materials present in the primary text with various Western "elite" theories simultaneously to prevent the separation of Third World texts and First World theories as well as to suggest the "limit and limitations" of the various theories she uses. Her aim is to produce scenarios in which the "teacher clandestinely carves out a piece of action by using the text as a tool . . . in celebration of the text's apartness (*être-à-l'écart*). Paradoxically, this apartness makes the text susceptible to a history larger than that of the writer, reader, teacher" (Spivak 1987, 268). Spivak's maneuver here allows her to rupture the totalizing gesture that would insulate Third World texts from First World theories that further the "current and continued subalternization of so-called 'third-world' literatures" (Spivak 1987, 241).[6]

The complex juxtaposed readings Spivak provides implicate her own position as a Third World informant whose accession to the ranks of the intellectual elite in the First World is guaranteed by her expertise in the esoteric theories of Derridean deconstruction, French feminism, and Lacanian psychoanalysis. In her concluding section, Spivak evokes David Hardiman's criticism of her reading of Mahashweta Devi's story. Hardiman indicts Spivak for wrenching Devi's story out of its immediate historical and social context, repudiating the "authentic" reading offered by the author itself, and imposing eclectic and olympian analyses on an apparently obvious realistic text. Hardiman therefore participates in the familiar and tiresome opposition between nativist "down to earth readings" and Third-World-intellectual in First-World's-elite reading.[7] He indicates once again the precarious position of anyone endeavoring to participate in cross-cultural exchanges. Not only is Hardiman guilty of, as Spivak puts it, "an ontological/epistemological confusion that pits subaltern being against elite knowing" (Spivak 1987, 268), but he also refuses to recognize Spivak's position as anything other than that of an elite guilty of an incriminating participation in the dominant, Western, male-centered sphere of intellectual performance that still dominates the U.S. academic scene. Hardiman dismisses Spivak's articulation of her position as a Marxist-deconstructivist-feminist-postcolonial critic who borrows eclectically from the various critical methodologies afforded by such a multiple plotting. This recognition of her own multiple negotiations between "internally created subjectivities" and "externally produced meanings" is an example of Spivak's refusal to engage in any epistemological paradigm that situates difference within a simple binary structure by insisting on a hierarchical dualism.

Unfortunately, despite her insistence to the contrary, Spivak has been valorized in the West (especially the U.S. academy) as *the* postcolonial critic. Though she has repeatedly denied the notion of a pure voice emitting from within a sanctioned essential notion of self based on a sovereign category—be it race, class, gender, sexual preference, or nationality—Spivak is, to use her own words, a "highly commodified, distinguished professor" (Spivak 1990, 86). Instead of functioning as an alibi for exclusion (as she herself presumes) in the rare circle inhabited by critics such as Fredric Jameson and J. Hillis Miller (two names that she evokes in the interview), her skin and nationality now in 1991 have increasingly ratified her position as the postcolonial critic (as opposed to 1989 when the interview was conducted). This identification contributes to the reification of the different and disparate voices in the margins into a Voice that is made to speak for and as the "other." The collection of interviews edited by Sarah Harasym increases my anxieties about the implications of producing a text that lends itself, perhaps completely unwittingly, to the production of an unmediated subject position in a space/place at the top. My interest here lies both in the interviews themselves, which more often than not are brilliant expositions of some of the most cogent and intelligent formulations of one of the leading theorists of our times, and in the commodification and marketing of Spivak as *the* postcolonial intellectual in the academic marketplace that such a collection under its given title facilitates.

The interviews cover a wide range of subjects even though each conversation does return, however tangentially or sporadically, to the situations of the postcolonial critic. The interviews are arranged chronologically, and they have all been published prior to their consolidation in this one space. The interviews range from discussions about the postmodern condition, its indifference and or relevance to practical politics, to the importance of engaging in a persistent critique of multicultural endeavors to prevent them from being homogenized by a benevolent audience. Spivak discusses important aspects of her work such as her belief in the possibility of using deconstruction to effect a politically directed "transformation of consciousness" similar to feminism, the crucial need to constantly problematize one's authority and given position as an investigating subject, the obligation on the part of teachers to examine their pedagogical responsibility as they disseminate various "isms" in the classroom, and the importance of scrutinizing self-representation carefully as one appropriates terms and categories from various disciplinary areas and, more importantly from other cultures.

My essay too participates in a feminist postcolonial critical historiography/epistemology. Feminist postcolonial practice is itself a subdivision in the already marginal category of postcolonial discourse, and some of the more recognized postcolonial critics are often oblivious to the way gender is deeply imbricated in their own production of oppositional discourses against Western hegemony. However, despite their individual limitations, as is the case with most areas of disciplinary studies, postcolonial discourse has produced its very own authoritative voices—critics whose various pronouncements on the efficacious role of the critical subject engage in the continuous dismantling of the paradigms of dominating and coercive systems of knowledge, as well as question the limited (read Western) horizons within which many current literary and cultural theorists operate. These critics occupy oppositional spaces in the academic arena and their disparate studies on various aspects of postcolonial societies function as strategic articulations of resistance to the insidious legacy of colonial occupation reconfigured as economic and political exploitation in today's global neo-imperial cultural economy. In the American academic scene, three names must necessarily inhabit an institutional reading list on postcolonial critics—Edward Said, Homi Bhabha, and Gayatri Chakravorty Spivak.[8] All three critics have participated and continue to participate in what Jenny Sharpe calls "an ethics of reading" that struggles to contend "with the problem of articulating resistance" to Eurocentric forms of knowledge, which shaped the grand narratives of imperialist maneuver (1989, 137). Through an inclusion of the disruptions produced by indigenous insurgent resistances, these critics investigate various aspects of colonial epistemologies and rupture the monolithic enterprise of Western master discourses. Their place in various anthologies on racism, feminism, and colonialism seems a given. However, Gayatri Spivak, above all, seems to have repeatedly been reified as the "Postcolonial Critic," especially in feminist-postcolonial and Third World feminist critical practice.

In a recent essay by Henry Louis Gates, these three names are evoked yet again in connection with their individual appropriations of Frantz Fanon. In the essay titled "Critical Fanonism," Gates takes us on the quest for the "true" Fanon through a circuitous ride that involves "Spivak's critique of JanMohammed's critique of Bhabha's critique of Said's critique of colonial discourse" (Gates 1991, 465). Though two other names appear on his list of postcolonial critics, the three are firmly in place.[9] It seems important to attend to the order of names—he begins with Spivak and ends with Said, who is not surprisingly preceded by Bhabha. In fact Gates's designation of Spivak as the first critic on his list confirms by claim regarding the commodification of the "Voice of Spivak" as the voice of the postcolonial critic. This valorization of a postcolonial critic in the American academic scene seems further validated by another one of Gates's claims in the same essay. Gates does provide a space for the contending voices in the increasing debates concerning the conflation of and distinctions between notions of cultural resistance and cultural alterity, and he is probably right in his assessment that "[t]here may well be something familiar about Spivak's insistence on the totalizing embrace of colonial discourse, and Parry's unease with the insistence" (Gates 1991, 466). However, his point that "what Jacques Derrida calls writing, Spivak, in a brilliant reversal, has renamed colonial discourse," and Gates's own rewriting of Spivak's *position* as a categorical denial of the possibility of signification "outside (the discourse of) colonialism" seems too sweeping a claim based on apparent surface similarities between the Derridean "mot, that there is nothing outside of the text," and Spivak's repeated insistence on the heterogeneous nature of every text and discourse. One sees a potentially dangerous move in Gates's essay when he states that "Spivak's argument, put in its strongest form, entails the corollary that all discourse is colonial discourse" (Gates 1991, 466). The privileging of colonial discourse as a signifier that subsumes all other discourses leaves almost no room for the very productive tensions that Gates argues for earlier in his essay. If all discourse is always already colonial discourse, any attempt to theorize a way out of its restrictive boundaries is necessarily futile. In fact, Spivak herself has stated that though she herself is deeply influenced by deconstruction (as practiced by Derrida) she does recognize its limits. Furthermore, deconstructive reading, a reading that addresses aporias, disjunctures, and is critical of binary oppositions, also resists totalizing gestures of the kind posited by Gates. My cautionary remarks are perhaps best borne out by Spivak herself: "The problem with the idea of deconstruction as a form of ideology-critique is that deconstruction is not really interested in the exposure of error. . . ." (Spivak 1990, 135). And again, in the same interview, she asserts that there is a real difference between her agenda with deconstruction and what other people do with Derrida's "stuff" since "[i]f you take the theoretical formulations of deconstruction, you have a stalling at the beginning and a stalling at the end (*differance* at the beginning and *aporia* at the end), so that you can neither properly begin, nor properly end. . . . I'm more interested in what happens in the middle. . . ." (136). It is this interest in the middle that precludes Spivak from the paralysis that underlies Gates's subsumption of all discourses under the rubric colonial, and in his attributing this maneuver to Spivak we have yet another moment in the renaming of Spivak as arch postcolonial critic.

The fact that Gayatri Chakravorty Spivak has been responsible for some of the most exemplary work on postcolonial theory and literature is irrefutable. Her contributions to the still marginal field of postcolonial studies, her emphasis on the need to change pedagogical methods in the teaching of postcolonial literatures, her commitment to the voice of the subaltern in its various aspects in colonial and postcolonial India has changed the face of critical and literary practice in American academics. Her commitment to feminist inquiry has not only produced brilliant critiques of the erasure of the body and subjectivity of the colonial woman from the history of both imperial domination and colonial resistance, but she has also analyzed crucial moments of violent epistemic shifts within the territorial imperialism of nineteenth-century India. She also articulates the crucial necessity of differentiating between the production of various colonial subjectivities under the aegis of a territorial expansive imperialism, and neo-colonial subjects—primarily women—in the era of postmodern, electronic capitalist imperialism. That imperialism continues to spread through the exploitation of primarily Third World women employed as cheap labor in transnational corporations that shape the economic system of contemporary postindustrial societies.

Nevertheless, while every discursive and literary field enjoys its special luminaries, the commodification of Spivak in a still-nascent field has prevented a productive critical engagement with some of her more ingenious arguments on the production of colonial and neo-colonial subjects. Her position of preeminence has to a certain extent understandably skewed the discourse of postcolonial studies. To my knowledge, with the exception of Benita Parry's article, there does not exist any substantive analyses of Spivak's critical positions. Two or three articles dealing with individual essays have appeared very recently,[10] but it appears that the power that apparently inheres in the use of her name guarantees its evocation only as a necessary credential for postcolonial critical practice, preempting any significant, lengthy critical discussion of her numerous essays.

The text, *The Post-Colonial Critic*, is offered to us as a package with the subtitle *Interviews, Strategies, Dialogues*. On the cover, which is black and white, we have an illuminated picture of an Indian woman with her long hair plaited, the traditional *bindi* on her forehead, and big round earrings hanging from pierced ears. What we are offered is a detail from a larger whole titled "Starry Night in Iowa"—the rest of the picture evokes substantial curiosity.[11] What does this image signify? A traditional Indian face among the cornfields of Iowa, perhaps? The postcolonial as Indian immigrant woman in the United States? Or perhaps (without the help of the title of the picture) the Indian subaltern woman whose voice is hard to retrieve, but which the postcolonial Indian intellectual "through that difficulty, discloses subalternity itself as a tropological move that threatens to silence the subaltern" (Sharpe 1989, 139). In whatever manner we view the picture, we must confront the title followed by a picture that figures the postcolonial critic as the Indian woman (read Spivak, or the texts produced by Spivak). Spivak is, of course, a feminist-Marxist-deconstructivist-postcolonialist critic, and she is an Indian. What then happens to other postcolonial critics who are not Indians and other postcolonial worlds when such a text with its particular cover begins to circulate in academic and nonacademic worlds? Benita Parry argues that in much postcolonial work "colonialism as a specific, and the most spectacular, mode of imperialism's many and mutable states . . . is treated as identical with all the variable forms" (Parry 1987, 34). Laura Chrissman, who cites this passage, observes that with this identification the "analysis of colonial discourse becomes self-contained, even hypostatised, a scene devoted solely to the supreme encounter with the Other removed from the network of domestic/ metropolitan and imperial discourses which informed it and which were informed by it" (Chrissman 1990, 39). She identifies this problem in some of Spivak's works, criticizing Spivak's "Imperialism and Sexual Difference" and "Three Women's Texts and a Critique of Imperialism," for unintentionally exalting one colony, India, which results in an erasure of significant and crucial differences between colonial worlds. Chrissman argues that even when Spivak deals with specific "domestic/metropolitan texts such as *Jane Eyre*" she tends to use India as a privileged site of representation and conceptual paradigm. This leads to the "indirect elision of 'black' presence" displacing blackness on to a "generalised otherness" (Chrissman 1990, 40). The valorization of Spivak could lead to a similar substitution and result in a precarious displacement of other marginal postcolonial voices.

Consider the preface to the collection of interviews where the voice of Sarah Harasym is heard only to be unheard. Harasym's preface exaggerates the figure of Spivak since it is a reductive editor's note that merely catalogs Spivak's contributions to the field of cultural studies. No doubt the interviews themselves function as "active critical commentary" (Spivak 1990, viii) and need few explanatory notes; however, the presence of Sarah Harasym (other than in her own interview of Spivak) is missing; also missing is a critical framework that situates the book historically and an examination of some of the controversies and contradictions generated by interviewers ranging from the Australian critic Sneja Gunew to the New Historicist Harold Veeser and a time span that covers a period of six or seven years in settings spread over three continents. The book hangs together by its name.

Spivak's position as a leading cultural and literary theorist requires us to engage critically with her various intellectual formulations that address in numerous ways the interconnectedness of the micro-politics of the academy and the macro-politics of imperialist narratives. If we fail to do so we are guilty of essentializing the position of a critic who above all rejects every notion of essentialism. For one example, there is an interesting relationship between the two interviews—"Strategy, Identity, Writing," conducted in Canberra, Australia, in 1986 and "The Post-colonial Critic," which took place in Delhi, India, in 1987. Although both discussions center on the problems and the politics of cultural self-representation and the need to critique one's position *vis-à-vis* the larger group within which one chooses to operate, the interview conducted by

the Indian women is seriously jeopardized by Spivak's refusal to respond directly to some of the more crucial questions concerning her privileged position as a renowned postcolonial critic in the First World. In the first interview, Spivak insists on a crucial factor essential in the "conscious struggle to win back the position of the questioning subject," not just in a "specific context" but in "terms of the much larger female constituency in the world for whom I am an infinitely privileged person. . . ." And it is in relationship to that broader constituency that one has to "unlearn" one's privilege so as to be able to speak to and be heard by "that other constituency" (Spivak 1990, 42). In the latter interview, Spivak is confronted precisely with a situation that should motivate the desire to unlearn her privilege—a challenging discussion with a group of Indian women intellectuals in India. Their first question sets the stage for what is now to me a familiar scene—you as opposed to us:
Q. "There are several questions that arise out of the way you perceive yourself ('The postcolonial diasporic Indian who seeks to decolonize the mind'), and the way you constitute us (for convenience, 'native' intellectuals)" (Spivak 1990, 67). Three corollary questions follow, raising issues of Spivak's position as a nonresident Indian *vis-à-vis* India, the "privileging of exile as a vantage point for a clearer perspective on the scene of postcolonial cultural politics," and finally the relationship between one's pedagogy and subject position in a markedly specific geographical-academic space. Spivak jumps on the initial binary opposition with which the Indian interviewers begin their interview—us the "native," you the "privileged" postcolonial Indian diasporic intellectual.

Spivak collapses the different spaces occupied by her and other less iconic postcolonial Indian-diasporic intellectuals in the United States and elsewhere. While I am not denying the importance of trying to undo these structures of opposition as a means of undermining the binary nature of Western enlightened discourse, Spivak's answer is problematic. She insists that she "constitutes" the Indian women intellectuals teaching/working in India "equally with the diasporic Indian, as a postcolonial intellectual." First, this suggests that the Indian woman intellectual working in India occupies a relatively analogous space to that occupied by Spivak in either India, America, England, or Australia. Spivak is absolutely correct when she asserts that "one can't quite articulate the space she herself inhabits" (Spivak 1990, 68). However, while it might be too facile a solution to "describe this relatively ungraspable space" in terms of us and them, or me and you, or even "I am thus and such and not thus"; what these "native" interviewers write and teach has greater immediate "political and actual consequences" given the Indian academic and political scene than what Spivak says and does either as a Professor in Columbia University or as a distinguished postcolonial scholar invited to occupy a visiting professorship at Jawaharlal Nehru University in India. Spivak does occupy a position of privilege, and in this interview she does not attempt to unlearn it. It is the interviewers' responsibility to gauge Spivak's resistance to the unanswered questions raised by the very notions of "distance and proximity between you and us" and move on to other issues.

Toward the end of the interview, Spivak once again reminds the interviewers to "meditate" on their own desires that seek to define her as a diasporic intellectual with the weight of "rarefaction and super subtlety" on her side so that they can define themselves as indigenous intellectuals whose realities "surely need connotations of a stronger and more formal intervention" (Spivak 1990, 71–72). Such a caution is well taken, and the interviewers move from the "solipsism of meditation" to the desire for a constructive communication with Spivak. Throughout this particular interview Spivak continues to shift the burden of investigation to the interviewers and never quite answers their questions so that the reader never experiences the kind of mutual, engaging, and dynamic discussions that she finds in the interviews with Sneja Gunew ("Questions of Multi-culturalism") and Angela Ingram ("Postmarked Calcutta, India"); the interviewers Rashmi Bhatnagar, Lola Chatterjee, and Rajeshwari Sunder Rajan are forced to move quickly and rather abruptly from one area of investigation to another. The subjects they introduce are provocative and should have generated a dynamic conversation; instead, Spivak dismisses a question about the inherent danger of the "regulative psychobiography for the Indian woman" as sanctioned suicide ending up as a master trope for the condition of the subaltern woman as being a mere "diagnostic point" of departure in her attempt to find an "alternative regulative psychobiography" that could operate outside both psychoanalysis and counter-psychoanalysis (Spivak 1990, 71). The interviewers try again, this time asking a question about the pragmatic usefulness of her recent work on the gendered subaltern subject. This too merits a brief, dismissive paragraph that does not really engage seriously with the issue raised. In this interview, a question is more often than not answered by another question.

Of all the interviews, "The Post-colonial Critic" is the least satisfying. Despite Spivak's admission that she wants to be instructed on how others "understand the complexities of [her] space as diasporic intellectual better than [she] can" (Spivak 1990, 69), she is annoyed and disturbed at the way she is perceived and her "space" examined and explained. In the other two interviews mentioned, "Postmarked Calcutta, India," and "Questions of Multi-culturalism," there appears to be a common ground between interviewer and interviewee that does allow for a mutually beneficial exchange of ideas—they (Spivak, Ingram, and Gunew) are all diasporic postcolonial intellectuals trying to engage in cross-cultural exchanges within the boundaries of a First World academic arena. The disagreements and conflicts between them are used as sources for further productive examinations of the differences and similarities between various multicultural discourses and the problems of cultural self-representations. When the indigenous Indian intellectuals search for a common ground with Spivak, it is not openly denied or negated but there is also no attempt made to discover such a space. Here Spivak's authority as a privileged diasporic intellectual invited to teach theory in India ends discussion and does not initiate dialogue.

In the interviews "Questions of Multi-culturalism," "Postmarked Calcutta, India," and "Practical Politics of the Open End," the authority of Spivak's personal experiences grounded in a material reality provide a boundary-breaking space, a "borderland" that allows the participants, who do not agree on all the issues, to "develop democratic processes for formulating collective postepistemological and postontological judgements." This then allows all participating in the discussions to learn "how to have *public* conversations with each other, arguing from a vision about the common ('what I want for us') rather than from identity ('who I am'), and from explicitly postulated norms and potential common values rather than from false essentialism or unreconstructed private interest" (Brown 1991, 80). On the other hand, in the interview "The Post-colonial Critic," a prevailing emphasis on identity politics leads to antagonism rather than a desire to argue "from a vision about the common."

However, even when one desires to argue from the position of "what I want for us," one needs also to be aware of the significant differences between the "I" and the "you" that constitutes the us. Unexamined benevolence is the danger. In the interview "Questions of Multi-culturalism," Spivak's anecdote of her encounter with an Air Canada employee at Heathrow who refuses to allow her to fly to Canada because she does not have a valid visa makes for an interesting exposition of the way one is variously perceived because of and despite one's nationality in different parts of the world. An Indian passport holder residing in the United States does not require a visa to enter Canada—"because of course an Indian resident in the United States would not, the thinking goes, want to become an illegal immigrant in Canada" (Spivak 1990, 65). She does not even require any other papers when she travels from Canada to London. However, the same person cannot enter Canada from London unless she has the proper entry visa—" 'Look here, I am the same person, the same passport . . .' Indian cultural identity, right? but you become different. When it is from London, Indians can very well want to jump ship to Canada" given the acceleration of racial problems in Britain (Spivak 1990, 65). The personal injury caused by such an insult—and the fact that Spivak could not attend her scheduled meeting in Canada—makes us aware of the problems inherent in dividing the world into us and them and predicating every "idiom of resistance" on the assumption that color and nationality act as universal, unchanging signifiers.

However, Spivak's bitter attack on the woman at the airport who recites the rules to her reiterates a structural politics based once again on the question "who I am." Spivak fails to take into account that the woman employee is a minor figure in an increasingly dictatorial bureaucracy and that she probably wields considerably less power in the global economy than Spivak herself. Asking the woman to change her words from "we can't accept you" to "the regulations are against it" might make Spivak feel better, but does it in any way change the status of the woman in question as Spivak suggests it does? The woman, who probably relies on the income generated by her job, will have to continue to maintain her status (if one can call it that) as a mere cog in a rather large and complex wheel. Are they then equal victims of a prejudicial government? Spivak's insistence on the necessity of using signification appropriate to the moment allows her to vent her bitterness on another white woman who, yes, would probably be shocked at the imperious bearing of a sari-clad woman telling her how to use the English language. On the contrary, one wonders if the Canadian representative is herself allowed the luxury for such careful semantic distinctions, and whether Spivak in this instance is not guilty of the kind of patronizing behavior that she so strongly argues against in other contexts of First World–Third World contact.[12] This anecdote, even while illustrating the denial of privilege based on one's ethnic/ political identity, raises serious questions about any politics of reading that ends up privileging one oppression over another. In this particular confrontation, race becomes the only criterion for the exploration of one's position in an exploitative system, thereby eliding the interrelatedness between race and class.

It is at this point in my analysis of Spivak's critical discourse of self-representation that I would like to insert the autobiographical account I referred to in the first section of this chapter. My desire to interrupt the straightforward analysis of Spivak's collection of interviews is motivated by a need to stop and suggest the importance of critiquing the category of personal "experience" by evoking one of my own. If, according to Spivak, it ought to be possible for cultural critics to "make visible the assignment of subject-positions" (Spivak 1987, 241), I would hope that a critique of my own failure to negotiate the structural complexities of identity formations might help identify the myopia inherent in her desire to erase crucial differences between variously negotiated subjectivities.

I returned to India after an absence of five years—a gruelling five years during which I obtained my Master's degree from one University, my Ph.D. from another, and finally a position as an Assistant Professor in a large state university. My time in India was spent entirely with my immediate family and the numerous relatives who took turns in inviting us for various meals—a traditional gesture of good will and hospitality. The space that I inhabited during my four-week stay was therefore largely homogeneous—most of my relatives and close friends belong to the upper middle class, are Westernized, and have either visited various parts of the United States and Europe themselves or else have very close ties with at least one person who lives abroad.[13] I of course inhabited this same space before I left in 1985; however, my presumption that I would be able to resume where I had left off was naive to say the least. Throughout my stay

there was a continuous struggle between my own desire to be perceived as the same and the resistance against this recuperative desire
that was the dynamic operative of the various individuals I inter-
acted with. Was this desire to return to an earlier mode of knowing
part of a larger desire to merely return home after a long stay of
absence or was it constitutive of the perennial problem facing those
who choose to live away from home? In Michael Ondaatje's words I
inhabited the space in-between, that space that epitomizes the anxious paradox of the postcolonial: "I am the foreigner. I am the prodi-
gal who hates the foreigner" (Ondaatje 1984, 79). I was repeatedly
designated not as a postcolonial, not even as an nonresident Indian,
but as a foreigner.[14] This designation was particularly shocking in its
complete unexpectedness. This was something that had never been
revealed to me in my conversations with friends and acquaintances
who had returned to India after a considerable period of absence. I
had heard numerous accounts of the distance that the nonresident
Indian is forced to face between her and the "resident" Indian—this
distance is not merely an analagous extension of the discrepancies
and differences that obviously underlie the experiences of trying to
mediate between separate cultural signifiers with their own configurations of meaning that the nonresident Indian is faced with on her
return home. It more crucially involves the circulation of the nonresident Indian in the circuits of a neo-colonial world as the fundamental signifier that can be quantified in terms of its economic
exchange value. Therefore the perception of nonresident Indians as
"loaded with money" because of the ever-diminishing value of Indian
currency is a common phenomenon in the homes and streets of
Calcutta. I was prepared for this; I thought I knew what to expect
and felt that I would be able to "deal with it" by representing myself
differently from those "other" Indians abroad. Within the immediate
circle of friends and relatives I was at least partially successful in
defending myself against allegations and perceptions that desired to
construct me as the "other." The conflict generated by my apparent
transgressive position in the discursive space delineated by those
that inhabited it from within the "resident" position participated in
the not unusual problematics defined by the structures of address
available in that space. There appeared to be only two positions that
I could take—either accept their vision of me as someone who must
have changed because of her alliances abroad or insistently question
their desire in wanting to perceive me as different. I attempted to

fracture the totalizing logic of their representational practices by othering myself from the stereotypical consolidation of the rich, nonresident Indian "subject." I did not own a home, I drove a second-hand car, I had not been able to return home for even a short visit in the five years as a student, and I probably would not be able to return for another three to four years. I was constantly engaged in decentering their ritual legitimation of the "true" Indian by deconstructing the horizon of their "social lifeworld" (Benhabib 1992, 226). I was always quick to undermine their single set of criteria by which they arrived at such universal consensus through a re-theorizing of the radical situatedness and contextualization of the "subject" which, I felt, might initiate an epistemological transformation in their discursive terrain of selfhood and identity. As is by now no doubt apparent, I was obviously very complacent about my ability to discursively reproduce my self in another temporal space. I completely failed to examine the ramifications and repercussions of my desire to situate my self through my "experiences" outside the boundaries of a geographically defined "Indian" space as both subject (agent) and object of a rationale for the transformation of representational practices. In trying to rupture the dialectic of a symbolic construction of identity based on the oppressive discourse constructed around the binary opposition of "us and them," I failed to acknowledge that my contestatory theory of "agency" was guided by a desire to be included in the community I had left behind as still "untainted" and yet contingent upon my differences from the nonresident Indian community that I claimed I was only marginally determined by.

Since returning to the United States, I have examined and reexamined the structural taxonomy that dictated what Keya Ganguly refers to as "the renovation of selfhood. . . . [she suggests] that the self is like a technology (in a Foucauldian sense) which, at any given moment, articulates a series of *realized* relationships" (30). My memory and investment in a past self and my desire to reaffirm it in a present continuous self reveals the contradictory and ambivalent nature of precisely such a desired mode of narrative construction.

What I still have failed to come to terms with, in an even half-hearted manner, is the attribution of the unacceptable (for me) apellation of foreigner. On the streets of Calcutta, whether I wore a saree, or jeans, or dresses; whether I was with my husband or with members of my family I was ninety percent of the time misperceived. As I would walk down Park Street, or Gaurihat, or Salt Lake I would hear folks around me whispering, *"bideshi, na Bideshi"* (foreigner, isn't she a foreigner?) or derogatorily *"dakh, dakh, shaada chamra"* (Look! white skin).[15] One incident was particularly painful: My mother and I after a long day of shopping were standing in front of a stall, drinking mango juice, when two men nearby started a heated discussion about my racial identity. One of them, certain I was a white foreigner, was trying to convince his friend who thought I could be part Indian (maybe a North Indian) about the infallibility of his position. When his friend continued to hesitate, he finally and forcefully asserted, "But look at her. Just look at her." His friend looked and was, I guess, convinced, since he nodded his head in agreement. In my desire to shock them out of their complacent assurance, I started to speak a little louder than usual in Bengali to my mother. I wished to stun them into recognizing me for a Bengali and thereby invalidate their assumptions about me. Their faces registered the desired shock, even perhaps a little shame at having been overheard and understood. I felt a sense of vindication, but too soon. As we started to walk away, I heard them marvelling at the ease with which, as a foreigner, I spoke Bengali. My use of the vernacular had not even come close to identifying me as an Indian, let alone a Bengali. I walked away chagrined and very unsettled about my position in a city that I had lived in for more than fifteen years, where I had received my Bachelor and Master's degrees at the University of Calcutta. I was not an Indian; I was not a nonresident Indian; I was not even a diasporic Indian. I was a foreigner who happened to be fluent in one of the many Indian languages.

The failure of recognition has resulted in a sense of loss, a displacement, that no autobiographical narrative can adequately explain and account for. However, my critical reaction to these and other similar encounters enabled me to question my investment in notions of an authentic, if you please, Bengali "self" that was natural and "given" and from which stable point I could then denaturalize my own position in a simultaneous yet differential plotting of multiple subject positions in academic critical discourses. The absence of any fixed term, in this case Bengali Indian, which had previously appeared to function as a transcendental signifier that could subsume as well as authorize a personal narrative that evoked the heterogeneous, multiple, and differential awareness of one's subject positions, produced a lacuna which made me examine the seriousness of the problem raised by Elizabeth Meese's concern that the "valorization of the personal . . . if elevated to law-in-itself, may become an exclusionary principle inhibiting other political actions—outside the private sphere, in the rest of or in other parts of the world" (Meese 1989, 253). In his reply to Meese's essay, R. Radhakrishnan explores the significances of a productive juxta-position of the personal and political through a critical examination of the spatial orientation of identities.

> I wish to argue that the structuralist rhetoric of "positionality" does not have to result in empty allegorical readings of his-tory, but instead can be used to sensitize our awareness of historical process as *chrono-topic*. . . . If one's sense of identity in "one's own time" endows the "self" with a sense of personal authenticity, a spatialized perception of one's own personal identity leads to the realm of the "political" which necessarily relativizes and/or sublates the *personal as such*. (1989, 281)

In response to Terry Eagleton's caution (quoted by Meese in her essay) that "political struggle cannot be reduced to the personal, or vice versa," Meese asks the question, "What then is the excess, the 'more than' the personal which constitutes The Political (not as reduction) or the political-taken-personally?" (Meese 1989, 254). Meese's answer suggests that we must constantly be critical of our complex relationships even as we inhabit the "site of struggle in/between the self and the world." Radhakrishnan enunciates the precarious predicament of each one of us trying to inhabit this tenuous space even as he explores the dialogical progressive poten-tial of this spatial tension.[16] The refusal to naturalize the "I," the deliberate undercutting of the notion of a single identity realized in the delineation of the constituted nature of one's subjectivity epito-mizes the crisis of living in tension and living as tension. However, the risks of self-absorption that often accompany the desire to talk about oneself can lead to only a superficial denial of the essential core that has for centuries characterized the humanistic definition of a pure self. It is not enough merely to implicate oneself in one's readings; the awareness of the critical interpreter's role in the continuous production of meaning as she chooses to position herself should affirm the cultural, racial, sexual, and political inter/intra reality of her identity and that of those around her. Spivak, in her interview "The Post-Colonial Critic," and in her recounting of her experience with the female official at the airport, fails to recognize and thereby affirm the simultaneity of oppressions, and the politics of her reading does not engage with the multilevelled, dialogical axes of organization of sexual, racial, cultural, national, and economic differences that construct one's subjectivity.

Just as the security provided by the symbolic economy of the autobiographical sentence needs to be constantly realized as heterogeneous to itself in order to prevent its reduction to a simplified trope; just as the failure to question the inherent essentialism rendered invisible in the authorizing account of one's "experience" erases the power imbalances made available through the very structures of address in a personal narrative, so too postcolonial intellectuals must realize that we are all spokespersons for our often conflicting and various points of view. And while we must unite to make visible hitherto unrepresented personal, social, and historical structures, we can do so by being critical and yet accepting of our differences and similarities, and not subsuming our own typographies and our own voices under one pure voice. I have provided in this chapter a few examples of the way in which Spivak's own texts can generate dialogues, and if the interviews were put into some kind of context with her other crucial and significant contributions, I believe that what Sarah Harasym suggests this collection might do would actually have been at least partially achieved—provide a "sustained critical discussion of her work" (Harasym 1990, vii)— something that is curiously absent in postcolonial theoretical and discursive analysis. Though the usefulness of her scattered and diverse interviews in one space is undeniable, the manner in which this collection is assembled promotes a further iconization of the postcolonial critic Gayatri Chakravorty Spivak. This prevents the necessary continuous interruption of the term "postcolonial."[17] We need to investigate our own status as subjects and objects of the postcolonial phenomenon. Postcoloniality is itself, as we know, an artificial and ultimately misleading conglomerate of radically disparate cultures and texts and its heterogeneity must regularly and arduously be affirmed.

POSTSCRIPT: When an essay originally published in 1992, and written in 1991, is to be included in a collection to be published in

1999, the question of beginnings is something that a writer must confront. In the preface to his book, *Beginnings: Intention and Method,* Said succinctly captures the dilemma of attempting to define beginnings. What makes a definition of beginnings difficult is its ideational connection to a whole "complex of relations" (Said 1975, 5–6) and its paradoxical theoretical and philosophical status as both a kind of action and an originary moment for future action. Thus "the beginning, then, is the first step in the intentional production of meaning" (Said 1975, 5) as well as "an activity which ultimately implies return and repetition rather than simple linear accomplishment, that beginning and beginning-again are historical . . . that a beginning not only creates but is its own method because it has intention" (Said 1975, xvii). I use Said's meditations on beginnings to open up a space wherein I can speculate not only on the makings of my earlier essay but also on the status of the postcolonial critic, which was ostensibly the subject of the text.

The initial essay was commissioned for a special issue on Philosophy and Language for *Hypatia: A Journal of Feminist Philosophy.* As a feminist postcolonial critic, the connections between a feminist theoretical and pedagogical practice and language is always at the center of any critical enterprise I undertake. Thus, an engagement with a collection of interviews titled *The Post-colonial Critic* seemed apposite precisely when postcolonial studies was being consolidated as an emergent discipline. The disciplinary status of a field of study can often be measured, as we all know, by a proliferation of various stances and its concomitant distillation in the voices of its central figures. I understood the publication of the scattered interviews of Gayatri Chakravorty Spivak as a textual production of one such seminal moment in U.S. academic history and thus wished to interrogate and contextualize its location through a postcolonial feminist praxis.

Since the publication of Spivak's interviews, however, one can identify a certain trend in postcolonial critical studies characterized by a failure to engage cogently with many of the key tenets articulated by Spivak, as significant for a politically charged postcolonial epistemology. At her best, Spivak's methodology skillfully combines scrupulous readings of Marx and Derrida with a politically nuanced international feminism that constantly negotiates the material grounds of theoretical productions without providing an easy and coherent narrative. It is perhaps the absence of portable definitions in Spivak's work that makes it impossible to package her neatly and transport her easily to other sites of critical examination. Often framing her investigations as questions—"Can the Subaltern Speak?"—or as negative assertions—"Not Virgin Enough to Say That [S]he Occupies the Place of the Other"—or as "negotiations" and "scattered speculations"—Spivak's theoretical exegeses cannot be easily recuperated in one's own examination of a cultural performance or fictional text.

This is not to say that other postcolonial critics are working with simpler concepts and that Spivak is more difficult than, say, Homi Bhabha. Homi Bhabha has recently been apostrophized as the "master of political mystification and theoretical obfuscation" (Dirlik 1994, 334–335, n.6),[18] however, it is also true that certain theoretical and epistemic categories produced by Bhabha have been easily accommodated into the conceptual vocabulary of postcolonial theory and analysis. A number of critics in postcolonial and cultural studies are completely comfortable working with notions of mimicry, hybridity, migrancy, and the pedagogical and performative narratives of nations, citing the requisite essay in which these ideas had been initially unfolded by Bhabha. In fact, it is the free-floating signification of these unanchored categories that more and more seems to mark a critical essay as postcolonial (or even better as transnational) rather than an informed material-based theoretical examination of an epistemic formation particular to a location.[19] The publication of Bhabha's collection of essays under the title, *The Location of Culture,* captures the singularity of thought that characterizes much postcolonial examination. Bhabha locates culture "in the realm of the *beyond*," in the theoretically innovative narrative of the space of in-betweenness that according to him provides the "terrain for elaborating strategies of selfhood" (Bhabha 1994, 1). Inasmuch as he locates his desire to interrogate the culture of Western modernity from the postcolonial perspective, that postcolonial perspective appears to be cathected to the necessary injunction that seems to demand both the presence and the erasure of the in-betweenness of the post-Cartesian subject. A particular moment in Bhabha's Introduction captures this paradox: "As literary creatures and political animals we ought to concern ourselves with the understanding of human action, and the social world as a moment when *something is beyond control, but is not beyond accommodation*" (Bhabha 1994, 12). Bhabha privileges the momen-

tary possibility of accommodation in the "[t]hird space of enuncia-
tions . . . that carries the burden of the meaning of culture" (Bhabha
1994, 38) in the various literary texts he reads, from Conrad to
Morrison, from Harris to Gordimer, in order to assert that it is in
this third space that one can begin to envisage "national, anti-
nationalist histories of the 'people,' . . . [that] elude the politics of
polarity and emerge as the others of our selves" (Bhabha 1994, 38–
39). I believe it is this ultimately benign and celebratory aspect of
Bhabha's postcolonial praxis that allows him to be situated as today's
postcolonial critic.[20] A special session at the 1994 MLA devoted to
Homi Bhabha and his book *Location of Culture* marked precisely
such institutional recognition.

It is not my purpose here to pit one postcolonial critic against
another to see who comes out on top. Rather, it is my intention to
suggest one possible reason for a shift in emphasis from one critic
to another in a field defined as postcolonial. Despite the publication
of Spivak's second collection of essays, *Outside in the Teaching
Machine* in 1993, Bhabha's *Location of Culture* seems to have become the privileged text. I would maintain that though Spivak's
critical vocabulary still resonates in certain feminist circles, primarily non-Anglo-American, Spivak's theorization of the relationship
between cultural, economic, and political systems of value, her
attention to the gendered and racialized face of global capitalism,
her interrogation of the responsibility of the "academic/intellectual/
artistic hybrid" (Spivak 1993, x) makes her the outside, dissident
voice not only in Marxist and deconstruction circles but also among
a number of Marxist and deconstruction influenced/oriented male
postcolonial critics. Her emphasis on the power of the structures of
violence that constantly seek to undo the third space that Bhabha
so valorizes is clearly articulated in her recent engagement with
the necessary crisis confronted by intellectuals desiring to produce
an ethical praxis of knowing the other. She insists on recognizing
that despite careful readings of the manner in which material and
epistemic differences structure our responses to a text designated
as "other," even the most responsible and accountable of critics has
to learn to acknowledge the impossibility of a fully revealed and
therefore a fully graspable episteme of alterity.

In her translator's introduction to *Imaginary Maps,* Spivak underlines the political valence of a radical epistemology that hinges
on this recognition. I quote at length below to clarify that Spivak's

insistence that "on the other side is the indefinite" (Spivak 1993, 176) not be read as a recipe for inter/intra/multi-cultural paralysis but be construed instead as a significant political statement that will allow for a more principled and disciplined engagement with the workings of a differentially stratified raced/classed/gendered agency. Spivak courageously asserts that a multicultural and/or postcolonial critic must admit that "to theorize the political, to politicize the theoretical, are such vast aggregative asymmetrical undertakings: the hardest lesson is the impossible intimacy of the ethical" (Spivak 1993, 171).

> "Ethical singularity" is neither "mass contact" nor engagement with the "common sense of the people." We all know that when we engage profoundly with one person, the responses come from both sides: this is responsibility and accountability. We also know that in such engagements we want to reveal and reveal, conceal nothing. Yet on both sides there is always a sense that something has not got across. This we call the "secret," not something that one wants to conceal, but something that one wants to reveal. In this sense the effort of "ethical singularity" may be called a "secret encounter." . . . In this secret singularity, the object of ethical action is not an object of benevolence, for here responses flow from both sides. It is not identical with the frank and open exchange between radicals and the oppressed in times of crisis, or the intimacy that anthropologists often claim with their informant groups. . . . This encounter can only happen when the respondents inhabit something like normality. . . . [I]t is impossible for all leaders (subaltern or otherwise) to engage every subaltern in this way, especially across the gender divide. This is why ethics is the experience of the impossible. (Spivak 1995, xxv)

This long quote returns me to my initial evaluation of the collection of interviews. My purpose there was: 1) To address the consolidation of the postcolonial critic by the compiler, who failed to provide an adequate theoretical argument framing the need and importance of precisely such a collection. I perceived the desire to let the interviews stand without much more than a prefatory editorial note as a failure to engage with the production of situated knowledges and as a sign of the systemic failure to engage productively with the body of Spivak's work; 2) to generate a critical conversation by broadly outlining some of the points of conflictual contact between different interviews and at times between interviewer and interviewee. In 1991 certain Spivakian phrases had gained tremendous currency, especially in feminist circles. Two, which still retain their critical popularity, are "strategic essentialism" and "unlearning one's privilege." In my assessment of two of the interviews, "The Post-colonial Critic," and "Questions of Multi-culturalism," I tried to raise issues crucial to feminist thinking about language and how to use it in a provocative and compelling way. I felt it important to point out that despite Spivak's periodic success at negotiating structural complexities of identity formations, the translation of an epistemological apparatus based on strategic essentialism and the dictum to unlearn one's privilege into politically fruitful practice is fraught with difficulty. I also believed and still do that Spivak in these two interviews had failed to confront or overcome her own myopia.

I read certain threads in Spivak's recent work as an endeavor to grapple her own theoretical way out of this particular miasma. In the interview that opens *Outside in the Teaching Machine,* Spivak underlines the particular historicity of the initial phrasing of the critical phrase "strategic essentialism" in relation to her evaluation of the work of the Subaltern Studies Group.[21] She then censures the easy proliferation of the term within mainstream U.S. feminism. Spivak issues a warning that could easily apply to her own previous unsuccessful use of the strategy *vis-à-vis* not only the Indian intellectuals who conducted the interview in "The Post-colonial Critic" but also in relation to Spivak's interaction with the white, female, Air Canada employee. She says, "[t]he strategic use of essentialism can turn into an alibi for proselytizing academic essentialisms. The emphasis then inevitably falls on being able to speak from one's own ground, rather than matching the trick to the situation, that the word strategy implies" (Spivak 1993, 4). She reminds us that "strategies are taught as if they were theories, good for all cases. One has to be careful to see that they do not misfire for people who do not really resemble us and do not share the situation of prominent U.S. universities and colleges" (Spivak 1993, 4).

It is in the spirit of my own careful and charged negotiations with Spivak's work and my indebtedness to her brilliant formulation that "the most intimate alterity or otherness defines and offers up our so-called selves to ourselves" (Spivak 1993, 142) that I added the auto-biographical anecdote. I hope my critique of Spivak's own lapses is balanced by a critical examination of the failure of the tools of postcolonial feminism to help me negotiate my own set of identities on my first return home after five years in 1991. My struggle with my own myopic vision is a daily one and I see my ability to incorporate a quite upsetting personal experience as my way of giving critical voice to the diurnal struggle of negotiating with the realization that even though essences may be merely a kind of content "all content is not essence" (Spivak 1993, 18).

--- NOTES ---

1. This essay is a revised and expanded version of an earlier review essay, "Shifting Subjects Shifting Ground: The Names and Spaces of the Post-Colonial," about Spivak's collection of interviews, *The Post-Colonial Critic*. The original essay appeared in *Hypatia: A Journal of Feminist Philosophy*.

2. Chandra Talpade Mohanty's essay "Under Western Eyes: Feminist Scholarship and Colonial Discourse" (1984) criticizes a similar maneuver resulting from the use of the term "colonization" to depict any relation of "structural domination, and a suppression—often violent—of the heterogeneity of the subject(s) in question" (333). This, Mohanty argues, had led to an often simplistic production of the category of "Third World Woman" colonized as a "monolithic subject" in a number of Western feminist texts on non-Western women. The desire to produce and participate in the production of knowledge is crucial to any analytical enterprise that one is involved in; however, one must resist the temptation to indulge in the gratuitous appropriation of "cutting-edge" critical signifiers in order to be a member of a particular discursive field. See also Mohanty's essay "Cartographies of Struggle: Third World Women and the Politics of Feminism," in *Third World Women And the Politics of Feminism* (1991). In this essay she engages with, among other issues, the ways and means by which knowledge is produced about colonized peoples and "which/whose history do we draw on to chart [the] map of third world women's engagement with feminism" (3).

3. Of course, certain referents are not available to every individual. For example, an African-American woman can never designate herself as even metaphorically "white," even though politically and socially she might

have a number of interests common to a feminist, white woman with a real desire to unlearn her privileged status as white woman and disrupt the increasing complacency of the dominant culture's fixed oppositions. Even if a white woman does not respond to the "other" as irrevocably different; even if, to re-contextualize Gloria Anzaldua's words, she highlights similarities, downplays differences, establishes a syncretic relationship by "rapprochment between self and Other," the designation "white" evokes a strategic power never available to a woman of color. I wish to thank Kevin Meehan for his help in articulating this point.

4. Within the immediate walls of the academy I definitely inhabit the margins, and therefore the need to constantly position myself in relation to various power structures that constitute and are involved in the running of a department is a strategic impulse and device that constantly foregrounds all my activities as a member of those very structures which desire simultaneously to both include and contain that which is indicated as marginal.

5. As Lata Mani points out, "the relation between experience and knowledge [is] fraught with history, contingency, and struggle" (26). I am greatly indebted to Lata Mani's article "Multiple Mediations: feminist Scholarship in the Age of Multinational Reception." She does a brilliant exploration of the "questions of positionality and location and their relation to the production of knowledge as well as its reception" (25) in the three very different places that her work has been received. The essay is a remarkable tour de force that constantly moves back and forth establishing hitherto unnoticed links between personal memories, and the broader/larger discursive arenas of academic learning with their various political allegiances.

6. Homi Bhaba in his essay "The Commitment to Theory" (1988) presents a very convincing argument against the "binarism of theory vs politics." He argues for a "Third Space" derived from the "semiotic account of the disjuncture between the subject of a proposition and the subject of enunciation," which he suggests would lead us out of the trap enforced by a dualistic structure that can only espouse an either/or situation—the belief that the "Olympian realms of what is mistakenly labelled pure theory" are assumed to be "eternally insulated from the historical exigencies and tragedies of the wretched of the earth" (5).

7. My use of the term Third World encompasses not only those countries whose economic and political structures have been permanently deformed because of colonial and neo-colonial processes, but also "to black, Asian, Latino, and indigenous peoples in North America, Europe, and Australia." See *Third World Women and The Politics of Feminism* (1991,

ix). My definition relies heavily on the way the above anthology and its editors choose to use this much-contested term.

8. Other names of course come to mind—Abdul JanMohammed, Benita Parry, Edouard Glissant, Anthony Appiah, Sneja Gunew, Bruce Robbins, Edward Braithwaite, Ngugi Wa Thion'go, Mary Louise Pratt, Chandra Talpade Mohanty, Benedict Anderson, and A. Sivanandan. This list is by no means conclusive. But the three names mentioned in the essay from a kind of triumvirate.

9. It is interesting, though not surprising, to note that Gates ignores two very important essays that also participate in the same debate about and around the appropriation of Fanon for general postcolonial theory. Jenny Sharpe's essay especially foregrounds Parry's critique of Spivak, and her validation of Bhabha's position over that of Spivak's. Sharpe herself defends Spivak's position, which, she argues, "not only addresses the overdetermination of the colonial scene by race, class, and gender differences, but it also accounts for the subaltern woman as one who cannot be simply reduced to her class and caste position" (138). Jenny Sharpe goes on to provide a brilliantly articulated example of the "problems with identifying sites of colonial resistance" (139) by deconstructing the subject position of the pankhawallah in the by now famous court scene in Fortser's *A Passage to India*. The other essay, by Ketu Katrak, though not directly evolving the subject of the debate over the correct appropriation of Fanon and the possibilities of oppositional politics within the colonial encounter, provides us through an analysis of Fanon's and Mahatma Gandhi's texts "certain theoretical models for a study of women writers that will expand the narrow conceptualization of theory. . . ." and how this model would "make our theory and interpretation of post-colonial texts challenge the hegemony of the Western canon" (158). Both these essays, significantly, appeared in a special issues of *Modern Fiction Studies* in Spring 1989 devoted to Post-Colonial Literature.

10. Benita Parry, "Problems in Current Theories of Colonial Discourse" (1987). See also Sylvia Tandeciarz's "Reading Gayatri Spivak's 'French Feminism in an International Frame': A Problem for Theory" (1991), Laura Donaldson's review essay, "The Miranda Complex: Colonialism And The Question of Feminist Reading" (1988), and Laura Chrissman's article, "The Imperial Unconscious? Representations of Imperial Discourse" (1990). Since the earlier essay was published, Asha Varadharajan's book *Exotic Parodies: Subjectivity in Adorno, Said, and Spivak* (1995) attempts to evaluate Spivak's contribution to a feminist postcolonial practice and its limitations through a critical usage of the tenets of the Frankfurt School, especially Adorno.

11. A version of what seems to be the entire picture that appeared in an earlier Routledge catalog raises even more questions, some disturbing.

I cannot go into a detailed explanation of the actual picture here, but the woman in the picture is cradling a bespectacled white man and in the background there looms a bear. Shades of "Gone Primitive."

12. For a criticism of another instance where Spivak is discomfortingly patronizing see Sylvia Tandeciarz's essay, "Reading Gayatri Spivak's 'French Feminism in an International Frame': A Problem for Theory" (1991), especially pages 76–81.

13. In this respect, my visit was perhaps different from those of Lata Mani, Chandra Talpade Mohanty, and Gayatri Chakravorty Spivak who had opportunities to interact with Indian feminists, historians, and other intellectuals and activists. See Mani's "Multiple Mediations," Biddy Martin and Mohanty's "Feminist Politics: What's Home Got to do with It?"; Spivak of course has numerous references to various experiences in India.

14. I was subject to this naming by strangers—the men/women working on the streets, shopkeepers, people in restaurants, officers working in the banks where I went to change currency and so on.

15. I am an extremely tall woman, standing six foot one without heels, and of course I was the same height when I left India. I am not however "fair" by Indian standards, not dark complexioned but not quite "fair" either (by fair I mean close to the Western "white" skin). Also, I was always told how I had very "Bengali" features, whatever that may entail. My husband is white, and so initially I thought that by association they perceived me as a Westerner as well. But even when he left, and I, wearing a saree, would walk down a busy street downtown with my mother and perhaps a nephew or niece, I would still be characterized as a "white" foreigner.

16. Radhakrishnan questions his own reaction to the movie *Out of Africa* in this essay. This example serves as an instance of the need for postcolonial intellectuals to not hide behind race, class, and cultural barriers, but be willing to question our own investments in attributing certain subject positions to ourselves and others.

17. Trinh T. Minh-ha's cautionary reminder is appropriate here. Minh-ha suggests that as the critic positions herself she must always be conscious that "the moment [when] the insider steps out from the inside she's no longer a mere insider. She necessarily looks in from the outside while also looking out from the inside. Not quite the same, not quite the other, she stands in that undetermined threshold place where she constantly drifts in and out. Undercutting the inside/outside opposition, her intervention is necessarily that of not-quite an insider and not-quite an outsider. She is, in other words, this inappropriate other or same who moves about with always at least two gestures: that of affirming 'I am like you,' while

persisting in her difference and that of reminding 'I am different' while unsettling every definition of otherness arrived at" (1990, 73).

18. For a critical response to Dirlik's essay, in particular his easy dismissal of poststructuralist-oriented postcolonial critics see the essay by Schwarz and Ray titled, "Postcolonial Discourse: The Raw and the Cooked" (1995).

19. For a critique of the concept of migrancy and the liberatory aspects of the performative narration of nations by migrants see my essay, "Rethinking Migrancy: Nationalism, Ethnicity and Identity in *Jasmine* and the *Buddha of Suburbia*" (1996).

20. Tellingly, in a recent collection, *Literary India: Comparative Studies in Aesthetics, Colonialism and Culture* (1995), editors Patrick Colm Hogan and Lalita Pandit have republished an interview with Homi Bhabha significantly titled "The Postcolonial Critic."

21. The term *strategic essentialism* first surfaced in an essay that sought to assess the work of a group of South Asian historians called the Subaltern Studies Group. The essay, titled "Subaltern Studies: Deconstructing Historiography," was subsequently reprinted in Spivak's first collection of essays *In Other Worlds* (1987). In this essay, Spivak reads the work of the Subaltern Studies against the grain to underline its deconstructive historiographical aspects. Reading their desire to retrieve subaltern consciousness as an interjection of both colonial and nationalist historiographies, Spivak asserts that she would characterize the methodology of the Subaltern Studies Group as "a strategic use of positivistic essentialism in a scrupulously visible political interest" (1987, 205).

--------- *REFERENCES* ---------

Benhabib, Seyla. 1992. *Situating the self: Gender, community and postmodernism in contemporary ethics.* London and New York: Routledge.

Bhabha, Homi K. 1988. The commitment to theory. *New Formations* 5: 5–23.

———. 1994. *The location of culture.* London and New York: Routledge.

Brown, Wendy. 1991. Feminist hesitations, postmodern exposures. *Differences* 3: 63–84.

Busia, Abena P.A. 1989. Silencing Sycorax: On African colonial discourse and the unvoiced female. *Cultural Critique* 14: 81–104.

Chrissman, Laura. 1990. The imperial unconscious? Representations of imperial discourse. *Critical Quarterly* 32: 38–57.

De Lauretis, Teresa. 1988. Displacing hegemonic discourses: Reflections on feminist theory in the 1980s. *Inscriptions* 3/4: 127–144.

Dirlik, Arif. 1994. The postcolonial aura: Third World criticism in the age of global capitalism. *Critical Inquiry* 20: 328–356.

Donaldson, Laura E. 1988. The Miranda complex: Colonialism and the question of feminist reading. *Diacritics* 18: 65–76.

Ganguly, Keya. 1992. Migrant identities: Personal memory and the construction of selfhood. *Cultural Studies* 6: 27–40.

Gates, Henry Louis. 1991. Critical Fanonism. *Critical Inquiry* 17: 457–470.

Hartsock, Nancy. 1989–90. Postmodernism and political change: Issues for feminist theory. *Cultural Critique* 14: 15–34.

Hogan, Patrick C., and Lalita Pandit, eds. 1995. *Literary India: Comparative studies in aesthetics, colonialism and culture.* Albany: SUNY Press.

Katrak, Ketu. 1989. Decolonizing culture: Toward a theory for postcolonial women's texts. *Modern Fiction Studies* 35: 157–179.

Kipnis, Laura. 1993. *Ecstacy unlimited: On sex, capital, gender, and aesthetics.* New York and London: Routledge.

Mani, Lata. 1990. Multiple mediations: Feminist scholarship in the age of multinational reception. *Feminist Review* 35: 24–42.

Martin, Biddy, and Chandra T. Mohanty. 1986. Feminist politics: What's home got to do with it? In *Feminist Studies, Critical Studies,* ed. Teresa de Lauretis. Bloomington: Indiana University Press.

Meese, Elizabeth A. 1989. The political is the personal: The construction of identity in Nadine Gordimer's *Burger's daughter.* In *Feminism and institutions,* ed. Linda Kauffman. Cambridge and Oxford: Basil Blackwell.

Miller, Nancy K. 1991. *Getting personal: Feminist occasions and other autobiographical acts.* London and New York: Routledge.

Minh-ha, Trinh T. 1990. Woman, native, other: Interview with Pratibha Parmar. *Feminist Review* 36: 65–74.

Mohanty, Chandra Talpade. 1984. Under Western eyes: Feminist scholarship and colonial discourses. *Boundary 2* 12: 333–358.

———. 1991. Cartographies of struggle: Third World women and the politics of feminism. In *Third World women and the politics of feminism,* ed. Chandra Talpade Mohanty, Ann Russo and Lourdes Torres. Bloomington: Indiana University Press.

Ondaatje, Michael. 1984. *Running in the family.* New York: Penguin.

Parry, Benita. 1987. Problems in current theories of colonial discourse. *Oxford Literary Review* 9: 27–58.

Radhakrishnan, R. 1989. Negotiating subject positions in an uneven world. In *Feminism and institutions,* ed. Linda Kauffman. Cambridge and Oxford: Basil Blackwell.

Ray, Sangeeta. 1996. Rethinking migrancy: nationalism, ethnicity and identity in *Jasmine* and the *Buddha of Suburbia.* In *Reading the shape of the world: Towards an international cultural studies,* eds. Henry Schwarz and Richard Dienst. Boulder: Westview Press.

Said, Edward. 1975. *Beginnings: Intention and method.* New York: Basic Books.

Schwarz, Henry, and Sangeeta Ray. 1995. Postcolonial discourse: The raw and the cooked. *Ariel: A Review of International English Literature* 26: 147–166.

Scott, Joan. 1992. Experience. In *Feminists theorize the political,* eds. Judith Butler and Joan W. Scott. New York: Routledge.

Sharpe, Jenny. 1989. Figures of colonial resistance. *Modern Fiction Studies* 35: 137–155.

———. 1991. The unspeakable limits of rape: Colonial violence and counterinsurgency. *Genders* 10: 25–46.

Spivak, Gayatri C. 1987. *In other worlds: Essays in cultural politics.* London and New York: Methuen.

———. 1988. The political economy of women as seen by a literary critic. In *Coming to terms,* ed. Elizabeth Weed. London and New York: Routledge.

———. 1990. *The post-colonial critic: Interviews, strategies, dialogues.* Ed. Sarah Harasym. London and New York: Routledge.

———. 1993. *Outside in the teaching machine.* London and New York: Routledge.

———. 1995. *Imaginary maps: Three stories by Mahasweta Devi.* London and New York: Routledge.

Tandeciarz, Sylvia. 1991. Reading Gayatri Spivak's "French feminism in an international frame": A problem for theory. *Genders* 10: 75–90.

Varadharajan, Asha. 1995. *Exotic parodies: Subjectivity in Adorno, Said, and Spivak.* Minneapolis: University of Minnesota Press.

Part Three

The Power of Masculinist Metaphors

Words that Keep Women in Place

Natalie Alexander

---------- *8* ----------

Sublime Impersonation

The Rhetoric of Personification in Kant

As for scholarly women, they use their books somewhat like a watch,
that is, they wear the watch so it can be noticed that they have one,
although it is usually broken or does not show the correct time.

—Immanuel Kant, *Anthropology*

Introduction

Immanuel Kant's ethic is well known for its universalism; Kant
insists that all human beings have dignity, intrinisc worth, as
autonomous rational agents (1959, 42). Yet Kant's works also contain many bizarre remarks about women and their nature. Despite
men and women's shared nature, which includes the potential for
rationality, they are characterized very differently by Kant; for
example: "A young wife is always in danger of becoming a widow,
and this leads her to distribute her charms to all men whose for-
tunes make them marriageable; so that, if this should occur, she
would not be lacking in suitors" (1978, 218). His views about women
have often been dismissed as merely reflecting the mores of his time.
Yet his contemporaries also often found his views extreme, and dismissed them as views appropriate to a crotchety old bachelor. At any
rate, Kant's misogynism has historically been conceived as unrelated
to his core philosophical theories (English 1977, v).

243

As a means of entering this issue, I explore Kant's use of a certain cluster of rhetorical tropes; I look, in particular, at a group of rhetorical figures, generally identifiable as forms of personification, in which Kant indicates aspects of human nature in general by referring to specific individuals. For example, here is a passage that uses two such figures, personifying both the human species and nature: *"The means that nature uses to bring about the development of all of man's capacities is the* **antagonism** *among them in society....* Man wills concord; but nature better knows what is good for the species: she wills discord" (Kant 1983a, 31–32; Kant's emphasis).

Such passages appear throughout Kant's works, but most commonly in works that explore conditioned, empirical human experience rather than aiming toward pure synthetic *a priori* conditions; most of the examples I cite come from Kant's *Anthropology, Metaphysic of Morals, Critique of Judgment,* and several short essays, in particular, "Ideas for a Universal History of Mankind," "Speculative Beginning of Human History," and "On a Noble Tone in Philosophy." I am concerned with how the gender connotations of these rhetorical tropes inform both Kant's views about women and his interpretations of the philosophical ideas represented by these personifications.

What "Man" Does

The first examples of personification I explore are Kant's various employments of an individual human figure, in particular "man," when referring to universal characteristics of the species. For example, Kant opens "What is Enlightenment?" with the following: *"Enlightenment is man's emergence from his self-imposed immaturity"* (1983c, 33).

I classify these examples according to four sets of oppositions relevant to Kant's use of this figure: first, I discuss how Kant uses this personified "man" to distinguish two senses of "man," one, emphasizing nature (senses, instincts), the other emphasizing reason; second, I distinguish between collective reference to "man" the species and distributive reference to each and every "man"; third, I distinguish references to "man's" static nature from references to "man's" development; and finally, I discuss the relation of Kant's seemingly gender-neutral references to those which distinguish gender-specific traits.

Kant's uses of "man" often serve the purpose of sketching out the contrast between acknowledging the animal nature of human beings, subject to desires and inclinations, and extolling our capacity as rational agents, capable of acting on principle.

> In pragmatic consideration, the universal, natural ... [signification] of the word character is two-fold. ... The first is man's mark of difference as a creature with senses or a being of Nature; the second is the distinguishing mark of a reasonable being endowed with freedom.

> We can therefore say the first characteristic of the human species is man's ability, as a rational being, to establish character for himself. ... (1978, 245)

His valorization of reason reminds us that, despite his brilliant reworking of the faculties of perception, empirical understanding, and critical reason, Kant remains a typical Enlightenment philosopher in his radical distinction between sensation, desire, and heteronomy on the one hand, and reason, freedom, and autonomy on the other.

Kant's uses of this trope can also be distinguished according to their distributive or collective application. Some uses of this figure apply collectively to the species as a whole, as in the "Enlightenment" example. Others evoke "man" as every-man, attributing characteristics distributively to each individual human being, as does the attribution of a twofold nature.

> Whatever is derived from the particular natural situation of man as such ... or even from a particular tendency of the human reason which might not hold necessarily for the will of every rational being ... can give a maxim valid for us, but not a law. ...

> Now, I say, man and, in general, every rational being, exists as an end in himself and not merely as a means to be arbitrarily used by this or that will. (Kant 1959, 43, 46)

Both of these examples also illustrate the separation of reason from nature.

Kant explicitly invokes the distinction between collective and distributive scope in the context of describing the development of human rationality: "Man only expects from Providence the education of the human species in its entirety, that is, collectively *(universorum)*, and not individually *(singulorum)*, where the multitude does not represent a system but merely an aggregate collected at random . . ." (Kant 1978, 245). Indeed, the relation between the distributive and collective uses can lead to some odd grammatical problems; for example, in the passage quoted earlier: *"The means that nature uses to bring about the development of all of man's capacities is the* **antagonism** *among them in society, as far as in the end this antagonism is the cause of law-governed order in society. . . .* Man wills concord; but nature better knows what is good for the species: she wills discord" (Kant 1983a, 31–32; Kant's emphasis). The reference to "man's capacities" is distributive (as is the antagonism) applying to the abilities and inclinations of every person; note the plural "them" which immediately follows. But it seems to me that it is the species "man" that wills against nature's wiser dictates. (The personification of nature also illustrated here will be discussed in a later section.)

Kant's figures of "man" can also be divided into structural and developmental applications. In some of the examples quoted above, Kant discusses "man's" characteristics in order to give a static description of human nature as subject to instincts and inclinations or, in the contrasting sense, as rational. In others, he discusses "man's" development in order to disclose the process by which these faculties, especially that of reason, have developed. Note that while the static, structural emphasis tends to be associated with the distributive use—"man" for every man's essential nature—the developmental emphasis can be applied either to "man" the species, as when, for example, Providence educates the collective man, or to each "man," as when Nature uses every man's antagonism to bring about societies in which each is governed rationally by law.

Finally, a fourth distinction can be seen in these illustrations, between applications of the trope in which "man" seems to stand in generic relation to all humankind—as all the prior examples have done—and applications in which "man and woman" make gender differentiation explicit. I offer two examples of gender-differentiated versions of this personification; I will discuss these and other such tropes in greater detail in a later section of this paper.

The first trope characterizes marriage by analogy to the relation of minister and monarch: "But since the husband must know best how he stands and how far he can go, he becomes like a cabinet minister who wishes, first of all, to express his dutiful compliance to a monarch (the wife) who is only intent on pleasure, and who has begun a festivity or the construction of a palace" (Kant 1978, 224). Here we can see all the oppositions I have drawn in play. The nature/reason contrast has not surprisingly become gendered, with the wife/monarch associated with inclination (nature). The metaphor is also used in a static and distributive context, to explain the underlying essential structure of each individual human marriage.

In a Genesis-based allegory, Kant discusses the development of rationality in the species as a whole: "Indeed, one must begin with man as a *fully formed adult,* for he must do without maternal care; one must begin with a *pair,* so that he can propagate his kind; and one must begin with *only a single pair,* so that war does not arise . . ." (Kant 1983b, 49; Kant's emphasis). Here, we see the beginning of an extended allegory evoking Adam and Eve in order to discuss how rationality develops through initial movements of desire, inclination, instinct. The allegory is used in a collective and developmental context, to explain how a natural animal species developed a capacity transcending nature, the capacity for reason.

The Personification of Man?

Before turning to a closer exploration of these gendered examples, I must confront a possibly serious objection to my treatment of these uses of "man" as a rhetorical trope of personification, the objection that surely people don't think of this usage as a metaphor or rhetorical trope when they use "man" in this way. Furthermore, even if it originally had figurative force, it has become so common and ordinary a way to use the term that any figurative force has been lost. After all, this sort of use is cited in numerous dictionaries as a possible meaning for the term in a whole host of Indo-European languages, including, of course, both English and German. Finally, what could be the point of calling it personification, when the beings so described are already persons? There is seemingly no need to personify persons.

Indeed, I admit that this particular figure has become such a common and mundane one that it often passes for one of the literal uses of "man." What can be said about the distinction between literal and figurative language? How finely can it be drawn, if at all? And what philosophical significance can be attached to the distinction? On one hand, I have to reject the distinction outright. All language is ultimately figurative; every semantic term or syntactic rule of grammar or pragmatic pattern of discourse has a penumbra of connotative meaning which often cannot be sharply distinguished from any "core" denotative meaning. Moving to a common deconstructive view of language, I would further concede that it is in the nature of discourse that significance shifts and transforms along lines of interrelations, through the interconnected chains of signifiers meanings undergo indefinite substitutions, slippage, and transformation, further transforming the significance of the entire discourse (Derrida 1973, 88ff.).

On the other hand, it seems quite plausible to me that in limited contexts of ordinary usage, this distinction remains a plausible and potentially useful one. By what criteria can more or less literal language be distinguished from the more or less figurative? The intentions of the language user cannot serve as a useful criterion of meaning; language, whether figurative or literal, always bears meanings (both denotative and connotative) that are public, rule-bound, shaped by shared patterns of language use, which the individual language user helps to shape and modify but cannot simply dictate (Wittgenstein 1958, 26e, 94e; Moulton 1977, 131, 135–136). The notion of literal language as a faded or dead metaphor—literal language as cliché—may prove useful, but it begs the question of the criterion. By what criteria do we distinguish dead from lively metaphors? Has some sense of freshness, of new connections, of rich connotations playing a forceful role been lost?

Lexical meaning might offer another available standard to apply, yet is in one way completely beside the point; dictionaries merely offer reports of how particular populations at particular times are using particular terms. They do not offer theoretical grounding concerning the underlying nature of language; nor do they reflect to any great degree the role of so-called secondary or connotative meanings in the usage patterns they report. A common term like "man" could have—indeed I argue does have—quite common uses that nevertheless continue to operate in figurative ways.

One important characteristic of literal uses of language is that the literal definition can be substituted for the word without significant loss or shift of meaning, whereas in more figurative language such substitutions would alter meaning in some way. In most other contexts of normal usage, the substitutivity criterion works sufficiently well, if not perfectly. A failure of substitutivity would be a failure of literalness, a mark of figurative language.

This criterion has the advantages that it is not dependent on the users' intentions, that common lexical entries may still fall short of the criterion, and that, outside of narrowly defined formal contexts, there will be degrees of substitution possible depending on connotative resonances of the terms. At stake here is not the failure of substitutivity which might be revealed through a long and intricate deconstructive intervention, but rather an immediate, short-term, small-scale, and obvious failure which would lead to obvious ambiguities in meaning and equivocations in arguments.

One way to demonstrate failure of substitution—failure of literalness—is to reveal that the so-called gender-neutral usage actually fails to refer "neutrally" to women as to any member of the species, or, in the usage we are employing here, to include women unambiguously in the personified figure of man, that is, to include women clearly as members of the human species.

A further complication arises when we turn to the German terms Kant was using. English and German terms—English "man" but German *Mann* and *Mensch*—have similar but not identical use patterns. Where English employs "man" both to refer to a male human being in a gender-specific usage and to refer in a supposedly gender-neutral way to any individual member of the human species, German employs two terms: *der Mann* refers to an individual male person (parallel to *die Frau* for an individual woman); *der Mensch,* on the other hand, refers to any human being, in a usage similar to "person" in English. Indeed, Kant rarely uses *Mann,* and in all the passages I have explored so far, the terms at stake have been *Mensch* or grammatical variations on that term (e.g., *menschligkeit)* (1956, 1957, 1964).

In order to demonstrate my thesis that, however faded into quasi-literal meaning, the trope of "man" for "humankind" remains rhetorical, I shall argue that this usage differs in significant ways from the literal uses of "man" to designate any individual man, and that, nevertheless it has one important feature in common with the so-called generic use of "man" for any individual human being—the failure of literal substitution. I argue further that this trope follows the standard rhetorical pattern of synecdoche, of naming the part for the whole. In the next section of this chapter, I show that Kant's alternative versions of the trope, using a male/female couple, make it clear that the German *Mensch,* while literally "neutral," evokes the figure of a male person to represent the species. These four claims further attest to the rhetorical nature of this common trope of the personification of "man."

In its most common literal designation "man" refers to some specific male person. Whether the context is definite—"John is the man who introduced us"—or indefinite—"I met a man on my walk today"—the referent is some specific, individual, human being. Explaining literal meaning as substitutability Bertrand Russell summarizes the significance this way. "I met a man" means "I met x; and x is human" (Russell 1905, 479; Moulton 1977, 132). Whether singular or plural ("I met some men"), my point here is that reference to one or more specific individual male human beings could successfully be substituted for these uses of the term. Still considered literal is the nonspecific use that refers to some (as yet unspecified) individual male—"They are auditioning for a man to play Hamlet"—in which the term could meaningfully refer to any one of a number of male individuals. Even the verbal uses such as "Man the oars!" refer to placing individual persons in position to do the designated work. There is also the so-called generic use of "man"—which is usually considered a literal meaning—for any individual human being whatsoever, male or female, e.g., "All men are created equal . . ." or, if we believe Bertrand Russell, "I met a man."

The particular passages in Kant that I have called personification differ from all of these clearly literal uses in referring to the nature or development of the human species itself rather than designating some given member of that collectivity. The reference is often to the structure or development of essential species-wide characteristics. The gender-neutral example given above is similar to some of Kant's passages, except that it attributes a universal characteristic of equality to the collection of all individuals, so "men" in that passage continues to refer to individual human beings. Closer to Kant's use would be the seemingly gender-neutral remark, "The Neander-thal Man was a hunter . . ." to refer to a characteristic of the species (Moulton 1977, 130).

Kant's trope has one important feature in common with this last example—the failure of substitutability—the failure to refer unambiguously to some individual (if still unspecified) human being. Kant's rhetorical trope of "man," I argue, is rhetorically a metonym, in which one term is substituted for another. More specifically, it follows the rhetorical pattern of synecdoche, in which the part is named for the whole, identifying " 'microcosm' and 'macrocosm' " (Burke 1969, 5078–508). Clearly, it is a synecdoche in which an individual person is named in order to refer to the species to which that individual belongs; it is the use of the singular "man" to refer not to individual persons but to their species' essential characteristics or development that I have called personification—the true referent is precisely not an individual "man."

I turn now to the question of gender-specific and gender-neutral usage. In her paradigmatic work on the so-called gender-neutral use of "man," Janice Moulton argues that the rules shaping "man" and "woman" (or "he" and "she") are in some ways similar to those shaping unmarked and marked adjectives such as "tall" and "short" or "old" and "young." Just as "tall" can be used either to refer to one extreme of height or the whole range, while "short" always refers to the other extreme, "man" can be used to refer either to males or to persons in general while "woman" always refers to females; furthermore, in such situations, the higher status term (at least at the time of language acquisition) is the one granted unmarked status (Moulton 1977, 128–130). Nevertheless, unmarked adjectives differ from the neutral "man" in that syntactic context always disambiguates whether the term designates the range or its end of the range. For example, "How tall is she?" or "He's five feet tall" request or specify a genuinely height-neutral position within the range, while "He's tall for his age," or "She's the tallest center in the league," clearly refer to the tall end of the range.

Moulton argues that, because there is no such disambiguating context, the so-called gender-neutral terms are not successfully gender neutral. "If Russell were correct, then parents familiar with his theory would have no cause for anxiety if their young female child, on arriving home several hours late from kindergarten, said 'I met a man' " (Moulton 1977, 133). "The Neanderthal man was a hunter" seems gender-neutral, unless one continues, "The Neanderthal woman was a gatherer" (Moulton 1977, 130). She concludes that the so-called generic uses of man, including both explicitly figurative and seemingly literal, are examples of Parasitic Reference whereby a term that refers to "a high status sub-set of the whole class, is used *in place of* a neutral generic term" (Moulton 1977, 135).

Does the German *Mensch* provide just the sort of disambiguating context that would be required for a genuinely gender-neutral usage? While grammatical gender has no literal relation to sex, it remains true in German as in other languages employing grammatical gender distinctions, that most nouns referring to males are masculine and most referring to females are feminine. *Mensch* is masculine, and may therefore carry some connotations of referring to a male person. But my argument need not rest on such vague suppositions.

I have already argued that Kant's usage in these passages is genuinely rhetorical—a synecdochal trope naming the individual man to refer to the human species, naming the part for the whole. I have indicated, and will support more fully in what follows, that the "part" so figured is male. I explore several tropes, in other respects similar to those discussed, in which Kant explores gender distinctions. This exploration serves two purposes. First, these tropes reveal Kant's views on sexual difference and men's and women's roles in marriage and in human development. Second, they reveal—at least on a connotative level—that it is the figure of an individual man (male person) who is used to personify the human species, while the rhetorical use of the female figure is reserved for other purposes.

Any-Woman and Every-Man

I have mentioned earlier that Kant's views about women seem so at odds with his universalism, his insistence on the intrinsic dignity of all rational agents, that many readers have dismissed them as personal quirks or cultural baggage. His contemporary Goethe seems to have expressed this view when writing about Kant in a letter:

> In spite of all the excellent, acute and delightful things in which our old teacher always remains faithful to himself, it

seems to me narrow in places and in some illiberal. . . . The assertion that young women try to please all men so that after the death of their husband they have another suitor in reserve is a gag such as poor wits may dish out in society, and proper only for such a confirmed old bachelor. (Goethe 1963)

I shall argue that, on the contrary, Kant's views about women have a strange coherence when read in terms of his rhetoric of personification. I shall explore two passages, both explicitly metaphorical and both gendering the contrast between nature and reason. The first is a static, distributive account of marriage relations; the second, a collective, developmental account of the awakening of human reason.

Discussing the character of the sexes, and in particular their differentiated roles in marriage, Kant portrays woman as dominating and man as wishing to be dominated; woman as freed by marriage and man as losing freedom; yet he holds also that a husband can have domestic domination only so far as he does not fail to fulfill any reasonable demands. Asking who should have the highest authority in the home, Kant answers: "I should say in the language of gallantry (though not without truth): the woman should reign and the man should rule; because inclination reigns and reason rules" (1978, 220, 223). This familiar association of man with reason and woman with inclination is followed by an explicit simile that casts the woman as a thoughtless monarch:

> But since the husband must know best how he stands and how far he can go, he becomes like a cabinet minister who wishes, first of all, to express his dutiful compliance to a monarch who is only intent on pleasure, and who has begun a festivity or the construction of a palace. The most high and mighty monarch can do everything he wants under the provision that the minister will lend him a helping hand in carrying out his wishes, even if at present there is no money in the treasury and even if certain more urgent needs must first be attended to. (Kant 1978, 224)

Several fascinating features of this simile must be noted. First, it seems to be a largely instrumental account of reason in the service of inclination which is atypical of Kant. Second, it portrays the woman as dominating the relationship, but also as incapable of reasoning out for herself either the means to her ends or the other more pressing needs. So, in marriage, the husband must not only devise means to the wife's ends, but must also find ways to suggest to her the ends she ought attend to. As one friend of mine succinctly put it: even though women dominate, men are in charge. This emphasis on women's domination is a constant theme in Kant's discussions of gender, and often seems in his writings to constitute a fundamental distinction between men and women, in conflict with Kant's explicit theory of a common human nature.

What accounts for the difference of character and of roles in marriage that Kant attributes to men and women, if, as he says, they have a common potential for rationality and a common set of basic inclinations? He writes that "if two people, who cannot do without each other, have identical ambitions, self-love will produce nothing but wrangling. In the interests of the progress of culture, one partner must be superior to the other in a heterogeneous way" (1978, 216). Note how strongly this view contrasts with the autonomy and mutual respect envisaged in the voluntary association envisaged for the realm of ends (1959, 39–44). He continues: "The man must be superior to the woman in respect to his physical strength and courage, while the woman must be superior to the man in respect to her natural talent for mastering his desire for her" (1978, 216). So, men desire sexual access and women gain dominance by fending them off. Kant describes a painfully familiar scenario of patriarchy: man pursues, woman refuses (1978, 216–225). She yields on the condition of marriage; he protects her from other men, while she remains jealous of all other women and a coquette with all other men. Yet this scenario is given a strange twist of masculine submission in Kant's descriptions.

Many of the features I have discerned here emerge also in a passage ostensibly describing the unjust lust for power, which he in fact describes only minimally. Instead, he writes extensively about women's "indirect art of domination," which he contrasts as justifiable to (men's?) unjustifiable lust for power, because

it holds no authority of its own, but rather it knows how to rule and to fascinate the person into submission through his own inclination. This is not to say that the feminine part of our species is free from wanting to rule over the masculine element (just the opposite is true), but it does not use the same means to this end as the masculine. The feminine sex does not use the quality of strength (which refers in this context to domination), but rather the quality of charm which directs itself toward the inclination of the other sex to submit. (1978, 181)

Why is the masculine inclined to submit? That is the condition (within civilized society) of fulfilling his desire to dominate through sexual access to her. It seems clear to me that the contrasting desires Kant attributes to men and women can, in fact, be reduced to the first difference he attributes, that of physical strength; both desire domination, but while men may dominate directly, women, being weaker, must do so indirectly. Once having submitted, the husband, like the cabinet minister, must also learn restraint and indirection in order to guide the unruly monarch, his wife.

This passage highlights another key feature of woman's role according to Kant. She holds no authority of her own, but in educating a man in restraint of passion, she makes possible his exercise of reason. But to understand the full significance of this role, we must explore Kant's view not of the status of men and women, but of the role these differences play in the development of our human potential for rationality.

Kant argues that while "the feminine sex has to develop and discipline itself in practical matters," the masculine learns "sociability and propriety" in response to women's modesty:

[W]omen mature early and . . . demand gentle and polite treatment from men, so that they [men] would find themselves imperceptibly fettered by a child due to their own magnanimity; and they would find themselves brought, if not quite to morality itself, then at least to that which cloaks it, moral behavior, which is the preparation and introduction to morality. (1978, 220)

One might think that Kant would praise women's superior ability to achieve rational agency without relying on teachers; but instead, as we saw in the opening quotations, he disparages women's application of reason as misplaced and trivial.

Indeed, Nature, not woman, is given credit for devising these roles. "All machines, designed to accomplish with little power as much as those with great power, must be designed with art. . . . Nature's foresight has put more art into the design of the female than the male . . ." (Kant 1978, 216). Here, indeed, in a trope of depersonification, woman is described metaphorically as a machine whose purpose, far from being an end in herself, is the propagation and the socialization of the species.

Kant applies this special role of women as moral educators not only to the development of the individual man but also to that of the whole species. He embellishes the trope by using the paired figures of an original male and female couple, based on Adam and Eve, to represent the human species, in particular to figure forth our collective development of rationality. Kant notes that "one must begin with a *pair*, so that he can propagate his kind" (1983b, 49). He cannot be intending this account literally, for he couches the entire essay as conjectural, using both "a holy document as a map" and experience as a guide, he takes a "flight of imagination" (1983b, 49, 60, n.1).

Furthermore, in the *Anthropology*, Kant casts doubt on the literal interpretation of Genesis:

> The assumption that an already developed first human couple was placed by Nature in the midst of food supplies, and not provided at the same time with a natural instinct which we in our present natural condition do not have, is difficult to reconcile with Nature's provision for the maintenance of the species. The first man would drown in the first pool he saw . . . (1978, 239)

This passage, which never quite explicitly denies the literalness of the Genesis story, turns upon the difficulties of accounting for the emergence of reason from natural instinct. In a nearby footnote, Kant does explicitly endorse Linné's quasi-evolutionary doctrine of gradual development of climatic variation and of plant and animal species, including, I presume, the human species (1978, 240, note).

Therefore, it is clear that Kant's use of the Genesis-based "original pair" is self-consciously rhetorical; yet, the usage is quite parallel to the seemingly gender-neutral tropes of "man" discussed earlier. That is, the allegory is a developmental account of the collective differentiation of reason from origins in instinct. In the opening passage which concerns us here, Kant elucidates four steps toward rational agency: First, the ability to eat fruit one imagines to be tasty rather than only that dictated by instinct; second, the ability to intensify sexual desire by use of coverings which incite imagination; third, the ability to anticipate the future; and fourth, the ability to see other things as means to one's ends, to see oneself as end in oneself (1983b, 50–53).

It is the second step that most concerns us here. "The fig leaf (Gen. 3:7)" by activating the imagination serves to prolong, increase, and make more constant human sexual attraction:

> For making a propensity become more internal and obdurate by removing the objects of the senses [from view] already displays consciousness of a certain mastery of reason over the impulses. . . . *Refusal* was the feat whereby man passed over from mere sensual to idealistic attractions, from mere animal desires eventually to love. . . . In addition, *decency*—a propensity to influence other's respect for us by assuming good manners (by concealing whatever could arouse the low opinions of others, as the proper foundation of all true sociability—gave the first hint of man's *[des Menschen]* formation into a moral creature. (Kant 1983b, 52; Kant's emphasis. Cf. 1991, 85–102)

This passage is explicitly allegorical. Like the seemingly neutral uses of *Mensch* discussed above, it is synechdocal—a part (the first pair or the first man) is named for the whole (the human species); it is personification, as the species is personified in the form of one original man, or one original pair—man and woman. Like many of the earlier examples, it is collective, developmental, and focused on the differentiation of reason and desire. This parallel attests to the non-literal nature of those earlier uses. And if, as I argue in what follows, the usage in this passage fails to maintain a consistent relation between universal and gender-differentiated humanity, it further attests to the same failure in the so-called neutral or universal tropes discussed above.

One of the first things one notices in this passage is the almost complete absence of personal subjects. Having begun the essay with a pair *(einem Paare)*, Kant immediately switched back to the singular *(der erste Mensch)*. Indeed, by the time he reaches the second step, the pair has so thoroughly disappeared that he must resort to somewhat awkward abstract and passive locutions (1964). We may well ask: Whose propensities and impulses? Whose refusal and decency? And who is concealing what from whom? What insights is Kant hiding from himself with the fig leaf of his abstract language?

Lest we should imagine that Adam veils himself modestly from Eve's importunate desires, I point out the only two places in which men and women are explicitly distinguished in this allegorical text. In a passage near the end of the essay, Kant remarks on the shift from a herding to an agrarian economy, by noting the temptation of luxury and the art of giving pleasure "in which the village wives [*Weiber:* women or wives] eclipsed the filthy desert girls [*Dirnen:* girls or prostitutes]" (1983b, 57; 1964, 83–102). The other reference is even more telling, for it follows as a direct result of the second step of refusal and decency; in the third step, Kant discusses the ability of the husband *(der Mann)* to anticipate the future in providing his mate *(eine Gattin)* and future children with food; while the wife *(Das Weib)* foresees "the difficulties to which nature had subjected her sex, as well as the additional ones to which the more powerful husband *[Mann]* would subject her. Both foresee a life of toil leading to death which arouses the hope of paradise; anticipation of the future is the third stage in human progress toward reason" (Kant 1983b, 52–53; 1964, 83–102). Somehow, Kant could not refer to a woman explicitly until—after the second stage—he had gotten her into her proper patriarchal place; only then was it safe to mention her.

Clearly then, Kant views this relation according to his version of the standard patriarchal pattern. It is men's sexual propensities that are altered, intensified but controlled, by women's refusal; it is men's desire, but women's bodies as sexual objects, that must be veiled for decency's sake. Kant's own veiled propensity to return to the singular *Mensch*, even more than his overt disparagement of women's capacity for reason, attests to the insight that it is man in the gender-specific sense to which he is truly referring in discussing *der erste Mensch*. Woman disappears behind the fig leaf of abstract and passive locutions, and reappears only when needed for some functional role. Once again, Nature, not woman, is credited for devising these steps of progress toward rationality. On the level of species, as of individual, women serve as Nature's mechanism—a means to the ends of man.

Kant and His Two Mothers

In this section, I will be working once again with the Kantian dichotomy between nature and reason. First, I discuss several passages in which Kant personifies nature, then I explore an explicitly gendered personification of Mother Nature as the veiled goddess Isis. Finally, I discuss a passage in which this same figure of the veiled goddess represents the rationality of moral law.

Kant discusses nature in two different but related ways—and uses personification in both; on one hand Kant writes of nature as human nature—for example, our emotions, desires, and instincts—in order to describe human character. On the other hand, he also writes of nature when referring to the entire phenomenal realm that people perceive about them. While they differ in scope, both pertain to the phenomenal, causal realm; both are that which human beings transcend through freedom, that is, through the development and practice of rational agency, practical reason. In both applications, Kant personifies nature, in order to describe human character and development in *teleological* terms and in order to evoke in students a proper awe and respect for nature as *sublime*.

I've tried here to follow the practice of most translators and capitalize "Nature" in cases of personification while leaving the literal use of the abstract noun as "nature." Nature, in this sense, is an abstract concept and therefore, like many abstract nouns in German, *die Natur* is feminine in its grammatical gender—and capitalized, like all German nouns; how then can some passages be identified as personification and others as literal uses of the term? I chose to consider uses as personification which attributed personal actions to nature, such as "voice," or deliberative action, forethought, plans to Nature as if a singular entity; in addition, references to "Nature's womb" or naming "the veiled goddess Isis" to refer to nature are clear cases of personification.

In the *Anthropology*, Kant discusses human nature as it pertains to the character of the individual person, of the sexes, of nations, of races, and of the species. In discussing individual character, Kant discusses various humors of natural temperament without resorting to personification, until he wants to distinguish a second sense of "character," one linked to the faculty of reason. "Here it does not depend on what Nature makes of man, but what man

makes of himself" (1978, 203). He then engages in a lengthy discussion of physiognomy, again without resort to personification.

In his discussion of the species, on the other hand, he informs us
of what "Nature has willed" and Nature's "plans" for "our departure from Nature" and war as "the device of Providence" to bring
us to a rational, law-governed society (1978, 238, 243, 248). But in
contrast, with reference to the character of nations, Kant romps
through the national and ethnic stereotypes of his day concerning
various European nations without any need for personification. He
does hold that the English have developed a national character,
having none "by nature," but this remark, however amusing, does
not meet the criterion for personification.

Kant's discussions of racial and sexual character are marked by
the almost constant appeal to a personified Nature. In discussion
of race, Kant holds that, in opposition of any "melting together of
various races, Nature has here made a law. . . . Nature has pre-
ferred to diversify infinitely the characters of the same stock . . . "
(1978, 236–237). In discussion of sex, Kant states that "we can only
succeed in characterizing the feminine sex"—the masculine sex is
apparently not in need of characterization—"if we use the principle
which served as Nature's end in the creation of femininity, and not
what we have devised ourselves as its end. Since this end must still
be wisdom according to Nature's design . . . these ends are 1) the
preservation of the species [and] 2) the improvement of society and
its refinement by women" (1978, 219). Notice that in the case of race
and sex, Kant poses these differences as relevant to someone's actions toward people so characterized, whereas with the national or
individual character (possibly of white men), similar differences were
not so characterized. Kant seems to resort to personification in precisely those places where he wants to justify an otherwise unjustifiable
distinction within the universal dignity of humankind.

Kant personifies our human nature, our place within the animal
kingdom, in order to evoke a natural teleology. Several of the passages in which previously I focused on the personification of "man"
also evoke this personified Nature. It is the personified Nature who
"wills discord," using human antagonism as a means to the development of a rationally governed society (1983a, 31–32). It is Nature
who has crafted woman to preserve the species and make individuals more civilized. "All machines designed to accomplish with little

power as much as those with great power, must be designed with art. Consequently, one can assume beforehand that Nature's foresight has put more art into the design of the female than the male . . ." (Kant 1978, 216). This passage resonates with an irony that is at once delightful and disturbing. Nature is personified as possessing reason—foresight, design, and art. Women are depersonified as being a machine, designed for a specific purpose—not fully an end in herself. Although the personified Nature is not explicitly gendered in this passage, the irony is doubled if we conceive of Nature here as Mother Nature.

In his Genesis allegory, Kant writes of the species' development of reason. His tropes slide from one to the next: "Instinct—that voice of God that all animals must obey. . . . this call of Nature. . . . the voice of Nature. . . . man's release from Nature's womb." (1983b, 49–53). Here it becomes clear that nature is personified as female—as Mother Nature. And like a good mother, she is raising humanity to become independent of her. As the human potential for reason, which is a natural potential, gradually becomes the actual practice of reason, Kant gradually shifts to a personified Reason as the agent of its own development: Not yet personifying reason, Kant argues that some experience with fruit "could have given reason the first occasion to play tricks on the voice of Nature" (1983b, 51). But after Nature's use of "the instinct for sex," Kant goes on to describe "Reason's third step" and "the fourth and final step that Reason took in raising mankind altogether beyond any community with animals . . ." (1983b, 52). Once again, here on the level of the whole species, we see the distinction between reason and instinct, and the developmental emphasis with the educative role belonging to a feminine figure.

So a familiar pattern emerges with a new twist. Kant uses the rhetoric of personification when he wants to emphasize the contrast between nature and reason, human (or does he mean men's?) development from nature to reason whether as individuals or as a species. A new element of that pattern is here brought to light; Kant uses the rhetoric of personification when he wants to justify a difference in treatment that could not otherwise be justified in terms of universal human dignity. The personified Nature's end for the personified Man, is man's escape from nature; Nature makes man fit for reason, gives us the potential, but the actual exercise of reason frees man from Nature's tutelage or bondage, frees man from Nature's womb. Like the sovereign who follows the minister's suggestions, like the wife who dominates only at the expense of refusal and indirection, Nature conspires in her own overthrow.

In addition to evoking a teleological aspect of nature, Kant also links nature with the sublime; as the dynamically sublime, for example, we represent God with images of nature's might (Kant 1969, 113). We experience the sublime when we represent something that is beyond the phenomenal through aesthetic (phenomenal) means, something *"absolutely great"* (Kant 1969, 106). Our imagination attempts to figure forth that which is unfigurable, beyond perception or phenomenal understanding. When we grasp a representation it is necessary that we comprehend it as a whole in intuition; yet that is precisely what is impossible. Therefore, the sublime evokes a feeling of respect, defined as "a vibration of repulsion and attraction," the "conflict of imagination and reason," or a "feeling of our incapacity to attain to [i.e., adequately represent] an idea that is a law for us" (Kant 1969, 105–109; Cf. Kofman 1982). In the last two tropes I will explore, evocation of respect for the sublime combines with Kant's view on women's roles in educating "man" (Cf. Kofman 1982; Alexander 1998). Kant employs the figure of a veiled goddess in two passages, one personifying nature, the other, reason. Although the fig-leaf has been replaced by a veil, the feminine nature of this figure is crucial to both tropes.

Rhetorical tropes, especially personification, appear rarely in *Critique of Judgment*. Yet, in a footnote, Kant offers a trope of personification: "Perhaps there has never been a more sublime utterance, or a thought more sublimely expressed, than the well-known inscription upon the temple of *Isis* (Mother *Nature*): 'I am all that is, and that was, and that shall be, and no mortal hath raised the veil from before my face.'" (1969, 179, n. 1; see also Kant 1979, 215; 2: 151). Here applied not to human nature but to the physical cosmos, to nature writ large, is the personification of nature as Mother Nature, further, as the goddess Isis. This representation is sublime in part because the universe represented by the veiled goddess cannot be fully expressed by the representation. Kant's footnote continues: "*Segner* made use of this idea in a suggestive vignette on the frontispiece of his Natural Philosophy, in order to inspire his pupil at the threshold of that temple into which he was about to lead him, with such a holy awe as would dispose his mind to serious attention" (1969, 179, n. 1). The holy awe is that oscillating attraction and repulsion of respect. The representation is sublime not only because the universe represented by the veiled goddess cannot be fully expressed by the representation, but also because it cannot be fully encompassed by the natural science through which the student attempts to lift her veil.

So, nature as a sublime object is characterized as a divine and perpetually veiled woman. Just as in the case of Eve and her fig leaf of modesty and decency, nature's reticence prompts more serious and rational attention. But is it legitimate to spin out and embellish Kant's personification in this way? Kant himself warns of the dangers of taking the representation too seriously.

I have already discussed the nature of gender relations as envisaged by Kant; clearly, the context is overtly heterosexual. If nature is the sublime veiled Isis, then the student standing before her in awe, trembling with a mixture of attraction and repulsion, must be male. Unpacking this personification, the student of nature, the knowing subject, is, for Kant, a man. Whether the specific term used is *Mann* or *Mensch,* the logic of the trope requires the male for whom the woman's body remains a mystery, at once desired and abhorred.

In his discussion of the sublime, Kant clarifies not only the dangers of representations, but also the distortion involved in taking any objective reality as sublime (1969). To evoke Mother Nature for nature is to invite distortion; similarly, to take nature as sublime is also ultimately a distortion, a displacement from which alone is *truly sublime:* the rational subject (1969, 91–92).

Kant again evokes the mother figure of a veiled goddess in quite a different context when he personifies the moral law of practical reason in "On a Newly Arisen Superior Tone in Philosophy" (1993, 71). He is arguing against the existence of an intellectual intuition or of a higher sentiment which could give direct aesthetic insight. In particular, his opponents are a group of Christian sentimentalists who have conceived a new "enthusiasm" for Platonism (Kant 1993, 72–75; see notes to the text for the historical background).

In this essay, Kant personifies reason itself as the commanding voice of duty: "Now, every human being finds in reason the Idea of duty, and trembles as he listens to its adamant voice when inclinations, which try to make him deaf and disobedient to this voice, arise within him" (1993, 68). The distinction between reason and inclination is sharpened by personifying reason, but not the inclinations; we can also observe here a distinct parallel with nature as the "voice of God."

Kant writes, perhaps somewhat ironically, of the conflict between himself and the enthusiasts: "But what is the good of all this conflict between two parties that at bottom share one and the same intention: to make people wise and virtuous?" (1993, 70). Adding in a now familiar trope of personification: "The veiled goddess before whom we of both parties bend our knees is the moral law in us, in its inviolable majesty. We do indeed perceive her voice and also understand very well her command" (1993, 71; see also Kofman 1982, 51–52). The similarities with the personification of nature are obvious; the differences, perhaps more subtle. Kofman argues, for example, that this trope fails to meet Kant's own criteria for an ethical and non-distorting representation of the sublime (1982, 50–53).

The figure is veiled—like Mother Nature—in order to represent the unrepresentability of the moral law. Also like Mother Nature, this figure employs a voice that commands obedience; but here, it is the not voice of God, but "the voice of reason"—of the moral law (Kant 1993, 68); Kofman 1982, 53). Furthermore, the figure is veiled—like Eve—in order to evoke a restraint, a civilizing influence. The context of gender relations so evoked remains overwhelmingly heterosexual. So, the parties kneeling before her—whether the philosophers of opposing schools or more broadly, all moral agents— are figuratively gendered male.

But unlike nature as Isis, whose veils the students lifted by study of science, this figure, the moral law as Isis, remains inviolable. One should not attempt to master or violate her. Yet, what precisely does this figure represent—the moral law, the nature of practical reason in the human mind, one's own rational agency. Whose rational agency? That of the men kneeling at her feet. So, the purpose of this image of a feminine goddess is to allow these men to worship their own rationality—to represent their capacity for moral law as sublime. Woman is again a means, a machine— if not a *deus ex machina* then a *dea qua machina*—for the production and self-admiration of men as rational agents. The inviolable and veiled goddess dominates; but, once again, the men are in charge.

Conclusion

Kant is so well known for his universalism, his insistence that all human beings have dignity, intrinsic worth, as autonomous rational agents, that his views about women have often been dismissed as cultural baggage, unrelated to his core philosophical theories. I am concerned with how the gender connotations of these descriptions inform both Kant's views about women and his interpretations of the philosophical ideas represented by these descriptions. Despite men and women's shared nature, which includes the potential for rationality, they are characterized very differently by Kant; why does he hold these views and how does he seek to justify them? Furthermore, Kant himself warns repeatedly against using aesthetic, perception-based representations to describe such philosophical ideas as humanity, nature, and moral law. Yet he continues to use such personifications as Man, Mother Nature, and the veiled goddess Isis. How do these gendered tropes both shape and reflect Kant's views about women and men? How do they inform and perhaps distort his very ideas of humanity, nature, and moral law?

In each of these tropes, a singular noun that would literally refer to an individual is deployed to refer to universal or general characteristics of the human species: for human nature: *Mensch,* literally, "person," usually translated "man"; for supposed sex-based characteristics: *Mann, Frau,* translated "man," "woman," or "husband," "wife," depending on context; for nature: "voice of God," use of feminine personal pronouns, the veiled goddess Isis; for moral law: "voice of reason," use of feminine personal pronouns, and again the veiled goddess.

While it can be applied either collectively or distributively, Kant uses this trope particularly in contexts where he contrasts reason from inclination, instincts, desires, aiming either to describe this contrast or to account for the development of reason (in either the species or individual). I argue that despite the seeming gender neutrality, this usage is not literal, but remains a rhetorical trope, a synecdoche, in which the part is named to refer to the whole. When we view this trope in its relation to Kant's explicitly gendered tropes, it proves to carry gender specific implications in Kant's works on the rhetorical if not on the grammatical level.

Kant does provide some theoretical context for his views about women, some of which even Goethe and other contemporaries found odd. In this context, Kant employs tropes—both explicitly gendered and explicitly metaphorical—to explain what he takes to be the nature of sexual difference. Women, for example, are driven by a desire to dominate, and hence try to be generally pleasing. In marriage, Kant holds, women reign, but men must (rationally) govern; this relationship protects women from becoming objects of sexual use and men from succumbing to their animal vices. Women are more finely crafted by nature, for they play a special role in developing (both in the species and in the individual man) the restraint, respect, and rationality required for civil and moral society.

I have argued that Kant's use of explicitly gendered pairs in contexts so similar and applications so parallel to the supposedly gender-neutral usage further attests to the rhetorical nature of the earlier examples and sets the stage for the failure of gender neutrality in the earlier examples. These tropes provide a useful perspective on some of Kant's more peculiar views about women, as well as on the role those views play in shaping the personifications by which Kant represents nature and the moral law.

Kant personifies nature (i.e., instinct) in order to describe human character and development in teleological terms and in order to evoke in students a proper awe and respect for nature as sublime; he also warns against losing the intelligible concept in the aesthetic representation. (The sublime is our feeling of both attraction and repulsion for that intelligible reality that goes beyond our perception or understanding.)

The correlation of women with nature and men with culture is a familiar one, but Kant's variation is fascinating. Nature works through human desires and antagonisms—including sexuality—in order to bring both species and individual to law-governed society and to principle-based morality. I argue that, for Kant, women serve a primary role as nature's means to bring about this developing rationality in men. Furthermore, it is as a woman that Kant's "Nature" conspires in her own overthrow by reason. Kant personifies nature as Isis, perpetually veiled. One's study of nature is never complete because it is inexhaustible by understanding; nature is sublime. If nature as sublime object is characterized as divine woman, then surely in Kant's heterosexual context the student of nature, the knowing subject, is male. For it is to a male within Kant's scheme that a woman's body is a veiled mystery.

Kant personifies moral law as the voice not of God but of reason, again evoking both teleology and respect for the sublime. Although by no means as common as the other tropes, Kant evokes the image of the moral law as veiled goddess precisely in the context of warning against the dangers of such representations, unless they are carefully contextualized under reason. He also argues that when we characterize nature as sublime we are in fact falling into the fallacy of subremption by attributing to an object of nature the human moral capacity as rational subjects. Properly speaking, only the moral law—which is to say, only practical reason, the human subject as rational agent, the good will—is truly sublime. So, while students of nature must lift her veils respectfully, students of the moral law must never imagine they could master her.

I argue that at this point the incoherence of Kant's views about women becomes clear. More finely crafted as nature's tools, women have a different relation to moral law, to rational agency, than men do. In Kant's schema of relation between the sexes, the woman must make of herself the object of respect; woman herself is primarily a representation for men; like Mother Nature, like moral law as Isis, women both are and are not representable. Women are sublime "objects." Again in the Kantian sexual schema, if the moral law can be understood as sublime object by being figured as divine female, the subject who represents must be understood as masculine. The image of the veiled goddess as moral law must give place to the intelligible idea of the autonomous subject; the feminine image only serves, for Kant, to represent the masculine subject's own rational agency. There is no real place in Kant's moral theorizing for women as subjects, either as agents of their own desires or as rational moral agents.

─────────── *REFERENCES* ───────────

I gratefully acknowledge the assistance I have received on this project from my writers' group—Martha Edwards and Janet Davis—as well as from my student assistant, Mark Dodds—and the unflagging support and encouragement from the editors of this volume. Any infelicities in this essay are, of course, my own.

Alexander, Natalie. 1998. Rending Kant's umbrella: Kofman's diagnosis of ethical law. In *Enigmas: Collection of essays on Sarah Kofman*. Ithaca: Cornell University Press (forthcoming).

Burke, Kenneth. 1969. *A grammar of motives*. Berkeley: University of California Press.

Derrida, Jacques. 1973. *Speech and phenomena, and other essays on Husserl's theory of signs*. Trans. David B. Allison. Evanston: Northwestern University Press.

————. 1993. *Raising the tone of philosophy: Late essays by Immanuel Kant, transformative critique by Jacques Derrida*. Trans. and ed. Peter Fenves. Baltimore: Johns Hopkins University Press.

English, Jane. 1977. Preface. In *Sex equality*, ed. Jane English. Englewood Cliffs, N.J.: Prentice Hall.

Goethe. 1963. Letter to Voigt, 19 December 1798. In *Kant*, trans. Gabriele Rabel. Oxford: Clarendon Press.

Kant, Immanuel. 1956–64. *Werke in sechs Bänden*. Ed. von Wilhelm Weischedel. Weisbaden: Insel-Verlag. [place and half-titles vary]

1956. Bd. 4 Schriften zur Ethic und Religions-philosophie. Wiesbaden.

1957. Bd. 5 Kritik der Urteilskraft und Schriften zur Naturephilosophie. Wiesbaden.

1958. Bd. 3 Schriften zur Metaphysik und Logik. Wiesbaden.

1964. Bd. 6 Schriften zur Anthropologie, Geschichtsphilosophie, Politik und Pädagogik. Frankfurt am Main.

————. 1959. *Foundations of the metaphysics of morals*. Trans. Lewis White Beck. Indianapolis: Bobbs-Merrill Educational Publishing.

————. 1969. *Critique of judgment*. Trans. James Creed Meredith. Oxford: Clarendon Press.

————. 1978. *Anthropology from a pragmatic point of view*. Trans. Victor Lyle Dowdell. London: Feffer & Simons.

————. 1979. *The one possible basis for a demonstration of the existence of God*. Trans. Gordon Treash. New York: Abaris Books.

————. 1983a. Idea for a universal history with a cosmopolitan intent. In *Perpetual peace and other essays on politics, history, and morals*. Trans. Ted Humphrey. Indianapolis: Hackett.

———. 1983b. Speculations on the origins of human history. In *Perpetual peace and other essays on politics, history, and morals,* trans. Ted Humphrey. Indianapolis: Hackett.

———. 1983c. What is Enlightenment? In *Perpetual peace and other essays on politics, history, and morals,* trans. Ted Humphrey. Indianapolis: Hackett.

———. 1991. *The metaphysics of morals.* Trans. Mary J. Gregor. Cambridge: Cambridge University Press.

———. 1993. On a newly arisen superior tone in philosophy. In *Raising the tone of philosophy,* trans. and ed. Peter Fenves. Baltimore: Johns Hopkins University Press.

Kofman, Sarah. 1982. *Le Respect des femmes: (kant et rousseau).* Paris: Galilée.

Moulton, Janice. 1977. The myth of the neutral "man." In *Feminism and philosophy,* ed. Mary Vetterling-Braggin, Frederick A. Elliston, and Jane English. Totowa, NJ: Littlefield, Adams & Co.

Russell, Bertrand. 1905. On Denoting. *Mind* 14: 479–493.

Wittgenstein, Ludwig. 1958. *Philosophical investigations.* Trans. G. E. M. Anscombe. Oxford: Blackwell.

Andrea Nye

9

Frege's Metaphors

The form of the sentence, as it is understood in contemporary semantics and linguistics, is functional. This paper interprets the metaphors in which Frege shows what the functional sentence means,
arguing that Frege's sentence is neither an adequate translation of
natural language nor of use in feminist theorizing.

F ew areas of establishment academic research in English-
speaking countries have been as closed to feminist influence as
philosophy of language has been.[1] The few women who have con-
tributed, such as Elizabeth Anscombe, were initiated into a male
club and agreed to play by its rules. No matter how "diverse" the
programs of philosophical associations now are or how "open" the
formats of some philosophical publications have become under feminist pressure, this hard core of "real" philosophy remains untouched,
only superficially garnished by concessions of space and print that
divert the heat of revolution. Let them have their sessions and
their journals, the "real" philosophers say: let them play, the poor
dears, with politics, with postmodernism; let them amuse themselves and leave us undisturbed to talk about truth and meaning.
The question of how to break into, or whether to attempt to break
into, this closed circle is not easily answered. Logical analysis remains buttressed by a formidable apparatus of graduate appoint-
ments, tenured positions, and publication policy. There is a tendency,
therefore, to return the concessions, to say: let them—the men, the
"real" philosophers—play; let them manipulate their truth functions,
endlessly entangling the arcane complexities of their formulas.

Against this separatist policy there are two things to be said. First, it leaves significant apparatuses of academic power intact. Second and, in my view, more important, it is essential to repossess the question of truth. When the form of truth-asserting sentences is taken as canonical, feminist critiques of ethics, political theory, or epistemology that do not follow that form are potentially discardable. When what it is to be an object about which something can be said, as well as what it is to say something true about that object, has been decided outside feminist theory, not only is feminist theory misunderstood by nonfeminists, but feminists themselves may be unsure of what it is to be understood or to agree among themselves.

One of the most painful misunderstandings of recent years has been between women of color and white feminists. Women of color have repeatedly cited the failure or refusal of white feminist philosophers to acknowledge or respond to what black, Hispanic, Asian women say. The charge is that even as they stand accused of ethnocentricity or racism, white academic feminists theorize, if only about the possibility of theorizing, and so continue to ignore the presence of women of color and what they are saying. Even more disturbing is what is sometimes taken as the only possible alternative to theorizing closed to response from others. Inspired in part by the postmodern and poststructuralist critique of reason and presence in language, some feminists give up on truth altogether, arguing that any theory or systematic assertion of truths is an imposition of authority on others, that the only nonoppressive expression is expression that makes no claim to objective or interpersonal truth, and that a feminist should speak only for herself, expressing her own feelings and beliefs and describing her own situation. If misunderstanding between women of color and white women or between lesbian women and straight women has hindered a viable coalitional politics, such a solipsism is likely to be fatal to that politics.[2]

What is this theorizing of which white women are guilty? What is this truth? What is the syntax of this language that cuts off response from others and imposes an impolitic authority? What sentences are these that necessarily impose monolithic truth and mark out, as their only alternative, personal expression with no claim to objectivity? How are such sentences put together? In the various complex and erudite answers to these questions in contemporary philosophy of language, there is one constant: whether meaning is analyzed as truth-theoretic or componential or determined by "conceptual role," the sentence that is the bearer of meaning and truth is a particular sentence, the sentence as it was reformed by the founder of modern logic and the forefather of contemporary philosophy of language, Gottlob Frege. At the most fundamental level, it is his sentences, combined according to logical rule, that constitute what contemporary philosophers take as the necessary form of truth-bearing theory.

In this paper, I try to understand Frege's sentences in the only way I believe in which sentences can be understood, as what the speaker, Frege, meant by them and tried to explain he meant by them. My hope is that such an understanding might begin to open a space for another kind of understanding and so indicate a way out of the painful dilemma of having to choose between the hegemonic theorizing of philosophers and personal expression with no claim to truth for others. Truth-bearing theory as it is understood in establishment philosophy of language descended from Frege has a particular purpose, one that feminists may not share. No small part of that purpose is the designation of theory's opposite—emotional and personal expression—as irrelevant to truth.

Most important, Frege's necessarily metaphoric explanation of what he means by the logical notation that is to reform natural language and exhibit the logical form of any meaningful sentence suggests that there may be other, semantically prior, kinds of explanation that are not hegemonic. It also suggests that logically structured theory may have no meaning or intelligibility independent of another evocative and figurative truth-speaking that does not involve the silencing of others but depends on their active participation. Given the necessity of that participation, an assertion of truth need not be an imposition of authority but can constitute an invitation to interpersonal understanding.

The purpose of the logical notation Frege devised, which in revised forms is now assumed to represent the form of any assertion, was to free language from dependence on interpersonal understanding. To do this, Frege argued, language has to be free from ambiguity. In Frege's "conceptual notation," or *Begriffsschrift*, each word is to have one reference, or one identifiable object to which it refers, each concept a clearly defined extension so that it is possible to say with no uncertainty whether a specific object "falls under" it or not.

Such a determinacy, Frege argued, demands a new form of sentence, in which the relation between what is said and what it is said about is modelled after the relation between a mathematical function and the quantities inserted into the function's variable places to produce different determinate values. This reformation of the sentence makes possible the translation of natural language into a logical notation of truth functions and quantifications, a translation that, in turn, allows the systematic presentation of truth inductively or deductively ordered.[9] Personal expression and emotional coloring have no place in such a language. Nor does metaphoric expression. What can be said must be said clearly, Frege explained. All that can result from metaphorical extension or transference of meaning is "piecemeal," "makeshift" definitions that retain old concepts while extending them to wider domains. Instead, in logic, as in science, a clean break must be made with all imprecise, inadequate concepts (LA 161).[4]

Metaphorical extension of a concept involves just that being true of something and not being true of it that logic forbids:

> logic cannot recognize as concepts quasi-conceptual constructions that are still fluid and have not yet been given definitive and sharp boundaries. . . . A definition once given cannot be expanded without contradiction. (LA 162)

Whatever the analysis of metaphor, metaphor's power to communicate depends on this kind of fluidity and ambiguity. If we call a woman a "doll," we extend the application of "doll" from inanimate object to animate. The ordinary meaning of doll—that it is not alive, for example—is elided but not eliminated, because the force of the metaphor depends on the literal meaning being there and not being there at the same time. The communication of metaphoric meaning is never completely assured; understanding depends on the active ability of the person addressed to catch a delicate nuance between literality and linguistic license.

Even though there can be no metaphors *in* the new "lingua characteria" that is to be the idiom of "modern," "scientific" truth-bearing language, Frege must resort to metaphor in order to explain the aim and meaning of such a language. Especially this is true after the poor reception given his logical notation's first formulation in the *Begriffsschrift* forced him to come to terms with the fact of his reader's lack of comprehension. It was not just the slowness or stupidity of Frege's fellow philosophers and logicians that made metaphoric explanation necessary. As Frege himself finally realized, even intelligent and informed readers might not find the fundamental elements in the new mathematical–logical idiom intelligible without such explanations.

Frege sometimes blamed the problem on a stubborn metaphoricity that infects all language. In one sense, he acknowledged, there can be no "lingua characteria," no pure language of thought, no pure literality in the sense that "letters" can exactly represent a thought. Expression that carries meaning, he complained, no matter how perfected its notation, must always take a "perceptible linguistic form" and so stubbornly retain something of the pictorial which is a characteristic of metaphor. As he expressed it metaphorically, no thought can be handed to a reader directly as if it were a "rock crystal" (T 13). But what is pictorial is logically improper. A picture cannot be true, cannot present a fact, cannot be compared with reality. Without a sentence or proposition (which are the only things that can be true or false), we do not know what to compare with what; no picture can be the same as reality (T 3). Saying something about something is not like drawing a picture, and even if a conceptual notation must use physical marks, its aim must be to eliminate the figurative element as much as is possible.

In order to communicate the very logical impropriety of metaphoric language, Frege must use metaphor. To be expressible, thought, which is invisible, requires a pictorial "clothing," a means by which it can be presented, but clothing can hide and disguise as well as reveal. Therefore, the "dressing" of thought must be done in a particular way; it is with this proper tailoring of the linguistic clothing of thought that the logician is concerned. If he frivolously "designs" he may cover over in flattering fashion the ill-fitting dress that previous logicians have devised. Boole, for example, put Aristotelian logic in new algebraic form, which only improved its appearance in a superficial way (ACN 93). To avoid such mistakes, the logician must begin not by dressing up a thought but by stripping off the poorly designed clothes of his predecessors to reveal thought's true form or body. The rippling, seductive, fluidly sensual pictorial clothing of natural language as well as outmoded logics that take grammatical categories for granted must be discarded. Switching the metaphor from fashion to navigation, Frege explained:

just as a sailor searches for landfall, the logician strains to "discover" an essential form that he sees in the beginning only "as through a fog blurred and undifferentiated" (FA viii). With his vision, the logician strips away "irrelevant accretions which veil (thought) from the eye of the mind" (FA vii). Then, having achieved insight into true logical form, he can proceed to properly re-dress, replacing the ill-fitting clothing of Aristotelian logic—and ordinary language—with a notation tailored to the structure of truth.

But that notation must still be made intelligible. It cannot be left as mere marks on paper, which were, unfortunately, all that many readers could see in Frege's unfamiliar schema. What does it mean? What is it for? It is at this point of incomprehension that Frege acknowledges that although there can be no metaphors *in* a truth-asserting logical language, he must use metaphors to explain its meaning and use.

> Metaphorical expressions, if used cautiously, may after all help towards an elucidation. (N 52)

> I must confine myself to hinting at what I have in mind by means of metaphorical expressions. (WF 115)

> We may express [the need for unambiguous concepts] metaphorically as follows: the concept must have a sharp boundary. If we represent concepts in extension by areas on a plane, this is admittedly a picture that may be used only with caution, but here it can do us good service. (LA 159)

The aim and purpose of the logical analysis of language cannot be presented logically, literally; in order to make it intelligible, Frege must revert back to the figurative language that the conceptual notation is to replace. This struggle to indicate or elucidate the point of a project so often misunderstood by Frege's contemporaries is evident in the introduction to the *Grundesetze* as well as in the explanatory articles written after the *Begriffsschrift*, "On the Aim of a Conceptual Notion" and "On the Scientific Justification of a Conceptual Notation." The exhibiting of logical form in the *Begriffsschrift* cannot stand alone and be understood; it might even, Frege realized, be seen as ridiculous. And so, not without some bitterness, he began again, to explain in a more fundamental way the aim and the purpose of the logical reconstruction of language. He uses the image of a tree:

> If I compare arithmetic with a tree which develops at the top into a multitude of methods and theorems while the root presses downward, it seems to me that the growth of the root is, at least in Germany, rather weak . . . the top growth soon predominates and even before a great depth has been reached, causes a bending upward and a development into methods and theorems. (LA 144)

In the nineteenth century, the tree of the mathematics that provides the idiom for science had proliferated unhealthily into new geometries, number systems, unfounded methods, and perhaps even alternative views of physical reality. The logician's job is not to contribute to the unseemly top growth of mathematical language or even to superficially prune, a procedure that might only contribute to further unregulated growth. The logician must "replant." Unfortunately, any "replanting" must take place in an existing environment, and it is with this further development of the tree metaphor that Frege is able to explain the poor reception given his logic. "It seems to me that any tree planted by me would have to lift an enormous weight of stone in order to gain room and light for itself" (LA 147). If Frege's logic was little read and little appreciated by his contemporaries, his insights languishing without any companion blossoming, the problem was with the poor intellectual soil in which it was planted. The environment into which a living organism is planted is always to some degree unpredictable, always more or less imperfect and so unable to support the intended shape of the planting, always more or less conducive to what is taken as disease or uncontrolled growth.

Frege does not further develop the image of the tree but turns to another metaphor, one more familiar in the history of philosophy. The logician does not prune a living organism or even replant a new one; rather, he erects an "edifice." In that case, logic does not have "roots" that are easily damaged or diverted, but a "base" that can be sound or unsound. No "tree" could be durable enough. Such an image might be appropriate for the uncontrolled, mortal productions of

Frege's contemporaries, but the logician's business cannot be any agricultural tending of a growing organism with a given life span. Concepts, proper in logic, do not "sprout in the individual mind like leaves on a tree," although unreliable and insubstantial ideas may (FA VII).

But Frege does not stay long with this Cartesian metaphor of the proper "construction" of knowledge. A conceptual notation should not be seen as a purely artificial construction either; as such, it might be taken as the logician's invention and of only formal interest. A better metaphor, Frege decides, is that of geography. The logician who defines number is not in the same position as the architect who designs a building. If the work of the logician in the foundation of mathematics and language is a construction, there is no point in saying that arithmetic embodies objective truth. An architect does not discover the building he constructs; logic cannot be a projection of the logician's ideas the way a building projects an architect's ideas. When a geographer makes a map, he does not invent or design the North Sea; he draws its boundaries, and it is in that North Sea whose boundaries he maps that we are interested (FA 34). The conceptual reality that the logician is to "map" already exists, and his logic is to be judged with reference to that reality. For this reason, the personality and even the aim of the logician are of no interest, but only the accuracy of the tools he uses. It is scientific "methods" that transcend any individual man and any intention he might have that guarantee his success. For this reason, it is never appropriate to inquire into the life of a logician, into his political or personal views, any more than it is necessary to trace the history of logic "as though everyone who wished to know about America were to try to put himself back into the position of Colombus" (FA viii).[5]

The geographer discovers the truth and must be judged on that basis. In the same way, the logician deals not with any personal, subjective ideas but with the real boundaries of "senses" and "references." Like the geographer, he cannot rely on his naked "eye"; he uses tools. Frege explains: it is like using a telescope to look at the moon. The eye is flexible and useful for many ordinary purposes; it is hopelessly inaccurate for the purposes of science because it produces only a subjective image. In contrast, the telescope produces an image that is the same for all "inasmuch as it can be used by several observers" or at least, "it could be arranged for several to use it simultaneously" (SR 60). Even though each might have a different "retinal image," even though each must look at the image or photographic record and so introduce possible defects in his personal vision, the telescopic image is objective and mechanically recordable. With such a mechanical intervention, uniformity is achieved in vision, and it is such a uniformity that it is the logician's task to produce, a mechanism that frames or records objects in such a way that subjectivity is eliminated. For this purpose neither the naturally blossoming tree, nor a physical building designed for human use, nor the flexible and moving human eye—all of which can be seen as analogous to natural language—is appropriate. Logic is a linguistic "instrument" that, like a telescope or a microscope, can produce a recordable, repeatable image. (ACN 105)

But here again, Frege realized, metaphor is misleading in some respects. Logic is more valuable even than the physical instruments whose images make it intelligible. Like the telescope and microscope, logic makes us less dependent on our unreliable senses, on those sensations that "blow" us where they will, set us adrift in circumstances that we cannot control (JCN 83). But microscopes and telescopes are also material things that can break down and malfunction. A logical notation, unlike a physical mechanism, will not wear out or break down. A representational system must take a physical form.

> Time and time again, in the more abstract regions of science, the lack of a means for avoiding misunderstanding on the part of others, and also errors in our own thought, makes itself felt. Both have their origins in the imperfections of language for we do have to use sensible symbols to think. (JCN 83)

But even though the logician cannot avoid the use of sensible symbols, he can use their physicality to his advantage: he, like the sailor, does not let his "sail" push him here and there, but manipulates it, "using the wind to sail against the wind" (JCN 84). The capricious, dangerous wind of human experience is reflected in the capriciousness of natural language, but with the cutting sail of logic, logicians turn the wind against itself to move about at will, "using the realm of sensibles itself to free ourselves from its constraint" (JCN 84). In the same way, the logician uses the very physicality of a notation to cut against the drift of thought and expression in natural language.

The purpose of logic is not to provide a passive image or reflection of reality but to actively grasp onto what is real in a certain way. What is needed, Frege explains in a final metaphor, is a language that is like a "mechanical hand," a device made of physical stuff but attached directly to human will. The natural hand, like natural language, is flexible, capable of gesture, affection, anger, anger, cruelty. The manipulatable mechanical hand of logic loses this flexibility but achieves in its place a solid "grip."

> We build for ourselves artificial hands, tools for particular purposes which work with more accuracy than the hand can provide. And how is this accuracy possible? Through the very stiffness and inflexibility of parts the lack of which makes the hand so dexterous. (JCN 86)

With this image of the mechanical hand, Frege explains the relationship between logical thought and his conceptual notation. The logician does not "have" a thought in the same way people have ideas, which implies a degree of indeterminacy, nor does he "see" a thought, which is to some degree dependent on what is external.

> A person sees a thing, has an idea, grasps or thinks a thought. When he grasps or thinks a thought, he does not create it, but only comes to stand in a certain relation to what already existed—a different relation from seeing a thing or having an idea. (T 18)

It is this uniqueness of the logician's relation to his "thoughts" that is to overcome both the pictorial qualities of representation and the difficulty of communication. Although logical thoughts cannot be grasped, observed, handed around like a "rock crystal," logic allows something "like" this. "Other men can grasp them just as much as I" (T 24). In natural language, we may express our ideas, respond to what others say, comment on what is happening, define objects of common interest. The mechanical hand of logic allows another kind of communication in which a thought is grasped onto securely and passed on intact. It is in this sense, Frege made clear, that thought can make a difference in the world. When we grasp a thought, we may act and cause others to act. Grasping a thought with the secure grasp of logic is like grasping a hammer, but even better than grasping a physical hammer, because a physical hammer in someone's grip "undergoes pressure and thus its density, the disposition of its parts, is locally changed" (T 29). A thought is not in any individual's possession, so it cannot pass over to another individual's possession, "for after all, man has no power over it" (T 29). Thought is a mallet that is neither breakable nor exhaustible. When it is grasped by another, it can change him, make him act, but it is never changed itself in the process. "There is lacking here something we observe everywhere in physical process, reciprocal action" (T 29).

With these images—geographer, astronomer, and finally mallet-wielder—Frege explained the purposes of the logic that has become the standard idiom for English-speaking philosophy of language. In the face of general incomprehension of his unfamiliar schema, Frege had no recourse but to explain. What is the point of speaking logically? Why must a theory be translatable into logical notation? What is a conceptual notation meant to do that natural language cannot? These questions no longer seem so pressing. Whether it is assumed that logical notation captures the cognitive content of any intelligible language or that logical notation is a "richer" and more exact metalanguage into which any language usable for the purpose of truth-telling must be translatable, mathematical logic is now taken for granted as the canonical form for semantic analysis.[6] The problem of the "intention" of logic lingers only as, perhaps, the "minor" technical worry about "intension," the troublesome translation of individual belief or intention statements into logical notation.[7] But questions of intention and aim, now muted by logic's familiarity, were not the only matters that required Frege's metaphoric elucidation. There was a further and even more fundamental problem that he saw as standing in the way of the correct understanding of modern logic: if a theoretical language is to be a reliable mechanical hand, its mechanism must be clearly indicated. How does logic "work" at the most elementary level, at the smallest unit of truth-bearing language, the sentence? The whole program of the *Begriffsschrift* and the authority of modern logic rests on Frege's functional interpretation of that sentence.

At the very beginning of philosophical reflection on language, Plato recognized that a truth-bearing sentence cannot be just a string of words. "Frege man" means nothing. Instead there must be the "fit" between subject and predicate that produces a meaningful, possibly true sentence. Words which, when spoken in succession, signify something, do fit together, while those which mean nothing when they are

> strung together do not. . . . The signs we use in speech to sig-
> nify being are surely of two kinds . . . one called "names," the
> other "verbs." . . . Now a statement never consists solely of
> names spoken in succession, nor yet of verbs apart from
> names . . . these words spoken in a string in this way do not
> make a statement . . . [but] the moment [you combine verbs
> with names], they fit together and the simplest combination
> becomes a statement of what might be called the simplest and
> briefest kind. *(Sophist* 261d–262d)[8]

It was the final breakdown in the late nineteenth century of the Platonic account of the "fit" between subject and predicate that made it necessary for Frege to devise a new logical idiom. Although Aristotle's logic made substantial revisions in Plato's metaphysics of Forms—for Aristotle, forms are no longer supersensual entities but essences embedded in substantial individuals—the Aristotelian syllogism that is the basis for most logics through the nineteenth century still reflects Plato's insistence that successful predication depends on the proper hierarchy and interlocking of essences or forms. This Aristotelian logic of universals persisted as the authoritative logic even as a classical metaphysics of essences and universals was replaced by a modern epistemology based on the methods of experimental science and as rationalism gave way to an empiricist psychology that understood the elements of thought as sense-data.[9]

The positivism that reflects these changes became a new orthodoxy in many quarters, including philosophy, but it was Frege's genius to see that the question of the nature of predication could not be circumvented. It is not possible to assume elementary and independent atoms of "sense-data" with pre-fixed truth-values that can be simply combined or calculated with logical connectives according to logical laws. The modern *Begriffsschrift* that replaces outmoded classicism has to be a "language," not just a calculus of preformed data. This requires that the very texture of linguistic expression be reworked at the most fundamental level. Empiricist epistemology itself could never accomplish this essential remapping of what it is to say something. First, inferences dealing with generality that the theory of the syllogism systematizes cannot be accommodated unless intrasentential relations between subject and predicate are analyzed. Second, as Frege saw clearly, if the basis for the truth or falsity of elementary propositions is taken as phenomenally given, logic is reduced to psychology and relativism and has no claim to a grasp of truth. Frege's logic, the first modern logic, combined a sentential calculus with the innovation of a dramatically new treatment of generality by way of quantifiers that made a clean break with the classical understanding of predication. The basis for the new logic is not the relatively superficial connectives between sentences—"and," "or," etc.—but the "discovery" of a new kind of sentence, formed from a new kind of "fit" between a subject and what is said about it.

The mistake, as Frege saw it, of previous logics influenced by Aristotle was to take subject and predicate as two things of the same kind that are linked together, an analysis based on grammatical constructions of natural language in which a subject in one sentence can be a predicate in another. ("Man is rational." "Frege is a man.") But, Frege insisted, natural language is the enemy of the philosopher.

> If it is a task of philosophy to break the power of the word over the human mind, uncovering illusions which through the use of language often almost unavoidably arise concerning the relations of concepts, freeing thought from that which only the nature of linguistic means of expression attaches to it, then my "conceptual notation," further developed for these purposes, can become a useful tool for philosophers. (CN 106)

In Frege's theoretical language, the grammatical distinction between subject and predicate is abandoned. Different grammatical structures may have the same content, as in passive and active voices: "The Greeks defeated the Persians;" "The Persians were defeated by the Greeks." The grammatical choice between a passive or active expression, Frege argued, is most often not a question of logic but a result of a reciprocal relation between speaker and hearer: "the subject place has the significance in the word-order of a *special* place where one puts what he wishes the listener to particularly heed; the speaker considers the listener's expectations and tries to put them on the right track even before speaking a (complete) sentence" (CN 113). For Frege, of course, such communicative considerations have no place in logic, where the purpose is to state necessarily universal truths for which no grammar, even Indo-European grammar, is a sure guide. Frege turned instead to mathematics. The new sentence would be composed not of subject and predicate but of argument and function. These two new components would fit together to make true or false sentences: names, which refer to objects, and function expressions, which refer to concepts. Unlike the grammarian's subject and predicate, object and concept are not interchangeable but play the essentially different logical roles that make saying something true possible. In all the elaborate permutations of twentieth-century logical semantics, this is the syntax assumed as the form of any sentence with a "truth-value."

Technically, it was a stroke of genius. The functional analysis of the sentence was essential to Frege's new device of quantification, which "handles" generality without recourse to abstract entities like universals. "Man is rational," Frege was able to show, is not about an entity that is the essence, form, or universal, "man," but can be analyzed instead: "for all objects, if it is a man it is rational." Or another way: for every x, if x "is a man," then x "is rational." This analysis makes clear that the predicate "man" is not a thing or an essence but a "function" with empty places into which variables can be inserted to produce values. In the case of a mathematical function, the value is numerical; in the case of a sentence, which is a special kind of functional expression, the value is a truth value.[10]

But for this functional analysis of the sentence to have substance, it must be possible to make a distinction between objects, which can take the place of variables, and functions, into which variables can be inserted. This crucial difference, presented but not explained in the *Begriffsschrift,* was, Frege realized, a major source of incomprehension on the part of readers used to the old distinction between subject and predicate. What were these new Fregean objects? What did these new functional concepts mean? These basic "elements" of sentences cannot be defined purely syntactically. This would be to make logic into a formal system, an arbitrary "construction" of rules and conventions with no "content." If Frege's logic was the first "formal" logic, its formalism could extend only to the body of logic, not to its most elementary constituents. Nor could the difference between objects and concepts be established as embedded in natural linguistic structure. Although Frege might have agreed that all truth-bearing language, at some level, aims at correct logical form, he also insisted that the imprecision and ambiguities of ordinary talk confuse the logician. Somehow, the primitive elements that make up the functional sentence have to be given independent content so that there is something for the logical geographer to "discover" and the logical astronomer to "grasp." A logical primitive like "and," or the negation sign that links together assertions, might be defined by rule. But primitive in a different and more substantial sense are the basic components of a meaningful sentence. These cannot be identified by way of a convention of use. To have significance, logic must have assertive substance; that substance, just as in natural language, is the saying something about something that makes a combination of words a sentence.

A concept is what is left when you take away the object about which it is predicated. The new technique of quantification made such an operation possible, not just for singular assertions ("Frege is a man," which can be analyzed "Frege," as the object, leaving "is a man," as the predicate), but also for assertions involving generality ("Man is rational," which can be analyzed as "for all objects, if it is a man, it is rational," so isolating rationality as a function which correlates every argument that is a man with the value True). But the question remains: how are you to know which is the object so as to take it away? In the statement "Man is rational," the surface structure of natural language gives no clue. Is the subject men, or is the subject something else: a concept, a way of thinking, made into an object about which to say something? It was clear to Frege that if logic is to have content, what is an object and what is a concept must be indicated in some way, even if concept and object cannot be, strictly speaking, defined.[11]

In the explanatory articles written to make the nature and aim of mathematical logic clear, Frege explained why the "definition" of object and function is impossible with a metaphor taken from chemistry.

> One cannot require that everything shall be defined, anymore than one can require that a chemist shall decompose every substance. What is simple cannot be decomposed, and what is logically simple cannot have a proper definition. (CO 43)

Concept and object cannot be "defined" by indicating various constituent elements because they are absolutely basic or simple. As with natural compounds, a thought cannot be broken down infinitely. Eventually, the chemist-logician reaches substantive elements that cannot be decomposed. To make things even more difficult, these simples may not be readily available in nature—logical subjects and concepts may not appear in the surface structure of natural language—and for this reason there will not be names readily available for them. The chemist must therefore coin a name for the new element.

> Now something logically simple is no more given us at the outset than most of the chemical elements are; it is reached only by means of scientific work. If something has been discovered that is simple, or at least must count as simple for the time being, we shall have to coin a term for it, since language will not originally contain an expression that exactly answers. On the introduction of a name for something logically simple, a definition is not possible; there is nothing for it but to lead the reader or hearer, by means of hints, to understand the words as is intended. (CO 43)

Because Frege cannot literally say what he means in a language shared with his critics, he must "point." But here the analogy with the chemist breaks down; we might suppose that the literal chemist has some phenomena or other in his laboratory to which he can point when words fail. Frege has no such recourse. He must use the old word "concept"—"we cannot come to an understanding with one another apart from language"—but not with its old meaning,—"But nobody can require that my mode of expression shall agree with Kerry's."[12] And there is no guarantee that another will understand the word "concept" in the same way as Frege does—"in the end we must always rely on other people's understanding words, inflexions, and sentence-construction in essentially the same way as ourselves." Frege can appeal to "a general feeling for the German language" (CO 45): when there is an object, we preface it with "the"—"the concept horse"; when there is a concept, we preface it with "a"—"a horse." Luckily, commented Frege, in this case there is a "good accord between the linguistic distinction and the real one" (CO 45). But predictably the fit is by no means perfect; the rule, Frege observed, does not work at all for the definite article in the plural. And so there is still no guarantee that a reader will grasp what it is to which Frege is pointing. A critic calls his criterion "unsuitable." The problem, comments Frege, is that "he is not taking the word 'concept' in my sense" (CO 46). There is no literal way in which this failure of understanding can be remedied.

Frege cannot *tell* his readers what he means; he can only give them a "hint" or a "clue," and this he tries to accomplish with another metaphor from chemistry. Like certain chemical substances, a concept is "unsaturated" or incomplete, an object is "saturated" (CO 47, 55). It is on the communication of this metaphor that the meaning of the mechanism that informs current philosophical understanding of truth-bearing theory must rest. Frege is fully aware of the danger.

> By a kind of necessity of language, my expressions, taken literally, sometimes miss my thought; I mention an object when what I intend is a concept. I fully realize that in such cases I was relying upon a reader who would be ready to meet me half way—who does not begrudge a pinch of salt. (CO 54)

> I must confine myself to hinting at what I have in mind by means of a metaphoric expression and here I rely on my reader's agreeing to meet me half-way. (WF 115)

This was the very subjective indeterminacy that a logical language was to eliminate. Because different people have different ideas, because there is an uncertain connection between any person's ideas and words, and because some people see differences where others do not, such differences can only be "evoked to each hearer or reader according to hints of the poet or speaker" (SR 61). For this reason, Frege ordained in "Sense and Reference" that where meaning and truth are concerned, "there will be no further discussion of ideas and experience" (SR 61). Indeterminacy cannot be allowed to mar the objective senses and references marked clearly in a theoretically adequate logical notation. But in order to explain what those senses and references are, Frege has to resort to that very metaphoric communication in which understanding is by no means guaranteed.

The problem goes beyond the deficiencies of readers who insist on understanding metaphor too literally, who begrudge Frege his "pinch of salt." Built into the very nature of language is the "obstacle" that makes it impossible for Frege to avoid a "certain inappropriateness of linguistic expression" (CO 55). This "obstacle" explains both the difficulty of explaining concept and object and the necessity of so doing. Again and again in "Concept and Object" Frege comes up against this stumbling block inherent in language. In order to maintain the distinction between concept and object in the face of counter examples such as "The concept 'horse' is easily learned," Frege must deny that the concept "horse" is a concept. "We are confronted by an awkwardness of language," he complains. "Language is here in a predicament" (CO 46). In other words, in the very nature of language is a phenomenon which, from the logical point of view, constitutes an essential and hardly superficial hitch. Not only is it possible to say something about something—to say that Frege is a man, for example—it is also possible to say something about what we say about Frege—about the concept "man." We can say that it is easily learned, or, more interestingly, we might say that it reflects sexist attitudes. In either case, the clear distinction between argument and function necessary for Frege's conceptual notation is lost. "One would expect that the reference of the grammatical subject would be the concept: but the concept itself cannot play this part, in view of its predicative nature" (CO 46). This puzzle makes metaphorical explanation of the distinction between object and concept necessary. The logical distinction between concept and object can be neither explained nor exhibited logically or literally, because language, with this reflective feature, blocks any such showing or saying. Worse, Frege admits, "on thorough investigation it will be found that the obstacle is essential, and founded on the nature of our language; that we cannot avoid a certain inappropriateness of linguistic expression; and that there is nothing for it but to realize this and always take it into account" (CO 55).[13]

The misfit between natural language and canonical logical form runs deep. It is not just that natural language is ambiguous or marred by surface structures with only rhetorical force or expressive of personal feeling, all of which might conceivably be "stripped" away by the logician-designer. In the very sinew of language is a barrier, an obstacle, to logic. The metaphors that Frege uses to explain what the logically analyzed sentence is meant to do also explain what that obstacle is. The functional sentence is like a chemical solution. It holds together a concept, which is an unsaturated substance that can take up into itself another solution—the object—to the point where it is itself saturated and becomes an object. The concept comes with empty places where it can be completed or saturated by suitable objects. The objects fit into the holes or spaces in the concept. Concepts and objects are made for this mechanism, in the same way the chemical structure of a compound makes it able to absorb another specific compound. Men fit into the spaces left for arguments in the concept "rational"; the concept "rational" has spaces left in it for certain objects, men; in fact, a concept just is the fact that spaces are left in it to produce certain truth-values. This is what Frege means by the requirement that concepts be determinate. "Thus there must not be any object as regards which the definition leaves in doubt whether it falls under the concept" (LA 159).

This is how logical language can act as the mechanical hand Frege meant it to be; this is how the gears of theory can be made to mesh without grinding or seizing up. This is also why theory of meaning can be understood as a theory of truth, and why semantics can be conceived as purely extensional with no reference to the beliefs, hopes, or desires of women or of men. Beliefs, hopes, desires are irrelevant to the determinate way in which a Fregean concept is saturated by its arguments to produce the saturated value-object True. The purpose of a concept is to map "objects" like men and women onto such a truth value. Insofar as language can be "perfected," insofar as more and more segments of natural language can be "tamed"[14] or translated into logical notation, truth can be reliably reproduced in the same way in which a mechanical hand can, time after time, without variation or sense and sometimes with disastrous results, accomplish the same physical movement.

In order to bring out the force of Frege's metaphoric elucidation of the aim and content of logic, a contrast with an alternative account of predication, more in keeping with the style of his explanation of the aim and meaning of conceptual notation, might be useful. Such an account might go something like this: In order to say something, there must be a subject about which we speak; this is not a logical object founded on any epistemological or ontological priority, but an object of interest between persons. There must also be a concept, something that we say about that subject that is not a correlation of arguments and truth-values but a saying something that is open to the response that calls what we say into question. When, for example, the comment is made by historians of culture that "Man is the tool-wielding animal," it is possible to answer: "The concept 'man' is sexist," bringing into question not the extension of the concept, not whether some other animal—apes or racoons, for example—use tools, but the predicate "man" itself as an object of interest to those who *believe* that women are oppressed or *hope* that their situation might be improved. Further, it may even be possible to predicate a concept of itself in such a way so that the concept calls itself into question. It might be possible, for example, to say, paradoxically but interestingly, "Rationality is irrational."[15]

It is not that language never functions in the way Frege describes. Talk and writing, whether informal or theoretical, often drearily grinds out what every one already knows. Those who engage in such talk or writing often do not acknowledge or listen to their readers or audience. Such talk and writing, however, rarely has the power to reveal any truth and, in fact, can occlude the truth as, with repetition, formulas lose meaning. Nor is this true only in ordinary nontechnical talk. Even if modern logic is taken as a language only for the sciences in which truth is determined, an alternative still might be preferable. The difference can be seen with an example used by another founder of contemporary semantics, Tarski. Challenged to give examples of how his post-Fregean theory of truth for formal languages might be useful, Tarski gives examples from what he calls the "special sciences." A psychologist, he argues, identifies "intelligence" with how many answers a subject gets right or wrong on an I.Q. test. Truth theory, then, can be used to make rigorous the psychologist's deductions about intelligence as correlated with a quantifiable value-range (Tarski 1944, 341–375). In an alternative account of theoretical language, the scientific "concept" of "intelligence" might itself be scrutinized as an object of interest and found to be racist, sexist, and/or ethnocentristic.[16]

In the alternative account, object and concept do not fit together as in a saturated solution. In fact, on this view, language may have the most power to reveal the truth when they do not fit together, when there is a dissonance between object and concept. At a point in the recent history of feminist politics, for example, one object of interest to women—calling mature women "girls"—did not seem to fit the concept, "harassment," as in "Calling mature women 'girls' constitutes sexual harassment." Nevertheless, such "indeterminate" theorizing, made new insights into the reality of women's condition possible and new legal principles available. It is not that the *content* of the concept "harassment" was vague, so that there was uncertainty whether or not a given "argument" fell under it, a vagueness that could be cured by a rigorous and determinate concept. In the alternative account of truth-asserting language, there is no way in which to identify a concept independently of the objects to which it is applied, or any way to identify an object independently of the interests expressed in what we say about it; instead, there is a moving interrelation between the objects we are concerned about and what we say about them. This is not to revert to either psychologism or Platonism; it is not to say that a concept is either an idea in someone's mind or an abstract entity. A concept might be better described as an ideal defined in reciprocal relation to objects of interest between people.

On the alternative view, a logically determinate concept in a law dealing with harassment or public morals might amount to no more than an *ad hoc* list of objects that happen to be repugnant to those in power. If this were the case, then the question of truth is eclipsed altogether. If, however, concepts like "corrupting" young persons or "harassing" employees are understood as acquiring meaning in relation to a series of specific objects—actions, speech behavior, etc.—as judges, lawyers, and citizens pursue a common interest in allowing persons to follow their interests without undue interference and in encouraging those who are impressionable to develop reliable moral standards, then there is some hope that what is, in truth, harassment and what is, in truth, corruption might emerge.[17]

Communication, in the sense of the alternative account, always requires what Frege hoped his readers would give his metaphoric explanations: "a pinch of salt." What we say about objects of interest cannot be passed hand to hand like a rock crystal or, more ominously, like mallets. What we say is not a repeatable processing of preformed information; its understanding requires that a reader, hearer, or interpreter come a step or two to meet us, that she attempt to understand and to "charitably" give us the benefit of the doubt, that she recognize that we may have a concept that is not hers.[18] Ironically, much as this language is hardly the logical language devised by Frege, it is the language Frege himself used to explain what his logical language is for and what it is.

Theorizing in the sense of the alternative account of language does not cut off the response of others. Its concepts do not mark determinate value ranges that make the only possible response additive. It is not personal expression either. It is not objective or rational in the sense that it is the remainder left over when the indeterminate personality, coloring, and imagery are taken out of language. If it is rational, it is rational in a different way than the functional sentence is rational because its rationality depends on the very barrier that blocks automated inferences between functional sentences. A concept—something said about something—can itself become an object of interest, and this is not simply to add on more previously sorted objects or mark more exactly which objects fall under the concept, but to introduce an understanding that changes the objects of understanding and so moves beyond a given restrictive universe of discourse.

Frege's metaphoric expressions constitute such a use of language, in which the meaning of what is said may, in the hands of a listener who has granted the necessary pinch of salt necessary for understanding, be transformed, creating new objects of interest. The object of interest in this case is logic itself, and "professional" philosophy based on that logic, understood as what Frege said about the logical form of sentences and theories: what he said about the saturation of its concepts, the hardness of its objects, the repeatable hammer blows of its inferences, the mechanical precision of its movements. What could I, or you, say about this object of interest?

Frege's functional sentence need not be the form of inference, feminist or other. Theories which purport to represent objective truth need not, perhaps cannot, involve functional relations between determinate objects and value-ranges by which they are sorted. To assert that something is true about an object can never close off a response that raises the inquiry to a new level of understanding. If any of these claims are true, then hegemonic theorizing and personal expression are not the only ways to speak truly, and feminist philosophers need not choose between alienated assertion and solipsistic withdrawal.

NOTES

1. One exception is Hintikka and Hintikka (1983). Noting the lack of feminist research in philosophy of language, the Hintikkas argue that

there are at least two ways of identifying objects across possible worlds: one, to which virtually all contemporary semanticists subscribe, that focuses on the identification of discrete objects typically by way of similarity, and another that, more holistically, looks at the functional role of individuals. The suggestion is then made on the basis of research showing sex-linked differences in the way boys and girls identify objects that the lack of interest in Jaakko Hintikka's "duality of cross-identification" is explainable as masculine bias in semantic research. As I see it, the problem with taking this line is the following: The semanticist is concerned with developing a theory of truth and is unlikely to be interested in psychological differences between individuals. Differences in women's behavior or attitudes are therefore irrelevant and can be easily dismissed as psychological, social, or linguistic disability. If contemporary semantics is defective, it is defective not because it is biased—biases may turn out to be true—but because it gives a flawed account of language.

2. Expressions of this dilemma can be found in many recent collections of feminist essays. In Claudia Card (1991), for example, see particularly Maria Lugones's essay, "On the Logic of Pluralist Feminism," and Joyce Trebilcot's "Greasing the Machine and Telling Stories."

3. Logical semantics remains as the syntax of theory through various rival epistemologies. Whether one is a foundationalist and believes that there are canonical anchor points for theory or whether a coherence view is taken, inferences remain as ordered by logical rules.

4. References in the text are to the following works by Gottlob Frege: "On the Aim of the Conceptual Notation" abbreviated (ACN), "On the Scientific Justification of a Conceptual Notation" abbreviated (JCN), reprinted in Frege (1972); *The Foundations of Arithmetic* (1959) abbreviated (FA); "Sense and Reference" (SR), "What is a Function?" (WF), "Concept and Object" (CO), "Conceptual Notation" (CN), and "The Basic Laws of Arithmetic" (LA) are in Frege (1970); "Thoughts" (T) and "Negation" (N) are in Frege (1977).

5. This position might not be accepted by those doing current research in the demographics and natural history of America for whom Columbus's racist and messianic attitudes are relevant in determining the physical as well as cultural boundaries of America. See, for example, Turner (1980).

6. Even when, under the influence of the later Wittgenstein, interest in "ordinary language" and the pragmatics of speech is revived, the propositional core of utterances governed by truth-functional logic and quantification theory is typically retained, only supplemented by a gloss of rules for what it is possible to "do with words" whose "locutionary" or truth-bearing meaning remains as represented in Frege's conceptual notation. Two well-known examples are Austin (1962) and Searle (1969).

7. The technical problem is to account for the fact that when propositions occur in an intensional context (for example, when "Frege was the founder of mathematical logic" occurs in the context "She knows that Frege is the founder of mathematical logic"), the mathematical-logical principle that truth conditions are preserved when equivalents are substituted may not hold (a number of definite descriptions may be equivalent to "Frege" with which the subject of the sentence is not familiar). Frege solved the problem by claiming that in addition to meaning or truth conditions, expressions have senses, or ways of identifying truth conditions (as argued in SR). This intrusion of unquantifiable meaning back into logic has been rejected by most contemporary philosophers of language, who solve the problem of intension using a variety of techniques. Davidson (1986), for example, argues that in intensional contexts "that" is a demonstrative pronoun that points to the sentence believed as a sentence to which the speaker would agree, so avoiding any reference to intensional meaning or sense.

8. This insight is crucial to what Plato sees as the future of philosophy. The Parmenidean emphasis on "what is" rather than what can be predicated of something else either reduced philosophers to silent affirmation ("what is is") or subjected them to a proliferation of frivolous refutation showing that nothing is anything else. See chapter 2 in Nye (1990) where I try to sort out the various strategies involved in Plato's dispute with those philosophers whose arguments are inspired by Parmenidean logic.

9. Boole's logic, perhaps the most influential logic of Frege's time, reflects the confusion. Although Boole introduced a kind of truth-functional calculus of elementary propositions, he interpreted his logical calculus in terms of the old syllogistic logic as interlocking classes.

10. That a sentence is the name for one of two truth-values—either The True or The False—just as a functional expression with argument inserted can be seen as the name of the same kind of thing as the argument—that is to say, a quantity or a number—is a counterintuitive consequence of the functional analysis of the sentence that later logicians have seen as an avoidable mistake. See, for example, Dummett (1981, 166 167).

11. Commentators on Frege have used various tactics to try to avoid the necessity of indicating the undefinable. See Dummett (1973, 235), who argues that what is a name can be defined independently and what is a predicate can be defined as what is left when you take a name away from a sentence; object and concept can then be defined as what names and predicates refer to. In subsequent explanations (1981, 235), Dummett admits that Frege never explicitly argued for such a sequence but always insisted

that concept and object are too simple to define. For another influential account, see Davidson (1986, 17): Frege tries to avoid an infinite regress of explanation with his metaphor, but this only "labels the problem." According to Davidson, Tarski's truth theory for formal languages, which separates an object language from the metalanguage in which the meaning of its sentences are described, can explain sentential meaning without reference to concepts and objects or even to meaning itself.

12. The immediate objection to which Frege responds in the article "Concept and Object" was from Beano Kerry who argued that a concept can sometimes be an object, as when we say "The concept 'horse' is easily learned." Frege argued that "the concept 'horse'" was indeed a name, but for that reason it could no longer be a concept but was a kind of shadow object that represents a concept.

13. It was not open to Frege to assert simply that concepts are never objects. To establish the logical foundations of mathematics, in particular to give a definition of number, Frege found it necessary to speak of classes and the value-ranges of concepts. He defined number as the value-range of a concept, a kind of correlate object thrown up by a function but kept separate from its predicative quality.

14. "Frege's massive contribution was to show how 'all,' 'some,' 'every,' 'each,' 'none,' and associated pronouns, in some of their uses, could be *tamed*." Davidson (1986, 29). Davidson's metaphors might also be profitably studied. The semanticist is involved in the gruelling and even dangerous adventure of subjecting natural language to truth-theoretic semantics. Because of the difficulty, he is often subject to "failure of nerve" (26). Commenting on Tarski's view that a theory of truth may not be possible for natural language, Davidson notes the semanticist's "conceptual anxiety" (28). Luckily, in this case, he argues, it is possible to carry on without "disinfecting" the site of contagion (28).

15. This, of course, is where the "obstacle" in language becomes not only an embarrassment but an impassable obstruction. The contradiction pointed out by Bertrand Russell, which Frege recognized as fatal to the assimiliation of mathematics and language, depends on self-reference. In an early letter to Frege, Russell pointed out the difficulty: "let w be the predicate to be a predicate that cannot be predicated of itself. Can w be predicated of itself? Every answer implies the opposite. Therefore, one must conclude that w is not a predicate. For the same reason there is no class (as a whole) of those classes as wholes that do not contain themselves" (quoted by Sluga [1980, 163]). Interesting and even truth-revealing in natural language, paradox is destructive in logic, which is founded on the principle of noncontradiction and the law of the excluded middle.

Although Frege was eventually convinced that the obstacle had been shown to be insurmountable and that the project of making a saturated solution of mathematics and language could not be carried through, logical semantics continued to flourish, the barrier elided by techniques such as Russell's theory of types, which rules that concepts, though objects, cannot be arguments in certain functions, and Tarski's truth-theoretic semantics, which cordons off talk about concepts in metalanguages, which are on a different level from object languages.

16. A similar criticism has been made of "moral development" as measured by the standard Kohlberg test as a concept that does not do justice to women's moral intuitions (Gilligan 1982).

17. I am indebted to an anonymous *Hypatia* reviewer for the analogy between corrupting public morals and harassment, as well as for a number of other helpful comments. She has pointed out that Fogelin, in one of the leading informal logic texts *Understanding Arguments*, uses as an example of impermissible vagueness a law forbidding all actions that tend to corrupt public morals, arguing that for the concept "corrupting public morals" there are too many "borderline cases." This analysis continues to assume, even for informal logical argument where rigor must be somewhat relaxed, the view that a concept should indicate (this time with as few borderline cases as possible) a range of objects whose identities are fixed. It is this assumption that I am questioning. If in the process of the legal interpretation of a law as it is applied to specific cases, no clear standards, arguments, or cases emerge, then it can be said that the law is too vague. This does not mean, however, that the concept of a law is meant to, or should, pick out a determinate set of given actions as illegal; rather, the concept of a law can be understood as providing a standard for judgment, which may change as it is applied and which may change the objects to which it is applied.

18. This charity can be distinguished from a logician's "charity." See, for example, Davidson's "principle of charity": "assign truth conditions to alien sentences that make native speakers right when plausibly possible, according, of course, to our own view of what is right" (Davidson 1986, 137). Davidson makes it clear that this is no compliment to human intelligence but a methodological necessity: "The methodological advice to interpret in a way that optimizes agreement should not be conceived as resting on a charitable assumption about human intelligence that might turn out to be false. If we cannot find a way to interpret the utterances and other behavior of a creature as revealing a set of beliefs largely consistent and true by our own standards, we have no reason to count that creature as rational, as having beliefs, or as saying anything" (137). I might point out that "alien," "native," "creature"—familiar from post-Quinian logical semantics—

are used to indicate speakers of our own language, as well as speakers of languages we do not understand.

————————————— REFERENCES —————————————

Austin, J. L. 1962. *How to do things with words.* New York: Oxford University Press.

Card, Claudia, ed. 1991. *Feminist ethics.* Lawrence: University Press of Kansas.

Davidson, Donald. 1986. *Truth and interpretation.* Oxford: Clarendon Press.

Dummett, Michael. 1973. *Frege: Philosophy of language.* New York: Harper and Row.

————. 1981. *The interpretation of Frege's philosophy.* Cambridge: Harvard University Press.

Frege, Gottlob. 1959. *The foundations of arithmetic.* Trans. J. L. Austin. Oxford: Basil Blackwell.

————. 1970. *Translations from the philosophical works of Gottlob Frege.* Ed. Max Black and Peter Geach. Oxford: Basil Blackwell.

————. 1972. *Conceptual notation and related articles.* Ed. Terrell Ward Bynum. Oxford: Clarendon Press.

————. 1977. *Logical invesgitations.* Ed. Peter Geach. New Haven: Yale University Press.

Gilligan, Carol. 1982. *In a different voice.* Cambridge: Harvard University Press.

Hintikka, Merrill, and Jaakko Hintikka. 1983. How can language be sexist? In *Discovering reality,* ed. Sandra Harding and Merrill Hintikka. Dordrecht: D. Reidel.

Nye, Andrea. 1990. *Words of power: A feminist reading of the history of logic.* New York: Routledge, Chapman, Hall.

Searle, John. 1969. *Speech acts.* Cambridge: Cambridge University Press.

Sluga, Hans. 1980. *Gottlob Frege.* London: Routledge and Kegan Paul.

Tarski, Alfred. 1944. The semantic conception of truth and the foundations of semantics. *Philosophy and Phenomenological Research* 4: 341–375.

Turner, Frederick. 1980. *Beyond geography.* New York: Viking.

10

Free Gift or Forced Figure?

Derrida's Usage of Hymen in "The Double Session"

Introduction

In his essay "The Double Session," Jacques Derrida introduces the term hymen to describe a concept of *in-betweenness* that reveals and undoes traditional metaphysical oppositions and classical economies of signification. Calling it "one of those *'beneficent figures'* " (261) because it can mean two or more things at once, Derrida takes and uses the word hymen as a metaphor for the undecidable. The anatomical *in-betweenness* of hymen as a vaginal membrane, physically or literally *in-between* the inside and outside of a woman, is as seductive to Derrida as the etymology of the word and its rich metaphoric associations. Archaically, hymen signified marriage, and the sexual act that proved the existence of a bride's hymen (and thereby destroyed it) also once served physically to consummate and legally to validate the contract of marriage. Metaphorically, then, hymen signified not only the concept of marriage, but also a woman's virginity as well as its loss, ideally a sacrifice for a fruitful matrimonial union. Rich both in literal and metaphoric terms, the neither/nor and both structure of hymen as *in-between* open/closed, membrane/marriage, virginity/consummation suits Derrida's agenda of using undecidable terms, such as *pharmakon, différance, supplément,* or *gift* to counter and deconstruct language's logocentrism and phallocentrism.

I will argue, however, that by inscribing hymen as one of his undecidables, Derrida willfully forgets that hymen's history is *decidedly* patriarchal and that its prior conscriptions have benefitted one sex—the male's—at the expense of an other's—the female's. I will critique Derrida's usage of the term hymen in "The Double Session" and, more generally, in his larger body of work to show that Derrida forcibly appropriates the term and uses it to yield "beneficent" textual figurations. In doing so, Derrida perpetuates a history where, both physically and metaphorically, hymen of woman has been appropriated and made through a form of forced labor— a forced metaphorical figuration—to reproduce the very institutions and discourses that further disseminate the masculine at the expense of the feminine. Thus the "phallogocentrism" that he pretends to oppose and undo, Derrida only violently reinforces and perpetuates.

I argue not against Derrida's project of deconstructing metaphysical and semiotic oppositions, but rather against the form his deconstructive strategy takes. His strategy is highly problematical and its effects dubious because it works to exclude the feminine and woman from the scene of representation, in particular from the acts of writing and reading. It also erases sexual difference for, as Kelly Oliver argues in *Womanizing Nietzsche,* Derrida's undecidables "operate within a larger economy of the proper/property, also known as an economy of castration" (65. See 65–82). Derrida seductively veils operations of a phallic economy, an economy that, as Oliver argues, either erases sexual difference or "operates according to the symptomology of fetishism" (65). Thus, while Derrida pretends to replace the phallus with the hymen, his hymen serves merely as a front for the phallus. And ultimately this is why Derrida fails in his deconstructive project: he allows for the economy of the phallus to continue its work at another more insidious level.

Graphic Properties of the Hymen in "The Double Session"

Even before attending to its complex content, one only has to look at the formal properties of "The Double Session" to see the workings of an economy driven by the phallus. Throughout the long, intricate, often beautiful, and seductively written essay, Derrida plays upon various themes of the crack, the fold, the crease, and the blank. Derrida uses these textual properties to lend form to his metaphor of hymen as undecidable and in-between. In turn, the structural and typographical properties corporealize the text as the body of woman. One such hymeneal crack structurally separates the first session from the second. Derrida originally presented to the *Groupe d'Etudes theorique* the material of "The Double Session" orally and in two parts in 1969. Subsequently *Tel Quel* published the sessions in two issues in 1970. Republished in *Dissemination* in 1972 (the English translation of which appeared in 1980), the work there received the title proposed by the editors, "La Double Séance." Derrida makes much of the split between the two sessions or "*séances*" writing that just as the double colloquia (originally) have no title, no authoritative "head" to dominate the rest of the text (177–179), neither do they have a "middle." "The Double Session" is "divided into two halves only through the fiction of a crease" (227). With this, Derrida calls attention to the spread of pages unfolding from the book's spine to separate structurally the two sessions (226–227). "The fiction of a crease," however, renders undecidable both the sessions' division and the difference between spoken and written representations.

Textual creases and folds also confuse (while calling attention to) the difference "*between* literature and truth" (183), absence and presence, representation and its reference. "In folding [writing] back upon itself," Derrida writes, "the text thus *parts* (with) reference, spreads it like a V, a gap that pivots on its point, a dancer, flower, or Idea" (239). Through strings of metaphors, Derrida turns the V-like spread of the text's pages into the spread of a woman's legs and the gathering of folded pages stitched into the book's spine into the hymen and its destruction. While Derrida sexes the book's form female, he figures it as both seductively "virginal" in its "closed feminine form" (259) and fecund in its open "womblike matrix of whiteness" (179). The "beneficent figure" of the hymeneal spread of pages offers for Derrida the "euphoria of a 'suspension'": it suspends "the opposition between the open and the closed" so that "both contradictory needs can be satisfied, successively or simultaneously" (247). The hymeneal text is both never and ever virginal for Derrida.

Structurally "decapitating" the text by suspending its title (178), spreading it apart at its middle, and giving over much of each page to "foot" notes, Derrida strategically divides "The Double Session" into smaller and smaller fragments. Derrida intends his textual splinterings to undermine traditional "phallogocentric" symbolic economies governed by transcendental signifiers and to effect a new "hymeneal economy" which perpetually suspends signification and disperses meaning. His formal strategy, however, works only to dismember the body of woman into fetishized parts. That Derrida dismembers not the authority of a phallic economy but rather the body of woman becomes graphically evident through his engagement with Stephan Mallarmé's work. Derrida appropriates many of the graphic textual metaphors of "The Double Session" from Mallarmó, and he snips and stitches them together with metaphors for the book and writing taken from literary critics who treat the theme of "the blank" and "the fold" in Mallarmé's work. For Derrida, Mallarmé's attention to the physical structure and typography of the book and writing illustrates a radically modern notion of mimesis. Mallarmé calls attention to writing as writing through an emphasis of syntax over semantics, position over meaning, and content through form. Using a short text by Mallarmé entitled *Mimique* from *Le "Livre" de Mallarmé* , Derrida shows *mimesis* as a system of representation that always illustrates " 'under the false appearance of a present' " (175, 200, and 211). Mimesis illustrates not the "presence of the other," but rather its lack (185). This Derrida illustrates by (re)marking (upon) the fold and the blank as otherwise unremarkable, marginal areas of writing. Derrida's focus on textual points of undecidability, however, effects a shift not from a phallic economy but rather to an economy that excludes woman from the scene of representation.

Topographically and typographically the exclusion of woman from the scene of writing and representation occurs when Derrida, after Mallarmé, inscribes the hymen as the " 'virgin whiteness' " of a blank page and the blank spaces of an already-written page (178–179). Figuratively as well as literally, the white blank areas of sheets of paper serve as the grounds of writing and reading. As such, however, Derrida's hymen/woman plays the role of a virginal wallflower: forever fading into representation's background, the ever-present absence of hymen/woman serves structurally to support the male writer's mark. Derrida variously describes the structural support of writing not only as sails, veils, canvases, bed sheets, and shrouds (260, 270), but also as other membranes including cauls (or birth-veils, 269) and vellum (270). Not unlike vellum or parchment—writing surfaces made from the flayed skins of animals—Derrida stretches the metaphor of hymen tautly to receive writing's marks. Derrida inscribes and uses hymen as the "propagation-structure" of writing (261) but only at the expense of the term from which he freely mines as a "[s]upplement, principle, and bounty [*prime*]" in what for him is the "baffling [*déjouante*] economy of seduction" (226). Since in French *prime* means either the first in a series or a free gift (bonus, premium, subsidy, or bounty), Derrida regards the loss of hymen as "bafflingly seductive"—like the playing out or spoiling [*déjouante*] of a mine.

While he sexes as female the formal structure of the book and its pages, Derrida sexes as male the acts of writing and reading. Both the writer and the reader approach the hymeneal text with a variety of sharp, pointed instruments which Derrida describes as phallic: pens, plumes, and quills (271–272) scatter "seminal spurts" (285) upon pages; sewing needles "pierce and join" together the text's tissues (213, 240); knives and letter openers "separate the lips of the book" and mark a " 'taking of possession' " of its " 'virginal folding back [form]' " (259, Derrida quotes Mallarmé). The operations of writing and reading mark the text in order to claim ownership and a stake in the text's physical properties. Derrida turns writing and reading into metaphors of sexual deflowering. Yet just as the "marking tip proceeds without a past upon the virgin sheet" (223), the hymen, when marked, virginally returns without a past to be re-marked: "[t]he unfailing return, the periodic regularity of the white in the text (*'indefectibly the white blank returns . . .'*) is re-marked in the *'virginity,'* the *'candor,'* and the *'nuptial proofs of the Idea'* " (178–179).

Derrida requires hymen to "readily" and "willingly" give itself up for written propagation: " '[t]he virginal folding-back of the book, again, willing/lends [*prête*] for a sacrifice from which the red edges of the books of old once bled' " (259). In this passage, cited again from Mallarmé, Derrida remarks that the "femininity of the virgin book is surely suggested by the place and form of the verb *'prête,'* clearly ready to offer itself as an adjective with the copula understood" (259). As a verb, *prête* means "lends"; as a feminine adjective, it means "ready" or "willing." Indeed, Derrida represents hymen or woman as not only "ready" and "willing" to "lend" itself in a bloody sacrifice to writing and reading but as having wanted and asked for physical violation. It/she brings violence against herself since, according to Derrida, "a blank that is written, blackens itself of its own accord" (260); the hymen "murders itself," Derrida writes, for writing (229). As soon as the hymen is marked or "marks itself," as Derrida puts it (to prove its virginity, for instance), it is torn and theoretically destroyed. Virginity loses itself in the operation that proves its existence. Yet "unfailingly," when Derrida's "beneficent" yet suicidal and masochistic figure " '*indefectibly . . . returns,*' " it returns a virgin, or at least simulating virgin. Never the worse for its wear, Derrida's hymen comes back with "periodic regularity" (178) for more of the same, further dividing itself into smaller and smaller white fragments upon the written page which, in turn, also give themselves up as " 'nuptial proofs of the Idea' " (178). Just as the structural "fold renders (itself) manifold but (is) not (one)" (229), the topographical blank divides "itself" into "next-to-nothing" in what Derrida describes as "a kind of multiple division or subtraction" (262) in the "squaring of writing" (265).

"Beneficent Figure"?

For Derrida hymen is "one of those 'beneficent figures' " (261) because it seems endlessly to give itself for propagative ends and to return eternally to reproduce more of the same. Throughout "The Double Session," Derrida celebrates the eternal return of hymen in written representations. Quoting from Mallarmé, for instance, he writes that the hymen reiterates the " 'return of the same—but almost other' " (228). When Derrida calls hymen "economically seductive" (226), then, it's hard not to imagine that the "economical" profits yielded by the figure—its free gifts—are not as real for Derrida as they are figurative. Derrida plays out his figuration of hymen as if he were extracting rich resources from an inexhaustible mine (263). Re-deploying the figure in his own writings, hymen not only illustrates but also produces and "disseminates" Derrida's deconstructive discourse.

The "free gift" ("*prime*" 226) of hymen's virginal returns affords Derrida never-ending opportunities to re-cast the figure (or that of woman or the mother) to play a featured role in a number of his texts including *Spurs: Nietzsche's Styles* (1978), *The Ear of the Other* (1982), and "The Law of Genre" (1980). In these texts, hymen produces and inscribes (often biologically figured) systems of reproduction, repetition, or *iteration*. Derrida's discussion of Friedrich Nietzsche's eternal return in *Spurs*, for instance, echoes his treatment of Mallarmé's " 'return of the same—but almost other.' " In "The Law of Genre," Derrida describes a similarly self-perpetuating narrative by Maurice Blanchot (*La Folie du jour*) whose end is always its re-beginning. Derrida's engagements with Mallarmé, Nietzsche, and Blanchot illustrate systems of representation that depend upon the double affirmation of woman who must say "yes, yes" to (her own) death in order to affirm the life of masculine representations.

In "The Law of Genre," for instance, Derrida shows Blanchot's figure of the Law *(La Loi)* to be both a woman and beautiful not only because the French noun is feminine but because women are "usually" the ones who say "yes, yes" (71), and women who say "yes, yes" to "affirm both life and death" are beautiful "creatures" (72). According to Derrida, "[b]eauty, the feminine beauty of these 'beings,' " is "bound up with this double affirmation" (72). From this line of reasoning, Derrida surmises that since he, too, says "yes, yes," he too is probably a woman and beautiful: *"I am a woman and beautiful."* (72). Casting himself in the part of her supporting role, Derrida mimes and mouths the words of woman who never is present and never can be present in his work because she "is only a figure, a 'silhouette,' " to whom *"he* gives birth" (73–74, my emphasis). *La Loi* issues from a "secret coupling . . . an odd marriage ('hymen')," which Derrida admits has "a hint of incest" to it since the father (who also plays the part of the mother) gives birth to *La Loi* and then attempts to seduce her: "he wishes to seduce the law to whom he gives birth" (74). Derrida's genealogical tricks pretend to neutralize the law of the father by making it the product of a marriage-bond (hymen) between the two genders *(genres)*. However, the nuptial contract to which "beautiful women" (through Derrida's voice) say their excessive "yes, yes" binds them to a marriage bed where they affirm the law of reproduction by birthing more of its representations.

In *Ear of the Other,* Derrida describes a similar genealogy, but the source of the double affirmation is the mother, an "ageless virgin," who, like the ever-present " 'silhouette' " of *La Loi,* is a

> faceless figure of a *figurant,* an extra. She gives rise to all the figures by losing herself in the background of the scene like an anonymous persona. Everything comes back to her, beginning with life; everything addresses and destines itself to her. She survives on the condition of remaining at bottom. (38)

The mother's affirmative response to eternity (to Nietzsche's "nuptial ring of rings" in *Thus Spoke Zarathustra*) affords him (i.e., Nietzsche, Zarathustra, or Derrida) endless returns. Citing Nietzsche in *Ecce Homo*, Derrida places himself between the dead father and the living mother: " 'I am . . . already dead as my father, while as my mother, I am still living and becoming old' " (15). As in "The Law of Genre," Derrida seems to bed the figure of the mother/woman in order for *her* to re-birth *him*. Yet she, the matrix, remains always at the "bottom," barely subsisting except to provide the fertile grounds for his eternal returns. When Derrida (Nietzsche, Zarathustra, or Mallarmé) returns to the woman's body, she goes further into debt leaving "no trace of woman" save for "the mother" who, according to Derrida, is "part of the system" of reproduction (38). Her repeated "affirmation (yes, yes) . . . affirms the return, the rebeginning, and a certain kind of reproduction that preserves whatever comes back" (20).

Like the figures of the hymen, *La Loi*, and the mother, the figure of woman in Derrida's *Spurs: Nietzsche's Styles* gives inexhaustible gifts (109–119). Indeed, according to Derrida, giving is woman's "greatest advantage" (111). Derrida writes about the relation of woman to truth by engaging a passage from Nietzsche's *Joyful Wisdom*. Nietzsche describes women as "so artistic" because "they 'give themselves airs' ('give themselves for'), even when they—'give themselves' " (69). In the phrase "giving-herself-*for*," Derrida notes that the "*for*" signals that the woman always "withhold[s] the gift of a reserve" (111). Because in "giving-herself-for," woman simulates or acts her part, Derrida argues that her self-sacrifice assures "the possessive mastery for her own self" (109). While in "The Double Session" hymen piques the desire of the critic or the philosopher "to regain that lost mastery" that the figure represents (230), the man in *Spurs* wants to take and to gain possession of what escapes his authority—the figure of woman or truth (109). The role of the woman is to "give-herself-for," but "man for his part takes, possesses, indeed takes possession" (109).

Property Rights over Language and Writing

Clearly the ever-returning hymen and the gift-bearing woman are " 'beneficent' " figures for Derrida and "*prime*" (free bonus) terms for him to use and re-use in his "baffling economy of seduction" (DS, 226). But what are they for women from whose bodies Derrida takes parts, as if there were "free gifts," to lend corporeal form both to the text as well as his own deconstructive discourse? Throughout his *corpus*, the same *corpus* to which hymen/woman "gives" body, Derrida denies hymen/woman property rights to the very language, voiced or penned, that his figure serves to ground and to produce. So while Derrida may locate the origin of the "proper name" in the mother (EO, 38), or the source of writing in the hymen, or the law in the beautiful woman, she, "losing herself in the background" (EO, 38) or "murdering herself" for writing (DS, 229), barely subsists except as a figure, a silhouette, a blank.

Derrida's *corpus* depends on and grows out of not the "presence of the other" but rather her lack (DS, 185). Indeed, in his hymen (or marriage), Derrida marries not an "other" (woman) but men. In "The Double Session," for instance, Derrida engages Mallarmé and Plato and weds their notions of mimesis for a fruitful "fraternal generation" "produced on the same stalk" (283). This occurs in the first hymeneal crack of the text where a white upside-down L-(*elle*)-shaped blank topographically unites/separates two excerpted passages (175). Arranged in adjacent columns on the opening page, a segment of Plato's *Philebus* corners Mallarmé's *Mimique* and edges it over, pushing the smaller text into the lower right corner of the page and leading Derrida to pronounce the "Hymen: ENTRE Platon et Mallarmé" (182). In this marriage, Derrida "grafts on the same stalk" (283) two men's discourses on mimesis. From Derrida's coupling of Plato and Mallarmé, he "illustrate[s] the mimetic system" as a "system of *illustration*" (183).

Ultimately, property rights over language and the body are at stake in Derrida's figuration of the hymen since the hymeneal contract he draws up, signs, and seals (using the blood of woman) ensures unlimited rights to linguistic reproduction for the male writer and reader over the dismembered and deadened body of woman. For woman, the physical implications of the nuptial contract are indeed grave since the bridegroom gains proprietary rights—sexual and reproductive—over her body, her hymen and the reproductive properties to which it is connected. As other (belonging) to language, hymen/woman/mother has no proper(ty) rights and no right to language: the hymen as propagation-structure belongs to language which belongs to man. Derrida takes hymen from woman while distancing her from the operations of language and writing. In Derrida's *corpus*, woman, with no right to speak or write her own words, only mouths his *"yes, yes."* The double affirmation sounds beautiful and "economically seductive" (DS, 226) to the male writer's ears since its enunciation validates a hymeneal contract that allows him to appropriate her reproductive rights as his own and to use them to produce and lend form to his own written propagation. By turning it into one of his trademarks for the undecidable, Derrida gains property rights over hymen's physical traits and properties—both metaphorically and legally. The figure of hymen supplements and enriches his written productions while copyright laws protect his "seminal spurts" (DS, 285) from being mis-taken as any "other's." Derrida brands hymen as his own and re-deploys it as one of his trademarks in his signature style of deconstruction.

Forced Figure

Derrida forces or forges the signatures of his affirmative women— the hymen, *La Loi,* the mother, the ageless virgin. He violently tears hymen in order to produce " *'nuptial proofs of the Idea'* " (DS, 178). With the blood he extracts from his figuration, he signs a "marriage-bond" or "hymen" that puts woman into debt: "Yes, yes," Derrida writes for the absent woman, "I approve, I sign, I subscribe to this acknowledgment of *the debt incurred toward 'myself,'* my-life—and I want it to return" (EO, 14). She turns over her life, gives it as a gift to her spouse and his offspring in exchange for her supposed "debt." As her "returns" diminish, however, his increase without end or frame until there is "no woman or trace of woman" (EO, 38) and "next-to-nothing of the hymen" (DS, 262).

Luce Irigaray eloquently argues in *Marine Lover of Friedrich Nietzsche* (1980) that Nietzsche and (implicitly) Derrida have no ears by which to hear the other's "no" to their nuptial contracts (83–84). She asks them: "why don't you give her leave to speak? From the place where she sings the end of your becoming, let her be able to tell you: no" (32). But brandishing " 'a knife, like a cook slaughtering fowls' " (as Derrida quotes from Mallarmé (DS, 259)), man (Derrida, Mallarmé, Nietzsche) violently forces the redoubled "yes" from woman's lips (*lèvres*) just as he makes "the red edges" of the book (*livre*) bleed by introducing a " 'letter opener, to mark the taking of possession' " (DS, 259). He separates and marks lips and books (*lèvres* and *livres*) in order to multiply his own properties in "a game of chance that follows the genetic program" (DS, 285). However, as Irigaray notes, only other males of the family can possess and pass on the genealogical and economic legacy (ML, 112). Irigaray writes:

> From this "yes" of her flesh that is always given and proffered to suit your eternity, you draw your infinite reserves of veils and sails, of wings and flight. . . . It is because she never says anything but "yes" to your all that you are able to go off so far, so high. . . . Once she is deflowered, you can draw infinitely upon her for your weaving, your painting, your writing, your music too . . . For the beauty you create. (ML, 33)

The deflowering act, the tearing of the hymenal membrane, the violation of "veiled lips" claims a writing surface, a sheet of skin, upon which man writes his signature and draws his representations to ensure his own immortality. Always in the background and forever at bottom of representation, woman "[f]rom this outside position" (ML, 91) grounds a phallic "economy of seduction" (DS, 226). What Derrida sees as the "seduction" of the other, Irigaray recognizes as a rape or a theft. She writes:

> Rape/rob the female one so that the other can indefinitely produce doubles for him. Take the female one for himself so that the other, all the others, distractedly, may continue the same operation but to his advantage. Multiplying his property. Indefinitely.

> The exile of woman outside herself leads her to engage in inexhaustible mimicry to the father's benefit. Her death—that she grounds, doubles . . . amounts to making her double anything. . . . (ML, 106)

Throughout his *corpus*, Derrida stalks woman "as if she were his prey" (ML, 117). As his "bounty" (*prime*) (DS, 226), he gains from her, Irigaray argues, "the drunken pleasure of being more, while remaining the same" (ML, 117): " 'the return of the same—but almost other' " (DS 228). The figure of woman re-doubles the male, "[i]increasing, without end(s)" and "without frame or term" (ML, 117). While Derrida's "dissemination *affirms* the always already divided generation of meaning" (DS, 268), the dispersal originates not from a marriage with the other, but rather from the phallus alone. Exiled from the scene and relegated to the background, hymen/woman leaves only a trace, a past presence that Derrida fetishizes to threaten castration while inspiring dissemination: "SPERM, the burning lava, milk spume, froth, or dribble of the seminal liquor" (DS, 266).

Since his whole system of representation depends on it, Derrida has an invested interest in hearing woman agree to a marriage proposal that diminishes her returns as his dividends increase. The forced hymeneal contract works to seal woman's last will and testament. The " *'nuptial proofs,'* " emissions of the torn membrane, consummate the marriage but also shroud or veil woman's death (DS, 260; see also ML, 28–31). As Irigaray puts it, Derrida has figured out a clever way to "finance the death of one's [man's] other" (ML, 79). His strategy disguises the contract he takes out on her life as a marriage contract, and he passes off his role as a "bounty" hunter (DS, 226; see also ML, 43) as that of the bride's groom. The conjugal rights ensured by the nuptial agreement cover up what in "The Double Session" Derrida calls the "perfect crime"— a rape-murder passes itself off as "the 'supreme spasm' " of a life-giving orgasm (DS, 201).

Rhetorical Strategies of Euphemization: Metonymy and Metaphor

Because his rhetorical strategies disguise and euphemize violence as love, Derrida's usury of hymen is particularly insidious. His euphemization depends on a forced forgetting of the social, economic, and political implications of hymen's history. A forced forgetting allows Derrida to re-deploy metonymical and metaphorical associations of the word without having to acknowledge or address its decidedly patriarchal history. As I will show, Derrida's forgetfulness turns hymen into a catachresis—rhetorically a forced figuration or a dead metaphor that, effaced of its history, passes as a "proper" way to refer to what otherwise has no properties of its own.

Linguistic associations, both metonymic and metaphoric, link hymen to biological and social systems of reproduction. Through metonymy, a linguistic trope that substitutes causes for effects and parts for tangential parts, hymen suggests biological reproduction. Metonymy associates the anatomical structure of hymen with one of its biological functions: facilitating conception. Located near a woman's reproductive organs, the hymen opens the vaginal enclosure and lines the outermost layers of the passage which also serves as birth canal. During sexual intercourse, the penis enters the "hymeneal" opening and, upon ejaculation, disperses semen onto the "hymen-lined" walls of the female's genital tract. Since the hymen is a mucous membrane, both penetration and conception are facilitated by its secretions which help both to transport and to provide a viable environment for sperm travelling toward the ovum.

Hymen's metonymical associations with sexual reproduction work at a physical and mechanical level involving substitutions of part for tangential part, part for the whole reproductive system (a synecdoche), cause for effect, and means for end. Because one term substitutes for another term, hymen metonymically becomes a mechanism of biological reproduction—a "propagation-structure" as Derrida calls it (DS, 261). But hymen can also be deployed as a metaphor for another type of reproduction: the reproduction of the social and symbolic through the institution of marriage. Archaically, Hymen was the "proper" name used to denote the socioeconomic institution of marriage.

The word's metaphoric reference to marriage can be traced from ancient Greece and Rome through the Renaissance. In ancient Greek and Roman mythologies, Hymen is the god of Marriage. Born either of a song between Apollo and one of his muses (thus an immaculate, noncorporeal conception), or fathered by Dionysus (whose excessive corporeality, as described by Irigaray, "lack[s] boundaries, limits—a skin" [ML, 123]), Hymen's genesis and biography are obscure. Supposedly so ideal was his marriage to an Athenian maiden (whom he had rescued from pirates), that thereafter Greeks and Romans invoked his name at wedding ceremonies and in nuptial hymns. Not always, however, were hymeneal incantations so joyous. In Euripides' *The Trojan Women,* for instance, Cassandra laments, "Hymen, my lord. Hymenaeus," as she prepares to sacrifice herself, in her father's name, to the enemy—a marriage "at the spear's edge." The mythic figure of Hymen symbolized social exchanges between men engaged in patrimonial power games in which women served merely as pawns to be moved to and fro.

In its various tropings, hymen fluidly turns from serving as a "proper" name for a mythical god to evoking abstract ideas of marriage; inversely, the idea of marriage reincarnates itself in Hymen as allegorical personification. As allegorical personification, Hymen appears in classical representations of weddings where, identifiable with his flaming torch and Cupid, his companion, he sanctifies matrimonial unions and emblematizes marriage as a sacred institution. Throughout the Renaissance and afterward, visual representations show Hymen forging the coats of arms of great patriarchal families, thus embodying the idea of a prosperous wedding—a fruitful union from the coupling of two sexes and of two familial social and economic units.

When it is forgotten that Hymen served as the "proper" name of an ancient mythological figure, or that capitalized, the word personified an allegorical idea, the historical implications of hymen's figuration as marriage fade into the background. Throughout the Middle Ages, the word primarily evoked associations of legal contract rather than mythological narratives. The archaic definition of hymen as the marriage contract (Derrida's " 'nuptial proofs of the Idea' " [DS, 195]) collapses or forgets distinctions both between anatomical organ and social institution and between the consummation of a sexual relationship and that of a legal contract.

Archaically, the legal consummation of a marriage involved the ritual act of breaking the bride's hymen to prove her virginity. In fact, customarily blood-stained bridal garments were submitted for legal inspection and public exhibition to provide evidence of her virginity, a property (or trait) given up for the marriage's consummation. These " 'nuptial proofs of the Idea' " (DS, 179) of marriage made a public spectacle out of the last traces of the hymen as membrane and its first emissions as a socially productive institution. What issued from the torn vaginal membrane (metaphorically a broken seal) sealed a marriage contract and guaranteed an untampered commodity. Only when the bride's groom marked in advance hymen's by-products as his own would a marriage gain proper legal recognition. The marriage's consummation recognized the man's staked claim over woman, her labor, her reproductive organs and, genealogically, their issue. Hymen was circumscribed by the patriarchical institution of marriage and forced to signify not only virginity and its loss, but also the legal consummation of a contractual relationship that equated sex with property and re-production—of the male order.

As continually re-deployed throughout history, the term hymen reclaims sexual acts as contractual acts. In its forced conscription (or figuration), hymen's uses and abuses within institutions of patriarchy are increasingly effaced until the term seems "naturally" to subsume and circumscribe biological reproduction within the institution of marriage. Yet the figuration of hymen as "propagation-structure" *and* "marriage" forcibly appropriates woman's properties and circumscribes them within a reproductive framework that benefits the male at the expense of the female. No longer is reproduction (biological, social, or symbolic) proper to woman; rather, through marriage/hymen, it belongs to the family of man, a patrilineal family in which properties can only be held and inherited by other males. Not unlike the copyrights that protect a writer's creations, property rights in the sexual/contractual union protect the husband's issue. Broken or unbroken, the hymeneal seal marks woman as another's property: her body—appropriated, claimed and branded—becomes an instrument of reproduction within patriarchal systems, both real and representational.

At moments when the physical coincides with figured meanings, it becomes apparent that the hymen as metaphor for marriage, a socioeconomic institution, already inscribes the "literal" or physical hymen as membrane "proper" to a woman's body. Patriarchal institutions have already determined hymen's significance in relation to biological reproduction, marriage, the family, and the sociopolitical economy. Likewise, a phallic economy determines woman's value as either virgin and potential commodity or property already consumed. Matrimonial *rites* consummate "conjugal *rights*": the "*right*" to sexual intercourse, which not so archaically the marriage contract guaranteed, implies both reproductive rites and "conjugal" rights. Not at the end, but from the very beginning the social re-writes the sexual, re-framing it within the terms of biological reproduction. As with other repeatable or *iterable* acts such as writing, the sociopolitical always already circumscribes biological reproduction. But the social has insinuated itself into the "natural" in ways that make it almost unrecognizable.

Popular beliefs surrounding the "loss" of a girl's "virginity" and the language that describes such events reveal traces of hymen's decidedly patriarchal history: man "deflowers" the virgin; he "takes" her virginity; he "makes" her a woman; she "loses" her virginity. . . . Luce Irigaray mimics this type of language in her work as a rhetorical strategy to reveal the insidious phallogocentrism of language and its social inscriptions. In her essay "When Our Lips Speak Together" (1980), Irigaray writes, *"between us* there is no rupture between virginal and non virginal. No event makes us a woman. . . . Your/my body doesn't acquire its sex through an operation. Through the action of some power, function, or organ" (211). Derrida similarly points out that the word hymen has no "natural," "literal," or purely physical referent: the value of the hymen "is worth nothing in itself; it is neither good nor bad" (185). He uses this fact, however, to willfully forget the history of hymen. As deeply imbricated within patriarchal systems of matrimony and the family as the hymen is, is it possible for Derrida to use the word as a tool to deconstruct logocentric and phallocentric systems of signification? His appropriation of the hymen as an antidote to the phallus as transcendental signifier only symptomizes the phallogocentric problem he pretends to oppose and deconstruct. Indeed, he perpetuates the phallic economy by further fetishizing the figures of woman and hymen and "suspending" them " *'between desire and fulfillment, perpetration and remembrance'* " (209). His fetishization disguises both the violence of his own symbolic economy (an economy based on the principle of castration) as well as hymen's violent history.

Catachresis: Forgetting and Euphemizing a Violent History

Derrida covers up the workings of his phallic economy by using hymen rhetorically as a catachresis. In his essay "White Mythology: Metaphor in the Text of Philosophy," Derrida shows philosophical language and metaphysics to work according to "a system of catachreses, a fund of 'forced metaphors,'" which have no relation to anything literal, natural, or physical (WM, see especially 255–257). Using Fontaniers's *Supplement to the Theory of Tropes,* Derrida explains catachresis as

> the violent, forced, abusive inscription of a sign, the imposition of a sign upon a meaning which did not yet have its own

proper sign in language. So much so that there is no substitution here, no transport of proper signs, but rather the irruptive extension of a sign proper to an idea, a meaning, deprived of their signifier. (WM, 255)

As the rhetorical trope of forced figures or dead metaphors, catachresis "irrupts" and "abuses" the code of signification by applying it, twisting it to produce symbolic value (256–257). When catachreses commonly circulate, repeated social usage (or usury) allows them to tacitly pass as " 'correct and natural' " (257), as "proper" ways to refer to things or ideas. Their forced figuration as " 'nontrue figures' " (256) collectively forgotten, catachreses come to be taken as the only possible means of reference. For instance, when we refer to the "arm" and "leg" of a chair we usually intend to suspend, for the sake of economy, the words' metonymical and metaphorical associations with the body. This is inevitable—a condition of language and philosophy—and nothing to get worked up over. However, when hymen, as repeatedly deployed throughout Derrida's work, begins to refer to the "undecidable," it is effaced of its physicality along with its *decidedly* patriarchal history. The violence that conscripts and forces hymen into labor, goes unrecognized as violence.

While the economic loss of meaning fascinates Derrida, who invokes etymological nuances of the word, he claims that the "lexical richness, the semantic infiniteness" of hymen is not what "counts" (DS, 220):

What counts here is the formal or syntactical *praxis* that composes and decomposes it. We have indeed been making believe that everything could be traced to the word hymen.... *The loss of the "hymen" would not be irreparable for* [Mallarmé's] *Mimique* [or for mimesis]. It produces its effect first and foremost through the syntax, which disposes the *"entre"* in such a way that *the suspense is due only to the placement and not the content of the words.* (DS, 220 [Emphasis mine])

Ultimately the content of the metaphor of hymen means nothing to Derrida. The social and linguistic practice of using hymen disperses and multiplies its signification, but the signifier itself, according to Derrida, " 'loses even a meaning,' becomes extenuated, devalued, mined out. Names no longer" (DS, 263). But "never min(e)d [*mine de rien*]," writes Derrida, which colloquially means that hymen's loss "is of no importance" to him but literally that hymen is "a mine full of nothing" and, thus, a vain loss (DS, 216; see also 262–267). Any other sign for deconstruction could easily replace hymen: *pharmakon, supplément,* or *différance.* Lifted to a metaphysical level, hymen's loss makes no difference to Derrida. Like other consumable properties, its abundant supply in his phallic economy ensures hymen's dispensiblity. Always available—"willing" and "ready" to "lend" itself—the (n)ever virginal hymen returns to disseminate more of the same.

Rather than its content, what "counts" for Derrida is hymen's "placement" between terms of symbolic exchange. Syntactically, this "placement" produces the "euphoria of a suspension" in men's exchanges. Place determines the meaning of the hymen and the value of woman as nothing in herself but as virgin or non-virgin in relation to the "tip" (*"le point"*—the prick) of the male: hymen/woman "is inscribed at the very tip [*le point*] of . . . indecision. The tip advances according to the irreducible excess of the syntactic over the semantic" (DS, 221). Derrida's symbolic economy places woman, like other commodities on the market, between an all-consuming " 'desire and fulfillment' " of men (DS, 175; see also 209–216).

Derrida's rhetorical exchanges of part for part and part for the (w)hole of woman insidiously veil his perpetuation of a tradition of violence against woman, both real and representational. Violence is rendered unrecognizable as violence in what Derrida describes as a "perfect crime," a crime that passes as "its opposite: an act of love" (DS, 214). This "perfect crime" or " 'barbarous simulacrum' " (259), which is "(at the same time or somewhere between) love and murder" (212–213), is illustrated in Derrida's reading of Mallarmé's *Mimique.* In Mallarmé's short text, a mime has murdered his wife, and he proceeds to mime or re-present his past crime in the present by playing both the roles of the husband and the wife, the murderer and his victim. The mime justifies murdering his wife with the claim that she turned him into a cuckold, but more importantly, he "felt like it": " 'I killed her—because I felt like it, I am the master, what can anyone say?' " (200). The mime tickles to death his wife, and she dies in a "supreme spasm" (201). Miming both pleasure and death, the mime re-presents the crime, the rape-murder, as if it were her own masturbatory suicide. Like Derrida's white blank page that "blackens itself of its own accord" or "murders itself" for writing, the violent murder of the woman goes unrecognized as a crime. Within the legal institution of marriage, a rape too easily passes as "love"; under the law, a wife's "no" may be too easily mis-taken as "implied consent." Thus the crime "has never been committed," and yet it "turns into [the woman's] suicide without striking or suffering a blow" (210). Derrida's law of representation turns a fact into "fiction" and an event into a "dream," thus obliterating the crime: "reference [of hymen] is lifted, but reference remains: what is left is only the writing of dreams, a fiction that is not imaginary, mimicry without imitation" (211).

Derrida's symbolic economy is driven by a decidedly phallic desire. "It is the hymen that desire dreams of piercing, or bursting," writes Derrida, "in an act of violence that is (at the same time or somewhere between) love and murder" (212–213). Desire fulfills itself (or suspends itself) not within a true marriage/hymen with an other, but in a wet dream that "abolishes" and "obliterates" her from the scene of representation. As Derrida describes it:

> Dissemination skims and froths the flight and theft of the seminal: a vain, blank loss in a wet dream in which the masthead, *pour qui le lit* [*for the one that reads / for which the bed exists*], blots itself into abysses of lost veils, sails, and children. *A«bo / lit.* The "*so white.*" (267)

Barbara Johnson, translator of "The Double Session," notes that *Abolit* means "abolishes," but it is also a homonym for *á beau lit* ("with/to a beautiful bed") and is aurally related to (*il*) *a beau lire* ("he reads in vain") (267). The superficially beautiful puns underscore Derrida's strategy of euphemizing his violent dis(re)membering of woman from the scene of representation.

Woman is not the only thing obliterated in Derrida's operation. Completely absent, without even a trace, is woman's desire. Derrida seductively plays with hymen as "between desire and fulfillment," repeatedly referring to the following Mallarmé quote:

> The scene illustrates but the idea, not any actual action, in a hymen (out of which flows Dream), tainted with vice yet sacred, between desire and fulfillment, perpetration and remembrance:

> here anticipating, there recalling, in the future, in the past,
> *under the false appearance of a present.* (175)

By now it is only too obvious "between" whose "desire and fulfillment" hymen is placed. A heterosexual male's desire occupies central stage, leaving woman's sexual desire and pleasure not even in the background, but completely unaccounted for. Never bothering to hear the *other* side of his "baffling economy of seduction" (226), Derrida writes-off woman's sexual pleasure from his books. His fetishization of hymen serves a phallic desire, threatening castration while supplying a fetish-substitute for the phallus: "the hymen as protective screen, the jewel box of virginity, the vaginal partition, the fine, invisible veil which, in front of the hystera, stands *between* the inside and the outside of a women, and consequently between desire and fulfillment" (212–213).

Derrida's fetishization of hymen and his excision of woman's pleasure from his accounts amounts to what Gayatri Chakravorty Spivak has described as a "symbolic clitoridectomy" ("French Feminism in an International Frame," 181). The real operation, still practiced in parts of Africa and the Middle East, excises all or part of a woman's clitoris in a ceremonial ritual that marks her a woman, makes her socially acceptable, and prepares her for marriage and childbearing. Like the real operation that cuts off the very organ associated with woman's sexual pleasure, the symbolic clitoridectomy in Derrida's economy obliterates an important symbol of the geography of woman's pleasure and sexual difference. Focusing only on vaginal penetration and the hymen, Derrida attempts to reestablish man's mastery over what otherwise "escapes reproductive framing"—clitoral pleasure (as Spivak argues, 180–181). Of course, as Irigaray has warned, it would be a mistake to attempt to remedy Derrida's omission by merely shifting the focus to woman's clitoral pleasure, for that organ would then serve only as another phallic substitute for a transcendental signifier. In "This Sex Which Is Not One," Irigaray instead argues for an economy that recognizes a far more diversified pleasure, "more multiple in its differences, more complex, more subtle, than is commonly imagined—an imaginary rather too narrowly focused on sameness" (28). Indeed, when Derrida replaces the phallus with the hymen, his operation merely exchanges one term for another allowing for the economy of sameness to remain driven by/toward a single sharp point (*le point*), by/toward a single prick: "It is the hymen that desire dreams of piercing, of bursting, in an act of violence that is (at the same time or somewhere between) love and murder" (212–213).

Ultimately, Derrida's willful memory lapse of hymen's violently phallocentric history allows him to sow his own seeds of dissemination under the " 'false appearance of a present,' " where the gift he makes of hymen passes as something "other" than the phallic signifier it really is. The history of the patriarchal appropriation of women's properties, including their bodies, their language, and their productive and reproductive rights, is forgotten. Man's past debts to woman, then, never fall due (*échéance*) in this mis-played game (*déjoue jeu*) where Derrida mis-takes hymen as "principle, and bounty [*prime*]" in a "baffling [*déjouante*] economy of seduction" (DS, 285; see also 226). For Derrida, this signifies unrequited love: "perpetual allusion that never breaks the ice or the mirror," . . . "in a pure medium of fiction" (DS, 210). His desire is sustained through "non-per(pen)etration," and fulfillment is contained within perpetual desire. What is unrequited love for Derrida who borrows the body of woman, for the woman is rape. His symbolic operations increasingly de-sexualize woman, and as the "differends" (DS, 210) are lifted, she is left *in-different* to either desire or fulfillment. In his hymeneal fable, woman's value along with the value of her pleasure are effaced, rubbed out, excised within an economy where hymen, forced into labor, serves merely as a front for the phallus.

--------------------- REFERENCES ---------------------

Derrida, Jacques. 1979. *Spurs: Nietzsche's styles*. Trans. Barbara Harlow. Chicago: University of Chicago Press; cited as S.

———. 1981. The double session. In *Dissemination,* trans. Barbara Johnson. Chicago: University of Chicago Press, 171–285; cited as DS.

———. 1981. The law of genre. In *On narrative,* trans. Avital Ronnell, ed. W. J. T. Mitchell. Chicago: University of Chicago Press, 51–77; cited as LG.

———. 1982. White mythology: Metaphor in the text of philosophy. In *Margins of philosophy*, trans. Alan Bass. Chicago: University of Chicago Press, 207–271; cited as WM.

———. 1985. *The ear of the other*. Trans. Peggy Kamuf and Avital Ronnell, ed. Christie McDonald and Claude Lévesque. Lincoln: University of Nebraska Press; cited as EO.

Irigaray, Luce. 1985. This sex which is not one. In *This sex which is not one*, trans. Catherine Porter. Ithaca: Cornell University Press, 23–33.

———. 1985. When our lips speak together. In *This sex which is not one*, trans. Catherine Porter. Ithaca: Cornell University Press, 205–218.

———. 1991. *Marine lover of Friedrich Nietzsche*. Trans. Gillian C. Gill. New York: Columbia University Press; cited as ML.

Oliver, Kelly. 1995. *Womanizing Nietzsche: Philosophy's relation to the "feminine."* New York: Routledge.

Spivak, Gayatri Chakravorty. 1981. French feminism in an international frame. *Yale French Studies* 62: 154–184.

Part Four

The Power of Feminist Metaphors

Words that Open Spaces for Women

Ewa Płonowska Ziarek

―――――――――――― *11* ――――――――

At the Limits of Discourse

Heterogeneity, Alterity, and the
Maternal Body in Kristeva's Thought

I

The intense debate around Kristeva's work among many feminist theorists indicates that her thought generates questions
of central importance to any feminist project devoted to revision of
culture and discourse. One of the most controversial among those
issues that Kristeva's theory incessantly confronts and submits "to
an interminable analysis" is the role of the maternal in the production of discourse. As she herself claims, it is not only a theoretical
enterprise but also a matter of ethics and, I would claim, of politics
as well. No wonder then that the explicit relation between discourse and the maternal body constitutes at once the most promising and the most problematic aspect of her work.[1] On the one
hand, her theory of semiotics opens a specifically feminine point of
resistance to the phallocentric models of culture. On the other hand,
because the semiotic is associated with the *prediscursive* libidinal
economy, the grounds and the effectiveness of that resistance appear problematic at the very least.

This controversy is reproduced in numerous interpretations of
Kristeva, which I am schematically organizing here into two groups.
The first one—for instance, Toril Moi (1985, 150–167), Jane Gallop

(1982, 113–131), Carolyn Burke (1987, 107–114), Mary Jacobus (1986, 169), and Susan Rubin Suleiman (1985, 366–371)—emphasizes different aspects of subversion in Kristeva's work. The second—Kaja Silverman (1988, 101–140), Ann Rosalind Jones (1984), Jacqueline Rose (1986, 151–157), Eleanor Kuykendall (1989, 180–195), Elizabeth Grosz (1989, 97), and Judith Butler (1990, 89–91)[2]—responds that such resistance rests on a problematic relation between the maternal and culture and in fact works to exclude women from the symbolic. More specifically, the questions generated in response to Kristeva's reliance on the prediscursive maternal economy have concerned the source of subversion, the political efficacy of her theory, the position of the female subject, and the issue of female agency. Does Kristeva, in spite of her intentions, blindly repeat the traditional cultural gesture that relegates women to a precultural, prediscursive position? Can her maternal source of resistance lead to any significant transformation of cultural paradigms? Does it empower the female speaker? Can it address the issue of female agency? And finally, does her elaboration of the maternal outside the symbolic order boil down to a crude version of essentialism, if not a mute biologism?

In order to advance the existing debate, it is more productive at this point to examine *how* Kristeva challenges the very distinctions between the prediscursive and the discursive, the precultural and the cultural, and to what degree her conceptual revision is effective. Kristeva's writings make it clear that these distinctions are not neutral or self-evident but are implicated in operations of exclusion, power, and control over the production and interpretation of discourse.[3] In other words, not only is the division between the linguistic and nonlinguistic shifting and open to revision, but also the decision about what aspects of signification fall on one or the other side of this divide is culturally produced and rests on gender presuppositions. As Kristeva constantly reminds her readers, linguistic analyses are not free from ethical and political decisions, especially when they refer to the role of the maternal in the production of discourse. In this context, I am particularly interested in the following issues: Why have the particular features of signification, coded as maternal, been relegated to the *prediscursive* position? How can we read this *prediscursive* in the larger context of Kristeva's theory of signification? Why does Kristeva need this *prediscursive* economy in order to arrive at a completely different understanding of what counts as *dis-*

cursive in cultural practices? Is it possible to comprehend the "prediscursive chora" as an attempt to disclose a signifying economy (the trace, negativity, and the rhythm) prior to the logic of the sign predicated on the separation and discontinuity between subject and object, signifier and signified? And if so, how does Kristeva negotiate the passage between this signifying economy and the maternal body?

Beginning with *Revolution in Poetic Language* (1984), Kristeva has insistently stressed the task of rethinking the maternal body as inseparable from the rethinking of language. In that first work, Kristeva opens her analysis of semiotics with avant-garde literature, as if to suggest that a different language lesson, provided by poetry rather than structuralist linguistics, is in order before one can refigure the cultural significance of the maternal body. Because poetry can perform "one of the most spectacular shatterings of discourse" and remain a linguistic practice nonetheless, it reveals for Kristeva "the limits of socially useful discourse and attests to what it represses: the *process* that exceeds the subject and his communicative structures" (Kristeva 1984, 16). By exploding the ideological constraints of the subject and discourse, poetic practice can disclose "the limits of formalist and psychoanalytic" approaches to language and bring into the open the signifying process that they exclude. And yet poetic practice is not revolutionary in and of itself. Kristeva asks a larger question: under what historical circumstances could this poetic process correspond to socioeconomic change, and under what conditions is it neutralized as a harmless "esoterism" and "aestheticism"? This approach to the maternal body, via poetry on the one hand and a larger socioeconomic analysis of the capitalist modes of production on the other, warns Kristeva's readers from the outset against the hasty conclusion that the attempt to think the maternal is a plunge into a mute biology, or a mere mystification of the prelinguistic unity between the mother and the child. Rather, I would argue, Kristeva's parallel discussion of poetry and the body suggests a displacement of natural primacy by a strategic redistribution of positions, a departure from natural origins. It implies from the outset that the question of the mother will be bound up with the task of the redefinition of language as a social practice rather than being simply an escape into a prelinguistic, narcissistic fantasy of the maternal paradise.

I would like, then, to repeat Kristeva's detour and focus on her theory of semiotics in order to underscore its two problematic aspects—heterogeneity and the prediscursive—which have not been sufficiently addressed in the numerous interpretations of her work. First of all, Kristeva's insistence on heterogeneity should be taken in a double sense: not only as the infolding of the body and language but also as the infolding of the two signifying economies. Kristeva attempts to think the processes of signification that are not reducible to semantics, symbolization, and the bipolar structure of the sign. By uncovering "disquieting" and heterogeneous elements of signification in a variety of disciplines (especially in linguistics, psychoanalysis, and phenomenology), Kristeva is concerned with the forms of otherness and multiplicity excluded by unifying orders of discourse. In this context, the thought of "irreducible" heterogeneity does not intend to ground language and culture in "a natural and pre-paternal causality" (Butler 1990, 89–91); rather, it anticipates a different understanding of language that takes into account interweaving of heterogeneous elements. In Kristeva's own words, such irreducible heterogeneity "goes by various names according to the conceptual framework of the theory that posits it and the level of its operations. *But the name always designates something irreducible, a disquieting heterogeneousness*, outside the transcendental enclosure within which we are otherwise constrained by phenomenology and its relative, linguistics" (Kristeva 1983, 40–41, italics added).[4] This analysis of the *traces* of heterogeneity in the linguistic and psychic economy aims to break away from the phenomenological constraints of both linguistics and subjectivity—that is, from the view of entities as clearly separated, distinct, and self-contained. As Kristeva argues in *Revolution in Poetic Language,* the inability to theorize the heterogeneity of linguistic practices leads invariably to positing of the transcendental ego as the implied subject corresponding to the symbolic order.[5]

Now I would like to turn to the second troublesome aspect of Kristeva's theory—the so-called move beyond language. For many feminist critics, Kristeva's association of the maternal with the prelinguistic moment evokes the most oppressive hierarchies of phallocentrism (the maternal body belongs to nature, the paternal law to culture)—hence the justified responses of caution, if not straightforward resistance, to that part of Kristeva's theory. Yet, if we situate Kristeva's analysis of "the maternal territory" in the larger context of poststructuralism, then her emphasis on the prediscursive is strategic: it indicates both the limitations of structuralist linguistics and the need to rethink the process of signification.

The thought of heterogeneity leads Kristeva to supplement the tradition of structuralist semiotics (which perceives language as a sign system) with the analysis of "what falls outside the system and characterizes the *specificity* of the practice as such" (Kristeva 1986b, 26). Her investigations in *Revolution in Poetic Language* and in her later work *Desire in Language* analyze what traditional linguistics excludes—"a crisis or the unsettling process of meaning" within the signifying phenomena—in order to produce a theory of signification based on the embodied speaking subject and the materialist historical process. In her critique of the "static formalism" of structuralism, Kristeva, like Adorno, claims that this ahistorical formalist approach to language is encouraged by the capitalist ideology. Kristeva passionately advocates a new linguistics (and later a new psychoanalysis) that would not only classify the signifying phenomena but also embrace within them moments of negativity, disruption, and undecidability. To carry out such analysis, she proposes to turn from the theory of language as a universal sign system to language as a "signifying process" in order to underscore both systematicity and transgression in every signifying practice, which she calls symbolic and semiotic disposition, respectively. Kristeva's signifying process defies the fundamental Saussurian distinctions between synchrony and diachrony, *langue* (language as a collective sign system) and *parole* (its individual usage), because each signifying practice is not merely a manifestation of a general code but results from the dialectic between the systematicity of signs and the transgression of drives. Therefore, only on the level of the specificity of signifying practices (which are invariably both more and less than underlying code) can we observe the traces of heterogeneity and transgression (Kristeva 1986b, 31). Kristeva's understanding of signification implies also a different understanding of culture, no longer conceptualized in terms of a general symbolic system but in terms of the specificity and multiplicity of signifying practices. Such decentering of the semantic/cultural field offers the most promising political implications (although not always explicitly elaborated by Kristeva) of her work.[6]

This turn from the theory of language as a sign system to the specificity of the signifying practices is not only advocated by Kristeva but also produced by her revision of the signifying process. Kristeva refers the symbolic level of language—that is, the dimension of sign, syntax, and, in the Lacanian terminology, the realm of the paternal law—to the presymbolic economy of the drives, characterizing the complex exchanges between the mother and the child prior to individuation of the subject and object. Like Lacan, Kristeva focuses primarily in her interpretation on the negativity of the death drive. Borrowing the term from Plato's *Timaeus*, Kristeva calls this heterogeneous and diffuse field of drives the semiotic maternal *chora* (the Greek word for space, place, locality).[7] Contrary to some interpretations of the chora as a return to essentialism and biologism, the chora is a cultural phenomenon for several reasons. First of all, *chora* already refers to the cultural ordering of the drives, which distribute energy according to social restraints exercised on the body: "they are arranged according to the various constraints imposed on this body—always already involved in a semiotic process—by family and social structures" (Kristeva 1984, 25). She thus resituates the Platonic chora on the level of the socialized body. Second, Kristeva stresses on numerous occasions that what is at stake here is *the structure* and *the economy* of the drives and not the mere presence of the biological body: "The position of the semiotic as heterogeneous does not derive from a desire to integrate, within a language . . . , a supposed concreteness, a raw corporeality, or an immanent energy" (Kristeva 1983, 36). More akin to rhythm and mobile traces than structure, it describes regulated movements and their "ephemeral" stasis, moments of gathering and irruptions, which lead to no identity, no body proper. And finally, and this is the least frequently commented aspect of her work, Kristeva reinterprets the destructiveness and repetition of the drives—the process of rejection and expulsion—in terms of the dialectical negativity. In so doing, she claims to give the Hegelian dialectic the materialist base by linking negativity to the movement of the heterogenous matter: "The logic exposed above will become materialist when, with the help of Freud's discovery, one dares think negativity as *the very movement of heterogenous matter,* inseparable from its differentiation's symbolic function" (Kristeva 1984, 113).

When Kristeva characterizes the specificity of the semiotic and the symbolic from the perspective of the genealogy of the subject, she points out that the choric rhythm of accumulation and dissolution is sublated at the moment of language acquisition into a thetic stage. Accomplished at two points—at the mirror stage and at the moment of the discovery of castration—the thetic phase corresponds to the bipolar division of the signified and the signifier and to the formation of syntax. In order to describe the transformation of the semiotic into the symbolic, Kristeva deploys the Hegelian concept of *Aufhebung*, which has a double meaning of "negation" and "conservation." Yet these references to Hegel underscore not only the fact that the symbolic is produced by a dialectical operation but also that this operation fails to subsume entirely the semiotic heterogeneity: no "signifier can effect the *Aufhebung* of the semiotic without leaving the remainder" (Kristeva 1984, 51). Because of these residues—or traces—of the first symbolizations, the symbolic level of language is just a certain stage, constantly open to the irruption of heterogeneity into the unity of the signifier: "All poetic 'distortions' of the signifying chain . . . may be considered in this light: they yield under the attack of the 'residues of the first symbolizations' (Lacan), in other words, those drives that the thetic phase was not able to sublate . . . by linking them into signifier and signified" (Kristeva 1984, 49).[8]

This irruption characterizing the economy of the drives *within* the symbolic level of language constitutes the third pseudo moment or level in Kristeva's dialectic—that is, a postsymbolic level of *every* signifying practice but most visible in poetic language, which is characterized as "a 'second-degree thetic', i.e., a resumption of the functioning of the semiotic chora within the signifying device of language" (Kristeva 1984, 50).[9] In Kristeva's account, then, the semiotic is both a presymbolic and postsymbolic moment. Clearly, the second moment attracts Kristeva's attention because the articulation of the drives can become a practice, a text, only when it enters language, "appropriating and displacing signifier." The only way we can access the semiotic on the level of cultural practices is by studying, or by performing, the "remodeling of the historically accepted *signifying device* by proposing a different relation to natural objects, social apparatuses, and the body proper" (Kristeva 1984, 126). Moreover, Kristeva will claim that the semiotic that precedes symbolization is only a theoretical presupposition, a theoretical fiction if you will, "justified by the need of description": "Only theory can isolate [the semiotic] as 'preliminary' in order to specify its functioning" (Kristeva 1984, 68). In other words, theory does not describe a psychic development but produces this genealogical description: "Theory can 'situate' such processes and relations diachronically within the process of the constitution of the subject because *they function synchronically within the signifying process of the subject himself*, i.e., the subject of *cogitatio*" (Kristeva 1984, 29). This is an extremely important point: here Kristeva postulates the theory of the chora in order to account for the moments of undecidability and transformation working always already within the subject and culture (on the synchronic level): "Language as social practice necessarily presupposes these two dispositions, though combined in different ways to constitute *types of discourses*, types of signifying structures" (Kristeva 1980, 134). The chora, then, can be read as a theoretical construction (rather than a natural stage) enabling us to see and to explain the constant disruptions of the symbolic stability (that is supposed to be secured by the paternal law) not as mere accidents or lapses into psychosis but as the necessary and regulated effects of the process of signification.[10]

II

Bearing in mind some of the conclusions of Kristeva's linguistic analysis, especially the fact that the semiotic is not just a simple return to the economy of the drives but the reinscription of the symbolic as such, let us turn to the other "site" of Kristeva's proceedings, the "site" of the maternal body. Such reinscription of the symbolic (the fact that the symbolic in the pure form does not exist) demands departure from the theory of language as a sign system to the analysis of the multiplicity and specificity of signifying practices. Otherwise, we will keep perpetuating the notion that Kristeva places the mother "beyond language" (i.e., beyond signification).[11] Clearly, in Kristeva's theory *both* poetry and the semiotic process of the maternal body have the potential to disrupt language as a social code:

> The speaker reaches this limit (of the symbolic) . . . only by virtue of a particular, discursive practice called "art." A woman also attains it . . . through the strange *form of split symbolization* (threshold of language and instinctual drive, of the "symbolic" and the "semiotic") of which the act of giving birth consists. (Kristeva 1980, 240–241; italics added)

We are encouraged to reconceptualize the maternal function as another instance of the infolding of the semiotic and the symbolic, as "a radical form of split symbolizations," which unsettles the positioning of both consciousness and body and introduces, in Kristeva's terms, "wandering" or "fuzziness" in place of semantic/logical connectives (Kristeva 1980, 136).

However, because it is very difficult to sustain this duplicity of/about the maternal body in her own discourse, Kristeva invariably produces in her interpreters signs of impatience and a desire to correct her texts, that is, to give one disposition—the semiotic or the symbolic—primacy over the other. Before suggesting my reading of the maternal body in Kristeva's texts, it would be useful to follow the course of one of the most compelling corrections offered by Kaja Silverman (1988, 101–140). The trajectory of Silverman's reading proceeds from a refutation of the chora as a prelinguistic origin to its placement within the symbolic as the negative Oedipus complex. The hypothesis of the negative Oedipus complex also radically revises both Freud's and Lacan's accounts of femininity because it transfers the little girl's erotic investment in the mother from the prelinguistic, pre-Oedipal to the symbolic level of language and desire. In this way, the chora receives clear representational support and therefore can challenge the paternal law "from within representation and meaning" (Silverman 1988, 123–124). If I nonetheless object to Silverman's interpretation, it is because I read the chora as already a signifying economy and because I claim that it is impossible to incorporate this maternal signification *without* deconstructing the symbolic order, which excludes semiotic signification in the first place. Moreover, I suspect that the inclusion of the maternal in the symbolic order compromises Kristeva's insistence on both the heterogeneity of linguistic practices and the otherness of the maternal body: *"it is imperative that we recognize the unconscious mother for who she is,"* that we "situate the daughter's passion for the mother . . . *firmly* within the symbolic" (Silverman 1988, 125, 123; italics added). The irony of this revision is indeed the "firm" assimilation of the choreic to the thetic operation and a foreclosure of Kristeva's most radical discovery—that is, the heterogeneity of discourse.

In order to underscore the insufficiency of the symbolic construction as a tool for both linguistic and psychoanalytical analysis, Kristeva introduces the notion of the semiotic as a material yet nonphenomenological trace. Like Silverman, Kristeva claims that the semiotic does not exist apart from the symbolic, but she insists that its status *within* the symbolic should be described as a nonphenomenological trace. The fact that the semiotic never becomes a part of the symbolic, that it never enters the nexus of the signs but instead disrupts their order, does not mean that it is not linguistic. On the contrary, for Kristeva the semiotic is perhaps the most important linguistic force. Yet what is characteristic about the semiotic trace is that it cannot be turned into either an alternative origin or an independent symbolic position:

> For to imagine the autonomy of the "trace," the "pictogram," or the "cryptogram" with respect to language's own thetic position, or to envisage some logical or chronological precedence to its impact, would be to give a helping—that is, a theoretical—hand to the maintenance of the notion of the maternal phallus. . . . Thus this semiotic mode has no primacy, no point of origin. When I heard it in echolalias . . . asyntactical and alogical constructions—in all of these divergences from codified discourse . . .—the semiotic chora appears within the signifying *process* as the trace of the *jouissance*. (Kristeva 1983, 36–38)

Kristeva demands that we read the semiotic chora neither as an alternative, more authentic origin (such an origin is indeed only a defensive fantasy of the Edenic image of the primary narcissism) nor as an alternative independent position within the symbolic, but as traces of alterity and heterogeneity operating *within* the linguistic and psychic economy.

Although articulated on the psycholinguistic rather than textual level, Kristeva's notion of the semiotic trace participates in a deconstruction of presence and the order of the sign similar to that of Derrida's trace. By pointing out this similarity, I'm not suggesting that these are isomorphic notions but, rather, parallel constructions. Like Kristeva, Derrida defines the trace as a mark of difference *within* every identity, a mark *"retaining the other as other in the same"* (Derrida 1974, 62; italics added.)[12] Kristeva finds Derrida's notion of the trace most promising in the project of deconstruction and acknowledges in "grammatology" a parallel attempt to think a signifying economy irreducible to the symbolic order and the concept of the sign. Through the notion of the trace Kristeva can find certain analogies—especially in the explorations of otherness, heterogeneity, and the critique of logocentrism—between semiotics and grammatology: Derridean trace and writing "both can be thought of as metaphors for a movement that retreats before the thetic but, sheltered by it, unfolds only within the stases of the semiotic *chora*." And, "we may posit that the force of writing [*écriture*] lies precisely in its return to the space-time previous to the phallic stage—indeed previous even to the identifying or mirror stage" (Kristeva 1984, 141, 143). Such status of the semiotic does not imply that it is ineffective or futile, but, I suggest, it questions the fundamental metaphysical notions of presence, origin, identity, and the notion of the sign itself. By insisting on these analogies between Derrida and Kristeva, I do not want to foreclose some important differences between their positions. For instance, Kristeva repeatedly criticizes Derrida for failing to address the subjective and sociopolitical implications of his theory. Nonetheless, deconstruction remains an important, though often unmentioned, context for assessing Kristeva's critique of structuralism.

The event of motherhood and pregnancy represents for Kristeva another resumption of the semiotic chora within the symbolic figuration of the body. Although Kristeva's account of pregnancy complements her analysis of poetic language, it also provides a new critical perspective. Specifically, it allows us to ask whether the heterogeneity of linguistic practice corresponds to a more radical conception of alterity—that is, otherness exceeding the subject/object dichotomy. And since Kristeva claims that the chora leaves the permanent traces in the economy of subjectivity, she conceives of the subject constituted and re-marked by the maternal otherness, which enables our ethical orientation in the world. She claims that the event of pregnancy splits the subject and asserts otherness within the intimacy of the self, shattering the symbolic inscription of the body that constitutes it as "mine" and separate from the others.[13] Kristeva's analysis of the maternal alterity is expressed most explicitly in "Stabat Mater," which appeared first under the telling title "Hérethique de l'amour" ("Love's Heretical Ethics") in *Tel Quel* (1977). As Mary Jacobus suggests, Kristeva wants to rewrite here the Christian representation of motherhood (and by extension the figurations of motherhood seen from the symbolic perspective) as an ethics of otherness, "emphasizing the difficult access to a radical Other demanded by maternity" (Jacobus 1986, 169). The entire effort of Kristeva's writing is to initiate a different discourse on maternity, transgressing the limits of the symbolic logic of separation on the one hand and the mystifications of unity and resemblance on the other. As Kristeva writes in "Women's Time," "pregnancy seems to be experienced as the radical ordeal of the splitting of the subject: redoubling up of the body, separation and coexistence of the self and of an other . . ." (Kristeva 1986c, 206).

Such is "motherhood's impossible syllogism": "Within the body, growing as a graft, indomitable, there is an other. And no one is present within that simultaneously dual and alien space, to signify what is going on" (Kristeva 1980, 237). What is peculiar in this description is the fact that the maternal body, the "site of splitting," becomes a space of othering, resistant both to symbolic inscription and to the "presence" of the signifying subject. Unlike it is the case with the famous Lacanian model of the sign—two doors bearing the inscriptions of Ladies and Gentlemen, where the signifying space is a destination of sorts, different for a little boy and a little girl[14]—no one can enter this maternal space, no one is there "to signify what is going on." When Gallop reads that particular passage from Kristeva, she stresses the fact that it is impossible to occupy that maternal position, that any posture of speaking from that site is a "fraud."[15] Or rather, I should say that any attempt to transform the maternal body into a coherent signifying position is a fraud, precisely because it is a heterogeneous site, constantly doubling itself and separating itself from itself. The maternal body, then, becomes paradoxically a nonsite, an impurity and a distance encroaching on the positionality of the symbolic language.

If, for Lacan, the first construction of bodily identity occurs at the mirror stage—that is, at the moment when the child recognizes for the first time his or her mirror image and receives from it a false sense of stable identity—then Kristeva's understanding of the maternal role can be described (to borrow the phrase from the title of Rodolphe Gasché's book) as "the tain" of this mirror. Such a reading is encouraged by Kristeva's claim that semiotic both precedes and exceeds the formation of the mirror stage. Similarly, the "tain" refers to the silver lining at the back of the mirror, which produces the specular stage of representation without itself appearing on it.[16] However, since Lacan does not acknowledge, at least in this particular text, the full implications of the maternal function on the specular stage of the mirror representation, her trace is barely marked in his text by such peculiar understatements as the "human or artificial support" of the infant or "the obstructions of his support." Curiously, Lacan would install on that stage a mechanical *"trotte-bébé"* rather than the figure of the mother (Lacan 1977, 1–2). Although erased from the moment of theoretical and specular reflection,[17] the maternal trace functions not only as a "support" of the infant but also as the silver lining of the mirror itself. However, at stake in Kristeva's theory is not only a gesture of acknowledgment of the maternal role in the construction of the subject, but also, and more important, a radical revision of the phenomenological model of reflection and the psychoanalytic model of identification. The maternal trace clouds the "purity" of the imaginary reflection and questions the possibility of a separate unitary identity closed upon itself.

This double approach to the maternal body as a nonreflective "site" of radical othering (thought as "infold" rather than non-coincidence and separation) and as a "site" of symbolic inscription is most visible in "Stabat Mater." Although the essay associates in a reductive way the feminist discussions of motherhood either with a rejection of motherhood as an institution or with an acceptance of its traditional representations, it does argue for a new, and a specifically feminist, understanding of the maternal. The difficult access to the radical discourse of maternity within the major symbolic articulations is dramatized by the form of the essay, split into two columns—one, a feminist critique of the Christian vision of virginal maternity as a necessary complement to the Word; the other, a poetic description of pregnancy and birth. I read the "poetic" column neither as Kristeva's desire to appropriate the style of creative writing nor as universalization of her own experience of maternity, but rather as a stylistic device recalling the analyses of poetry in *Revolution in Poetic Language*. In short, the form of the essay represents Kristeva's methodology evident in all of her writings: it demonstrates that the space for an alternative feminist discourse on maternity can be cleared only after rigorous interrogation of the cultural representations of motherhood. As Carolyn Burke argues, the essay performs "both an examination of the conceptual and social limits imposed upon 'motherhood' in Western culture and a reimagining of that central relationship" (Burke 1987, 113).[18]

According to Kristeva, the Christian construction of virginal maternity represents a curious compromise. On the one hand, Christianity explicitly supplements the internal coherence of the Word with the heterogeneity of the maternal body. Yet because of this dangerous addition, the heterogeneity of the maternal body is consistently neutralized, purified, and eventually homologized to the symbolic order of the Word. The development of the Marian cult, and especially the dogma of Immaculate Conception and Assumption, aims to foreclose the gap between the flesh and the Word: "the Virgin Mother occupied the tremendous territory hither and yon of the parenthesis of language. She adds to the Christian trinity and to the Word that delineates their coherence the heterogeneity they salvage" (Kristeva 1986a, 175). This ordering of the maternal libido results in the powerful and soothing construction of the unique virginal maternal body that does not know sin, sex, or death.

In contrast to this religious discourse (but also in contrast to the dominant scientific and psychoanalytic discourses as well), the poetic language might be better equipped to sustain painful and joyful "lucidity" about motherhood against the indolence of its habitual representations:

A mother's identity is maintained only through the well-known closure of consciousness within the indolence of the habit, when a woman protects herself from the borderline that severs her body and expatriates it from her child. Lucidity, on the contrary, would restore her as cut in half, alien to its other— and a ground favorable to delirium. (Kristeva 1986a, 179)

Perhaps inseparable from this "closure of consciousness" or "indolence of habit," the dominant cultural constructions of motherhood continuously skirt the traces of maternal *jouissance*, submit it to the stability of paternal law, and misconstruct the othering process as the maternal bond of the generality of the species. Similarly, Kristeva argues that the Freudian account of the desire of motherhood in terms of the desire for a penis is insufficient and perhaps falls prey to the same indolence of habit.

How does this indolence of habit and consciousness restrict understanding of otherness that the experience of maternity reveals? At the end of her essay, Kristeva seems to say that from the perspective of the symbolic order otherness can be read in only two ways. On the one hand, the articulation of otherness is determined by the topography of the sign with its gap between the signified and the signifier: "discontinuity, lack, and arbitrariness: topography of the sign, of the symbolic relation that posits my otherness as impossible" (Kristeva 1986a, 184). Dictated by the structure of the sign, this thought of alterity is comprised under the rubric of separation and noncoincidence. In the symbolic order of language, the Other is inaccessible and unattainable. For Lacan, it leads to the "excentric" notion of the subject, split between the "the place I occupy as the subject of the signifier" and "the place I occupy as the subject of the signified" (Lacan 1977, 165). Entirely subordinated to the theme of (decentered) identity, this thought of alterity functions as a reference point from which a separate subject position can be established. On the other hand, alterity is perceived as natural, as "resembling others and eventually the species." Outside the field of language, otherness is neutralized in terms of resemblance.[19]

Yet, maternal lucidity rests on neither of these approaches and demands the articulation of otherness beyond the symbolic/natural opposition. It pursues the thought of otherness to a point where no "identity holds up": "The child, whether he or she, is irremediably an other. . . . I confront the abyss between what was mine and is henceforth but irreparably alien. Trying to think through that abyss: staggering vertigo" (Kristeva 1986a, 179). The vertigo of thought points to the impossibility of thinking the otherness of the child (and, consequently, the mother's "sameness") in terms of relations; the alterity is neither inaccessible to me nor similar to me, but radically interrupts "my relation" to myself, to "my" body. Unlike the clear separation and noncoincidence between the signifier and the signified, the subject and the Other, the maternal body requires the thought of alterity in terms of *infolding*, as the imprint of the other *within* the same. As a site of infolding of the "other" and the "same," the maternal body renders the fundamental notions of identity and difference strikingly insufficient—these crucial philosophical categories indeed no longer "hold up." Therefore, such an inescapable imprint of otherness makes the maternal body impure, turns it into a "catastrophic fold of being."

Such articulation of the maternal in terms of othering places Kristeva's thought in the tradition of heterology (from Platonic *symploke* as the interweaving of heterogeneous strands, to the contributions of Nietzsche, Heidegger, Freud, and Derrida, to mention just a few thinkers directly discussed in her work). In most general terms, heterology can be defined as a theory of the Other. This tradition represents various attempts of thinking otherness, which resists incorporation into the unifying orders of discourse but on which both thought and discourse depend for their possibility. What is at stake here is not only a departure from the homogeneous notions of thought and language (understood as a system/order) but also a different approach to otherness. As Rodolphe Gasché argues, heterological thinking articulates otherness prior to the principles of contradiction and negativity (which anticipates dialectical resolutions) and independently from the process of self-definition.[20] Rather, otherness is perceived as always already inhabiting every identity and interrupting every principle of thought. Likewise, Kristeva's refiguration of the maternal in terms of this radical alterity inevitably leads to a "catastrophe" of both the signifier and dialectics: "no signifier could uplift it without leaving a remainder"; she is "a catastrophe of being that the dialectics of the trinity and its supplements would be unable to subsume" (Kristeva 1986a, 182–183). From this perspective, the maternal body is not merely a form of embodiment and a kind of primordial shelter but, as Suleiman emphasizes, a primordial site of division (Suleiman 1985, 368): always already a nonnomadic body subject to internal splitting, "a crossroads of being," which the event of pregnancy intensifies and "brings to light and imposes without remedy."

The process of division in the maternal body implies not merely a separation of the mother and the child but also an inscription of alterity and distance into every identity and linguistic practice: "A mother is a continuous separation, a division of the very flesh. And consequently of language—and it has always been so" (Kristeva 1986a, 178). Because for Kristeva pregnancy is the most radical ordeal of the splitting of the subject, it can be a basis for a demystification of "the identity of the symbolic bond itself."[21] Just as the maternal body is interrupted, imprinted, and increased by grafts and folds of otherness, so Kristeva postulates a similar interruption in the construction of every identity: "This process could be summarized as an *interiorization of the founding separation of the socio-symbolic contract*, as an introduction of its cutting edge into the very interior of every identity whether subjective, sexual, ideological, or so forth" (Kristeva 1986c, 210).

Moreover, Kristeva explicitly claims that such resumption of the maternal economy within language is quite distinct from erecting the myth of the archaic mother as an alternative origin or a lost presence. She denounces the nostalgia for the presence of the maternal body as a phantasm, as a narcissistic myth, or as a utopian "belief in the omnipotence of an archaic, full, total englobing mother with no frustration, no separation, with no break-producing symbolism" (Kristeva 1986c, 205). Kristeva's construction of motherhood as an impossible space of radical othering where "no one is present to signify," where no "identity holds up," indeed "challenges precisely this myth of the archaic mother."

In the context of Kristeva's analysis of the maternal body that so strongly emphasizes both the shocking discovery of the abyss in the mother's relation to her child and inscription of otherness in her relation to her own body, the only continuity between the mother and the child is the paradoxical "continuity" of love and pain:

What connection is there between myself, or even more unassumingly between my body and this internal graft and fold, which, once the umbilical cord has been severed, is an inaccessible other? My body and . . . him. No connection. (Kristeva 1986a, 178)

One does not give birth in pain, one gives birth to pain: the child represents it and henceforth it settles in, it is continuous. Obviously you may close your eyes, cover up your ears, teach courses, run errands . . . think about objects, subjects. But a mother is always branded by pain, she yields to it. (Kristeva 1986a, 167)

For Kristeva pain registers this abyss within the self, the wound within the maternal body, as well as the "intimate" inaccessibility of the child. Pain registers on the emotional level a disconnection in the relation of the mother to herself and to her child. Like the negativity of *jouissance*, pain accompanies a maternal lucidity that embraces her borderline existence as a "continuous" distancing from herself and from her child. But for Kristeva pain is inseparable from joy and laughter as a certain overflowing of identity and difference. There can be no unity between mother and child *"except for"* this pain and this mutual "overflowing laughter where one senses the collapse of some ringing, subtle, fluid identity or other, softly buoyed by the waves" (Kristeva 1986a, 179–180).

Having brought Kristeva's two privileged sites of semiosis in such a close proximity, I should also stress their continuous drifting apart. Kristeva suggests that although both poetic practice and the semiotic process in the maternal body disrupt the fragile symbolic stability, our response to them is fundamentally different. Since semiotic discontinuity is so much more threatening to the mastery of the subject and the stability of social codes when it is associated with the mother, maternal lucidity is constantly erased and subordinated to the demand for the presence of the maternal body as a form of embodiment and a warranty of symbolic coherence:

> On the other hand, we immediately deny it; we say there can be no escape, for mamma is there, she embodies this phenomenon; she warrants that everything is, and that it is representable. . . . Because if, on the contrary, there were no one on this threshold, if the mother were not, that is if she were not phallic, then every speaker would be led to conceive of its Being in relation to some void, a nothingness asymmetrically opposed to this Being, a permanent threat against, first, its mastery, and ultimately, its stability. (Kristeva 1980, 238; italics added)

This strategy of fetishistic denial and daring thinking in the terms of hypothetical otherwise ("because if, on the contrary") is symptomatic of Kristeva's own discussion of motherhood. Because a similar denial coupled with a demand for presence is not directed at poetic language, because we are more likely to bracket poetic practice as marginal deviation from the "normal" patterns of communication, Kristeva's (and her critics') analysis of poetic semiosis is much more radical than her discussions of maternity, which surprise us with occasional notes of timidity and retrenchment. Kristeva's semiotic analysis of the maternal body inscribes, after all, the abyss and alterity into the very site of domesticated normalcy (or what is perceived as such) and into the construction of every subject. Therefore, if the avant-garde poet can be easily thought of as a modern Dionysus, pregnant Madonnas invading that Nietzschean position still evoke the specter of monstrosity.[22] Kristeva herself occasionally claims that the potentially dissident role of motherhood has to be counterbalanced with its more traditional role of preserving the social order.

In spite of these reservations, I think that Kristeva's work is still of considerable importance to feminism. First of all, her theory provides conceptual tools for diagnosing the limitations of what counts as discursive, especially in the context of representations of the feminine and the maternal. Second, like Lyotard, Kristeva in her early work claims that what is at stake in the analysis of culture from the perspective of sexual difference is, indeed, a destruction of metalanguage—that is, a turn from the all-embracing symbolic to the multiplicity of socio-linguistic practices. Even though her later work vacillates between this notion of linguistic practice and the more anthropological conception of the symbolic as the sacrificial order (see, for instance, "Women's Time"), Kristeva's early texts provide theoretical resources for moving beyond an impasse generated by the opposition between "culturalism" and "formalism"—an impasse in which the debate between psychoanalysis and feminism still remains caught. But the most promising aspect of Kristeva's thought is that it provides the ground for renegotiating the position of the feminine speaker. By postulating a subject-in-process, or a subject-on-trial, and leaving open what this process/ trial could mean for female subjectivity, Kristeva demystifies the "nature of the symbolic bond" that places women in a subordinate position. Her theory of language as encompassing both the maternal and the paternal signifying economies makes it possible to question and revise rigid notions of sexual identities and subject positions in culture. Similarly, her theory of the subject re-marked by otherness from within and inserted into multiple discursive practices not only supports the argument for the multiplication of differences within the concept of femininity—"I am in favor of a concept of femininity which would take as many forms as there are women" (Kristeva 1989, 114)—but also leads to a rethinking of the group formation and to the alternative logic of the community based on such differences. And indeed, it is this aspect of her theory I find most productive.

---------------------------- *NOTES* ----------------------------

This essay was originally published in *Hypatia* 7 (1992): 91–108.

1. Kristeva has also been criticized for her apparent antifeminism and her unclear relation to feminist politics. What is at stake here is Kristeva's valorization of the "third generation" of feminists who seek to subvert the very notion of sexual identity over both the liberal feminists postulating equality and the feminists postulating specificity of the female identity. For further discussion, see Kristeva (1986c, 187–214) and Grosz (1989, 63–70).

2. One of the most important questions that Butler raises is about Kristeva's exclusion of the figure of the lesbian.

3. In this sense, Kristeva implicitly elaborates the questions of discourse and power raised by Foucault (1972, 215–239).

4. This is one of the few articles in which Kristeva, while paying homage to Lacan, reiterates the differences between her position and his. Her critique of Lacan is precisely addressed to his homogeneous concept of language: "*la langue* . . . is nevertheless homogeneous with the realm of signification, even going as far as to assimilate what the dualism in Freudian thought regarded as strangely irreducible" (Kristeva 1983, 35).

5. At this point we should recall Kristeva's ongoing engagement with the thought of Husserl in an attempt to uncover the systematic complicity between *the presence* of the transcendental consciousness and the linguistic operations of sign and syntax. She stresses the fact that every signifying act, in addition to being the expression of meaning, reasserts the presence of Being because "it simultaneously posits the thesis (position) of both Being and ego" (Kristeva 1980, 132–135).

6. This point differs radically from the usual negative assessments of Kristeva's politics. Judith Butler, for instance, claims that "by relegating the source of subversion to a site outside of culture itself, Kristeva appears to foreclose the possibility of subversion as an effective or realizable cultural practice" (Butler 1990, 88). However, this criticism does not take into account that for Kristeva, culture—like signification—is no longer reducible to the realm of the symbolic paternal law but manifests itself through the multiplicity of signifying practices.

7. In *Timaeus*, Plato gives his account of cosmology twice. Revising the first story, Plato introduces the third category—"chora"—in addition to the prior distinction between the eternal pattern and the created copy. "Chora" not only functions as a receptacle receiving the created forms but also "in some mysterious way partakes of the intelligible, and is most incomprehensible" (Plato 1969, 1178). Concerning Kristeva's appropriation of the

Platonic term, Jacqueline Rose reminds us that Plato describes the chora as maternal because the mother is seen in his text as "playing no part in the act of procreation" (Rose 1986, 153–154). Yet Kristeva is interested in the term because already in the Platonic text it is caught in a "bastard reasoning," which on the one hand insists on the distinction between the passive and the active, but on the other hand describes chora as both the passive receptacle and the active movement. For a more detailed discussion, see Kristeva (1984, 239–240, nn. 12 and 13).

8. This aspect of Kristeva's work is emphasized by Lewis (1974, 29).

9. In her earlier article, Domna C. Stanton interprets these irruptions of the semiotic as manifestations of negativity and dissidence (Stanton 1987, 75).

10. Judith Butler argues that what Kristeva discovers as a natural prediscursive maternal subversion is in fact an effect of culture rather than its "secret cause." From that she concludes that by placing the source of subversion outside culture, Kristeva forecloses the possibility of the effective subversion as a cultural practice (Butler 1990, 90–93). As I try to demonstrate, Kristeva quite self-consciously starts her analysis from the effects of disruptions already within the culture and accounts for them not as mere accidents befalling the symbolic but as necessary consequences of the process of signification.

11. See, for instance, Rose (1986, 154): "It seems to me that the concept of the semiotic, especially in those formulations which identify it with the mother and place it *beyond language*, is the least useful aspect of Kristeva's work." The irony is that of course Rose is right—Kristeva indeed does take us beyond language thought as structure and system in order to propose a new logic of signification based on the signifying practice. It is the failure to explain the relation between language and signifying practice, the relation that is not reducible to distinction between *langue* and *parole*, that results in such conclusions.

12. See Kristeva (1984, 140–146) for a critique of Derrida's deconstruction.

13. Elizabeth Grosz, on the other hand, interprets Kristeva's emphasis on the maternal alterity merely as "the overtaking of woman's identity and corporeality by a foreign body," ignoring in this way Kristeva's effort to demystify the very notion of identity and rigid sexual difference (Grosz 1990, 161–163).

14. Lacan revises Saussure's model of the sign (the arbitrary connection between signifier and signified) in order to stress the primacy of the

(phallic) signifier and to inscribe the sexual difference into the very structure of language. The image of the two identical lavatory doors demonstrates that it is the signifier alone that inscribes the sexual difference into signification (Lacan 1977, 151).

15. Jane Gallop interprets this point as Kristeva's attempt to dephallicize the mother and reveal behind this reassuring construction an empty space that no one can occupy (Gallop 1982, 117).

16. Gasché employs the phrase to indicate the substructures underlying the philosophy of reflection: "This book's title, *The Tain of the Mirror*, alludes to that 'beyond' of the orchestrated mirror play of reflection that Derrida's philosophy seeks to conceptualize. *Tain* . . . refers to the tinfoil, the silver lining, the lusterless back of the mirror. Derrida's philosophy, rather than being a philosophy of reflection, is engaged in the systematic exploration of that dull surface without which no specular and speculative activity would be possible" (Gasché 1986, 6). In a similar way, Kristeva's exploration of the maternal categories examines that "dark continent" without which no specular/speculative activity of psychoanalysis would be possible.

17. Kristeva analyzes the mode of withdrawal of the maternal economy from the constitution of the subject as the process of abjection. What is original in her analysis is that the mode of maternal disappearance is not neutral: it is a violent process of expulsion, a spasm of vomiting that consumes also the subject and destabilizes the boundaries of subjectivity (Kristeva 1982, 3–10).

18. By contrast, Domna Stanton sees limitations of this revisionary project and asserts that the maternal "I" in "Stabat Mater" is an exception to a more typical articulation of the mother as "a passive instinctual force that does not speak" (Stanton 1989, 164).

19. Although she interprets only the "natural" aspect of otherness in motherhood, Susan Rubin Suleiman suggests that it can provide "a privileged means of entry into the order of culture and of language" (Suleiman 1985, 367).

20. For an excellent discussion of heterology in the philosophical context, see Rodolphe Gasché (1986, 81–105). Gasché argues that Derrida's heterology opposes "the uninterrupted attempt to domesticate" otherness in the history of philosophy. Although Kristeva situates her analysis of otherness on the level of psychoanalysis and linguistics rather than philosophy, the implications of her arguments are very similar.

21. Carolyn Burke likewise stresses Kristeva's critique of the very notion of identity and her subsequent rejection of that brand of feminism that is "caught in the concept of a separate identity" (Burke 1978).

22. This last image I owe to Fred Dallmayr, who, during our discussion about Kristeva, attempted to compare her theory with Nietzsche's.

————————————— REFERENCES —————————————

Burke, Carolyn Greenstein. 1978. Report from Paris: Women's writing and the women's movement. *Signs: Journal of Women in Culture and Society* 3: 843–855.

————. 1987. Rethinking the maternal. In *The future of difference*, ed. Hester Eisenstein and Alice Jardine. New Brunswick, N.J.: Rutgers University Press.

Butler, Judith. 1990. *Gender trouble: Feminism and the subversion of identity*. New York: Routledge.

Derrida, Jacques. 1974. *Of grammatology*. Trans. Gayatri Chakravorty Spivak. Baltimore: Johns Hopkins University Press.

Foucault, Michel. 1972. *The archaeology of knowledge*. Trans. A. M. Sheridan Smith. New York: Pantheon.

Gallop, Jane. 1982. *The daughter's seduction: Feminism and psychoanalysis*. Ithaca: Cornell University Press.

Gasché, Rodolphe. 1986. *The tain of the mirror: Derrida and the philosophy of reflection*. Cambridge: Harvard University Press.

Grosz, Elizabeth. 1989. *Sexual subversions: Three French feminists*. Sydney: Allen and Unwin.

————. 1990. *Jacques Lacan: A feminist introduction*. New York: Routledge.

Jacobus, Mary. 1986. *Reading woman: Essays in feminist criticism*. New York: Columbia University Press.

Jones, Ann Rosalind. 1984. Julia Kristeva on femininity: The limits of a semiotic politic. *Feminist Review* 18: 56–73.

Kristeva, Julia. 1980. *Desire in language: A semiotic approach to literature and art*. Ed. Leon S. Roudiez, trans. Thomas Gora, Alice Jardine, and Leon S. Roudiez. New York: Columbia University Press.

————. 1982. *Powers of horror: An essay on abjection*. Trans. Leon S. Roudiez. New York: Columbia University Press.

————. 1983. Within the microcosm of "the talking cure." In *Interpreting Lacan*. Vol. 6. *Psychiatry and Humanities*, ed. Joseph H. Smith and William Kerrigan. New Haven: Yale University Press.

———. 1984. *Revolution in poetic language.* Trans. Margaret Waller. New York: Columbia University Press.

———. 1986a. Stabat mater. In *The Kristeva reader*, ed. Toril Moi. New York: Columbia University Press.

———. 1986b. System and the speaking subject. In *The Kristeva Reader*, ed. Toril Moi. New York: Columbia University Press.

———. 1986c. Women's time. In *The Kristeva Reader*, ed. Toril Moi. Columbia University Press.

———. 1989. Talking about *Polylogue*. In *French feminist thought: A reader*, ed. Toril Moi. New York: Basil Blackwell.

Kuykendall, Eleanor H. 1989. Questions for Julia Kristeva's ethics of linguistics. In *The thinking muse: Feminism and modern French philosophy*, ed. Jeffner Allen and Iris Marion Young. Bloomington: Indiana University Press.

Lacan, Jacques. 1977. *Ecrits.* Trans. Alan Sheridan. New York: Norton.

Lewis, Philip E. 1974. Revolutionary Semiotics. *Diacritics* 4: 28–32.

Moi, Toril. 1985. *Sexual / textual politics: Feminist literary theory.* New York: Methuen.

Plato. 1969. *Timaeus.* Trans. Benjamin Jowett. In *The collected dialogues of Plato*, ed. Edith Hamilton and Huntington Cairns. Princeton: Princeton University Press.

Rose, Jacqueline. 1986. *Sexuality in the field of vision.* London: Verso.

Silverman, Kaja. 1988. *The acoustic mirror: The female voice in psychoanalysis and cinema.* Bloomington: Indiana University Press.

Stanton, Domna. 1987. Language and revolution: The Franco-American dis-connection. In *The future of difference*, ed. Hester Eisenstein and Alice Jardine. New Brunswick, N.J.: Rutgers University Press.

———. 1989. Difference on trial: A critique of the maternal metaphor in Cixous, Irigaray, and Kristeva. In *The Thinking Muse*, ed. Jeffner Allen and Iris Marion Young. Bloomington: Indiana University Press.

Suleiman, Susan Rubin. 1985. Writing and motherhood. In *The (m)other tongue: Essays in feminist psychoanalytic interpretation*, ed. Shirley Nelson Gamer, Claire Kahane, and Madelon Sprengnether. Ithaca: Cornell University Press.

Lisa Walsh

12

Writing (into) the Symbolic

The Maternal Metaphor in Hélène Cixous

On dit que la vie et la mort sont au pouvoir de la langue. Dans mon jardin d'enfer les mots sont mes fous. Je suis assis sur un trône de feu et j'écoute ma langue.

—Hélène Cixous, *Dedans*

The psychoanalytic assertion that femininity exists, or does not exist, merely as a boundary between the rational order that stabilizes our reality and the psychotic chaos that threatens it is increasingly belied by the many contemporary feminine voices that have shattered the symptomatic silence of the Freudian hysteric through the production of a feminine discourse and the consequent dethronement of the Lacanian phallus. Writing her most important theoretical texts in the seventies, Hélène Cixous thematizes a feminist revision of the psychic structure of the speaking subject so as to allow for the possibility, and in her own case, the creative reality, of a maternally motivated movement within language that might account for the vocalization of a feminine imaginary—a logical impossibility according to psychoanalytic orthodoxy. By metaphorically shifting the originary connection to the maternal body into a boundless symbolic future, not through substitution or destruction but through remembrance and love, Cixous's maternal, as metaphoric fourth to the Oedipal triad, dislodges the paternal third from its position of absolute supremacy and presence, thus

347

reestablishing the severed maternal bond as a newly disembodied and symbolic connection based now on desire rather than need. This temporal, tropic loop reminiscent of Lacan's *futur antérieur* rewrites the Oedipal drama, in-completes the psychic shift into language, and enacts the fulfillment of a discourse that exists as a reply to/from the (m)other, a truly connective, limitless discourse with substantial political and ethical implications.[1]

Any attempt to grapple with the texts of Hélène Cixous, or those of other so called French feminists,[2] requires an understanding of their somewhat curious relationship to Lacanian psychoanalytic theory. American feminists tend to experience an understandable concern when confronted with a politics grounded in a seemingly clotured dialogue between "feminist" theory and a highly esoteric brand of psychoanalysis. Because much of the "French feminist" project is concerned with undermining systems of representation, Lacan's linguistically informed revision of Freud provides at most a theoretical framework, at least a useful point of departure. Cixous's notion of an *écriture féminine* situates her at the end of the theoretical spectrum furthest from Lacanian orthodoxy (to risk a contradiction in terms). While she appropriates (*vole*) certain Lacanian terminology, in a truly "feminine" gesture she refuses to accept any conceptual baggage that might inhibit her emancipatory flight (*vol*).[3] She bypasses the "*limite historico-culturelle*" posed by Lacan's "*mystification phallique*" to theorize and ultimately en-gender an *écriture* that refutes the exclusive mastery of the paternal Symbolic and opens into the possibility of an inclusive connection with a maternally inspired expression of a self always already indebted to her (m)other.

Cixous's free engagement in/with psychoanalytic discourse in both her "fictional" and "non-fictional" works (she would certainly refuse this distinction), might lead to a rather simple, though in my reading equally unwise, tendency to impose this coherent theoretical grid onto her texts and interpret them accordingly. Cixous refuses to play under the rule(s) of the logocentric game (*jeu*); in borrowing (*volant*) from a certain philosophical system she does not necessarily adhere to any or all of it. In fact, for Cixous, psychoanalysis simply re-presents a cleverly disguised mimesis of the sociocultural superstructure ultimately responsible for its production.

Because, if psychoanalysis is constituted through woman, and the repression of the femininity (a repression which, men show, is not altogether successful) of masculine sexuality, it confirms an idea difficult at present to refute: like all of the "human" sciences, it [psychoanalysis] reproduces the masculine of which it is one of the effects.

Car, si la psychanalyse s'est constituée depuis la femme, et à refouler la féminité (refoulement qui, les hommes le manifestent, n'est pas si réussi que ça), de la sexualité masculine, elle rend un compte à présent peu refutable; comme toutes les sciences "humaines" elle reproduit le masculin dont elle est un des effets. ("Rire," 46)

Cixous's acceptance of the Lacanian model of psychic development, or any of the terms therein, is far from unqualified. In fact, such a theoretics, no matter how playful and incomprehensive (in both senses of the word), does not comprehend Cixous's poetics of the feminine.

Among the most common critiques of Cixous's *écriture féminine* is the charge that her "theory" is both utopic and naïve.[4] After all, if the Symbolic orders all signifying processes, how can the feminine imaginary find expression within its all-encompassing, and therefore non-existent, parameters? Luce Irigaray in particular, though her project in many ways resembles Cixous's, argues that we must first forge a space within (or outside) the Symbolic order before we can even begin to actually create a uniquely feminine "self"-expression, one able to speak the "feminine corporeal."[5] Cixous, however, accepts neither Lacan's Symbolic nor its universally circumscriptive limitations. She squarely situates this notion of the Symbolic within a psychoanalytic tradition that excludes the feminine and worships the phallic; how could this theory but reflect its sociocultural reality? For Cixous, "Their 'symbolic,' it exists, it has the power, we, the destroyers of order, we know it all too well. But nothing obliges us to deposit our lives in its banks of lack. . . ." ["Leur 'symbolique', il existe, il a le pouvoir, nous, les désordonnantes, nous le savons trop bien. Mais rien ne nous oblige à déposer nos vies à ses banques de manque . . ."] ("Rire," 47). Cixous emphasizes the caution with which feminists should approach Lacanian dicta of language by setting the symbolic off within inverted commas and de-universalizing it with the parenthetic insertion of the possessive pronoun.[6] The(ir) Symbolic does not belong to "nous, les désordonnantes" but to they (*eux*) who (*qui*) "have theorized their desire for reality" ["ont theorisé leur désir pour de la réalité"] (47). Although Cixous does concede both the existence and the power of the Lacanian Symbolic (as such), she opens up the possibility of "our" symbolic—a space within which an equally if not more powerful feminine can inscribe itself as other than silence. In "Sorties" she asks: "Is the system flawless? Impossible to bypass?"[7] Her political-poetic project lyrically responds that it is not.

Cixous's theory/practice of a disruptive, feminine poetics ex-poses the decidedly male order of the Lacanian paradigm of psychic development. For Lacan, an unabashed Freudian in this respect, the child (male or female) must irrevocably reject the body of the mother in order to enter into the socio-symbolic order of the father.[8] Cixous, however, re-writes this scenario grounded in the mother's lack, replacing Freud's phallic mother with a maternal jouisseuse situated at the very locus of a uniquely feminine writerly creation.[9] By affirming a "maternally" motivated *"venue à l'écriture"* and denying the phallus its centrality in the signifying process, she transforms the problematic relation of woman to the Symbolic. For Cixous, the maternal metaphor represents an all too often absent feminine economy capable of exploding the "Empire of the selfsame" inherent in the masculine One ("Sorties," 78–83). Cixous's conception of the "mother" is worth quoting at some length:

> The *mother* is also a metaphor: [. . .] the attachment to the "mother" *as* delight and violence is not severed. Text, my body: crossing of singing streams; understand me, this is not a mother who clings, who is clung to; she is, touching you, the equivoice that affects you, pushes you from your breast to come to language, projects *your* strength; she is the rhythm that laughs you; the intimate destination that makes all metaphors possible and desirable, body (bodies?), no more describable than god, the soul, or the Other; the part of you that enters into you opens you up and pushes you to inscribe your style as woman in language.

> La *mère* aussi est une métaphore: [. . .] le rapport à la mère *en tant* que délices et violences n'est pas coupé. Texte mon corps: traversée de coulées chantantes; entends -moi, ce n'est pas une "mère" collante, attachante; c'est, te touchant, l'equivoix qui t'affecte, te pousse depuis ton sein à venir au langage, qui lance

ta force; c'est le rhythme qui te rit; l'intime destinataire qui rend possibles et désirables toutes les métaphores, corps (le? les?), pas plus descriptible que dieu, l'âme, ou l'Autre; la partie de toi qui entre en toi t'espace et te pousse à inscrire dans la langue ton style de femme. ("Rire," 44)[10]

By means of a qualifying "aussi" here, Cixous challenges the Lacanian "paternal metaphor," a reformulation of the Oedipal drama whereby the child (boy?) must *substitute* the law of the father for the love of the mother.[11] Cixous's mother, as metaphor, accesses an otherwise indescribable feminine imaginary, most vividly "represented" in Cixous's own "style de femme."[12] In both her fictional and theoretical texts, she strategically redeploys a multitude of patriarchal myths and images, multi-temporally creating and filling a space within language where a maternally inspired *écriture féminine* can be born.

Shifting slightly now from the theory to praxis, in her first "novel," *Dedans*, Cixous weaves an oneiric poem in prose of her own "*venue à l'écriture*."[13] At first glance, Cixous reproduces Freud's version of the Oedipal journey. The daughter (narrator) rejects her mother's stifling materiality and seeks communion with her dead, and therefore bodiless, father—the bearer of the phallus, of signification. In the course of the novel, the mother gradually, silently disappears; the father(s) insistently, vocally reincarnate(s). Cixous, however, reinvents the very nature of the daughter's entrance into the symbolic, one which does not entail submission to the Law of the father, erasure of the feminine self. Although the (nameless) narrator is seduced by the language of the father and repulsed by the voice of the mother,[14] she manages to successfully break the "cord" that prevents her linguistic flight (*vol*); she affirms and re-affirms a maternal/feminine entrance into language/writing.

Within the context of the novel, the distinction between mother as embodied "role" and "mother" as metaphor clearly emerges as the former disappears and the latter evolves. From the beginning, the actual (biological) mother of the narrator is in the process of vanishing into the future, realizing the aporia of the metaphoric is/is not:

My mother was disappearing, she never asked for anything, she was running, things slipped quickly between her fingers and since she forgot to speak, nothing was left to us in her absence but the echo of her footsteps. We were free. As our mother fled into the future, we remained there.

Ma mère disparaissait, elle ne demandait jamais rien, elle courait, les choses se déplaçaient vite entre ses doigts et comme elle oubliait de parler, il ne nous restait, en son absence, que l'écho de ses pas. Nous étions libres. Tandis que notre mère filait à l'avenir, nous restions là. (*Dedans* 15)

This maternal refusal of the present, of the father's existence, provides the initial impetus for the daughter's rejection of her mother. Unlike the dead father whose legacy lingers in the form of language, or more precisely "*les mots*," the only audible remains of the mother are the sounds of disappearance as she flees the paternal present. Within the memory of the fictional autobiographer, the mother does not fully exist in the present, and the use of the past imperfect in this passage again underscores the ephemeral quality of her actuality. She finally erases her mother's presence altogether: "BECAUSE I HATE HER, MY MOTHER NO LONGER IS. What I call hate is what most resembles death in the world where the living circulate; and death is the provisional disappearance of a well-known being" ["PARCE QUE JE LA HAIS, MA MERE N'EST PLUS. Ce que j'appelle la haine, c'est ce qui ressemble le plus à la mort, dans le monde, où circulent les vivants; et la mort, c'est la disparition provisoire d'un être bien connu"] (65). And in fact the mother does "die" as the daughter makes her way into the world of the father(s). This mother's position remains unambiguous; she has/had no voice as a speaking subject. Hers is the voice ironically, and conspicuously, absent from the daughter's inner world (*dedans*), a space (to be) infused with the (m)other. To reach the metaphoric maternal, however, she must first fuse with and ultimately transcend the seductive father.

In keeping with the Freudian Oedipal plot, this "fictional" daughter views her father as a love object. He is not only her father but her god, her husband, her lover. The father also offers access to and closure within the(ir) Symbolic. While this would seem to constitute, then, a fictional re-presentation of the Lacanian scenario, the narrator's expression of a complex, dynamic relation to language creates multiple fissures in the Symbolic "prison," allowing for the potentiality, even inevitability, of escape. In the first part of the novel, the narrator psychically revisits her childhood to verbally, sensually (re)create herself and her intimate connection to the world of words. Although the discourse of the father does manifest the almost mystical, necessarily phallic power of the(ir) Symbolic, its liberating (from the maternal body?) force remains questionable. The narrator recalls the incomprehensible quality of her father's voice:

> [T]hey were the most caressing sounds I had ever heard, and they breathed into my body a fire that I took for that joy that permits human beings to fly. My father's words, then, were made with the carrying wind whose name I did not know? I sprang forward.

> [C]'était les sons les plus carressants que j'aie jamais entendus, et qui insufflaient à mon corps un feu tel que je le pris pour cette joie qui permet aux êtres humains de voler. Les mots de mon père étaient donc faits avec le vent qui transporte et dont je ne connaissais pas le nom? Je m'élançai. (*Dedans*, 31)

Although the narrator does access the symbolic realm by way of the father, she clearly now recognizes what she did not as a child. What she took (*passé simple*) for the joy that allows (*présent*) humans to fly (*voler*—conceptual absence of "time"), the words of her father, provides merely an illusion of freedom, one she must punctuate with a question mark. Nevertheless, she does throw herself forward—only to be brutally snapped back.

During her first attempt at flight, the narrator discovers the invisible restraints of a process of signification incapable of expressing an incorporated feminine imaginary. While her brother (*toi*) asserts the inescapability of the oppressive, hierarchical nature of this structure, he remains unable to convince her of her lack of freedom: "my brother asserts that there is no dog without a leash, and no leash without a master. But, says my brother lowering his head, you can't always see the master because he is always behind you" ["mon frère affirme qu'il n'y a pas de chien sans corde, et pas de corde sans maître. Mais, dit mon frère en baissant la tête, on ne voit pas le maître parce qu'il est toujours derrière"] (39). The (veiled?) invisibility of the master does not negate his/its existence. Although she does manage to leave the ground, to enter the imaginary, "I was barely separated when I felt the cord [leash]; every part of my body, even every one of my hairs was fastened to the ground by invisible ties there must have been millions of them. I fell freely" ["à peine étais-je détachée que je sentis la corde, chacun de mes membres, et même chacun de mes poils était fixé au sol par des liens invisibles il devait y en avoir des millions. Je tombai librement"] (41). Afterward, she attributes her fall to an inability to carry her body with her into flight; the female body, the feminine imaginary cannot be inscribed in the(ir) Symbolic. So, she and her brother "resigned we allow our bodies to hold us down. For the moment" ["résignés nous laissons nos corps nous attacher. Pour l'instant"] (42). In order to truly achieve flight (*voler*), she must transcend the masculine economy of the(ir) Symbolic and its exclusion of a feminine which is not simply a specularization of the masculine, a repetition of the Same.

According to the Lacanian scheme of psychic development, birth into the Symbolic by way of the father supplants the physical birth connection to the mother; the syntactic thread, "*ce fameux fil,*" substitutes for the umbilical cord.[15] For Cixous, however, this metaphorical replacement is neither desirable nor inevitable. Explaining the failure of her attempted flight to her brother, she contradicts his assertion that the cord has prevented her flight: "There is no cord here. Only our bodies hold us back" ["Il n'y a pas de corde ici. Seul le corps nous retient"] (42). But, as we have seen, unlike the (metaphoric) cord, the body constitutes only a momentary, voluntary constraint ("*pour l'instant*"). A disruptive feminine discourse, precisely by writing this body, exploring feminine *jouissance*, breaks the metaphoric cord, allows for the potential reconnection of the maternal cord, and surpasses the limitations of the(ir) Symbolic.

Feminine power is such that carrying away syntax, breaking that famous thread (just a tiny little thread they say) that men use as a substitute for the cord to reassure themselves— without which they can't come—that the old mother is still well behind them, watching them play phallus. Women will move toward the impossible.

Telle est la puissance féminine, qu'emportant la syntaxe, rompant ce fameux fil (juste un tout petit fil, disent-ils) qui sert aux hommes de substitut de cordon pour s'assurer, sans quoi ils ne jouissent pas, que la vieille mère est bien toujours derrière eux, à les regarder faire phallus, elles iront à l'impossible. ("Rire," 48)

The narrator, as she re-writes herself, ultimately overcomes the death-driven, phallic order of a discourse designed to repress, albeit not altogether successfully, any autonomous expression of "femininity." By writing herself (in) a time/space free from the restrictive confines of the(ir) Symbolic, she becomes able to communicate through the medium of language without simply re-producing the "Empire of the selfsame" ("Sorties," 78–83).

Cixous's notion of a disruptive practice of feminine writing does privilege voice—the rhythmic, lyrical potential of writing to act as the locus of subversion.[16] This does not, however, mean that the feminine imaginary can be expressed only outside the structuring limits of the symbolic. For Cixous, while an anarchic, formless vocal expression can be empowering, women should by no means limit themselves to this arguably primal mode of expression.[17] Initially, in attempting to break into the paternal order of self-expression, the narrator of *Dedans* experiences the scream as the only means of moving out of the pure materiality of the maternal connection and into speaking subjectivity. Addressing her dead father in both the second and third person, she writes:

I scream, it's simple, I am all scream, I wait for him to respond, as long as you don't respond I scream, I scream forward, backward, I scream five thousand seven hundred and some years ago, I scream in nineteen hundred and some, I scream *there where you are*, screams have no age, I scream where there are no men, under crusts of ice, at the ends of the earth, and the ends of the waters I scream you in five thousand seven hundred and some years, an often lived day, I am my scream, I scream I am, prove to me that you are, the first one to be silent has lost, it's only normal, I screeeeeeeeeam . . .

[J]e crie, c'est simple, je suis tout cri, j'attends qu'il réponde, tant que tu ne réponds pas je crie, je crie en avant, en arrière, je crie il'y a cinq mille sept cent et quelques ans, je crie en mil neuf sept cent et quelques ans, je crie *là où tu es*, les cris n'ont pas d'âge, je te crie là où il n'y a pas d'hommes, sous les

croûtes de glace, aux bords de la terre, aux bords des eaux je
te crie dans cinq mille sept cent et quelques ans, un jour
souvent vécu, mon cri est moi, je crie je suis, prouve-moi que
tu es, moi je te prouve que je suis, le premier qui se tait a
perdu, c'est normal, je criiiiiiiiii . . . (86)

For Freud, as for Lacan, "*là où tu es*" is the position from which the
subject speaks, the paternal space of the Symbolic, the locus of
the Other. The locational ambiguity of this position with regard to
the narrator and her paternal addressee calls into question the
fixity of the Self/Other (*moi/toi*) relation in the extra-Symbolic
speech act: Is "*là où tu es*" the destination or the source of the
disruptive scream, or perhaps both at the same time? As she awaits
the response of the Other to ascend to the status of coherent
subjecthood, the screamer occupies a somehow timeless, spaceless
locus outside the Symbolic, yet contained therein by the very act of
fictional autobiography inscribed on the written page. In "Le Rire
de la méduse," Cixous expresses in more explicit terms the importance of exploding the Symbolic from within:

> Now, I-woman am going to make the Law explode; an explo-
> sion henceforth possible, and inevitable; and let it be accom-
> plished immediately, *in* language. . . . We don't need to leave
> them a place that isn't any more theirs than we are . . . it is
> time that she break up this "*in*," that she explode it, turn it
> inside out and seize it, that she make it her own.

> Maintenant, je-femme vais faire sauter la Loi; éclatement
> désormais possible, et inéluctable; et qu'il se fasse, tout de
> suite, *dans* la langue. . . . Il ne faut pas leur laisser un lieu qui
> n'est pas plus à eux seuls que nous sommes à eux . . . il est
> temps qu'elle disloque ce "dans", qu'elle l'explose, le retourne
> et s'en saisisse, qu'elle le fasse sien. (48–49)

This production of a feminine text, the expression of a feminine
imaginary necessarily restructures the symbolic, disengages the
phallus from its ordering centrality in the creation of meaning, and
institutes a non-threatening, "feminine" other (though perhaps safely
distanced in the future) whose voice might potentially constitute a
less restrictive version of the paternal Other. Any such "mater-

nally" motivated entrance into language necessarily challenges the primacy of the phallus, the logic of the Same.

Cixous's *écriture féminine* refutes the simplicity of a rational tradition seeking structure uniquely in a system of binary oppositions. For Cixous, within this definitional hierarchy the feminine exists only to re-affirm the masculine: "Either woman is passive or she does not exist. What is left of her is unthinkable, unthought" ("Sorties," 64). Since women occupy a privileged space in relation to writing as a result of their proximity to the maternal, Cixous returns to the maternal metaphor to "theorize" a feminine economy that does not negate/exclude the (m)other. In "Sorties" she asks, "How could the woman who has experienced the not-me within me, not have a particular relationship to the written? To writing as giving itself away (cutting itself off) from the source?" (90). Cixous might (too) easily be accused of biological essentialism here, of reducing woman to her reproductive function. The "not-me within me" does signal the fetus as metaphor, but more significantly, it refers to the inclusion of the (m)other in the self: "within woman, the productive force of the other always maintains itself, in particular that of the other woman. . . . In woman, latent, ever ready, there is a source; and a place for the other" ["en la femme toujours se maintient la force productive de l'autre, en particulier l'autre femme. . . . En elle latente, toujours prête, il y a source; et lieu pour l'autre"] ("Rire," 44). This Cixousian feminine economy through its rejection of the paternal Other as constitutive of symbolic existence or functionality does not destroy the other as source of creation and voice. Rather, the revision of the Oedipal myth metaphorically re-instates the originary maternal bond in the future, a bond that connects the speaking subject to the maternal past via the metonymic "echo" of the maternal body. The other woman, then, as writerly source, opens up a space in the present, a bridge between the materiality of the past and the disembodiment of the future, wherein woman might begin to re-present herself from without, both to and from the (m)other.

This maternally induced "not-me within me" finds its most explicit narrative expression in Cixous's refusal of a traditional unified subjective voice in her "fictional" texts. The narrator of *Dedans* weaves fluidly in and out of different subjectivities, speaking the other within herself; for her, writing is far from a monologic exercise. She is not only the mouth but the ear: "I am only myself, ear of the last generation, of the knowledge of my fathers ... I am the son, the daughter, my father, his father, and my own son, without ever ceasing to remember myself" ["je ne suis que moi-même, oreille de la dernière génération, au savoir de mes pères ... je suis le fils, la fille, mon père, son père, et mon propre fils, sans cesser de me souvenir de moi-même"] (120). As she rewrites herself, she does indeed speak the son, the daughter, her father, his father, his mother, and implicitly, her own son (her "immortality").[18] The pronomial confusion endemic to this narrative strategy reinforces the instability of the subject/object dichotomy so essential to logocentrism. Because all of her "characters" remain nameless, as she slips in and out of multiple identities, the reader can easily become confused as to who is speaking, who is the "subject"—who is "I"? From the beginning of the novel, the narrator affirms: "... I knew that there was me and that there was you, and that I could be one or the other" ["... je sus qu'il y avait moi et qu'il y avait toi, et que je pouvais être l'un ou l'autre"] (25). Within the feminine imaginary, the "I" and the "you" are no longer conflictually bound.[19]

As she progresses toward the realization that she can use words and language without becoming a prisoner of her father's Symbolic, the nature of the relation between the self (I) and the other (he) becomes increasingly confused. Responding to "his voice in me," she affirms that she will return from her reunion with her father: "Because I know who you are. Because I know who you are not. And who I am and who he is and who we are, youmeyou, and who we are mehimme" ["Parce que je sais qui tu es. Parce que je sais qui tu n'es pas. Et qui je suis et qui il est et qui nous sommes, toimoitoi, et qui nous sommes moiluimoi"] (197). Through this juxtaposition of stress pronouns, the narrator again challenges any notion of absolute, static identity that precludes inclusion of the other. This simple explication of the first person plural pronoun, signifying both the "I" and an "other," puts identity into question; the "nous" (visually) re-presents either the "moi" in "toi" or the "lui" in "moi"—the "not-me within me." At this point in the novel, just as the narrator begins to write, the reliability of pronomial identifications are at their most unstable. In the end, the "not-me within me," the father in this case, once again takes up the position of the speaking "I," but this time from a space inside the "you," the daughter, the narrator.

Although the father and his power in relation to language has allowed the daughter to enter the(ir) Symbolic, in order to write herself, to speak the feminine imaginary, she must ultimately "abject" the father.[20] As the novel comes to a "close," the narrator recognizes that she cannot allow herself to become trapped in the Symbolic "prison" of the paternal Other. She credits her father with the gift of language: "He planted in my soul the seeds of immortality" ["Il m'a planté dans l'âme les graines de l'immortalité"] (200). The gift, however, is not freely given.[21] His words, his Symbolic, threaten to extinguish the feminine imaginary: "Those words in his mouth were graceful. In mine these words swallow my tongue" ["Ces mots dans sa bouche étaient gracieux. Dans la mienne ces mots m'avalent la langue"] (198). So, while her father repeatedly beseeches her, "let's go into prison," she must refuse if she is to write herself, to escape the domination of a closed, death-driven discourse. She ultimately chooses to transcend the boundaries of death and words represented by the language of the father:

> Now I'm fed up with the edges of death and I'm fed up with substitutes. And although I am the princess of times past, and the daughter of a dead god, and the mistress of tombstone inscriptions, of books of stone, of dresses of the sea, I am not happy . . . I rejoice in my ability to speak, whether I'm ten, thirty or sixty, and in my ability to say shit shit shit to death.

> Or j'en ai marre des bords de la mort et j'en ai marre des remplaçants. Et bien que je sois la princesse des avant-temps, et la fille d'un dieu mort, et la maîtresse des inscriptions tombales, des livres de pierre, des robes de mer, je ne suis pas contente . . . je me réjouis de pouvoir parler, que j'aie dix ans, trente ans ou soixante, et de pouvoir dire merde merde merde à la mort (208).

In the last instance, the narrator rejects the Symbolic of the father and embraces the metaphorical body of the "mother" to make a move into language, into a "space" of writing, where the feminine imaginary is no longer bounded by a signifying system regulated by a morbid, exclusionary logic.

In the end, Cixous's theoretically fictional writer refuses to subordinate the sensual maternal body to an abstract paternal discourse. By displacing the phallus with the "maternal metaphor" as site, source, of writerly creation, a feminine poetics as theorized and written by Cixous succeeds both conceptually and structurally in subverting the circumscriptive closure of the(ir) Symbolic. For Lacan, movement into language, into the Symbolic, always involves the metaphoric, matricidal gesture of absolute substitution: the father supplants the mother. Lacan's paternal metaphor, substitution of the father for the mother, of one term in the Oedipal triangle for another, predicates an exclusionary poetics of absence and loss whereby the Imaginary remains forever under phallic mastery. Rather then simply replace the paternal metaphor with a maternal version of the same, yet another substitutive gesture, Cixous moves beyond this notion of metaphor altogether. By positing the "maternal metaphor" as an alternative locus for a poetics of the feminine, Cixous rewrites the finality of the paternal third term as eternally present (and therefore without a future) and the consequent erasure of the mother-child dyad as tragically lost in the past by instituting a maternal fourth term that exists in the seeming impossibility of the past future.[22] The maternal metaphor, then, establishes a renewed access to the symbolic based on a sort of temporal loop that simultaneously shifts the speaker into the (future) infinitude of the realm of the other, always a step ahead or beyond the self, and a re-connection to the equally boundless body of the mother, the (past) umbilical link, whose echo incarnates the maternal fourth term. The "maternal metaphor," then, in traditional terms, is not really a metaphor at all.

The maternal metaphor, in this light then, revises the Lacanian Feminine as other than ontological limit, extra-Symbolic disturbance. For though the feminine voice of an *écriture féminine* does indeed incite an incursion of the pre-Symbolic Real into the rigid confines of the paternal order of signification, thus decentering the phallus, it does so from a temporal beyond that posits the maternal origin as always already signified in and through the symbolic. Cixous's maternal fourth term sets up a psychic paradigm that acknowledges the necessary developmental detachment from utter dependence on the maternal body yet refuses an absolute amnesic rejection of the mother-child dyad. As both source and destination of the feminine voice, the (m)other seeks neither to define nor limit, though as tropic figure she exists decidedly within the (self-)expressive realm of signification. No longer bounded by the myth of phallic omnipotence and paternal Law, a true feminine expression begins to emerge from the maternal breast, the *seinbolique*, as we allow ourselves to recognize the echo of the maternal footstep as projected into the future, yet always already inscribed in our bodily memories of the past.

────────────── *NOTES* ──────────────

1. For a fascinating discussion of the Lacanian *futur antérieur* in the context of the Cause of the subject see Slavoj Zizek, *The Metastases of Enjoyment: Six Essays on Woman and Causality* (London and New York: Verso, 1994), especially chapter two.

2. Though Cixous and other French women theorists, most notably Julia Kristeva and Luce Irigaray, have been dubbed "French feminists" due to certain commonalities in their respective research, I qualify this identification in recognition of their non-French origins as well as their (non-collective) refusal of the "feminist" label. I also wish to avoid a misguided assimilation of their at times deceptively similar philosophies of "femininity" and its role in the determination of individual subjectivity.

3. *"To fly/steal*, is the gesture of woman, to fly/steal in language, to make it fly/steal. Through flight/theft we have learned the many techniques of art, after centuries of not having access to it except through *flying/stealing* [. . .]. It is not by chance that 'to fly/steal' plays out between two flights/thefts, coming from one to the other and derailing the agents of meaning."
"*Voler*, c'est la geste de la femme, voler dans la langue, la faire voler. Du vol, nous avons toutes appris l'art aux maintes techniques, depuis des siècles que nous n'avons accès à l'avoir qu'en *volant* [. . .]. Ce n'est pas un hasard si 'voler' se joue entre deux vols, jouissant de l'un et l'autre et déroutant les agents du sens." See "Le rire de la méduse," in *L'arc* 61 (1975), 49. All translations are mine unless otherwise indicated.

4. The editors of *New French Feminisms*, for example, place Cixous's "Laugh of the Medusa" in a section titled "Utopias." See *New French Feminisms*, eds. Elaine Marks and Isabelle de Courtivron (New York: Schocken, 1981).
Augustin Menard argues that the utopic vision necessarily entails the negation of a foundational lack, a negation of time, a certain *malaise* inherent in any social structure. According to this definition, then, Cixous's refusal of castration as the driving force of signification might well identify her as a utopian. Augustin Menard, "Le lien social en psychanalyse," unpublished lecture, Conférence de l'Association de la Cause Freudienne Voie Dominitienne, Montpellier, October 21, 1995.

5. See Luce Irigaray, *This Sex Which Is Not One,* trans. Catherine Porter (Ithaca: Cornell University Press, 1985).

6. See also Morag Shiach, "Their 'symbolic' exists, it holds power—we the sowers of disorder, know it all too well," in *Between Feminism and Psychoanalysis,* ed. Teresa Brennan (London and New York: Routledge, 1989).

7. Hélène Cixous and Catherine Clément, *The Newly Born Woman,* trans. Betsy Wing (Minneapolis: University of Minnesota Press, 1986), 78.

8. Julia Kristeva also sees the "abjection" of the mother, or more precisely the "maternal container," as necessary for the child's entry into the socio-symbolic realm. For Kristeva, the experience of a sense of physical repulsion, or "abjection," toward the maternal body serves as an impetus for the child to leave this otherwise safe haven. To avoid a perpetual state of psychosis, the child must "abject" the mother and embrace the Law of the father. See Julia Kristeva, *Pouvoirs de l'horreur* (Paris: Seuil, 1980).

9. According to Cixous, this may be a particularly frightening proposition for men. She writes: "Too bad for them if they crumble upon learning that women are not men, or that the mother doesn't have one. But isn't this fear convenient? Isn't the worst, wouldn't it be, isn't it, in truth, that woman is not castrated . . . ?" ["Tant pis pour eux s'ils s'effondrent à découvrir que les femmes ne sont pas des hommes, ou que la mère n'en a pas. Mais est-ce que cette peur ne les arrange pas? Est-ce que le pire, ce ne serait pas, ce n'est pas, en vérité, que la femme n'est pas castrée . . . ?"] ("Rire," 47).

10. For an incisive critique of the maternal as metaphor in Cixous's fiction and theory, see Domna C. Stanton, "Difference on Trial: A Critique of the Maternal Metaphor in Cixous, Irigaray, and Kristeva," in *The Thinking Muse,* eds. Jeffner Allen and Iris Marion Young (Bloomington and Indianapolis: Indiana University Press, 1989).

11. Jacques Lacan, "The agency of the letter in the unconscious or reason since Freud," *Ecrits: A Selection* (New York: Norton and Company, 1977), 146–178. See also Elizabeth Grosz, *Jacques Lacan: A feminist introduction* (London and New York: Routledge, 1990), 98–105. I use "metaphor" metaphorically here. In both cases, the tropic and the psychic, the movement is one of substitution.

12. Notice in the above citation for example that she disrupts not only the syntactic but also the syntagmatic axis, "rompant ce fameux fil [le syntaxe] . . . qui sert aux hommes de substitut de cordon . . ." ("Rire," 48).

13. Hélène Cixous, *Dedans* (Paris : des femmes, 1986). The semi-autobiographical nature of the novel raises the question of fictionality from a slightly different angle. Isn't all autobiography fiction and all fiction autobiography? Cixous has also written a "non-fictional" version of her entry into writing entitled "La venue à l'écriture," in Hélène Cixous, Madeleine

Gagnon, Annie Leclerc, *La venue à l'écriture* (Paris: Union Générale d'Editions, 1977).

14. Slavoj Zizek argues that while the voice (as opposed to the written word) maintains a uniquely subversive potential with regard to the symbolic order, in its most conventional modes of expression, it renders signification culturally functional, and therefore in a sense completes and assures the reign of the phallus. The voice is "an irreducible supplement of the (written) law. Only the voice confers a performative dimension upon the law, renders it operational: without this support of the voice, the law would be an ineffectual written text, not obliging anyone to do anything" ["un supplément irréductible de la loi (écrite). Seule la voix confère à la loi sa dimension performative, la rend opérante: sans ce support de la voix, la loi serait un écrit inefficace, n'obligeant personne à rien"]. According to this reading of the *écrit/parole* split, then, the original mother/father dyad in this novel would quite effectually initiate the child into a fully coherent and ultimately stable submission to the symbolic order, the law of the father. See Slavoj Zizek, "La voix dans la différence sexuelle," *Le dire du sexe* (Paris: l'Ecole de la Cause freudienne, 1995), 86.

15. "Rire," 48. Luce Irigaray similarly remarks: "No longer omnipotent, the phallic erection could, then be a masculine version of the umbilical bond." See Luce Irigaray, "The bodily encounter with the mother," in *The Irigaray Reader,* ed. Margaret Whitford (Oxford: Basil Blackwell, 1991).

16. Zizek makes a similar remark with regard to the history of music and its relation to Lacan's notion of *"joui-sens":*

The history of music can be read as a sort of counter-proposition to the derridean history of western metaphysics in that in the former, voice supplants writing: one never ceases to find in music a voice that threatens the established order and which, for this reason, should be kept under control, subordinated to the rational articulation of the spoken word, fixed in writing.

L'histoire de la musique peut se lire comme une sorte de contre-proposition à l'histoire déridienne de la métaphysique occidentale en tant que la voix y supplante l'écriture: on ne cesse en effet d'y trouver une voix qui menace l'ordre établi et qui, pour cette raison, doit être tenue sous contrôle, subordonnée à l'articulation rationnelle de la parole dite et écrite, fixée dans l'écriture. (*Le dire du sexe*, 82)

17. Julia Kristeva also insists on the necessity of remaining within the Symbolic, though in much more traditionally Lacanian terms. See especially Julia Kristeva, *La révolution du langage poétique* (Paris: Seuil, 1974).

18. Cixous, like Irigaray, does not see birth as only the biological, reproductive process. Explaining what she has learned from her psychic journey into the past, the narrator of *Dedans* remarks: "Apparently, it is a question of births just before or just after the exit from the belly. Before or after? It was impossible for me to determine" ["Il s'agit apparement de naissances juste avant ou juste après la sortie hors du ventre. Avant ou après? Il me fut impossible de déterminer"] (121). In "The bodily encounter with the mother," Irigaray writes: "It is also necessary for us to discover and assert that we are always mothers once we are women. We bring something other than children into the world: love, desire, language, art, the social, the political, the religious, for example" (*Reader*, 43).

19. Irigaray makes a similar and equally poetic gesture in "Quand nos lèvres se parlent," in Luce Irigaray, *Ce sexe qui n'en est pas un* (Paris: Editions de Minuit, 1977): "Already, I carry you with me everywhere. Not like a child, a burden, a weight. Even loved, even precious. You are not *in* me. I neither contain nor retain you: in my belly, my arms, my head. Nor my memory, my mind, my language. You are there, as the life of my skin. The certitude of existing on this side of all appearances, all surfaces, all designations. The assurance of living because you redouble my life. Which does not mean that you give or subordinate your own. The fact that you live makes me feel alive, but only if you are neither my replica nor my mime" ["Déjà, je te transporte avec moi partout. Non comme un enfant, un fardeau, un poids. Même aimé, même précieux. Tu n'es pas *en* moi. Je ne te contiens ni te retiens: dans mon ventre, mes bras, ma tête. Ni ma mémoire, mon esprit, mon langage. Tu es là, telle la vie de ma peau. La certitude d'exister en deça de toute apparence, tout revêtement, toute dénomination. L'assurance de vivre parce que tu redoubles ma vie. Ce qui ne veut pas dire que tu me donnes ou subordonnes la tienne. Que tu vives fait que je me sens vivre, à condition que tu ne sois ni ma réplique ni mon mime"] (215).

20. See note eight for a brief explanation of Kristeva's use of the verb "abject."

21. Cixous has written substantially on the subject of the "gift." See "le Rire de la Méduse," *The Newly Born Woman*, and Hélène Cixous, "Le sexe ou la tête?" in *Les Cahiers du GRIF* (13), October 1976.

22. Kristeva theorizes negativity as a fourth term in the Hegelian dialectic. See *Révolution*, especially pages 101–105.

REFERENCES

Cixous, Hélène. 1975. Le rire de la méduse. *L'arc* 61: 39–54.

———. 1976. Le sexe ou la tête? *Les Cahiers du GRIF* 13: 5–15.

———. 1986. *Dedans*. Paris: des femmes.

Cixous, Hélène and Catherine Clément. 1986. *The newly born woman*. Trans. Betsy Wing. Minneapolis: University of Minnesota Press.

Cixous, Hélène, Madeleine Gagnon, and Annie Leclerc. 1977. *La venue à l'écriture*. Paris: Union Générale d'Editions.

Grosz, Elizabeth. 1990. *Jacques Lacan: A feminist introduction*. London and New York: Routledge.

Irigaray, Luce. 1977. *Ce sexe qui n'en est pas un*. Paris: Editions de Minuit.

———. 1985. *This sex which is not one*. Trans. Catherine Porter. Ithaca: Cornell University Press.

———. 1991. The bodily encounter with the mother. Trans. David Macey. In *The Irigaray reader*, ed. Margaret Whitford. Oxford: Basil Blackwell.

Kristeva, Julia. 1974. *La révolution du langage poétique*. Paris: Seuil.

———. 1980. *Pouvoirs de l'horreur*. Paris: Seuil.

Lacan, Jacques. 1977. *Ecrits: A selection*. Trans. Alan Sheridan. New York: Norton and Company.

Marks, Elaine and Isabelle de Courtivron, eds. 1981. *New French feminisms*. New York: Schocken.

Menard, Augustin. 1995. Le lien social dans la psychanalyse, unpublished lecture. Conférence de l'Association de la Cause Freudienne Voie Dominitienne. October 21, 1995. Montpellier, France.

Shiach, Morag. 1989. Their 'symbolic' exists, it holds power—we, the sowers of disorder, know it only too well. In *Between psychoanalysis and feminism,* ed. Teresa Brennan. London and New York: Routledge.

Stanton, Domna C. 1989. Difference on trial: A critique of the maternal metaphor in Cixous, Irigaray, and Kristeva. In *The thinking muse,* eds. Jeffner Allen and Iris Marion Young. Bloomington and Indianapolis: Indiana University Press.

Zizek, Slavoj. 1994. *The metastases of enjoyment: Six essays on woman and causality*. London and New York: Verso.

———. 1995. La voix dans la différence sexuelle. *Le dire du sexe. La Cause freudienne: Revue de la psychanalyse* 31: 82–92.

Cynthia Baker

13

Language and the Space of the Feminine

Julia Kristeva and Luce Irigaray

A marked contemporary trend within Anglo-American feminism involves the polarization of feminist analysts of philosophical, literary, and other cultural texts around one or another feminist theorist. As a consequence, it is sometimes maintained that a particular body of work offers both a superior and more useful analysis of women's oppression and a preferable theory of change. Two French feminist theorists loom especially large in the divisive Anglo-American debates: Julia Kristeva and Luce Irigaray. In considering some of the major themes woven throughout the bodies of their work, this paper takes a position contrary to those seen in critiques that would have us choose between Kristeva and Irigaray.[1] For in their respective concerns with the explorations, theorizations, and critiques of women's relationship to language within phallogocentric culture, as well as in their analyses of the discourse-based structure of feminine subjectivity and oppression within Western culture and representation, both Kristeva and Irigaray make significant contributions to feminist attempts to think beyond the goals of liberal feminism. Both bodies of thought are therefore useful to Anglo-American feminists working within a generally Marxist or Left tradition of scholarship; both function to point feminism in a new direction, serving as crucial internal critiques of early feminisms that stressed equality with men as an overriding value while failing to account either for how women's oppression is actually constructed, why that oppression is structurally so hard to combat, or why women feel that their own particular set of values continues to be repressed and devalorized even in the wake of huge achievements in the area of "equality." By examining Kristeva's and Irigaray's respective positions in terms of the following: 1) subjectivity, language, and the feminine; 2) psychoanalysis, feminine agency, and the body of the mother; and 3) formalism and pragmatism, each thinker's analysis of Western culture can be shown to target the structural and linguistic roots of women's oppression in projects that, while they ought not to be collapsed, are neither incompatible nor mutually exclusive, but rather, complementary and important for Anglo-American thought.

Subjectivity, Language, and the Feminine

In her 1974 account of Chinese women under Maoism, *About Chinese Women*, Kristeva spelled out quite extensively a position on feminism which since that time has remained stable in most of its major tenets. Therefore, despite her rapid development as a thinker since 1974, it is worth taking a brief look at what she had to say then about feminine subjectivity and language in order to discover how her views might be compatible not only with 1990s feminism in general, but also with Irigarayan feminism. In the work on China, Kristeva examines, in a precisely historical way, how monotheistic religion uses the division of the sexes into two unequal parts, both subordinated to phallogocentric language, in order to create and support a masculine economy that takes as its starting point the "absence" of maternal jouissance. For Kristeva, it is this repression and silencing of feminine jouissance that leads to the situation in which woman becomes the other of the same, that is, in which female libidinal economy is repressed to the extent that a specifically feminine pleasure can only be located in the baby/penis itself.

Comparing Chinese and Western approaches to the establishment of sexual difference, Kristeva points out that in both cultures "a cleavage or abyss opens up" within discourse to separate men from women (141). In her view, Chinese Confucianism, like Western Christianity, has traditionally stressed the principle of sexual difference to such a degree that a different relationship to the law, both religious and political, emerges between the sexes, paradoxically becoming the "very condition of alliance" between men and women (141). "Monotheistic unity" is thus "sustained by a radical separation of the sexes: indeed, it is this very separation which is its prerequisite. For "without this gap . . . it would have been impossible to isolate the principle of One Law—the One, Sublimating, Transcendent Guarantor of the ideal interest of the community" (141). Kristeva's concern with historicizing, and thus "denaturalizing," the difference between the sexes is clear in this piece, as she seeks to locate sexual difference specifically within cultural practice, language, and textualization. Furthermore, as she draws these parallels between China and the West, Kristeva frames the question of sexual difference in a manner quite similar to the way in which Irigaray will frame her analysis of the suppression of the feminine in Western culture.

Like Kristeva, Irigaray conceives of language as the root of the Law and tries to show how women might overcome their relegation to what Kristeva terms "the aphasic" (CW, 145) by locating and naming a specifically female *jouissance*. Furthermore, where Kristeva finds that the economy of the phallogocentric/ monotheistic system "requires that women be excluded from the single true and legislating principle, namely the Word" (143), Irigaray's desire to formulate a woman's language is inspired by similar perceptions. It is also important to recall that, for Irigaray, the formulation of a specifically woman's language is not something to be "invented" helter-skelter, but is rather intended to be both strategic and transformational over time at the levels of the Imaginary, the Symbolic, and of representation, precisely the levels at which Kristeva locates the separation between the sexes.

Another place in which the two thinkers parallel each other becomes evident through the examination of another early, seminal Kristevan piece, "The System and the Speaking Subject" (1973). Illustrating her longstanding commitment to a radical project of cultural transformation, Kristeva introduces in this piece the theory and technique of semanalysis, which are concerned with analyzing meaning as a signifying process that may be able to account for ruptures and changes that are both transgressive and transformative of culture (29). In this article, Kristeva not only challenges traditional linguistics as being both limiting and ideological, she also begins to think out the idea of subjectivity as a process.

This idea of the subject in process posits the subject as an always historically conditioned entity that may become useful to radical movements for change only if such movements are able, in praxis, to locate the speaking subject within the relations of production (32). Thus, for Kristeva, our greatest hope for social transformation may lie within the theoretical project of "reshaping the status of meaning within social exchanges" (32). Such reshaping locates social struggle at the level of the individual and of language and symbolic production. Illustrating one way in which social struggle may take place within symbolic production in *About Chinese Women*, Kristeva discusses how Christianity "associate[s] women with the symbolic community, but only provided they keep their *virginity* " (145). This assumption of "virginity" thus comes to function as a type of social contract for women.

While she does not share Kristeva's concern with careful historical analyses, Irigaray nonetheless similarly locates women's oppression at our particular historical juncture within a discursive structure that, although in decay, remains basically Judeo-Christian and Monotheistic in origin. In building her arguments, Irigaray analyzes aspects of cultural texts that reinforce women's oppression, such as the Catholic cult of the virgin, playing with them in a game of mimesis meant to free the female subject from her relegation either to silence or to strictly phallogocentric representations within the symbolic order.

In "Belief Itself," for instance, Irigaray, like Kristeva in *About Chinese Women* (and later on, in "Women's Time"), discusses the issue of women's unique relationship to time, noting that there exists another time "that has not, or has not yet, been loosed by all that is too bound, too secondarily bound, thereby leaving so-called free energy chained up, in the crypt" (BI 25). She then suggests that "perhaps that energy is merely deprived of the space-time it needs to decathect, unfold, inscribe, play" (BI 25). Here, as elsewhere, Irigaray uses poetry and stylistic devices to create a mysterious linguistic realm in which words, like "woman," exceed the superficial "meaning" of the text in which they are embedded. Irigaray's words attempt to capture the mystery of the Eucharist and women's unique relationship, through Mary and her martyred son Jesus, to Catholicism when she describes in the opening sections of "Belief Itself" the mysterious and disturbing problem experienced by one of her own psychoanalytic patients: at the point in the Catholic mass when it is time to take holy communion, the patient bleeds. For Irigaray, this "hysterical" moment is a symptom of this woman's (and of women's in general) incongruous placement within the symbolic order, in which the experience of subjectivity "takes place both outside and inside the game [of culture] . . . in a radical hemorrhage of herself" (27). The patient's bleeding during the sacrifice thus symbolizes woman's hidden and silenced presence in the ceremony as veiled background.

Such a "veiled" presence of woman within the Western symbolic is also evident for Irigaray in the story of little Ernst, Freud's grandson, who, in Freud's view, uses a wooden reel tied to a string to experiment with his ability or need to control his mother's presence or absence, symbolically throwing her away in the form of the reel and then drawing her back with the string as he repeatedly tosses the reel into his curtained cot and then retrieves it by pulling on the string. Irigaray, however, notes that little Ernst's game is probably related as much to his developing conception of God and death as to his desire to control his mother's presence or absence. In other words, the game involves his need to bring himself into presence by learning how to separate from and return to his mother, quite literally without dying. For Irigaray, then, Ernst's game actually teaches him how to be present within discursive space, since, in some sense, it is really Ernst who disappears behind the curtain or veil when the reel is thrown, and Ernst who reappears when it is retrieved. Little Ernst is learning that the mother, like the unconscious, is veiled, and that to remain in the space of her body and language is to be invisible, dead, silenced, while to leave is to appear, to take up a position as a speaking subject—*Fort . . . da*. And yet the mother retains within this game the awesome power over life and death for which she is feared and punished by phallogocentric culture; for Ernst fears that he might indeed disappear into her permanently if he loses control.

Like Irigaray's adult female patient, Little Ernst unconsciously realizes that Western ontology is grounded simultaneously upon the body and the silencing of the feminine. "This does not prevent him from wanting to master her," however, "reduce her little by little to nothing, by constructing for himself all kinds of new enclosures, new homes, new houses, directions, dimensions, foods, in order to break the bond with her" (34). But her power cannot ultimately be tamed: for "behind all these substitutes lies the belief that she stands, she stands there all-powerful" (34). This little boy's game thus takes on an important new symbolic dimension that goes far beyond Freud's original interpretation, signalling both Ernst's entry into phallogocentric culture and his ultimate self-positioning within masculine language as a phallic subject.

Ernst's phallic subjectivity is thus grounded upon, indeed dependent upon, the repression of his relationship with his mother and the fear of her power that drives his desire to repress her. In "Body against Body," therefore, Irigaray wonders: "Does the father replace the womb with the matrix of his language?" And she answers herself: "But the exclusivity of his law refuses all representation to that first body, that first home, that first love. These are sacrificed and provide matter for an empire of language that so privileges the male sex as to confuse it with the human race" (14). This phallic empire built on top of a feminine body that covers over emptiness is what Little Ernst is attempting to come to terms with in his game. Finding himself dependent on what cannot be symbolized within the language that draws him away from his mother, Ernst must create in his imagination this misty realm guarded or enveloped by the silenced, veiled mother in order not to be scared to death.

Irigaray suggests in this piece, however, that there is a way out of fearing the mother when she identifies the emptiness behind the veil as the realm of the angels, of belief. She thus rewrites Freud's classic case study of his grandson in order, not merely to illustrate how the repressed and silenced mother forms the backdrop for Western culture, but also to show how the mother's supposed darkness might be brought into the light, acculturated, by means of the concept of "angels." The angel's primary role is to "announce." And Irigaray envisions a time when a heterosexual couple might actually communicate with the beyond of the angel as they engender life, likewise announcing their intention to respect that life, mediating with the sacred as they create. This mediation would place human experience between the space of the angel, the "feminine" space of language, and the space of culture, masculine in the contemporary Western world. Irigaray feels, too, that such a renewed relationship to the silent space of the feminine would create a new kind of world and humanity: "Doesn't the angel announce, in some way, that she is also an angel and that she will bring an angel into the world?" (BI, 39). The concept of the angel, which seems disturbingly anti-modern, can be seen primarily as a metaphor for what the veiled feminine might be able to return to phallic culture in its

role as "messenger." The angel also provides a feminist alternative
to the diabolical imagery of the voracious mother with which the
feminine realm has always been symbolized within phallic culture.
Irigaray's angels, as Margaret Whitford points out, may even be
seen as "an alternative to the phallus" (PF, 163).

While talk about angels might be antithetical to Kristeva's way
of looking at the world, her theorization of Western culture's grounding upon the silencing of the mother nonetheless resembles
Irigaray's. Indeed, like Irigaray in "Belief Itself," Kristeva points
out in "Motherhood According to Giovanni Bellini" (1977) that
Western discourse has traditionally offered only two possible discursive spaces for the body and *jouissance* of the mother: that of
science, and that of religion—discourses which, for Irigaray, correspond to that of Freud theorizing his grandson's game, and to that
of her female patient's physical manifestation of a psychological
intuition. For Kristeva, however, Bellini's paintings exhibit signs of
an actual representation of the mother as the infinite grounding of
culture. This grounding of culture by the feminine represents, in
her view, both the otherness of woman within Western textuality
as well as her function as the ontological ground from which language is born. Furthermore, Kristeva finds evidence in the unfo-
cused gaze of the late madonnas for the unnamable experience of
feminine *jouissance*. Like Irigaray, she notes that this grounding of
language upon the silenced maternal body and its pleasure works
to stave off the absolute unknown of the unconscious and its drives:
this realm "is a whirl of words, a complete absence of meaning and
seeing; it is feeling, displacement, rhythm, sound, flashes, and fan-
tasied clinging to the maternal body as a screen against the plunge"
(240). Whereas Irigaray posits that women are in a unique position
to theorize the beyond the veil (the beyond the mother) as the
realm of angels, thus disarming that realm of its horrifying power
and, hopefully, symbolizing or bringing into representation some of
the unsymbolized contents of the Imaginary, Kristeva believes that
the realm of the mother has already been represented to some
extent within Western art. She points out that "crafstmen of Western art reveal better than anyone else the artist's debt to the
maternal body and/or motherhood's entry into symbolic existence—
that is, translibidinal jouissance, eroticism taken over by the language of art" (243). Bellini's madonnas exemplify his retention of
"the traces of a marginal experience, through and across which a

maternal body might recognize its own, otherwise inexpressible in our culture" (243). For Kristeva, the language of Bellini's paintings speaks the maternal body and *jouissance.*

As a contrast to Bellini's "textualization" of the mother, Kristeva also undertakes in this piece a detailed examination of Leonardo's madonnas. For Kristeva, Leonardo, like Freud, expresses an incipient bourgeois "scientific" and phallic view that all experience can be captured and represented. She portrays Leonardo as a "servant of the maternal phallus" inasmuch as his paintings display "this always and everywhere unaccomplished art of reproducing bodies and spaces as graspable, masterable *objects,* within reach of his eye and hand" (246). Somewhat like Little Ernst, Leonardo attempts to fill up this unspeakable space with objects that can be named, identified, controlled. Leonardo's style is thus portrayed as a precursor to commercial art and related to Western culture's overall concern with the object and its mastery: "Body-objects, passion for objects, painting divided into form-objects, painting-objects: the series remains open to centuries of object-oriented and figurable libido, delighting in images and capitalizing on artistic merchandise" (246). Furthermore, if Leonardo paints phallic madonnas whose delight exists only in the possession of the penis/baby, then he perfectly captures the distorted form of feminine *jouissance* that is most commonly represented in Western culture; that is, Leonardo portrays woman as the other of the same, who delights in her baby as though he were a penis.

Bellini's technique, on the other hand, "suggest[s] a different interpretation" (246). "The face of his Madonnas are turned away," notes Kristeva. They are "intent on something else that draws their gaze to the side, up above, or nowhere in particular, but never centers it in the baby" (247). These madonnas do not locate their pleasure in the domination of an object (the baby). Rather, their pleasure exists somewhere outside the painting and its representations, in a realm that is not represented by the objects in the painting: "The maternal body not covered by draperies—head, face, and eyes—flees the painting, is gripped by something other than its object. . . . It rather seems as though he sensed a shattering, a loss of identity, a sweet jubilation where *she* is not" (247). This pleasure is, in fact, nonrepresentable as such. Rather, it is contained only within the folds of draperies, the dazzling contrasts of color, the "limitless volume resolving into a contrast of 'hots' and

'colds' in an architecture of pure color" (248). This ecstasy of color opens up color itself, "a last control of vision, beyond its own density, toward dazzling light" (248). Light, folds, contrasts, color appear like eruptions of the semiotic, representing both woman as ground of being and her unnameable pleasure.

Although Kristeva does not claim that Bellini is a feminist,[2] she is very concerned in this analysis, as elsewhere in her work, to discover within art (though normally within avant-garde art) the presence of the semiotic, that is, the normally unrepresented, and ultimately unrepresentable, realm of the pre-Oedipal drives, which are associated with the maternal. For Kristeva it is precisely within the fissures and cracks opened up by representations like Bellini's within privileged Western discourses (which are displayed in phallic textualizations like those of Freud and Leonardo) that possibilities for revolution and change exist. Such subjective and historical representational processes are also material processes that may serve historically to open up spaces within discourses and to reshape "the status of meaning within social exchanges" (SSS, 32). Kristeva thus examines privileged discourses in order to explore how reshaping them might be accomplished, suggesting that a contractual commitment to acknowledging, both materially and discursively, culture's debt to monumental time and maternity might be one way of beginning to reshape the meaning of social exchanges.

Psychoanalysis, Feminine Agency, and the Body of the Mother

In "The True-Real" (1979), written for her seminar at the *Service de psychiatrie, Hôpital de la Cité Universitaire* in Paris, Kristeva reveals a critical, Hegelian-Marxist bent that illustrates an overarching concern with theories of social change, a consistent commitment to many of the major tenets of Leftist thought and praxis, and a powerful reconsideration of psychoanalysis and its potential role in addressing the issue of agency in post-Freudian culture. Revealing in this piece an overriding interest in how patterns of linguistic structure and change might be brought to the service of radical movements for broadly democratic social change at the level of culture and the individual, she addresses the disruptive lack of common codes within the contemporary Western symbolic order, attributing this lack to the progressive deconstruction of a Western ontological/ epistemological system.

Rooted in Classical philosophy, this system was then refined and developed through the Enlightenment and up to Modernity by Judeo-Christianity. The artistic and literary disruptions of Modernism, identified as symptomatic of that breakdown at the start of the twentieth century, are thus termed instances of the eruption of the "true-real" in which the (Lacanian) "real" breaks through the "truth" of a symbolic order in decay. That is, the breakdown at the advent of Modernism of linguistic and cultural forms associated with the deterioration of Christianity enabled new linguistic forms to break through a previously closed symbolic system, leading to radical transformations at the level of cultural texts as artists attempted to formalize the breakthroughs they perceived. The relatively controlled disruptions of Modernist texts are then compared to psychotic texts as Kristeva questions whether the "true-real" they both express can be plausibly and broadly socialized within culture apart from mysticism or madness.[3] For inasmuch as the decay of structured codes teaches us that all social codes are structured and therefore malleable, psychotic language teaches us that structure and order are also necessary.

Illustrating the flow of codes as she traces the history of Western philosophy from Plato to the present, then, Kristeva also attempts to account for their breakdown. Describing classical notions of truth, for example, she traces their gradual deconstruction from the Renaissance through early Modernism, placing Freud as the culminating figure for modernity and identifying perhaps the major post-Freudian problematic as the plausible socialization of the "true-real." In her view, while they do not offer a panacea, historical eruptions of the "true-real," such as those associated with Modernism, may provide opportunities for conscious human control over some aspects of the formulation of the symbolic, as we learn to play with and to direct the unconscious materials bubbling up from the "true-real" through the fissures in Western symbolic structures.

This early Kristevan notion of the "true-real" has, of course, undergone a good deal of refinement over the course of a long career. What is important for feminism within this particular work is, however, its analysis of the symbolic crisis of the West as it is revealed within the various phenomena of modernity; for this crisis has split traditional Western discursive structures at several points, allowing for the disruptive entry of a variety of new discursive positions, one of which is feminism. Kristeva sees within these splits a great deal of potential for revolutionary developments of all kinds, locating feminism, not as the central moment within a radicalized modernity, but rather as one focal point within a large-scale cultural transformation that might be taken in a broadly democratic and peacefully transformative direction. Unlike Freud, then, she valorizes radical social change, affirming it consistently throughout her work.

Nonetheless, Kristeva remains close enough to the Freud of *Civilization and Its Discontents* to emphasize consistently the potentially dark side for culture inherent in the symbolic eruptions she analyzes. If the expansion of the "true-real" offers the potentially positive result of broadening narrative and subjective possibilities, therefore, the confusing plethora of existing narratives to which they might potentially attach themselves may also make it difficult for individuals, or for radical movements, to map reality or to formulate symbolic identities strong enough to "control" the "true-real's" irruptions into socialized space. The Western symbolic crisis, therefore, also places limits on social movements such as contemporary feminist attempts to valorize and represent the feminine body within phallically structured cultures and languages (228); for in the absence of symbolic structures that would contain linguistic protest, the contamination of the symbolic by the imaginary may simply leave holes that are then filled by hysterical and hallucinatory textualizations (such as those seen in mass religious movements), which may ultimately be of limited value.

Indeed, related as they are to psychotic texts, the languages of modern art and literature point to the increasing incidence of the "true-real's" unstructured eruption into discourse, possibly indicating an ever more schizoid cultural pattern in which fewer and fewer subjects are able successfully to enter our fluid symbolic order. Kristeva's main concern is not to make value judgments about these changes; rather, she is interested in the meaning for culture that the loss of the sense of identity and centered subjectivity, which reached their final apotheosis in the Modernist period, imply. She thus stresses, not any kind of false need to maintain the Romantic subject (a favorite theme of Jean Baudrillard's), but rather the constant need to maintain plausible speech, and she views psychoanalysis as a method (not as a totalizing world view), that can help maintain it. These themes, introduced nearly twenty years ago, have been continually honed and developed throughout her work, remaining, in fact, major concerns of the recent book *New Maladies of the Soul* (1995).

In that work, she stresses that our contemporary era's cultural issues continue to revolve around the problem of "plausible speech," since in the absence of normative codes, individuals, in order to maintain their position as social beings, that is, in order to avoid psychosis, must constantly work toward maintaining their ties to an increasingly individualized and alienated discursive space. It must be remembered, however, that "plausible speech" does not mean normative speech. Quite the contrary, if Kristeva holds, with Lacan, that, in order to formulate a functional self, the child must enter the Oedipal crisis, which imposes the phallic third term of language on the child and incites him or her to reject the realm of the maternal (a potentially psychotic realm within Western culture), she nonetheless seeks to lead her patients to discover freer discursive orientations and greater degrees of mastery over their personal lives. That is, within the limits imposed upon all subjects by the existing culture, which *is* phallic and Oedipal at this historical juncture, Kristeva acknowledges and plays with the plethora of discursive spaces available within the fluidity of culture that coexists with an Oedipal structure in decay. She therefore encourages her patients, who are in pain because they cannot find the language to speak some crucial aspect of their experience, to seek out and formulate discursive spaces into which they may enter in a non-normative way as speaking subjects in process. "Freud has staked out a path that all innovators must respect if they lay claims to psychoanalysis," she notes (NMS, 36). That path, a narrow one, is one in which "sexual experience [desire] resists language . . . [leading] to repression and to the related necessity that we use language in order to interpret hidden unconscious signs" (NMS, 36). As of 1995, then, Kristeva continues to use psychoanalytic methods and ideas in her writings, and Freudian principles to guide, but not to dominate, her work.

Without adopting a narrow Freudian (or Lacanian) vision of the world, then, Kristeva finds along the psychoanalytical path a way to move toward a freer space of personal existence in which, through the analyst's guidance, the patient may achieve a greater degree of control over his or her language and symbolizations and a higher level of personal empowerment. For Kristeva, furthermore, the discursive methods of psychoanalysis (the transference) might easily be utilized in a broader way within culture in order to increase our "capacity for signification" (NMS, 36). Psychoanalytic methods are useful because "the eroticization of language within transference allows us to convey sexual experience and to relieve symptoms" (NMS, 36). Like Irigaray, Kristeva retains a long-term commitment to discovering new means of renovating speech, in part by using the methods of psychoanalysis as she seeks out discursive positions that might empower individuals and help them to heal from ancient wounds rooted in once-ossified symbolic structures. Without denying the importance of feminist discourse, then, she does not privilege that discourse, emphasizing instead the multiplicity of discourses to which all individuals belong and encouraging the already decentered people she treats in her practice to search out new spaces for their existence.

In *New Maladies of the Soul*, therefore, Kristeva develops and refines the analysis seen in embryo in "The True-Real," questioning whether, at this historical juncture, we can even discuss human beings or "the individual" as we have been accustomed to do in the West for the past several centuries. This line of argument, though not explicitly feminist, is important for feminism because of its radical questioning of traditional Romantic notions of subjectivity. What Kristeva offers feminism in this and other linguistic analyses, is the possibility for a critique of the unified subject that would include a critique and deconstruction of the *feminine* subject too. And this is precisely where it might be argued that her position is incompatible with Irigaray's. Despite upholding somewhat different positions on the future direction of feminine agency, however, Kristeva and Irigaray make very similar critiques of psychoanalysis, working within basically deconstructive perspectives in which they explore the complex cultural interaction of language and subjectivity in an attempt to argue for human (and not just feminine) empowerment within language and representation.

How Irigaray's writing and speaking strategies relate both to her own critique of psychoanalysis and to Kristevan thought can be examined through a close reading of "The Poverty of Psychoanalysis" (1977). Although Irigaray does not concern herself in this piece with theorizing and describing the modern discursive space in the systematic way that Kristeva does, she shares several of Kristeva's key concerns about psychoanalysis and its relationship to human agency. This piece also illustrates how Irigaray's strategy is often more tactical than it is traditionally theoretical, with her refusal of traditional theory functioning as an important part of her critique of and challenge to Western textuality.

In fact, Irigaray aims this particular critique of psychoanalysis both at psychoanalysts themselves—just as elsewhere she critiques specific philosophers—and at certain practices of psychoanalysis that negate feminine experiece and disempower women by trying to reduce them to "the same," attempting to impose phallic norms upon their behavior. She thus directly challenges institutionalized psychoanalysis in order to deconstruct its phallic practice, particularly as it is utilized in the analysis of women. In doing so, she charges that not only is psychoanalytic discourse *not* politically neutral, as it would claim, it is, rather, politically *charged*, enforcing the repression of women in the name of a discourse valorized as "scientific." This aspect of her critique is aimed, not so much at Lacan himself, nor even at Freud, but rather at what has been made of Freud's and Lacan's theories by many contemporary practitioners, especially male ones, who are concerned to normalize their patients. In fact, she reminds these psychoanalysts that Freud never forgot to listen to and learn from his patients, to let them reveal their discourse (83). She thus shows how certain psychoanalytic practices attempt to impose phallic concepts upon female analysands (and analysts) who are thereby deprived of their own language and experience, made to conform rather than helped to heal or become healers.

As she criticizes the practitioners of psychoanalysis themselves, Irigaray charges that psychoanalysts are often, if not actually reactionary, highly supportive of the (phallic) status quo, which disempowers women. She therefore makes a commitment to deconstruct traditional psychoanalytic positions on women, arguing that only by rethinking the feminine and feminine sexuality in non-ideological ways can psychoanalysis gain a place as a "science" that actually addresses the "real," as opposed to the male-defined, needs of women. Irigaray's critique of psychoanalysis is not, therefore, a wholehearted rejection of the discipline at all, but rather an urgent demand that it live up to its own ideals and stated goals. Like Kristeva, she uses the very method of psychoanalysis to critique the discipline. She carries this critique, not farther than Kristeva takes hers, but rather in a different direction.

For instance, Irigaray announces in this highly charged piece of writing not only her intention to break with establishment psychoanalysis, but also her commitment to formulating a theory of the feminine, feminine language, and feminine sexuality, with the broader goal of empowering women. As she speaks/writes the article, then, she simultaneously illustrates the primary technique she plans to utilize in her efforts to rethink the feminine by taking on the speech of the hysterical patient who is so disturbing to these analysts, adopting, with every sentence, a harsher and more "hysterical" tone until, toward the end, one can literally hear her sounding shrill. This method illustrates quite plainly how she uses technique as strategy, as she implies that psychoanalysts and their practice create in a (any) woman the voice of a hysteric, since every way you try to enter phallic discourse "differently" you are either repressed or charged with insanity or hysteria.

This article thus draws a convincing portrait of an analysis gone awry, since Irigaray here takes up the position of a female analysand defending herself in front of a stodgy group of old men who want only to dismiss and label her. Despite her mimed adoption of a hysterical discourse (or perhaps because of it?), however, Irigaray demands that she be acknowledged as a serious psychoanalyst. Furthermore, she makes a public commitment to actively reform the psychoanalytic position on women and the feminine, challenging her "colleagues" to join her in thinking through a specifically feminine language and pleasure. "If that is all there is to the sexual relation—man's fascination with the nothingness she veils," she cries at one point, "then we are defenceless against the most negative elements of nihilism" ("Poverty of Psychoanalysis," 87). Rather than aiming for a traditionally theoretical critique, Irigaray creates a feminist declaration of independence from bourgeois psychoanalytic practice, marking, not so much her desire to sever relations with psychoanalysis, as her determination to start the journey anew.

Related to the issues of feminine agency and women's oppression within psychoanalytic practice is the concern expressed by both thinkers to work out the meaning of women's relationship to the maternal as an alternative system of time and space. Kristeva, in well-known works such as "Women's Time" (1979), for instance, outlines a dual system of time that functions within the Western symbolic order, analyzing its effects on women's agency. In a closely related piece, "Stabat Mater" (1977), she combines her concern with the two levels of time within Western culture with a critical analysis of motherhood, particularly as it relates to French Catholicism and its cult of the Virgin Mary. Irigaray, too, going beyond her specific critique of psychoanalysis in "The Poverty of Psychoanalysis" (1977), has been deeply concerned in virtually all of her subsequent work with women's relationship to the maternal, consistently arguing for the need to acknowledge the existence of "two sexes" and criticizing Western culture's repression of the maternal. In part by rethinking the cultural significance of Western textualizations of the mother, therefore, Irigaray hopes to develop a more coherent speaking position for women.

Kristeva's analysis in "Women's Time," like many of Irigaray's analyses of the maternal,[4] argues for the existence of two distinct kinds of time or timekeeping and emphasizes that post–World War II societies need to come to terms with the existence of these two different systems of time, which exist simultaneously within the Symbolic order. The historical/linguistic and symbolic splits she perceives mirror the split between production and reproduction within Western economies. Kristeva defines the two time systems, therefore, as linear time, which corresponds to nationalistic history, everyday language, and production, and monumental time, which corresponds to cyclical and universal history, artistic and literary language, and to reproduction. For Kristeva, women's particular reproductive function gives them a privileged (though not necessarily exclusive) access to monumental time, which means, among other things, that modern women may be in a better position than men to transcend national boundaries in defining their personal and historical concerns. Kristeva thus believes that a primary task of feminism is to think through the problem (and privilege) of women's partial participation in an alternative system of time.

Using this vision of two times to sort through various issues of twentieth-century feminism, Kristeva relates the schisms to be found within the women's movement to a fundamental split in Western culture between these two times, historical or linear versus monumental time, arguing that women, in order to keep from falling into mysticism or madness, must find a third way of peacefully existing within both realms simultaneously. Her article thus depends upon a dialectical structure, a structure which is, in "Stabat Mater," physically represented on the page by the use of two columns of text, one linear, rational, and structured, and the other poetic, free, and open. Like Irigaray, who often depends upon a free, poetic style, Kristeva thus employs in "Stabat Mater" various writing styles and techniques in order to strengthen her critiques and to express a dissident position with respect to twentieth-century bourgeois culture, showing how linear time, as the time of project, language, and civilization, both challenges and depends upon cyclical time, valorizing itself at the expense of cyclical time while simultaneously depending upon the maternal relationship as the ground for the development of spatial perceptions (WT 191–192).

"Women's Time," on the other hand, depends, not upon poetic speech, but rather upon a more traditional use of dialectics, as Kristeva contrasts linear time as thesis with monumental time as antithesis, proposing a synthesis within subjectivity and praxis as a major project not only for feminism but for Western radicalism in general. She goes on to illustrate, then, how the early women's movement in the West, because it emphasized specifically linear goals such as equal job opportunities and equal pay for equal work, soon came up against a real limitation at the level of the body as space, and of time as women's relation to the maternal and to its different, or cyclical, time. She thus points out the dangers of pursuing a women's movement that concentrates solely upon women's future "as men," stressing that women need to include as an inherent part of feminism a reconsideration of their relation to monumental time that might then be expressed through a renovated relation to the symbolic at the synthetic level of social contract (199–200). Kristeva implies here, as elsewhere, that a particular kind of women's movement may lead to the development of a new relationship between human beings, both male and female. In making such arguments, however, she is always careful to emphasize the potential for violence and brutality inherent in any movement that posits us-versus-them as a founding principle, including some strains of feminism. Although it may not be immediately evident, Kristeva once again parallels Irigaray quite closely in these views. For Irigaray, despite her constant insistence that we "think the feminine" in the direction of delineating two sexes, always remains clear that she hopes her kind of praxis will lead, not to a society of independent Amazons, but rather to a world in which both sexes, by being simultaneously separate in their genders and together within a shared culture will achieve mutual relations of equality and respect.[5]

Unlike Irigaray, however, Kristeva encourages the adoption of synthetic thinking from the start. Rather than attempt to work out feminine specificity, as Irigaray does, she suggests that women attempt to arrive at a synthesis between women's time and the "reality principle," as outlined by Freud. Like Irigaray, she suggests that an attempt to develop a new cultural code of ethics ought to serve as the guiding principle for a "third wave" of feminism, which would be capable of acknowledging the ethical interdependence of the sexes. Although Kristeva clearly opposes feminisms that are either openly separatist or hostile to men, she nonetheless supports attempts by women "to break the code, to shatter language, to find a specific discourse closer to the body and emotions, to the unnameable repressed by the social contract" (200). Kristeva is careful to note, though, that she is not speaking about a specifically woman's language "whose (at least syntactical) existence is highly problematical and whose apparent lexical specificity is perhaps more the product of a social marginality than of a sexual-symbolic difference" (200).

Despite appearances, however, this Kristevan position on women's language may not actually represent a direct critique of Irigaray. In any case, it does not diminish Irigaray's position on language, since, in keeping with her primarily tactical feminism, Irigaray never attempts to "scientifically" develop a specifically feminine language structured around a particular grammar. Indeed, she does not, strictly speaking, attempt to *write* a new language at all. Rather, she uses existing differences in speech between men and women in basically mimetic fashion, taking up the feminine position as the negative of the male so as fully to expand its logic. In this manner, she hopes to broaden the contradictions of phallic speech, both in order to reveal its limits, and, hopefully, in order to clear a possible space for the emergence of a form of feminine speech that she believes may be hidden or repressed within male logic. Such feminine speech might indeed be marginal, as Kristeva implies above. But its marginality has very little to do with whether or not it might be tactically co-opted in order to support Irigaray's project of creating feminine cultural representations.

Formalism versus Pragmatism:
Textualizing Change, Exploding the Present

The solutions Irigaray offers to the problem of how to represent the feminine, then, though they may differ from Kristeva's, are nonetheless compatible with them if one understands the underlying concerns of each thinker's project, her particular textual and institutional practices, and especially the different emphasis each one places on historical accuracy and faithfulness to traditional methods of scholarship. That is, Irigaray's thinking of the feminine is concerned with identifying within the gaps of Western textuality a specifically contemporary form of the bourgeois family and women's role in it, in order to explode its structure from within. Because, in her view, Western culture textualizes contemporary conceptual space in order to contain it, she sees the Western Symbolic as a historical complex of textualizations that tend to remain consistent in the present mostly because of the difficulty involved in penetrating or changing them. Her particular view of how the Symbolic is structured thus helps explain why Irigaray often "ventriloquizes" texts rather than identifying and engaging with them according to generally agreed-upon academic standards (IR, 9). Irigaray's point is not to analyze specific texts or use them to support her arguments, which would merely add another layer of culture to them. Rather, by using a mimetic strategy, she seeks to expose the preconceptions revealed within the interstices of textualized discourses. Kristeva's theories, on the other hand, while they never embrace a totalizing Western ontology either from the Right or from the Left, are concerned not only with contemporary history, but also with projecting and attempting to trace contemporary trends beyond the moment. The scientific and systematic examination of discourse formation is thus crucial to her goal of exploring our particular contemporary discursive structures and examining how they might be directed in a broadly democratic way.

Irigaray, on the other hand, always formulates her critiques of Western culture and representation so that they reveal various aspects of women's oppression. For example, she posits the notion, derived from Lacanian linguistics and psychoanalysis, that Western sex roles and conceptions of gender are basically forms of masquerade and can only be so, since women have traditionally been defined within Western discourse, not as anything positive, but simply as the negative of the male. She therefore claims that women's negative definition makes mimicry or mimesis of a male-defined feminine realm the only possible way for women to behave, since women lack Symbolic access to what they *are*, because what they positively are is absent from representation. And yet traces do exist: "Woman ought to rediscover herself, among other things, through the images of herself already deposited in history . . . ," she notes, "rather than through the work itself or its genealogy" (SD, 169).

Irigaray's mimetic strategies, then, which range from postioning herself as the challenging "lover" of major Western philosophers like Friedrich Nietzsche or Emmanuel Levinas to the positing of a feminine "religion," and the thinking of female genealogies, center her work, underscoring her radical rejection of traditional academic discourses, which she views as textualizations of feminine oppression. Therefore, as Whitford notes, "Precise theoretical references are on the whole absent from her work" (IR, 4). This lack of references should be seen as a crucial part of her technique, which is self-consciously anti-academic. In a style that consistently reminds us of her debt to Derrida, she takes well-known canonical texts, particularly those from Western philosophy, and tries to discover their blind spots, cracks, and crevices, making them speak their unconscious as she lays the groundwork for the development of a female Imaginary, feminine philosophy and language.

Irigaray thus offers her ideas, not as alternatives to phallic discourse or structure, but rather as guidelines from which women might develop their own discursive spaces within contemporary bourgeois culture. "To speak *of* or *about* women," she notes, "may always boil down to, or be understood as, a recuperation of the feminine within a logic that maintains it in repression, censorship, nonrecognition." This means that "the issue is not one of elaborating a new theory of which woman would be the *subject* or *object*, but of jamming the theoretical machinery itself, of suspending its pretension to the production of a truth and of a meaning that are excessively univocal" (PD, 126).

Kristeva, for her part, would not so much disapprove of Irigaray's desire to explode Western discourses in order to expand and develop women's discursive position within them as she would urge people to think beyond such projects. For Kristeva sees a discursive realm which may already have left the Romantic, centered subject so far behind that gender may simply be on its way to becoming just one of a series of interconnected discursive problematics involving race, class, group identification, internationally variable family structures, and cultural factors of all kinds. This means that Irigaray's project may figure less importantly in, for example, certain "Third World" or emerging feminisms, than it would in contemporary bourgeois French, American, Australian, or English practices of feminism.

Nonetheless, Kristeva has often been open to an Irigarayan-style thinking of the feminine, as she acknowledges in *About Chinese Women*, even if in her own work she has always refused to privilege such an approach. Discussing the Virgin Mary and her symbolic role in the formation of feminine subjectivity, for instance, Kristeva notes that between the historical constraints imposed upon women by their textualization and "the myth of the Virgin impregnated by the Word there is a certain distance, which will be bridged by two psychoanalytic methods: one is relative to the role of the mother, the other to the function of language . . . .The first consists in ceasing to repress the fact that the mother is *other*, has no penis, but experiences *jouissance* and bears children" (ACW 26). For Irigaray, "the/a woman who does not have *one* sex . . . which will usually have been interpreted as meaning no sex . . . .Woman's sexuality therefore cannot be inscribed *as such* in any theory, unless it is standardized to male parameters" (VC, 61). These statements, in which Kristeva and Irigaray express a deep concern with rethinking the position of women and their role within culture, serve to illustrate both how close the two thinkers often come to one another, as well as where they remain forever separated. They also illustrate the different degree of emphasis and value each one places upon psychoanalysis and traditional academic methodologies.

Kristeva clearly remains fully committed to adapting and developing academic discourses, to working out scientifically "the function of language" through the analysis of carefully chosen historical and discursive moments (the specific situation of women in Maoist China as compared to that of French women, for instance). She is, furthermore, consistently committed to revealing the textualized structures of subjectivity and to delineating the role these structures have played in the West's self-understanding.[6] With her faithfulness to academic accuracy and to Western traditions of scholarship, Kristeva's textual analyses are invaluable in coming to understand the insertion of any group, including women, within the Western Symbolic and ought to figure strongly in feminist theories about how the Symbolic and Imaginary realms function to oppress women and to rob them of their agency.

Irigaray, on the other hand, in her desire to "jam the theoretical machinery," reveals her continuing commitment to a kind of guerrilla warfare against a Western and bourgeois notion of "universal" truth, itself partially expressed within the conventions of the academic methodologies that Kristeva values. Irigaray thus uses to her own advantage whatever aspects of whatever discourses are convenient for her in making her points, assuming that no one discourse can really contain or represent her voice in its radical Otherness to phallic culture.

Irigaray, however, like Kristeva, would reject any suggestion that women attempt to replace the masculine *logos,* its discourses or religions, with feminine ones, for neither thinker intends to portray feminism as an alternative to phallogocentrism, or indeed to reify a feminist project by defining feminism in some kind of permanent way. "It is not a matter of toppling [the phallocratic] order so as to replace it," points out Irigaray, "that amounts to the same thing in the end—but of disrupting and modifying it, starting from an 'outside' that is exempt, in part, from phallocratic law" (PD 118). In the final analysis, she believes, "Architects are needed. Architects of beauty who fashion *jouissance*" (FC, 214). Kristeva would not disagree.

Conclusions

The Anglo-American feminist tradition seems, for the most part, to remain caught in the kind of egalitarian feminism that Kristeva and Irigaray criticize. Therefore, both Kristeva's and Irigaray's linguistic and cultural theories are indispensable to feminists from that tradition (and others) who have seen the limitations of feminisms inherited from the past and undertaken the daunting task of rethinking their projects. While feminists like Claire Duchen, in her book *Feminism in France,* remind us that the project(s?) of French feminism deal with a specifically French discursive structure and therefore cannot be blindly adopted by other feminisms, it seems equally correct to say that neither can other feminist projects afford to ignore the contributions of French feminism. Both Kristeva's and Irigaray's rethinking of language, discourse, and their role in the formation of subjectivity provide important critical bodies of work; both can provide a powerful theoretical background for all Western feminisms. It thus seems strangely misguided, if not phallic, to argue that Anglo-American feminists (or any other feminists) must choose one theorist at the expense of the other, and we should be aware of the risks of doing so.

As Whitford points out in her introduction to *The Irigaray Reader*: it is all too easy to neutralize a woman thinker, thus eliminating her intellectual contributions (1–2). Such reductions of Left women thinkers should not come from within the movement itself. Rather, we should retain the best, most useful thought of each participant as we think beyond a simplistic egalitarian feminism to explore oppression at the levels of language and discourse. This discussion of Kristeva's and Irigaray's feminist positions has thus attempted to stress the importance of both thinkers to the project of Western feminism and to show how, despite their differences, both agree in significant ways about how language, feminine subjectivity, and women's oppression are related within Western culture.

Thus, if Kristeva is often faulted for her failure specifically to theorize a separate feminist movement, her feminist-oriented theorizations of language and discourse become a crucial counterpart and balance to Irigaray's strategic attempts to challenge, rethink, and recontextualize contemporary feminine language and representations. She reminds us, too, that the need outlined by Irigaray to "think two sexes," to develop a way of speaking as a woman, is itself a historically conditioned discourse like any other. Kristeva thus places contemporary feminist thought in its historical situation of being caught up as a participant in a reality burgeoning with emergent discourses of liberation, many of which intersect with the women's movement without adopting or wishing to adopt Irigaray's emphasis on deconstructing bourgeois feminine experience. While Irigaray undertakes the important project of engaging with the philosophers, challenging their master discourses and rethinking their meaning for certain groups of Western women, then, Kristeva traces a method of cultural analysis that attempts to theorize the precise way in which the repressed enters history, bubbling, or sometimes erupting, through the cracks to drive it forward. This realm, far from neutral, contains the potential for positive change as well as virtually unlimited destructive potential. We are thus balanced between it and the need for structure, which, Kristeva always reminds us, cannot be done without.

──────────── NOTES ────────────

1. Symptomatic of this type of polarizing trend with Anglo-American analyses of French feminist thought is the position taken by Elizabeth Grosz in *Sexual Subversions*, in which she notes that Kristeva's and Irigaray's "positions are extreme poles apart when judged from a feminist point of view" (104). Indeed, discussing "Lacan and Feminism" in *Jacques Lacan: A Feminist Introduction* (1990), Grosz maintains that Kristeva has failed to challenge the psychoanalytic establishment at all, remaining a "dutiful daughter" of psychoanalysis who "enacts for herself and reproduces for other women the roles of passivity and subordination dictated to women by patriarchal culture and affirmed by psychoanalysis" (167). Irigaray, on the other hand, is described in almost hyperbolic terms as a woman who has heroically taken on the psychoanalytic establishment through her critiques of philosophy and psychoanalysis, her rethinking of the mother-daughter relationship, and her attempt to formulate a female imaginary. Irigaray is thus held to be a feminist thinker who both opposes and surpasses Kristeva both as a philosopher and a feminist.

2. In fact, she would see him as being incapable of participating in a discourse like feminism which was not a part of his historical period.

3. With the term "plausible socialization" she means to extend the comparison between Modernist textualizations of semiotic eruptions and those occuring within psychotic language in order to emphasize that, although it may be desirable to change linguistic codes, there also exists a dark and dangerous underside to rapid transformations of cultural codes, which Left-oriented movements may be incapable of containing symbolically.

4. For Irigaray's most coherent discussions of the maternal see "Belief Itself"; "Body against Body: in Relation to the Mother"; and "The Bodily Encounter with the Mother."

5. See her analysis of these issues in *Je, tu, nous: Towards a Culture of Difference.*

6. See *Tales of Love*, for instance, which represents a sustained effort to trace the concept of love within Western texts.

———————— REFERENCES ————————

Duchen, Claire. 1986. *Feminism in France: From May '68 to Mitterrand.* London: Routledge.

Grosz, Elizabeth. 1989. *Sexual subversions: Three French feminists.* Sydney: Allen and Unwin.

———. 1990. *Jacques Lacan: A feminist introduction.* London: Routledge.

Irigaray, Luce. 1991. The bodily encounter with the mother. In *The Irigaray reader,* ed. Margaret Whitford, trans. David Macey. New York: Basil Blackwell, 34–46.

———. 1991. *Marine lover of Friedrich Nietzsche.* Trans. Gillian C. Gill. New York: Columbia University Press.

———. 1991. The poverty of psychoanalysis. In *The Irigaray reader,* ed. Margaret Whitford, trans. David Macey. New York: Basil Blackwell, 79–104.

———. 1991. The power of discourse and the subordination of the feminine. In *The Irigaray reader,* ed. Margaret Whitford, trans. Catherine Porter with Carolyn Burke. New York: Basil Blackwell, 118–132.

———. 1991. Questions. In *The Irigaray reader,* ed. Margaret Whitford, trans. Catherine Porter with Carolyn Burke. New York: Basil Blackwell, 133–139.

———. 1991. Questions to Emmanuel Levinas. In *The Irigaray reader,* ed. and trans. Margaret Whitford. New York: Basil Blackwell, 178–189.

———. 1991. Volume without contours. In *The Irigaray reader,* ed. Margaret Whitford, trans. David Macey. New York: Basil Blackwell, 53–67.

———. 1993. Belief itself. In *Sexes and genealogies,* trans. Gillian C. Gill. New York: Columbia University Press, 25–53.

———. 1993. Body against body: In relation to the mother. In *Sexes and genealogies,* trans. Gillian C. Gill. New York: Columbia University Press, 7–21.

———. 1993. The fecundity of the caress. In *An ethics of sexual difference,* trans. Carolyn Burke and Gillian C. Gill. Ithaca: Cornell University Press.

———. 1993. *Je, tu, nous: Towards a culture difference.* Trans. Alison Martin. New York: Routledge.

———. 1993. Sexual difference. In *An ethics of sexual difference,* trans. Carolyn Burke and Gillian C. Gill. Ithaca: Cornell University Press.

Kristeva, Julia. 1980. Motherhood according to Bellini. In *Desire in language,* ed. Leon S. Roudiez. New York: Columbia University Press, 237–270.

———. 1986. *About Chinese women.* Trans. Anita Barrows. New York: Marion Boyars.

———. 1986. Freud and love: Treatment and its discontents. In *The Kristeva reader,* ed. Toril Moi, trans. Leon S. Roudiez. New York: Columbia University Press, 240–271.

———. 1986. Stabat mater. In *The Kristeva reader,* ed. Toril Moi, trans. Leon S. Roudiez. New York: Columbia University Press, 160–186.

———. 1986. The system and the speaking subject. In *The Kristeva reader,* ed. and trans. Toril Moi. New York: Columbia University Press, 24–33.

———. 1986. The true-real. In *The Kristeva reader,* ed. Toril Moi, trans. Séan Hand. New York: Columbia University Press, 241–237.

———. 1986. Women's time. In *The Kristeva reader,* ed. Toril Moi, trans. Alice Jardine and Harry Blake. New York: Columbia University Press, 187–213.

———. 1987. *In the beginning was love: Psychoanalysis and faith.* Trans. Arthur Goldhammer. New York: Columbia University Press.

———. 1987. *Tales of Love.* Trans. Leon S. Roudiez. New York: Columbia University Press.

———. 1995. *New maladies of the soul.* Trans. Ross Mitchell Guberman. New York: Columbia University Press.

Whitford, Margaret. 1991. Introduction. In *The Irigaray reader,* ed. Margaret Whitford. New York: Basil Blackwell, 1–15.

———. 1991. *Luce Irigaray: Philosophy in the feminine.* London: Routledge.

About the Contributors

Natalie Alexander is Assistant Professor of Philosophy at Truman State University in Kirksville, Missouri, where she teaches contemporary continental philosophy, feminist theory, and history of philosophy. Recent work includes "Rending Kant's Umbrella: Kofman's Diagnosis of Ethical Law," in *Enigmas: Collection of Essays on Sarah Kofman* (forthcoming), and "The Hollow Deconstruction of Time" in *Derrida and Phenomenology* (1995). Her current research interests involve developing a postmodern reading of Sartre's *Being and Nothingness* and further exploring the works of Sarah Kofman.

Cynthia Baker is a *summa cum laude* graduate in Political Science and Spanish from the University of New Mexico and holds an M.A. degree in Latin American Studies from the University of Texas at Austin. Currently, she is completing a doctorate in Latin American Literature at the University of Texas at Austin, where she teaches Spanish and Portuguese. As an integral part of her studies in Brazilian and Spanish American literature, she also writes and speaks about French feminism, literary theory, and cultural studies. The main focus of her work, as well as the subject of her doctoral dissertation, is the fictional world of Brazilian writer Clarice Lispector.

Susan David Bernstein teaches literature and women's studies at the University of Wisconsin-Madison. She has published *Confessional Subjects: Revelations of Gender and Power in Victorian Literature and Culture* (1997) as well as several articles on topics ranging from confession and feminist psychoanalytic theory to women, primitivism, and Victorian sensation fiction.

Jane Hedley is Professor of English and Chair of the English Department at Bryn Mawr College in Pennsylvania, where she teaches Renaissance/Early Modern literature and regularly offers courses in British and American poets. She is the author of *Power in Verse: Metaphor and Metonymy in the Renaissance Lyric* (Penn. State Press, 1987), and she has published articles on Renaissance tropological strategies and on language activism in the work of contemporary American women poets in *ELR, Style, Genre,* and *Narrative.*

Christina Hendricks is a doctoral candidate in Philosophy at the University of Texas at Austin. She is currently working on a dissertation considering the political role of the intellectual in Michel Foucault and Julia Kristeva, focusing especially on the use of language and its liberatory and/or oppressive potential.

Elissa Marder teaches French and Comparative Literature at Emory University. She has published articles in *Diacritics, Camera Obscura, Yale French Studies,* and *Hypatia.* She is currently completing a book entitled *Dead Time: Temporal Disorders in the Wake of Modernity.*

Sara Mills has co-written *Feminist Readings/Feminists Reading* (Harvester), and she has edited *Language and Gender: Interdisciplinary Perspectives* (Longman) and *Gendering the Reader* (Harvester). She has written *Discourses of Difference* (Routledge) and *Feminist Stylistics* (Routledge). She has just finished a book on discourse theory. She is Professor in Cultural Studies at Sheffield Hallam University, Sheffield UK.

Andrea Nye is the author of a number of books including *Words of Power: a Feminist Reading of the History of Logic.* She teaches philosophy and feminist theory at the University of Wisconsin-Whitewater.

Kelly Oliver is Associate Professor in Philosophy at the University of Texas at Austin. She is the author of *Family Values: Subjects Between Nature and Culture, Womanizing Nietzsche: Philosophy's Relation to "the Feminine,"* and *Reading Kristeva: Unraveling the Double-Bind.* She is the editor of *The Portable Kristeva* and *Ethics, Politics and Difference in the Writing of Julia Kristeva.*

Sangeeta Ray is Associate Professor in the English department at the University of Maryland at College Park where she teaches postcolonial and U.S. ethnic literatures and critical theory. She has published various essays in journals such as *Genders, Modern Fiction Studies, Ariel,* and *South Asian Review* as well as in anthologies. Her book *En-gendering India: Woman and Nation in Colonial and Postcolonial Narratives* is forthcoming from Duke UP. She is also co-editing *The Blackwell Companion to Postcolonial Studies* with Henry Schwarz, forthcoming in 1998.

Lynne Tirrell is Associate Professor of Philosophy at the University of Massachusetts Boston, and was formerly Associate Professor of Philosophy at the University of North Carolina at Chapel Hill. She has published papers on the theory of metaphor, the power politics of language, Nietzsche, Simone de Beauvoir, aesthetics, and feminist theory. She is currently writing a book on the discursive practices and power associated with derogatory terms.

Georganna Ulary is a graduate student in Philosophy at Duquesne University. She is writing her dissertation on the notion of recognition in Kristeva and Hegel: rethinking the production of human subjectivity.

Lisa Walsh is currently completing her dissertation, titled "You Are Not Your Self: Toward an Alternative Ethics of Maternity," at the University of Texas at Austin. She has published short essays on Luce Irigaray and Julia Kristeva and intends to continue her interdisciplinary research in the field of feminist ethics.

Roberta Weston is a doctoral candidate in Art History at the University of Texas at Austin, and is writing a dissertation on the theme of the gift examining artists' gifts, symbolic and real exchange, and economies of signification in postwar American art.

Ewa Płonowska Ziarek is Associate Professor and Director of Graduate Studies in the English Department at the University of Notre Dame. She has published numerous articles on Derrida, Kristeva, Levinas, Foucault, Kafka, Benjamin, Joyce, and Marianna Hauser. She is the author of *The Rhetoric of Failure: Deconstruction of Skepticism, Reinvention of Modernism* (SUNY Press, 1995) and the editor of *Gombrowicz's Grimaces: Modernism, Gender, Nationality* (forthcoming from SUNY Press). Her current book project is devoted to postmodern feminist ethics.

Index